SIR GEORGE GOLDIE
and the Making of Nigeria

Sir George Goldie, from the portrait by Herkomer

WEST AFRICAN HISTORY SERIES

General Editor: GERALD S. GRAHAM

Rhodes Professor of Imperial History, University of London

SIR GEORGE GOLDIE
AND THE MAKING
OF NIGERIA

BY

JOHN E. FLINT

LONDON

OXFORD UNIVERSITY PRESS

IBADAN   ACCRA

1960

Oxford University Press, Amen House, London E.C.4

GLASGOW NEW YORK TORONTO MELBOURNE WELLINGTON
BOMBAY CALCUTTA MADRAS KARACHI KUALA LUMPUR
CAPE TOWN IBADAN NAIROBI ACCRA

Preparation and publication of this series has
been made possible by the generous financial
assistance of West African Newspapers Group,
Lagos, Accra, Freetown, and London

PRINTED IN GREAT BRITAIN
BY WESTERN PRINTING SERVICES LTD BRISTOL

To
Alfred Edgar Flint

PREFACE

To the general public the name of Sir George Goldie is almost unknown. Yet he was the man who revived the chartered company as a method of acquiring and ruling territory, added the most populous of all the tropical African colonies to the British Empire, and contributed vital techniques to British administrative policies. Few Englishmen know nothing of the life of Cecil Rhodes, yet in many ways Goldie pioneered in West Africa the road which Rhodes was to take in the south. That Goldie's name is largely unknown is almost entirely a result of his own efforts. Before his death he systematically destroyed all his papers, forbade his children to write anything about him or assist anyone who wished to do so, and threatened to haunt them after his death if they disobeyed him. Confronted by the ashes of his papers and the prospect of visitations from his uneasy ghost, it is perhaps not surprising that no historian has been eager to write the history of this man and his works. To date, only one person has attempted to convey a picture of his enigmatic character. Dorothy Wellesley, Duchess of Wellington, was a child when first she met Goldie, who discerned in her an unusual sensitivity and perception and talked to her in a way which was later to give her an extraordinary insight into his mind. These impressions she set down in 1934 in her book *Sir George Goldie, Founder of Nigeria*. Stephen Gwynn, who had known Goldie in a less intimate way as a journalist, contributed an introduction which was not without disclosures. But this book cannot be regarded as definitive, or even as serious history. It is written in a spirit of indignant defence of Goldie; it ignores his opponents and enemies, and presents, in near-poetical terms, merely one facet of Goldie's many-sided life as interpreted by one who was still enthralled by his almost hypnotic personality. It should be treated, as I have tried to treat it, as a document.

Dorothy Wellesley's book, and a few articles scattered here and there, remained the sum total of what was known of Goldie's life until 1952. In that year the Government decided to open its records for the years from 1885 to 1902, which had up to then remained confidential. At one stroke the major portion of Goldie's correspondence, and that which most clearly revealed his political life, lay open to inspection, and it is these papers which form the basis for this biography. But other sources, by dint of extraordinary good luck, came my way. In 1956 Mr. Cecil Holt, of John Holt and Company (Liverpool) Limited, asked me to sort and catalogue a great series of documents connected with his firm's history. These papers, besides being of first-rate importance for the history of the commercial penetration of West Africa, contained, to my great delight, practically all the letters exchanged between Goldie and his opponents in Liverpool, laying bare with astonishing frankness and detail the complicated economic rivalries which lay beneath the political struggles on the Niger. I am most deeply indebted to Mr. Cecil Holt and John Holt and Company (Liverpool) Limited for permission to use and quote these papers.

I must also thank Mr. Ronald Norman, who, though in very poor health, gave me all his valuable personal knowledge from a close friendship with Goldie, and used every effort to gather in information and documents. It was through Mr. Norman that I obtained most gracious help from the Earl of Scarbrough, who put aside time from a very busy public life to give me his own memories of Goldie, and to make available to me the Goldie-Scarbrough correspondence. My debt to Lord Scarbrough can be judged from the important part which these, some of the few really intimate letters written by Goldie which remain, play in my narrative.

I am also much indebted to Sir George Goldie's nephew, Captain J. W. L. Fry-Goldie-Taubman, for his very kind hospitality in allowing me to see the Nunnery, and for the pains he has taken to give me his knowledge both of his uncle's life and character, and of the history of his family.

I am very conscious of my debt to the staff and officials of many organizations which serve the inquiring and troublesome historian: to the Registrar of Joint Stock Companies who

accorded me facilities above those he is obliged to afford; to the
Church Missionary Society; and to the officials and attendants
of the Public Record Office and the British Museum, I can only
express my sincere thanks for the great kindness I have received.

Many kind friends helped me to produce this book, giving me
advice and criticism which are largely responsible for whatever
merits it may possess. I would like to thank Dr. Evelyn Martin
for initiating me into the techniques of historical research; Professor G. S. Graham for reading and commenting on the manuscript and for his wise advice in so many things which have
vitally affected my work; Miss Margery Perham for the great
amount of time and energy she has given to helping me at a time
when her own work was very pressing; and Dr. Roland Oliver
not only for detailed criticism and advice, but for showing me a
wider and deeper Africa than that of the official records.

Much of the spade-work for this book was done during a prolonged stay in hospital. It could not have been done but for the
many friends who went to much trouble to bring me books and
copies of documents at that time, particularly Miss C. Gertzel
and Dr. J. F. Ajayi, nor without the skilled supervision of the
medical and nursing staff of St. Ann's Hospital, London, and
the facilities which they provided, which allowed me to study
and write whilst undergoing treatment.

Finally I must thank my wife for the help she has given me in
every way.

                                              J.E.F.

King's College,
London,
18 December 1959

CONTENTS

ILLUSTRATIONS

MAPS

LIST OF ABBREVIATIONS USED
IN FOOTNOTES

A.A.	African Association
B. of T.	Board of Trade
C.M.S.	Church Missionary Society
C.O.	Colonial Office
C. of C.	Chamber of Commerce
conf.	confidential
D.D.F.	*Documents Diplomatiques Français*
F.O.	Foreign Office
G.P.	*Die Grosse Politik der Europäischen Kabinette*
enc.	enclosing
J.H.P.	John Holt Papers
L.O.	Law Officers of the Crown
mem., mema.	memorandum, memoranda
N.A.C.	National African Company
P.P.	Parliamentary Paper
P.R.O.	Public Record Office
R.N.C.	Royal Niger Company
U.A.C.	United African Company
W.O.I.D.	War Office Intelligence Department

I

Early Years

THE Isle of Man is one of the most beautiful of all the islands which lie off the British shores. Its great hills rise sharply and majestically from the sea. On stormy days the waves lash against the rocky southern shore sending up white ramparts of foaming water; on dull days, when the mountain tops are covered with grey mist, the effect is one of Celtic mystery. On days of bright spring sunshine the mountains to the northward may still be capped with snow, and from these heights, with the wind roaring in the ears, the whole island seems to tilt downward as though about to tumble into the sea. Across the waters on a clear day all the four countries of Britain can be seen as faint shadows on the horizon. The feeling of power, and of distance eradicated, is an exhilarating experience.

It is small wonder that this little island has produced more than its fair share of conquerors and dreamers, adventurers, swashbuckling pirates and smugglers, and builders of empire. In the twelfth century, exploiting its strategic position in the Irish sea, the Kingdom of Man held sway over the isles of western Scotland, and ruled eastern Ireland, including Dublin itself. When the English came, and independent feudal lords ruled the island from its ancient capital of Castletown, Manxmen turned their energies to fishing and trading on the high seas. By the eighteenth century, when the English system of mercantilist protective duties was at its height, the Manx, with their independent customs duties, used their advantage to the full, and a rich group of trading families, with fortunes built from the lucrative smuggling trade between England and

B

Ireland, began to impart a tone of leisured civilization to the island. By 1765 the Manx traders were such a thorn in the side of the English customs system that the government of the island was purchased compulsorily from its Lord, the Duke of Atholl, and the island was reduced to the status of a colony.[1]

The result was ruin for many of the hitherto prosperous Manx families. The island was not very productive and trade had been the basis of their wealth. Many of them emigrated to England or the colonies, or to the United States after the American Revolution. Some stayed and went into decline, to be reduced to the status of small farmers. The Taubman family fared better. According to the Duke of Atholl, writing in 1813, it had been the Taubman family's 'extensive smuggling transactions which had been the principle means of my family being deprived of their rights in the island'. When the British had taken over the government of the island the Taubmans had been caught with large stocks of tea, wines and spirits intended for smuggling into England. These goods could not now be exported, but they had paid no duties and were cheaper than goods imported into the island after 1765. The Taubmans were thus able to unload them at a lucrative profit, with which they bought up large amounts of land at a low price, for the island was thought to be ruined. Thus the family moved into the nineteenth century as the wealthiest interest on the island.[2]

It must not be imagined that they were an uncouth lot of jumped-up traders, nor were they narrow in their interests or connexions. The family was not purely Manx; the name Taubman is German in origin, and there are instances of its presence in England in the seventeenth century. In the eighteenth century the family had become allied with the Goldies of Dumfriesshire, and from this time carried this name on with their own. The family also had connexions with the Senhouses of Cumberland, and through them with Fletcher Christian, the most famous of the *Bounty* mutineers. The tone of life in the family

---

[1] The best modern history of the island is Kinvig, R. H., *A History of the Isle of Man*, University Press of Liverpool, 1950.

[2] Atholl Papers in the Manx Museum, X/29/3rd. Duke of Atholl to Lord Sidmouth n.d. 1813.

was definitely aristocratic, and descent from Edward I was claimed and proved. In the nineteenth century the Taubman sons followed military careers, and fought and died in the Peninsular and Crimean wars, while the head of the house played his part in the government of the island and was usually Speaker of the House of Keys, the lower house of Tynwald, the Manx parliament. Early in the century the Taubmans began to build a house which would reflect their status in the island. A site was chosen on rising ground behind the port of Douglas, and there above splendid lawns and gardens the magnificent grey stone house which is called the Nunnery, after ruins which still lie in the grounds, was constructed. It is still today the most elegant and beautiful residence on the island, and has only been rivalled by Castle Mona, once the Douglas house of the Dukes of Atholl, but now a hotel.

George Dashwood Goldie Taubman, better known as Sir George Goldie,[1] the most famous and remarkable of this truly remarkable family, grew up in this house and throughout his life spent much time in it. George Goldie was the youngest of four sons. His father, John Taubman Goldie Taubman, had married twice, and from the first marriage had issued the future head of the family, John Senhouse Goldie Taubman, Speaker of the House of Keys from 1867 to 1898, who was destined to play a key part in introducing Goldie to the River Niger. From the second marriage there were three sons, all of them destined for the army.

George was born in 1846. Of his early life almost nothing is known. There is a bad portrait of him and his brothers in the Nunnery, but the children are pictured angelically against the sky, with formless features which tell us nothing of his character as a child. Undoubtedly the boy was gifted with a touch of genius even at this time. The family used to visit London

[1] He changed his name in 1887, upon receiving his knighthood, to Sir George Dashwood Taubman Goldie, and dropped the Taubman thereafter. His reason for so doing is not clear, though it may have been that he regarded the German-sounding name as awkward for the leader of a British chartered company. To avoid confusion I have referred to him as 'Goldie' throughout this book, though strictly this is inaccurate before 1887. In footnote references I have retained the accurate names.

frequently, and George, like many other boys of his day, was fascinated by the Aquarium at Westminster (now the Central Hall). Here were displayed all kinds of wonders, freaks and marvels, both animal and human. When George was about eight years old he went on his own to see one of these, a 'Calculating Man'. This gentleman possessed a miraculous arithmetical mind, and challenged his audience to call out mathematical problems which, without pencil or paper, he would answer with amazing speed. Young George, witnessing the display, became aware that he too possessed this gift, and with childlike enthusiasm innocently began to shout out the answers before the 'Calculating Man', much to the delight of the rough cockney audience. The occasion became something of a riot, the boy had to be ejected rapidly, and the attendants were instructed never to admit him again. He retained this gift of rapid calculation throughout his life.

Goldie's youth was wild and turbulent. In the 1860's he trained for two years at the Royal Military Academy, Woolwich. But he was full of tensions and frustrations:

I was like a gun powder magazine. I was blind drunk when I passed my final examination for the engineers, two years later a relation died, leaving me his fortune. I was so elated by the freedom that this gave me that I bolted without sending in my papers, and leaving all my belongings behind. I went straight to Egypt.[1]

His stay in Egypt, about which very little is known, was undoubtedly one of the formative periods of his life, which turned him definitely towards Africa. In Egypt he met an Arab girl with whom he fell deeply in love, and the two went up to the Egyptian Sudan, where for three years they lived an idyllic and isolated life which Goldie was to describe as a 'Garden of Allah'.[2] He learned fluent colloquial Arabic from his mistress, and began to penetrate into the life of the peoples among whom he lived. He ordered books from England, and used to go into Suakin to collect them. Goldie's life now began to turn towards the Niger. He met the Hausa pilgrims and scholars who were on

[1] Wellesley, Dorothy, *Sir George Goldie, Founder of Nigeria*, London, 1934, p. 94.
[2] *Ibid., loc. cit.*

their way to Mecca, and they showed him that the Egyptian Sudan where he lived was but the fringe of the vast Sudanic belt extending from the Niger to the Nile. He obtained and digested Barth's *Travels*,[1] five volumes packed with historical and geographical information on the western Sudan. The idea of the unity of the Sudanic region began to form in Goldie's mind, later it was to become one of his fixed principles and he was to dream of British expansion from the Niger to the Nile as fervently as Cecil Rhodes believed in linking Cape Town and Cairo.[2]

After three years of the 'Garden of Allah' Goldie gave up his curious existence and returned to England. Why he did so is not clear. There are stories that his Arab mistress died of tuberculosis,[3] on the other hand a reliable witness told this author that she lived on, and that Goldie created a trust fund in Cairo to provide for her. Whatever the reason, his return did not betoken a transformation to more sober ways; instead he lead 'a life of idleness and dissipation'[4] in England. Then, returning to the Nunnery, he entered a course which was eventually to sober him and settle him down in marriage. But even this was done in what was in Victorian times a scandalous and shocking way, offending the accepted class-structure and code of sexual morality. He became infatuated with the family governess, Mathilda Catherine Elliot, and induced her to run away with him to Paris where they began a tempestuous love affair. Then politics stepped in to alter the shape of both their lives. The year was 1870. On 2 August war broke out between the French Empire of Napoleon III and Prussia; within a month the Prussians had forced the French armies and their Emperor to surrender, and by 20 September Paris was surrounded by Prussians. The lovers were caught in the trap. For four months the capital was besieged, and Goldie and Mathilda Elliot witnessed

[1] Barth, H., *Travels and Discoveries in North and Central Africa*, 5 volumes, London, 1857.

[2] Much of my information on Goldie's stay in the Sudan is based on oral accounts and memories given to me by witnesses who heard Goldie speak of this phase of his life. I am particularly indebted to Mr. Ronald Norman for information on this period of Goldie's life.

[3] This is the view of Dorothy Wellesley, *op. cit.*   [4] *Ibid.*, p. 94.

all the horrors of the terrible investment. Not until February 1871 were they able to return to England. By this time both were unalterably 'compromised'. On 8 July 1871 they were married quietly at St. Marylebone Church in London. Thereafter, though Goldie was not a faithful husband, deep bonds of sympathy grew between them, and Mathilda's death in 1898, at a time of acute crisis in her husband's affairs, came as a cruel and savage blow.

At the time of his marriage Goldie was nearly thirty, and without a career. His personal life had apparently taken a disastrous turn, and he had abandoned the army. His life hitherto had been noted for its licentious and irresponsible character. Though he had a small private income, and a wealthy family to back him, he could not hope to use these to make a public career as a servant of the state or in politics. He could enter commerce, but lacked the kind of character which could work up from a subordinate position. Moreover he was fiercely intelligent and he knew it; his was the kind of intelligence which prompted high ambition rather than academic study.

Looking at him, the impression immediately received was one of incredible gauntness; his body and his face were both of them long, straight and severe. His high forehead set off the bony features of his face, which were relieved only by the generous military moustache which covered his upper lip. Most striking of all his features were his eyes, intensely bright and metallic, they radiated aristocratic pride and disdain, yet managed to twinkle with humour at the same time. His laugh was open-mouthed and uninhibited. His appearance was unusual, his life hitherto had been lacking in respect for the conventions, and his opinions matched the man. He was totally devoid of religious belief of any kind, not an agnostic but a convinced atheist. God did not exist, and this reality he insisted on facing and accepting. His philosophy, so far as it was derived, was that of Huxley, Darwin and Winwood Read. Culturally too he played the rebel, boasting his admiration for the scandalous Ibsen and the un-melodic Wagner. Such tastes and opinions, and perhaps rumours of his private life, were to bar him from many spheres of Victorian high society. He never gained access, as did many a lesser man, to Queen Victoria's tea-table. He was never on terms of intimate personal friendship with any of the great political families of the day. Where he built influential con-nexions that became close friendships, as with Lord Aberdare and later with the Earl of Scarbrough, he did so initially through his work on the Niger. Social snobbery aside, he was not an easy man to know or like. His temper was atrocious and he would fly into rages over a trifle. He could be self-righteous and pompous to a degree which infuriated even his well-wishers. He never under-stated a case, but would inflate a weak argument to grotesque proportions in trying to overcome reason with aggressive assertion. He made few friends, but those he did make were steadfast and devoted to an intense degree. Some people seem almost to have been permanently hypnotized by him. In subordinate employees, and often in African servants, he could engender a fanatical loyalty. And if he often made himself look ridiculous where trifles were involved, he was masterly in dealing with big issues. Here he could persuade not only his bitter enemies, but statesmen and diplomats who possessed more experience of bargaining than he. Though he would never admit error or defeat on a quibble, he could abandon a long held position taken on a vital issue with perfect ease, and quickly take up a new, and usually superior, position as if he had planned the move years before. Often this gave an impression of almost purposeless opportunism, but this was a false judgement. His atheism was not a negative thing; he was a materialist who held that civilization was a necessary product of advancing material prosperity, and that man's duty was to assist that process.

In 1875, when Goldie was nearly thirty, his opportunity came, and it came through family connexion. His eldest brother, John Senhouse Goldie Taubman, now head of the family, had married in 1860 a Miss Amelia Grove-Ross. Her father, Captain Joseph Grove-Ross, had become the secretary of the small firm of Holland Jacques and Company, which had begun trading on the Niger in 1869. By 1875 the firm was in serious financial difficulties and Grove-Ross appealed to his son-in-law for help. The Taubman family may have seen this as an opportunity for George, or Africa may have fired him to persuade his eldest brother to let him take his chance. Whichever the case, Goldie took over the company, and resolved to go once more to Africa, this time to the Niger, to see for himself why Holland Jacques were losing money, and, if possible, to cross Africa from the Niger to the Nile and see the whole of the Sudanic region.

2

Trade and Politics on the Niger River

TRADE and politics had always been intimately connected in the regions around the Niger River. Africans had always understood this, Europeans perhaps less so. Goldie was to bring trade and politics together as a unity. Within two years of his visiting the Niger he had created a trading empire on the river, seven years later the British Government gave his company a charter to rule the region. Goldie's desire for political power on the Niger arose directly from his analysis of the difficulties of the Niger trade; without political power there could be no stable commerce with Europe, and no secure profit.

To understand why this should have been so in the 1870's it is necessary to look more closely at the way in which British traders had penetrated Nigeria, and at the attitude which the British Government had adopted towards their activities.

There had been trading contact between Europe and West Africa for many centuries, and as the contact increased so the slave trade had increasingly become preponderant. By the eighteenth century West Africa was an integral part of the British commercial empire of the Atlantic. The West Indies were the vital productive unit in that empire, and the west coast of Africa furnished the slave-labour supply for West Indian sugar plantations, at the same time increasing the profits of colonial trade and strengthening the merchant fleet. But despite the crucial importance of the slave trade, the British Government had found no need to establish a territorial empire in West

Africa. Slavery of a kind was a native institution, easily adapted to satisfy the wants of the Europeans, and the African states on the coasts exploited their position to act as middlemen, and to arm themselves with European weapons against their rivals in the interior.

In the Niger region the lion's share of the slave trade had been concentrated in the hands of the merchants of Liverpool. It was thus a disastrous blow for them when in 1807 Parliament made the slave trade criminal, and imposed drastic penalties for those found guilty. The Liverpool traders had much capital tied up in West African shipping, and had built up a costly system of contacts with the African rulers of the coast. They were now forced to try to save something from the wreckage of their fortunes by developing a 'legitimate commerce'.

Coincidence gave them their opportunity. In the first half of the nineteenth century the demand for cleanliness in Europe revolutionized the soap industry; life was becoming dirtier, and washing essential to health. The researches of the French chemist Chevreul laid the foundations for the application of mass-production techniques to the soap industry. The main fat used to make soap was tallow, but it was found that in order to make a good lather the fat had to be blended with vegetable oils, and the best of these was palm oil. The foundations of the industry in England were already laid in and around Liverpool and the Mersey; by 1850 Liverpool was producing nearly 30,000 tons of soap every year, more than any other English town, and one-third of the total British output. The development of machinery in industry at the same time produced a demand for palm oil as a lubricant.

The Liverpool traders were thus able to turn over their shipping and capital resources to the development of the trade in palm oil. The oil was obtained from the fruit of a particular kind of palm (*Eloeis Guineënsis*) which grew wild in the forest belt which lay behind the mangrove swamps of the coasts on either side of the delta of the Niger River. Progress was rapid; in 1806 only 150 tons of oil had been shipped to Liverpool, by 1819 the figure had risen to 3,000 tons, and by 1839 imports stood at

13,000 tons.[1] The region soon became known as the 'Oil Rivers'.

Though the trade prospered (it reached a bulk of 30,000 tons by the 1870's and a value which rarely fell below the level of £1 million per annum),[2] and although it seems within a generation to have driven out the slave trade from the Oil Rivers, the development of a 'legitimate commerce' made no revolution in the basis of Afro-European relations. The elaborate system of native middlemen through which the slave trade had passed was adapted to the palm oil trade in the same way that the Europeans had adapted their own organization. The pattern of trade remained the same.

Indeed, there was no alternative for the Europeans. The mangrove swamps lay between them and the regions where the palms grew and the oil was collected by the local peoples, and this fever-ridden coastal belt was deadly to Europeans. The slavers had soon learned to lie off the coast, using the local peoples as middlemen, and the legitimate traders had of necessity to continue this system. In such conditions the interior 'markets', where the oil was collected naturally came to be dominated politically by the coastal towns, and gradually, after a long series of wars between the towns, the markets were delimited into regions over which a particular coastal town had asserted its predominance. The Liverpool firms, dependent for oil upon the coastal rulers, became implicated in their policies, supporting them both internally and externally. Until the 1880's they made little effort to obtain a direct access to the producing regions, despite the fact that quinine had made this possible in the 1850's. Vested interest held any such move in check. David Livingstone's brother, at the time British consul in the Oil Rivers, described the position in 1871:

Gladly would the nearest oil producers come and trade direct with the whites to the advantage of both, and most willingly would some white and many black traders go up to the markets of the oil producers, but the black brokers are strict protectionists and allow no

[1] P.P. 1845, XLVI, MS. p. 481.
[2] Dike, K. O., *Trade and Politics in the Niger Delta*, Oxford, 1956, analyses the growth of the palm oil trade, pp. 97–127.

trade with white or black except what passes through their own hands, and each tribe on river or coast does the same with its next inland. All are protectionist and ever have been. Savage Africa is the home of protection and heathen.[1]

Two deadly vices indeed in the opinion of a Christian free-trading Englishman!

Though the strength of the middleman system prevented direct access to the oil producing regions by way of the Oil Rivers until the 1880's, the Niger itself was destined to have a somewhat different history. It must be remembered that until 1830 it was not realized that the Oil Rivers were in fact, many of them, merely mouths of the Niger, comprising its delta. The Niger was known from the writings of such travellers as Mungo Park who had struck its course inland, but who had failed to discover either its sources or its mouths. The tales of the explorers as to the tremendous length of the river, its great width and navigability at places many hundreds of miles from the sea, of the civilized Muslim populations living on its banks, only intensified the aura of legend and myth which had surrounded the river since the time of the Romans.[2] In 1830 the problem of the mouth of the Niger was suddenly and dramatically solved by the Lander brothers, who succeeded in sailing down the river from Busa, emerging into the open sea from what had hitherto been known as the River Nun, one of the Oil Rivers.[3]

The gathering of knowledge about the interior by these early explorers soon began to affect the thinking of the powerful humanitarian group in England, violent opponents of slavery and the slave trade, and influential in the councils of the Government. The explorers had all stressed that the Atlantic slave trade was based on the inland regions for its sources of supply, and they had also shown that the slave trade with the Arabs of North Africa was as important as the trade with Europeans. But in addition the explorers had all laid great stress on

[1] P.P. 1875, LXV, MS. p. 3.
[2] Bovill, E. W., *The Golden Trade of the Moors*, London, 1958. See esp. chap. 20, p. 203.
[3] Lander, Richard and John, *Journal of an Expedition to Explore the Course and Termination of the Niger*, London, 1832.

the existence of a vast 'legitimate' trade in goods between the Muslim states of the western Sudan and the Mediterranean coast via the Sahara by caravan. Now that the Niger was seen to flow into the Bight of Benin, could not its mouth, already worked by the African middlemen as part of the Liverpool palm oil trade, be used as an entrance by which Europeans might penetrate the interior of Africa? The purpose would be to intro- duce civilized commerce, thereby extinguishing the slave trade by competition. It was also hoped that the supposedly vast trans- Saharan trade could be diverted into British hands, using the cheaper transport by sea around the coast to the Mediterranean.

The Landers' discovery immediately excited the imagination of MacGregor Laird, a member of the famous Birkenhead ship- building family. He was so fired with enthusiasm that he retired from his father's firm to concentrate on the Niger. Undoubtedly he was lured by the prospect of adventure, but he also visualized the spread of legitimate commerce into the interior of Africa as 'a mortal blow to that debasing and demoralizing traffic which has for centuries cursed that unhappy land'. He 'aspired to be the means of rescuing millions of . . . fellow men from the miseries of a religion characterized by violence and blood, by imparting to them the truths of Christianity.'[1]

Laird went on to form a company in Liverpool, and Richard Lander joined him, agreeing that there was a good prospect of very profitable trading, particularly in ivory and indigo. Two vessels were especially constructed for the venture. One of them, the S.S. *Alburkah*, made maritime history, for she was the first vessel constructed entirely of iron to complete a successful ocean voyage. In October 1832 the little flotilla, one sailing ship and the two steamers, arrived on the Niger coast, ready to make the first organized, direct commercial contact between Europe and the Africans of the Niger valley.

These, the first British traders, were not beginning to write on a blank slate. The African peoples they were to meet had already evolved commercial and political systems of their own,

[1] Howard, C. and Plumb, J. H., *West African Explorers*, Oxford (World's Classics), 1951, p. 388. The authors are quoting Laird's own words.

systems shaped by geography and the realities of power politics among the African states. All were intensely competitive in the pursuit of wealth or power, and struggles between states which had already been pursued for many decades were still taking place, and unresolved. The Europeans thus entered as another element to complicate the situation, and the Africans were quick to attempt to make use of them.

On entering the Niger, Laird had first to pass through the coastal belt of mangrove swamp. This was a region which was itself unproductive; the undrained soil refused to grow yams and cassava, the staple diet of the inhabitants. In the dim past these people had come as fishermen, but as the population increased they had been forced to turn to trade, using the profits to buy food, and maintain warriors and a river navy of war canoes. At first they had traded with the Portuguese in slaves, and from the frequency with which they repeated the phrase 'Ba-ra-sin', meaning that a price offered was too low, their towns and the country around them came to be called 'Brass' by Europeans, though its African name was Nembe or Nimbe. In the early nineteenth century, like the people of the rival cities farther along the coast, the Brassmen turned to palm oil and the trade with Liverpool, signing treaties with Britain in which they agreed to cease the trade in slaves. When Laird entered the Niger in 1832 the Brassmen were attempting to build up a monopoly on the Niger, harassed by rivals from New Calabar, and by the truculence of the interior rulers, who were naturally averse to committing themselves to one buyer. Richard Lander was well aware of these rivalries; the Brassmen had once ransomed him from captivity on an earlier voyage and he knew them well, and Lander persuaded Laird not to enter into competition with the Brassmen for the palm oil trade, but to concentrate on the region to the north of the palm oil belt. By accepting this advice Laird obtained co-operation from the King of Brass, who helped to guide them up the network of creeks leading to the main Niger.[1]

---

[1] For the early traditional history of Brass see Tepowa, A., 'A Short History of Brass and its People', *Journal of the African Society*, London, Vol. VII, 1907–8, p. 32. For R. Lander's captivity see Howard, C. and Plumb, J., *West African Explorers*,

When the expedition reached the oil producing regions Laird was quick to appreciate the significance of the struggle between the Brassmen and the people on the river banks who collected the oil for sale to the Brassmen. These people welcomed competition, and encouraged men from Bonny to come and trade despite intimidation from the Brassmen. With a truly prophetic insight Laird imagined the impact of a regular traffic by steamship direct to Liverpool. With support from European traders, he thought, the people of the interior would dispense with the middlemen of the coast, and monopolize to themselves the trade with Europeans.[1] Though his real goal was the north, Laird realized, as all the traders after him were forced to do, that trade on the Niger would have to be based upon the palm oil regions for a reliable profit, and that the inevitable hostility of the Brassmen would have to be faced.

This analysis was borne out by Laird's first contact with the north; he made a journey into Nupe, only to find his high hopes of diverting the trans-Saharan trade dashed by the prevalence of revolution and anarchy.[2] The whole of the north was in fact just emerging from a period of religious and political turmoil. For centuries the indigenous people had been organized politically in the seven Hausa states, with the so-called 'bastard states', states which were often not Hausa by race and language, lying to the south bordering the Niger and Benue. In many ways these states were the most sophisticated political organism which Africans had yet attained, they had evolved elaborate systems of taxation, advanced military techniques, and a comparatively complex social system based on what was for Africa an intensive agriculture. As early as the fifteenth century an alien people, the Fulani, had begun to penetrate the Hausa states. They came bringing cattle and 'books on divinity'. The cattle were welcomed and allowed to graze on the fields after the harvests so as

1951, pp. 330–9. Lander contrasted the generosity of the Brassmen with the meanness of an English shipmaster at Brass, who refused to advance him the money to repay the King of Brass.

[1] Laird, M. and Oldfield, R. A. K., *Narrative of an Expedition into the Interior of Africa, by the River Niger . . .*, etc., London, 1837, 2 vols. Vol. I, p. 97 and p. 103.

[2] *Ibid.*, pp. 155–6, see also Oldfield's description of the situation on the Niger in Vol. II.

to fertilize the ground; the religious teachings were assimilated by a people already well under the sway of the Muslim religion which they shared with the Fulani immigrants. By the end of the seventeenth century the Fulani had many colonies in Hausaland, some of 'cattle Fulani' preserving an ancient pastoral life, some in the towns where Fulani made good as traders, teachers, and even as political advisers. But the Fulani had a puritanical streak which never blended well with the more easy-going and tolerant Hausa. The Hausa had taken Islam piecemeal, and their religion was mixed in with much superstition and with remnants of older beliefs in spirits which lived in rocks, trees, rivers and the like, or in animals or people. Hence tensions between the races began to flare up by the beginning of the nineteenth century. The revolt of the Fulani began in the far north, in Gobir, where the Hausa ruler tried to limit the privileges and immunities of the local Fulani, and in particular to control the preaching of a certain Uthman dan Fodio. Uthman replied by declaring a *jihad*, or holy war, against all the Hausa rulers, giving flags to emissaries sent to raise the other states. By 1809 the Fulani, under Uthman as *Sarkin Musulmi* or Commander of the Faithful, were supreme in Hausaland proper. Later the country became divided into Emirates under Uthman's successors, each Emir owing feudal services to the Emir of Gandu or to the Sultan of Sokoto, the twin heads of the new empire. In 1810 the revolutionary contagion reached Nupe in the shape of Dendo, a *mallam* or priest of Islam, who in that year began wandering and preaching in the country. He soon gathered a large following among the Fulani who lived in Nupe, and also attracted support from mercenary soldiers and the merchant classes in the towns in northern Nupe. In 1818 the death of the Nupe ruler, and a dispute among his sons for the succession, was the signal for the repetition of the Fulani *jihad* in Nupe. By the 1830's Mallam Dendo was the real ruler. Laird and Lander were able to meet him on their first trade venture in 1832;[1] a year later the old man had died, and chaos and anarchy once more visited the country as Dendo's four sons fought for

[1] Laird and Oldfield, *op. cit.*, Vol. II, p. 65.

the succession.[1] One of these sons, Masaba, had the political insight to appreciate the significance of the entry of the Europeans, and to use it and exploit the resources which the traders could provide, to end the anarchy in his country, and to make Nupe the most powerful state on the lower Niger. Masaba was later to be a factor to be reckoned with in the policies of Gladstone's government and in the ambitions of George Goldie.

Laird's first trading venture laid bare to the traders of Europe the possibilities on the lower banks of the River Niger, and the framework of African politics into which that trade would have to penetrate. At the mouth, the Brassmen, jealously guarding the palm oil 'markets' in their rear; behind them the peoples of the river banks wishing to establish direct contact to cut out the middlemen; and in the north, religious and political turmoil in a potentially rich area producing shea-butter (another vegetable oil product) and ivory. Yet in other ways Laird's venture had not been a success. It had not produced a trading profit, but much worse was the toll taken by disease. Thirty-nine of the forty-eight Europeans employed did not survive.[2] Laird did not return to the Niger until the use of quinine gave Europeans at least a fair chance of returning to England alive; meanwhile he used his shipbuilding experience to help build iron steamships which pioneered the Atlantic routes.

Others were less cautious. Thomas Fowell Buxton, the successor to Wilberforce as leader of the British anti-slavery movement, seized upon the evidence of Laird and the other explorers to develop the legitimate trade thesis to a disastrous practical conclusion. Starting from the conviction that the efforts of the Royal Navy to stop the slave trade by sea were of little use so

[1] The full history of the Fulani *jihad* in northern Nigeria has yet to be written. The above account is based on the *Kano Chronicle*, translated by H. R. Palmer in his *Sudanese Memoirs*, Lagos, 1928, Vol. III, pp. 98 ff. and on the contemporary accounts of European travellers, such as Clapperton, Barth, the Landers, and Laird himself. For Nupe I have made particular use of Nadel, S. F., *A Black Byzantium. The Kingdom of Nupe in Nigeria*, with a foreword by Lord Lugard, Oxford, 1942, reprint 1946, where the account is largely based on oral traditions acquired during field work.

[2] Burns, Alan, *History of Nigeria*, 4th ed., London, 1948, p. 90.

C

long as the sources of slave supply remained untouched, Buxton gathered together all the evidence he could find in the writings of the explorers to try to prove that, but for the human wastage of the slave trade, West Africa was potentially a wealthy area. In 1839, a year after the victory of the humanitarians in extinguishing the last vestiges of the status of slavery in the West Indies,[1] Buxton published *The African Slave Trade and the Remedy*.[2] The remedy, he suggested, lay in fitting out a large trading expedition to ascend the River Niger and convince the inhabitants by practical example that 'legitimate commerce' was more profitable than the trade in human beings. Now at the height of his influence, Buxton was able to get Government support for the venture, despite warnings from Laird, and the opposition of the Liverpool coastal merchants, who resented the idea of Government help in diverting the Niger produce from the hands of their African middlemen of the Oil Rivers.[3] The story of this Niger Expedition of 1841 needs no further recapitulation here;[4] the disastrous mortality (forty-eight of the 145 Europeans died) reinforced the dreadful lesson of Laird's attempt, and merely strengthened the arguments of the Liverpool traders that the system of African middlemen should be preserved and developed.

The failure of the 1841 Niger Expedition retarded progress for a decade. Not until the 'fifties did British Governments begin to show renewed interest. In an effort to lessen the risk from disease, they sent Richardson, Heinrich Barth and Overweg across the Sahara to explore the Niger Sudan. Heinrich Barth, a German by nationality, was perhaps the greatest of all the European explorers of Africa. The British Government could not have summoned a better emissary to preach the morals of Europe

---

[1] From 1833 to 1838 the ex-slaves in the West Indies had been constrained to work for the planters as 'apprentices'. This had been intended as a transitional status pending the establishment of a free labour market.

[2] Buxton, T. F., *The African Slave Trade and the Remedy*, London, 1839.

[3] See P.P. 1845, XLVIII, MS. p. 39. *Papers relative to the Expedition to the River Niger*.

[4] For the full story see Allen, W., and Thomson, T. R., *A Narrative of an Expedition sent by Her Majesty's Government to the River Niger in 1841*, 2 vols., London, 1848.

to Africa, and reveal the secrets of Africa to Europe. His greatest virtue, greater than his courage in wandering through so-called savage lands without military protection, greater than his instinctive flair for diplomacy in the intricate politics of African courts, greater even than his industry, was his curiosity. He was interested in all things African, in politics, religion, housing, economics, sports, flora, fauna, history, languages, social structure, in fact, everything about Africa. His curiosity, coupled with his industry, led to the publication of the five volumes of his *Travels* which Goldie read so assiduously during his stay in the Egyptian Sudan. The work is still a classic, and an essential study for any serious student of West African history.

The news that Barth had crossed the Benue River, the great tributary of the Niger which flows into it from the east, led to the re-entry of Macgregor Laird to the Niger. He was given a Government contract to build and equip a vessel which could ascend the Niger in an attempt to link up with the explorer. The command was first given to the British consul in Fernando Po, but he died before the voyage up the river could begin, and the command reverted to a naval officer, William Balfour Baikie.

Baikie's expedition was the greatest step forward in Nigerian commerce with Europe since the Lander brothers had made their revolutionary discovery of the mouths of the river. Baikie began the regular trade on the river. His was the first venture to trade at a profit. From this time forward Europeans appeared on the river every year. Moreover, this commerce was no longer monstrously costly in human lives. By administering regular doses of quinine to his men Baikie kept disease at bay, and they all returned alive.[1] He too was an exponent of the 'legitimate commerce' theory, and his writings strengthened the connexion between anti-slavery sentiment and the Niger trade. He again gave the impression, which Barth's writings were to reinforce, of the vast wealth waiting to be tapped:

[1] Burns, *op. cit.*, p. 94. Baikie, W. B., *Narrative of an exploring Voyage up the Rivers Kwora and Binue in 1854*, London, 1856. 'Kwora' or 'Kworra' was commonly used at this time to describe the River Niger above its confluence with the Benue.

We have met on friendly terms with numerous tribes, all endowed by nature with what I may term the 'commercial faculty', ready and anxious to trade with us, and to supply us from their inexhaustible stores, with immense quantities of highly prized articles. . . . We can also indicate a most important outlet for home manufactures, as the unclad millions of Central Africa must absorb thousands of cargoes of soft goods, eagerly bartering their raw cotton, their vegetable oils, and their ivory for our calicoes and cloths.[1]

But there were higher motives; a 'noble task' was in store for those who 'will pioneer the way of civilisation and Christianity' and help to stamp out 'the unnatural traffic in human beings'.

The only real method of effectively checking this detestable trade is by striking at the root of the supply, by going directly to the fountain head. . . . For these purposes no auxiliary is more effectual than commerce, which, to minds constituted like those of the Africans, is highly intelligible. Prove to them that they can derive more benefit by cultivating the ground and by selling their grain, their cam-wood, their palm-oil, their shea-butter, than by living in a state of perpetual warfare.[2]

Trade now began in earnest. Laird was given a Government subsidy for five years, on condition that at least one vessel visited the Niger above its confluence with the Benue every year. But though the aim was clearly the north, the south with its palm oil was soon seen to be more profitable. The hulks moored at Abo and Onitsha each did a brisk trade; that at Lokoja made little profit. Abo and Onitsha were right inside the palm oil producing region, which had by this time come under the domination of the Brassmen, who were quick to realize the danger to their hard-won monopoly. In 1859 Laird's steamer on its way down-river laden with produce, was attacked by tribes allied to Brass. He had barely had time to appeal for naval protection when his station at Abo was sacked.[3] This pattern of hostility became fixed in the decade of the 'sixties; the riverain tribes, coerced and armed by the Brassmen, made trade more and more violent and difficult. The struggle was not simply one between Africans and Europeans, for behind the Brassmen was

---

[1] Quoted from Baikie, *op. cit.*, in Howard and Plumb, *op. cit.*, p. 529.
[2] *Ibid.*, p. 531.   [3] Dike, *Trade and Politics in the Niger Delta*, pp. 171 ff.

the active support of the Liverpool merchants who supplied the
arms and ammunition, in an attempt to keep what they regarded as their own. The situation was made worse by the death
of Laird in 1861, and the retirement of Baikie due to ill-health in
1864. The Brassmen began to arm their up-country allies with
cannon and rifles, and the British traders had to rely on annual
naval expeditions and regular bombardments to keep the river
open to them.[1] This savage struggle had its counterpart in England on a more sophisticated level. When Laird's executor, supported by the anti-slavery movement, attempted to obtain a
renewal of the Government subsidy for a company to continue
Laird's work, the Liverpool merchants, now organized as the
'African Association' to protect their interests, canvassed the
merchants of Bristol and London, and their protests succeeded
in wrecking the scheme.[2]

The West African policy of the British Government in the
nineteenth century could easily be pictured as one of vacillation
and blundering, of decisions shirked or reversed, or as no policy
at all. To do this would be unfair. The agencies of government
were not well-informed of the facts of African life, and such
blundering and vacillation as occurred often arose from sheer
lack of information, or from the swiftly-moving kaleidoscope of
events in Africa outside the Government's control. In reality the
Government had a policy, or at least a firmly held set of attitudes
upon which policy was based. The remarkable fact is that the
bases of British policy remained fixed and almost unalterable
until nearly the end of the century, and it was this rigidity of
attitude which was to give George Goldie his opportunity for
free-lance colonization. The British attitude towards West
Africa was really very simple and straightforward, it rested
upon two bases which were accepted almost without question by
politicians, civil servants, and the general public; these bases

[1] *Ibid.*, p. 174.
[2] See P.P. 1864, XLI, *Papers relating to the grant of a subsidy to the Company of African Merchants.*

were, firstly that the effort to stamp out the slave trade must be continued, and secondly, that it was the duty of the British Government to give all reasonable assistance to the legitimate traders. The doctrine of the humanitarians that legitimate trade would drive out the slave trade by its own inherent superiority made these two attitudes complementary, and also fitted perfectly the dominant economic theory of the time—the belief in free trade. In fact the doctrine of legitimate commerce was simply free trade morality adapted to the conditions of West Africa.

The idea of expanding British territory, or establishing colonial regimes, was not a part of this policy. At times, however, the establishment of a colony might become a technique used to aid the expansion of legitimate trade. Lagos had been annexed in 1861 because the local ruler had revived the slave trade and reduced the flow of legitimate commerce to a trickle. The new colony was intended both to coerce the slave traders, and to attract to itself the legitimate trade of the Yoruba people in the hinterland.[1] But ordinarily annexation was avoided wherever possible; the officials at home, besides being convinced on theoretical grounds that territorial expansion was unnecessary, had little incentive to encourage the creation of colonies in fever-ridden areas where their own friends and colleagues might be sent to meet a painful and inglorious death. Instead they raised the usual free trade objections, and urged that the private efforts of legitimate traders were enough gradually to kill the slave trade. If the legitimate traders needed support, then the occasional gunboat could provide it.

Behind the reluctance of the officials there were groups in Parliament whose activities could intensify the prejudice against establishing new colonies in Africa. There had long been a strong undercurrent of opposition to the humanitarians, and failures like the Niger Expedition of 1841 always produced a Select Committee of Inquiry. The spirit behind this attitude was

---

[1] Burns, *op. cit.*, Chap. XI. Biobaku, S. O., *The Egba and their Neighbours 1842–1872*, Oxford, 1957, discusses the annexation and its background in his Chap. 4, and on pp. 68–69.

not anti-imperialist, in fact its leaders, like C. B. Adderley, were often 'Colonial Reformers' and violent partisans of colonization in Australasia. They had old scores to pay off against the humanitarians who had supported the Maori in New Zealand, and they could muster support among the rank and file in the Commons because of the almost megalomaniac concern which those gentlemen always evinced for economy in Government expenditure. Reverses and scandals in the Gold Coast produced such an inquiry in 1865, and a committee pronounced upon the results of British rule in West African settlements. Its report advised economies in administration, the preparation of local peoples for self-rule, and insisted that no further expansion should be undertaken.[1]

Though most of its recommendations were never seriously attempted, the policy laid down by the 1865 Committee had important repercussions on the Niger. The scheme for resurrecting Laird's subsidy had already fallen through. Baikie, who had held a vague official position 'in command of the Niger expedition', was replaced by a consul at Lokoja in 1867, but the man appointed turned out to be an inveterate drunkard, and the post was abolished in 1869.[2] All that remained in the way of an official link with the Niger was the annual naval expedition, sent to overawe the opposition of the coastal middlemen and their allies. The British Government now began to consider how to get rid of this crude 'protection'. On the coasts the middleman system had provided a framework through which legitimate commerce could be carried on, at no expense to the British Treasury. The attempt to get behind the middlemen on the Niger had reduced the banks of the river to anarchy, but could not some substitute (having all the convenience which the middleman system provided on the coast) be effected in the interior, so that British traders could proceed unmolested, and the naval expeditions be withdrawn? It was natural that the British should look to the power of Nupe as a possible substitute.

---

[1] P.P. 1865, V. *Report of the Select Committee on the State of British Settlements on the West Coast of Africa.*

[2] Burns, *op. cit.*, p. 135. See minutes on FO 84/1551 Simpson to F.O. 21.11.71.

Here was a state which was recognizable as a state in the eyes of an Englishman; it had a central authority in the person of the Emir or *Etsu* (as the Nupe preferred to call him), a standing army, a treasury and taxation system, and a body of law—all of which recalled to Englishmen the systems of government of the Muslim states of the Middle East or India, and were in marked contrast to the institutions of the tribal communities lower down the river, as yet unopened to the understanding of Europeans by the interpretations of even the amateur anthropologists.

It was therefore decided that an attempt should be made to carry on the trade under the protection of Nupe, and to withdraw British naval protection. In June 1871 W. H. Simpson sailed from Liverpool with instructions from the Foreign Office to negotiate with the Emir of Nupe to secure such protection.[1] So the first step in the effective British penetration of the river was to make British subjects the 'protected persons' of an African ruler.

That ruler was Masaba, a son of Mallam Dendo and a Nupe mother; Masaba, who had won his uneasy throne after decades of struggle with Fulani and Nupe rivals. His genius lay in recognizing the part which the British traders now appearing on the Niger could play in consolidating his own power in Nupe. He had supported all extensions of British influence on the river, provided no inroads were made into Nupe territory. He had welcomed the consulate at Lokoja, had befriended Baikie, and defended his settlement with troops. His aim in so doing was to draw to Nupe the bulk of the trade of the north, particularly ivory, and to bring the British traders to Egga in search of it. In return for the ivory and for locally produced shea-butter, the Europeans were to barter not gin and rum as they did in the south, for these were forbidden to Muslims, nor Manchester cottons, for the locally produced hand-woven textiles were cheaper and better, but European arms and ammunition. In 1833 the Nupe forces were armed with swords, knives and poisoned arrows.[2] In 1871 there was a flourishing trade with

---

[1] FO 84/1351 Simpson to Granville 21.11.71 (narrative report).
[2] Laird and Oldfield, *op. cit.*, Vol. II, pp. 86-7.

several English firms, whose imports to Nupe consisted almost entirely of arms and powder. The Nupe army was organized around a nucleus of 2,000 mounted men armed with European rifles, and Masaba's arsenal at the capital city of Bida boasted eight cannon, two of them six-pounders.[1] Nupe's time of troubles was over, and Masaba was ready to begin her expansion.

Simpson's task of persuading the Emir to give protection to the British traders was thus not a difficult one. Masaba confessed that he 'could never sleep with gunboats on the river' and viewed the prospect of their departure with some relief. Nevertheless he would not give his protection gratis. His price was no less than the creation of a middleman system on the upper part of the river; his aim was 'to monopolize and retain at Egga the whole of the British trade above Onitsha', and Nupe traders would act as middlemen to supply the north with British goods. The aim was ambitious—Nupe was to control the commercial intercourse between Europe and the western Sudan, and consequently dominate the surrounding areas with European firearms (the re-export of which was already prohibited).[2] To all these plans Simpson gave his approval[3] and the Emir then signed a letter to the Foreign Secretary in which he agreed to protect British traders on the Niger between Idah and Egga, and to open up the Benue to trade.[4] Thus Britain encouraged Masaba to create an African empire, in the hope that this would provide a regime strong enough to assist the development of British trade.

The inauguration of this policy undoubtedly stimulated the British Niger trade, and in the next few years its value doubled and redoubled. The value of ivory taken out of Nupe was £13,500 in 1871, by 1876 it had risen to £24,000, and in the next two years it rose to £52,000. No less important was the

[1] FO 84/1351 Simpson to Granville 21.11.71, p. 3 and p. 21.

[2] Ibid., see esp. pp. 3, 12, 17–21.

[3] E.g. in the way that he persuaded the West African Co. not to try to open up trade on the Benue, but to buy through Nupe agents. Ibid., p. 18.

[4] FO 84/1351 Masaba to Granville 22.9.71.

rise in the exports of shea-butter. Chevruel had conducted experiments with shea-butter in the 1830's and found it a perfect substitute for palm oil, but the real exploitation of Nupe's resources of this crop only began after 1871. In that year the traders had exported only 120 tons, valued at £4,800, in 1876 they exported £25,460 worth, by 1878 they were taking away 1,500 tons valued at £58,500.[1]

This prosperity naturally increased the competitive nature of the Niger trade (as Masaba had intended); the price paid for ivory increased by 60 per cent between 1871 and 1878. What worried the Europeans more, and was eventually to lead to real difficulties, was the multiplication of European firms engaged in the trade. In 1869 only the London firm of Holland Jacques and Company, then run by Goldie's relative Captain Grove-Ross, and the West African Company of Manchester, shared the trade. Holland Jacques were newcomers, but the West Africa Company had been some years on the river, and was heir to tradition of humanitarian 'legitimate commerce'. Among its shareholders was Samuel Ajayi Crowther, the Yoruba ex-slave who was consecrated Bishop of the Niger Territories in 1864. His shares were not his personal property, but represented funds invested by the Church Missionary Society.[2] In the 1870's the Bishop's son Josiah Crowther was put in charge of the company's trade on the Niger, and all the Europeans except the engineers and ship's captains were dismissed, another example of the curious phase of 'self-rule' after the 1865 committee.[3]

---

[1] It is fortunate that three estimates, based on the returns of the Niger traders, were made in 1871, 1876, and 1878, and these figures are taken from them. It is safe to presume that they are reasonably accurate, they were given to British officers in confidence at a time when there was no British taxation on the trade to be avoided. They can be found in FO 84/1351 Simpson to Granville 21.11.71, p. 10, *Estimates of Niger Trade 1871*; FO 84/1498 Conf. Print 3029, Journal of 1876 Niger Expedition by Comdr. W. H. Hewett, enc. 1 in Admiralty to F.O. 13.12.76, *Estimates of Niger Trade 1876*; FO 84/1508 Consul Hopkins to F.O. 18.11.78, *Produce shipped from the Niger 1878*. Figures used hereafter in the text for these years come from the appropriate source referred to here.

[2] C.M.S A3/04(a) 1879 Crowther to Hutchinson 16.10.79.

[3] FO 84/1508 Hopkins to F.O. 18.11.78 discusses this move and praises the African staff. The arrangement for Masaba's 'protectorate', Samuel Crowther's appointment as bishop, and the regime of African self-government by committee in Abeokuta are all examples of this attempt to support the recommendations of the

Though these firms might have preferred to concentrate on the north, the experience of Laird was constantly re-emphasized, and it was not found possible to ignore the palm oil trade; in fact one-half to three-fifths of the Niger trade was palm oil taken from the lower river, hitherto the preserve of the African coastal middlemen. In fact the very rigidity of the monopolistic system on the coast was driving new firms into the Niger for palm oil. The early history of the famous firm of Miller Brothers is a case in point. Millers were a Glasgow firm which had attempted to break into Liverpool's preserve in 1869 when they had tried to start a 'factory' at Brass; within a year they had been forced to retire in face of the Liverpool stranglehold.[1] They obtained another footing in the Oil Rivers by seizing, with a determination characteristic of their persistence and opportunism, the chance created for them by African politics in the city-state of Bonny, which still controlled the largest share of the producing regions behind the coast. In 1869 civil war had broken out, and Ja Ja, the most skilful trader in Bonny, seceded with his followers to found the new settlement of Opobo. Millers gave Ja Ja their entire support, and Ja Ja was assisted in his successful attempt to capture much of the Bonny 'sphere of influence'. The palm oil then began to flow into Glasgow.[2] This success emboldened Millers to move into the Niger. They built a new steamer, aptly named the *Ja Ja*, and in 1871 this vessel made four Niger voyages, three to Onitsha for palm oil, and one to Egga in search of Nupe shea-butter. She was the largest ship on the river, and captured about a quarter of the Niger exports of 1871. By 1876 Millers held the dominant position in the Niger trade, running two large steamers and a steam launch, which together made seventeen voyages, eleven for palm oil on the lower river, and six to Nupe.[3]

1865 committee. It came to an abrupt end in the 1880's when European protectorates were established. There is a most interesting discussion of this phase in Ajayi, J. F., 'Christian Missions and the making of Nigeria, 1841–91', unpublished Ph.D. thesis, 1958, in the University of London Library.

[1] FO 84/1407 Miller Bros. to F.O. 31.12.74 recounts their early history.
[2] *Ibid.* See also Dike, *op. cit.*, pp. 182 ff., Chap. X, 'The Rise of Ja Ja'.
[3] FO 84/1351 Simpson to Granville 21.11.71 inc. List of Vessels and Owners. FO 84/1498 Conf. Print 3029, Cmdr. Hewett's Report.

The voyages of the other firms displayed the same reliance on palm oil; by 1878, to a total export trade of £309,100, palm oil contributed a value of £195,000. The coastal Africans were no more inclined to accept this competition than they had been in the days of Laird. Their case was ably put in a letter from King Ockiah of Brass to the Foreign Office, written in 1876:

Many years ago we used to make our living by selling slaves to Europeans, which was stopped by your government, and a treaty made between you and our country that we should discontinue doing so; and that we should enter into legitimate trade . . . this we did and our trade gradually increased until we shipped an average of about 4,500 or 5,000 tons of palm oil per annum.

To do this we had to open up places on the Niger, trading stations, or markets as we call them, up as far as a place called Onitsha. . . .

Some years ago the white men began trading in the Niger . . . they did us no harm as long as they went up a long way further than we could go in their steamers, and also bought a different kind of produce. . . . But lately, within the last six years, they have been putting up trading stations at our places . . . (now) we do not send 1,500 (tons of palm oil) per annum. . . .

It is very hard on us, in all the other rivers . . . the markets are secured to them, and why should a difference be made for this my river. We have no land where we can grow plantains or yams, if we cannot trade we must starve.

What we want is, that the markets we have made between the river and Onitsha should be left to ourselves.[1]

The Brassmen did not confine their opposition to mere verbiage, but invoked their alliances with the riverain tribes. In 1871 a Holland Jacques steamer was attacked, forced up river, and then cleverly sent to the bottom on her return down the river after she had spit herself on a sunken spike placed there for the purpose.[2] In 1875 the same company had a ship whose fo'c'sle was smashed by a nine-pounder shell, and in the same year Millers' best steamer, the *Sultan of Sockotoo* was attacked by Africans instigated by the Brassmen and armed by the Liverpool traders.[3] The Niger traders demanded protection on the lower

[1] Ockiah and other chiefs of Brass to F.O. 7.7.76 forwarded in FO 84/1498 Admiralty to F.O. 13.12.76.
[2] FO 84/1351 Holland Jacques and Co. to F.O. 12.7.71.
[3] FO 84/1498 Admiralty to F.O. 13.12.76.

river, and gunboats went up in the high water of 1876 and bombarded and burned several of the offending villages.[1] Despite protests from the Liverpool traders,[2] naval protection was given to the Niger traders with ever-increasing frequency after 1876, but it was confined to the lower river, outside the region which Masaba had promised to protect.

The Niger traders had other difficulties. In 1871 Simpson had commented on 'excessive competition' among the firms, and prophesied failure if it were not restricted.[3] His warning was justified by the experience of the next seven years. The increases in prices paid were not crippling, but the competitive basis of the trade was obviously wasteful. By 1878 the three main companies had all established an identical chain of trading posts along the river; where one broke new ground, the others were quick to follow, at each place the three competed for produce.[4] The worst sufferer was naturally the smallest firm, Holland Jacques and Company, and by 1875 it was in such difficulties that the secretary, Captain Grove-Ross, made his appeal to his son-in-law, John Senhouse Goldie Taubman, for financial help. The response of the Taubman family has already been noticed.[5] The family bought out the entire assets of the company and George was given the control and the task of putting the business in order. He and another brother, Alexander, planned to visit the Niger and see for themselves the conditions of trade.

Before this journey began George had made a diagnosis and begun to prescribe a remedy. Over-competition was the disease, and monopoly the only cure. Such a monopoly could not be won by Holland Jacques alone, for the company was too small; it would have to be achieved by persuading all the other traders to come together. The first move took place in May 1876, when Goldie reorganized the structure of the company. This he did by forming a new company, the Central African Trading Company Ltd., of which he and Grove-Ross were the sole directors. This new company now bought the assets of Holland Jacques

---

[1] *Ibid., loc. cit.*, discusses these expeditions.
[2] FO 84/1499 African Association to F.O. 1.12.76.
[3] FO 84/1351 Simpson to Granville 21.11.71, p. 6.
[4] FO 84/1508 Hopkins to F.O. 18.11.78.   [5] See Chap. 1, pp. 7–8.

and Company, owned by Goldie, in return for shares of the face value of ten pounds each. Goldie now owned 1,135 shares in the new company, his brother Alexander 401, another relative, Helen Erskine, 268, and Grove-Ross and four others each held one share to make up the statutory seven persons needed to form a company. The purpose of this manœuvre may be found in the memoranda of association of the new company; one of its objects was to be:

The making and carrying into effect of arrangements with respect to the union of interests, or amalgamation, either in whole or in part, of the company with other companies.[1]

Shortly afterwards Goldie and his brother set off to the Niger, intending to travel overland to the Nile. This plan had to be abandoned, for Alexander fell ill in Nupe and had to return home.[2] No doubt what he had seen further convinced Goldie that amalgamation was the only salvation for the Niger trade. Negotiation with the other firms were already under way before his return. In May 1877 the West Africa Company reformed itself as the West African Company, giving the new company power to amalgamate with other companies.[3] There were two other firms on the Niger, Miller Brothers and James Pinnock, a free-lance from Liverpool who specialized in the trade of Benin, but these were not incorporated as companies, and so did not need to take special powers to amalgamate.

The way was now clear for amalgamation. The moving spirit behind the idea was Goldie, and it is an indication of his skill in bringing it about to note that his company was the smallest of the three main companies involved. He did not emerge from the amalgamation with any dominant financial control of the new company; yet the leadership was his, throughout the company's history until his retirement. Here is perhaps the most graphic illustration of the almost hypnotic influence which he could

---

[1] R.J.S.C. 10605 Central African Trading Co. Ltd., Mem. of Assn., Arts. of Assn., Agreement between G. D. Goldie Taubman and Central African Trading Co. Ltd. 31.5.76. Capital and shares 24.1.77.

[2] Mary Kingsley, *The Story of West Africa*, London, 1899, pp. 150–1.

[3] R.J.S.C. 11464 West African Co. Ltd., Mem. of Assn. 16.5.77. Capital and shares 12.9.77, Articles of Assn.

exert over others; in 1879 he was completely 'green', without more knowledge of the Niger than that provided by one brief visit, with no experience of trading or shipping, or even that which another career might have given him; nor could he force his will upon the others by financial power. Yet the amalgamation of the Niger firms meant that a group of tough hard-headed business men, fighters like the hard-bargaining Scot Alexander Miller, men like John Edgar of the West African Company with widespread interests in cotton, palm oil, chemicals, and the manufacture of ice, or individualists like James Pinnock, put their trust in a young man of no proven talents, known to be something of a profligate, who had already bungled an army career and made an unfortunate marriage, and who was as yet only thirty-three years old.

The technique of amalgamation was the same as that used in the previous manœuvres and floatations. On 20 November 1879 the United African Company was formed with limited liability and a nominal capital of £250,000. As with the other floatations no actual cash was introduced. The new company then made a series of agreements with the Niger firms in which it bought all their assets and rights on the river. The payment took the form of shares in the new company which were considered to be fully paid up shares. As each of the old firms received shares in the new company proportionate to the assets it had sold, the new United African Company was in fact an alliance. No group emerged with a controlling number of shares. Miller Brothers received the largest allotment, 5,400; the Goldie family, as proprietors of the Central African Company, obtained 4,400 and the interests of the West African Company, now in the hands of John Edgar and a few of his relatives, 4,320. Pinnock, the sole representative of Liverpool, obtained 960. Thus the control rested with any two of the three larger groups. In fact all the three large holdings co-operated together throughout the company's history, the only internal conflict was to be with Pinnock, whose small interest could safely be ignored.[1]

[1] R.J.S.C. 13209 United African Company Ltd., Capital and shares 20.11.79. Agreement with Miller Bros. 5.8.79, with Pinnock 8.8.79, with John Edgar 9.7.79, with Central African Trading Co. Ltd. 8.8.79.

The monopolistic character of the new company was revealed in the articles of association. Article 15 stipulated that no shareholder was permitted to trade on the Niger, Tchadda (Benue), Nun (Niger mouth) or Brass rivers, within a thousand miles of Akassa; or in any affluent or branch of these rivers within twenty-five miles of them (this allowed Pinnock to continue his Benin trade and Millers to continue at Opobo in the Oil Rivers). If these rules were broken the offender would forfeit his shares, which could be re-allotted by the directors as they saw fit. The power of the directors was dictatorial and complete. They were named in the articles of association and made irremovable for seven years, regardless of shareholders' voting. Moreover shareholders' rights were severely limited; for the first three years of the company's life shares could not be transferred except to another shareholder, and when this time had elapsed any prospective seller had first to offer his shares to the directors, if they refused his price he could not thereafter sell for less than that price.[1]

In short, the formation of the United African Company was based on an agreement between all the Niger firms to cease competition, to pool their ships, stores and staff into one organization, and to share the resultant profits proportionately between themselves.

This was the company which was about to embark on a career not only of commercial, but of political, expansion. This company was to become Britain's imperial agent on the Niger. Its structure is therefore worth closer examination. The most influential annalist of late-Victorian imperialism asserted that 'the dominant and directive motive was the demand for markets and for profitable investment by the exporting and financial classes';[2] if this be so then there was not much of imperialism about the United African Company. Not one of its shareholders

---

[1] *Ibid.* Arts. of Assn. see esp. clauses 23, 24, and 59. The directors named were W. Dixon, J. Edgar, C. B. Edgar, for the West African Company; J. S. Goldie Taubman, A. H. Goldie Taubman, and G. D. Goldie Taubman, for the Central African Company; Alexander Miller, Geo. Miller, A. MacEachen and J. Croft, for Millers; and J. Pinnock.

[2] Hobson, J. A., *Imperialism, a study*, 3rd ed., London, 1938, pp. v–vi.

could claim to be a member of the 'exporting and financial classes'. The company's main exports were fire-arms and alcoholic liquors, mainly gin and rum, but no armament interest was represented in the shareholders, and the liquor was manufactured not in Britain, but in Rotterdam and Hamburg, and re-shipped from Liverpool. In fact the exporting function was secondary, these were barter goods to obtain the African produce. Not even the ubiquitous Manchester cotton exporters were as yet represented in the new company. If the directors were not exporters, still less were they financiers looking for opportunities to invest. The Taubmans were minor landed aristocrats, the rest were small merchants, all of them specialists of the West African trade, and of the Niger trade in particular. Economically their function was neither to provide an outlet for surplus capital (for they had none and could attract none), nor to foster British exports. If they had a precise function in world economics it was to supply the developing soap and chemical industries of Lancashire and Cheshire with tropical raw materials.

If Goldie already had plans for obtaining political powers, the company had a long way to go in 1879. There were no close links with the British Government, and no close ties of influence or friendship. The Foreign Office was informed of the amalgamation after it had taken place,[1] but took no part in shaping its form. In a general way the Government was prepared to support the Niger traders; it was not prepared to hamper them in order to favour the Liverpool interests, but any idea of establishing a colony, protectorate, or British administration on the Niger was, in 1879, utterly remote and fantastic.

[1] FO 84/1611 U.A. Co. to F.O. 19.1.81.

3

Towards Political Power

PERHAPS Goldie imagined that the formation of the United
African Company in 1879, and the inauguration of a system of
monopoly by agreement, would prove a final solution to the
difficulties of the Niger traders. If so he was to be rudely dis-
appointed on the very morrow of his success. There were grave
weaknesses in the new conception. The success of a monopolistic
policy was of itself a new incentive to renewed competition, for
the object of amalgamation was to strengthen the bargaining
power of the Europeans in order to reduce the prices paid to
Africans for their produce. If the policy succeeded, and prices
fell on the Niger, then the Niger trade would naturally begin to
draw the attention of merchants buying produce in other areas
where competing Europeans had to pay more for produce. Thus
new traders would appear in the Niger and competition would
recommence. Of course, the newcomers might be bought out, or
persuaded to join the amalgamated company, but these were
techniques which could not be used indefinitely, and in a sense
they were defeatist, in that they admitted rivals to a share in the
trade on equal terms.

In fact new competitors appeared on the Niger almost before
the United African Company was in existence. If the newcomers
had been simply a fresh influx of British traders the United
Company might have been a dismal failure. But the interlopers
were French, and this entirely altered the situation; it made it
more dangerous, but it also provided new opportunities which
Goldie was prepared to seize, and delicate situations which he
was prepared to exploit. Though French competition was at first

apparently purely commercial, on the Niger there could never be 'pure' commerce; trade and politics were inseparably mixed together. The French intervention translated the Niger question from the level of the balance-sheet to the level of the diplomatic note, and Goldie from an obscure business man to a familiar name in the Foreign and Colonial Offices.

The history of French activities in West Africa at first sight bears superficial resemblances to that of the British. In the 1870's while Britain was attempting to implement the recommendations of the 1865 Committee, France was similarly reluctant to assume responsibility for ruling African territory; officials were withdrawn from French stations,[1] and France seriously considered the abandonment of all her West African colonies except Senegal.[2] Nevertheless there were fundamental differences in the French approach. Since the time of Napoleon III France had looked to the interior of Africa for markets and material, her coastal stations were regarded as bases from which to penetrate the interior rather than part of a finished commercial system. French traders were not committed to African middlemen on anything like the scale of British traders. Moreover France was not a free-trading country, her industry was backward and uncompetitive in comparison with Britain's, and the arguments against colonies born of the free trade theory did not therefore carry much weight. It was very well for Britain to argue for the preservation of the African systems of government, no colonies, and free trade for all, when in fact this meant virtually a British monopoly of the trade. France must look to colonies in which she could set up tariffs against her rivals. In the years after 1879 such thinking began to have an increasing effect on French policy. The pioneers were the French traders, who had preserved French influence in the seventies, and now assumed a more aggressive role. Private treaties were signed with African rulers, railway schemes for linking scattered outposts advocated, and private missions sent off to the interior, particularly to the upper Niger to look for its

[1] E.g. Assiné, Grand Bassam and Dabou, in 1872. See Masson, P., *Marseilles et la colonisation française*, Paris, 1912, p. 404.
[2] Blet, *France D'outre Mer, L'œuvre de la Troisième République*, Paris, 1950, p. 9.

sources.[1] Their activities were soon reflected by the French Government; in 1879 a commission began to inquire into the feasibility of a railway from Senegal to Algeria, official treaty-making expeditions began to wander over the upper Niger, and in 1881 the first section of the railway from St. Louis to the Niger was sanctioned.[2]

Goldie was not therefore over-suspicious when he assumed a deeper political purpose behind the appearance of French traders on the lower Niger in competition with the newly formed United African Company. Taken as part of the general renaissance of French political and commercial activity in West Africa, the move seemed ominous; particularly in the light of French activity far up the river near its sources, and the well-known French predilection for grandiose plans for linking scattered possessions on interior lines. What better method of linking could there be than the Niger, one of the longest and most navigable rivers in Africa?

The French intervention on the lower river began in 1878 with the visit of the Compte de Semellé. This journey was exploratory, but thorough; the Count visited Nupe and obtained a promise from Umoru, who had succeeded as Emir on the death of Masaba in 1873, that the French might trade freely in Nupe.[3] At the same time he acquired land on which to build trading stations.[4] Returning to France, Semellé then succeeded in forming the *Compagnie française de l'Afrique equatoriale* to exploit these concessions.[5]

In his absence the British company had been busy; negotia-

[1] Olivier de Sanderval advocated the occupation of Futa Jallon, near the sources of the Niger, before 1870. Later he argued that Futa Jallon should be a jumping-off point for expansion down the Niger and the eventual acquisition of Lake Chad. In 1880 he obtained permission from the ruler of Futa Jallon for a railway linking it to the coast. C. A. Verminck, a self-made merchant and industrialist from Marseilles, sent Zweifel and Bayol on a mission to the Niger sources in 1879. Masson, *op. cit.*, pp. 396–400.

[2] Blet, *op. cit.*, pp. 135–6.

[3] C.M.S. C.A5/04 Bishop Crowther to Ed. Hutchinson, 28.8.80.

[4] *Ibid., loc. cit.*, same to same 6.9.78.

[5] Masson, *op. cit.*, p. 407. Hanotaux G., and Martineau, A., editors, *Histoire des colonies françaises et de l'expansion de la France dans le monde*, Tome IV, Paris, 1931, p. 311.

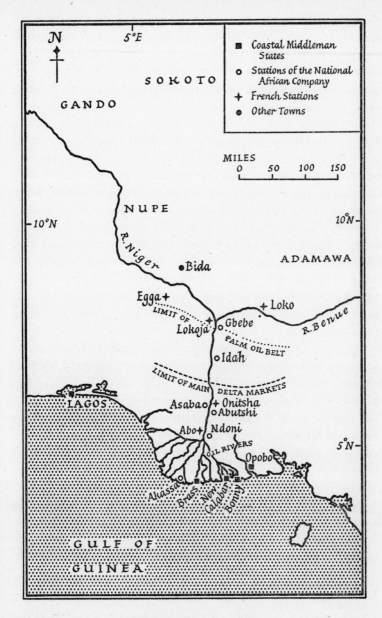

1. Trading Situation 1880–4

tions with Umoru gave the United African Company a monopoly of Nupe's trade with Europeans, and when Semellé returned to Nupe in 1880 he received a cold reception and was told that his concession of the previous year was now rescinded, and that he had no right to trade.[1] Nevertheless the Frenchman persevered, and set up stations outside Nupe proper at Abo, Onitsha and Egga on the Niger, and at Loko on the Benue,[2] all of them at places where the United African Company had stations. His death on this trip did not prevent his company from continuing to attract financial support from merchants and simple investors in Paris and the French maritime towns, and its capital was now increased to three million francs.[3] Semellé's death also gave a distinct political twist to the rivalry, for now the French War Ministry lent the services of Commandant Mattei to direct the company's operations on the Niger, and the Foreign Ministry gave him the status of *agent consulaire*.[4] Within a few months Mattei had succeeded in breaking the United Company's monopoly both in Nupe and in the palm oil trade of the lower river.

In Nupe Mattei's success in overcoming the Emir's previous refusal to allow the French to trade was achieved by direct political means. As soon as Umoru announced that he had tied himself to the British company, opposition arose to it among his subjects. A group of dissaffected army chiefs seized on this issue to raise a rebellion, demanding free trade with the French. The rebels produced a pretender to the throne and the country was soon in chaos. But there was little to daunt Umoru in this, the forty-second rebellion in the past fifty years of Nupe history, and he soon re-established himself, defeated the rebels, and killed the pretender. The commercial grievance, however, still remained, and it was this which almost immediately caused a second, more serious, revolt, which contemporary observers agree came with-

[1] C.M.S. C.A3/04 Bishop Crowther to Hutchinson 16.8.80, see also C.M.S. C.A3/01 Bishop Crowther to Rev. Lang 31.12.82.

[2] C.M.S. C.A3/04 Bishop Crowther to Hutchinson 7.10.80.

[3] Masson, *op. cit.*, p. 311. R.J.S.C. 17049, Vol. I, gives a list of the French shareholders and their allotments in the United Company in 1884.

[4] Hanotaux and Martineau, *op. cit.*, p. 310. Masson, *op. cit.*, p. 407.

in an ace of destroying the regime in Nupe. This second revolt
was the work of the Kede people. The Kede held a strange but
powerful position in the economic life of the country. They were
the 'ferrymen', responsible for the carriage of goods across the
Niger. They thus controlled the sole means of communication
between the two halves of the country. No sooner had the army
rebels been defeated than these people rose in revolt. Their first
move was to seize every canoe between Rabba and Egga, thus
cutting off the Emir from his sole source of arms and ammunition—the British company. By the early months of 1882 the
Kede were in absolute control of the river banks and the Emir
was impotent in his capital at Bida. Without the huge canoes of
the ferrymen the Emir was unable to get his cavalry across to
the southern side of the river to tackle the Kede. He therefore
turned to the British company for help. As soon as the news was
received the United Company agents loaded up a steamer with
rifles, three large cannon, and a Gatling gun, and steamed her
up the river to tackle the rebels. At this point Mattei, seeing the
drift of events, insisted that a French ship join the demonstration. The Kede were no match for this display of European
power; the steamers put their canoes to flight, embarked the
Emir's cavalry aboard, and shipped them across the river, where
they defeated the rebels in open battle.[1]

The revolt in Nupe was a political manifestation of the
impracticability of the system of monopoly by agreement which
the formation of the United Company had been designed to
secure. By assisting the Emir the French secured re-entry into
the Nupe trade. On the lower river their position was already
established in the palm oil trade, by 1882 the French had established seventeen floating stations on the lower river, with their
headquarters among the British company's enemies the Brassmen. Nor were the French the only rivals to Goldie's company.

[1] This narrative is built from two main sources; the oral evidence put forward by
Nadel in *A Black Byzantium*, which is somewhat inaccurate as to dates and names,
and the written evidence of missionaries, particularly the eye-witness Rev. C. Paul,
whose description can be found in C.M.S. G.3 A3/01, no. 129 of 1883 entitled
The Rebellion in Nupe. Under the same reference, see also no. 65 of 1882 Archdeacon
Johnson to Bishop Crowther 19.3.82, and 95 of 1882 Rev. John to Bishop Crowther
2.5.82.

In 1882 two Liverpool firms began trading with small launches, and gave passages to African traders from Sierra Leone and Lagos, whom Goldie had barred from passage on United Company boats.[1] The problem of competition from the Brass traders was even more formidable.

'They came last year in shoals,' wrote the African Archdeacon Johnson to his Bishop, 'and were underselling the Company, when Mr. McIntosh (the chief agent) gives one case of gin for a measure, Brassmen give two cases, McIntosh immediately ordered three cases to be given . . . the relation between the Company and the Brassmen was becoming strained. The latter were preparing to defend their position *with arms* if need were.'[2]

It must have seemed to Goldie as if his entire scheme to end competition had failed, and the situation of the years before 1879 had returned. By the end of 1882 the French company was equal, if not superior in strength. As before, Goldie turned to negotiate with his rivals to try to bring the French into the United African Company.[3] At the same time he began a commercial war on the Niger to try to force the French to come to terms; prices paid to Africans were increased by twenty-five per cent and a large expansion in the number of the company's stations was undertaken.[4]

But this was a policy born of desperation, and could not be a final solution. Even if the French could be bought out and a second amalgamation take place, there still remained the other British firms already coming into the Niger, and the others which would follow whenever prices were low. A third amalgamation, or a fourth, would carry the process to absurdity. Even if all the European rivals could be bought out successively and indefinitely, there then remained the African competition which could not be bought, whether it were from Brass, or from Sierra

[1] C.M.S. G3 A3/o1, no. 15 of 1882 Bishop Crowther to Rev. Lang 31.12.82.
[2] *Ibid.* 37 of 1882, Johnson to Crowther 7.1.82. Italics in the original.
[3] PRO 30/29/269 (Granville Papers) F.O. Conf. Print 4825, *Oil Rivers and British Protectorate*, Part II, C.O. to F.O. 6.1.83 with enclosures p. 2. From here on F.O. confidential prints will be referred to by their serial numbers. They can be found in the Granville Papers.
[4] *The Times* 10.12.85. Special Report of National African Company Ltd.

Leone and Lagos. Some new method would have to be found to secure the monopoly, though meanwhile negotiations with the French traders could continue.

There was a solution in British colonial history. Before the days of free trade the normal way to obtain a commercial privilege or monopoly was to acquire it from the Crown by Royal Charter. Though many companies had been incorporated by charter, the technique was particularly characteristic of colonial companies. It was used extensively in the settlement of America, and had achieved its apogee in the eighteenth century with a plethora of chartered companies which held sway over the slave trade, the fur trade of Canada, and the trade of the East Indies. But the nineteenth century movements for political reform and free trade gradually got rid of these bastions of political privilege and protection until only the mammoth East India and Hudson's Bay Companies survived. Even these eventually lost their political rights, the former in 1858, the latter in 1869. Could Goldie hope to obtain a charter giving him a monopoly on the Niger from a Liberal Government like that of Gladstone which had come into power in 1880? Surely the idea was absurd. Chartered companies were outmoded, they had been proved by experience to be corrupt, oligarchic, supporters of privilege in England and oppression in the colonies, and, what was more important, enemies of free trade.

Nevertheless there is evidence as early as 1879 that Goldie believed that a charter would prove the answer to all his problems on the Niger. Immediately before the announcement of the formation of the United African Company Bishop Crowther heard rumours on the Niger 'that the Company is contemplating to get a charter of the Niger trade to the exclusion of others entering', but he was too sensible to believe 'sayings afloat . . . got up by some busybodies to stir up the feelings of the public'.[1] Goldie himself said in later life that he had asked for a charter in 1881, and that it was refused on the ground that the company had not enough capital, but the records show no trace of this

[1] C.M.S. C.A3/04(a) Bishop Crowther to Hutchinson 16.10.79.

episode.[1] Then, just as Goldie was pondering this idea of a charter, and no doubt reflecting that the whole idea was somewhat fantastic in the political climate of the day, an event occurred which overnight revolutionized the position, and fully determined him on his course. This was the grant of a charter to the British North Borneo Company in November 1881. Goldie was immediately struck by the similarity of the problems of this remote company operating on the northern shores of Borneo, and those of the Niger trade. The Borneo Company based its claim to rule on concessions from local Muslim rulers, it asked for and obtained monopolies of specific articles, and it, too, was facing foreign pressure, in its case pressure from Holland and Spain. All this was revealed by Parliamentary Papers which were published and on sale in the bookshops within a few months of the grant of the charter. These papers[2] were eagerly bought by Goldie, and carefully studied. The United Company's solicitor was called in, and an eminent lawyer, Sir Hardinge Giffard,[3] brought in to give specialist advice. Conferences were held at which Goldie and the two lawyers thrashed out all the legal problems involved in the exercise of political power by commercial companies.[4] The conclusion was that the company should now make the attempt to obtain powers of government over the region where it traded, and that this was

[1] *Daily Telegraph* 5.7.99. This interview is the basis for statements in C. W. Orr, *The Making of Modern Nigeria*, p. 24, and in Wellesley, *op. cit.*, p. 20, and in most books which discuss these years in Nigeria. There is no trace of such a request in F.O. and C.O. papers or in any of the private collections I have studied. My reading of the correspondence with the United African Company suggests that Goldie's memory was at fault, the correspondence entirely lacks the intimacy which such a request, even if refused, would have produced. Possibly Goldie informally approached some Liberal politician, such as Dilke or Chamberlain, and was advised to increase the company's capital before asking officially, but there is no trace of this in their biographies.

[2] P.P. 1881, LXXXI, *Papers relating to affairs of Sulu*, etc., Pt. I, *Claims of Spain.* P.P. 1882, CXXXI, MS. p. 59, Pt. II, *Claims of Holland.*

[3] Hardinge Stanley Giffard, 1823–1921, created First Earl of Halsbury and Viscount Tiverton 1898, created Baron Halsbury 1885. Called to the Bar (Inner Temple) 1850, made his legal reputation as leading counsel for Governor Eyre, accused of murder in 1868 and as second counsel for the Tichborne claimant 1871–1872. Solicitor-General 1875, Lord Chancellor 1885 and 1886, and 1895–1905, leader of the 'die-hards' in the House of Lords against the Parliament Bill of 1911.

[4] Revealed in FO 84/1880 Goldie Taubman to Wright 8.1.86.

legally possible, either through a charter from a European power, or even without a charter, by obtaining its powers by treaty with the local rulers and chieftains. This latter course was suggested particularly by the Borneo papers. The Foreign Secretary, Lord Granville,[1] in facing critics of the Borneo charter, had argued that the Borneo Company was perfectly entitled to rule its territories even without a charter, under concessions which it held from local sultans, and that if the promoters had registered themselves as an ordinary limited company they would have been entitled to the protection which any British company enjoys in the pursuit of its lawful ends. The charter merely gave control over the Borneo Company to the British Government.[2] Assuming such a theory to be valid, then it ought to be perfectly feasible for the United Company to rule the banks of the Niger by virtue of concessions from the local chiefs, in fact the arrangement with Nupe of 1880 might almost be interpreted as a concession of sovereignty. For Nupe to concede a monopoly of trade to the United African Company was clearly analogous to the concessions made by the Sultans of Sulu and Brunei to the Borneo syndicate of rights to farm taxes, upon which the claim to a charter had been based. There remained two legal difficulties however, connected with the structure of the existing United Company. Could a company already incorporated under the Companies Acts receive a charter, for charters were usually instruments of incorporation? Sir Hardinge Giffard ruled that it could, and that a charter might simply be an instrument conferring or recognizing new powers.[3] And secondly, assuming that a charter could be granted to an existing company already incorporated, could the United Company, under its present legal constitution, accept such a charter, and failing a charter, could it exercise power by other means? Here the lawyers had their doubts, and urged that the company be entirely reconstituted before the attempt was made.

[1] G. G. Leveson-Gower, 1815–91, succeeded as Second Earl Granville 1846, Foreign Secretary 1851–2, 1870–4, and 1880–5. Colonial Secretary 1868–70 and 1886.
[2] P.P. 1881, LXXXI, no. 197, Granville to Morier 7.1.82, and *Hansard*, 3rd series, CCLXVII, Speech of Granville 13.3.82.
[3] FO 84/1880 Goldie Taubman to Wright 8.1.86.

In June 1882 this reorganization took place. A new company was formed by the directors of the United Company, and it proceeded to purchase the assets of the old company. The new name was significant—the National African Company. It was formed with the avowed intention of governing the region with which it traded, of excluding competition by political means, either through a charter from a European government, or by concessions from the native rulers. The operative clause in the new Memoranda of Association allowed for every possibility of obtaining political rights. The National African Company was empowered

> To apply for, acquire, and hold any charters, Acts of Parliament, privileges, monopolies, licences, concessions, patents, or other rights or powers from the British Government, or any other government or state, or any potentate or local or other authority in Africa or elsewhere; to exercise, carry on, or work any powers, rights or privileges so obtained, and to constitute or incorporate the Company as an anonymous or other society in any foreign country or state.[1]

This was the fundamental change arising from the reorganization, but to be able to undertake such responsibilities the company needed an impressive balance sheet, and more actual capital. The former was produced by a technique known on the Stock Exchange as 'watering'. The nominal capital of the old United Company in 1882 was £250,000; of this £106,000 was in theory 'fully paid up', for it represented shares issued to the original interests forming the amalgamation in payment for their assets in 1879.[2] These assets, stations, steamers, produce on hand, and the like, were now valued at £110,274.[3] For these

---

[1] R.J.S.C. 17049 Memorandum of Association of National African Company Ltd. 3(d) 8.6.82.

[2] R.J.S.C. 13209 return of U.A.C. capital 1884.

[3] R.J.S.C. 17049 Mem. of Agreement between United African and National African companies, 7(b)2. *The Times* 16.4.83, gives

Steamers	£16,629
Stores	1,400
Factories	20,300
Goods, etc.	71,945
Total	£110,274 based on a valuer's report.

assets the National African Company paid the United African Company £250,000 (£135,000 for the assets, and £115,000 for 'goodwill') in the form of shares in the new company valued at £10 each and considered as 'fully paid up'.[1] This was the basis for a balance sheet which looked solid. The nominal capital of the new National Company was £1,000,000, of which the £250,000 paid to the shareholders of the old company was 'fully subscribed'. A further 66,675 shares were issued on the stock market with a call of £1 per £10 share.[2] Thus, though possessing in assets £110,274 and new capital subscribed £66,675, only £176,947 in real values, the company was able to represent a return of £316,675 'fully paid'.[3]

Goldie took the opportunity of the reorganization to try to extend the influence of the company in high places. Hitherto the United Company had corresponded with the Foreign Office about affairs on the Niger, but in cool, formal and distant tones. There are no intimate little private notes between directors and officials or politicians in the records before 1882. If the company wanted a charter it must find names of repute and influence to grace its board of directors, 'if possible all peers and baronets' advised W. S. Gilbert.[4] The position of Chairman was of course particularly important, and Goldie finally persuaded Lord

---

[1] R.J.S.C. 17049 Mem. of Agreement between United and National African Companies, Clause 9.

[2] *Ibid.* return of National Company shareholders 21.11.82.

[3] It should be noted that such manœuvres were not unusual or remarkable at this time. 'Watering' was an inevitable result of English company law, which insisted upon a par value being placed upon a share, an absurd restriction, for a share is a 'share' in the company's assets, and is therefore essentially variable in value. At the same time the law placed no restrictions on those who wished to exploit this insistence on a share having a par value by 'watering'. In actual fact the Niger traders used far less 'water' than many of their contemporaries. The British South Africa Company was at times almost entirely 'water', with no actual cash or assets at all! The 'watering' of the National African Company, however, had some importance when the question of compensating the company for the loss of its charter arose at the end of the century. See pp. 309–310.

[4] When he satirized company floatation in *Utopia Unlimited*, 1893. The complete verse is very apt:

> Some seven men form an association,
> (If possible all Peers and Baronets),
> They start off with a public declaration
> To what extent they mean to pay their debts.
> That's called their Capital.

Aberdare to invest £800,[1] and stand at the head of the company. Aberdare was a close personal friend of both Gladstone, the Prime Minister, and of the Foreign Secretary, Lord Granville. He had been a prominent Liberal politician, and had served Gladstone as Home Secretary in his first Ministry, but had retired from politics with its defeat in 1874. In 1881 he had become President of the Royal Geographical Society. His wealth was solid, his integrity unquestionable, and his reputation of the highest.[2] Other newcomers to the board of directors were less well-known to the public, but as influential as Aberdare in quieter backwaters. Charles W. Mills, who invested £1,500, was a partner in the old private banking firm of Glyn, Mills and Currie, who were also the National Company's bankers; a firm with a long connection with imperial finance, particularly in Canada.[3] James F. Hutton, subscribing £500, was a Manchester cotton exporter, a Member of Parliament, President of the Manchester Chamber of Commerce, and an expert on African affairs who had the ear of the Colonial Office and connexions in almost every European capital.[4] One new shareholder who was not a director deserves notice. Joseph Chamberlain, not yet the imperial politician whose policies were to bring Goldie's rule in Nigeria to an end, invested £950 in the new venture.[5]

The building up of these new connexions with British politicians and officials occurred at a most opportune time for Goldie. Shortly after the National African Company had been formed, French moves in West Africa became more extensive and more ambitious, and began to take on the appearance of an attempt to win from the British by political means their position of commercial supremacy in the Niger and Oil Rivers. At first the

[1] R.J.S.C. 17049, Vol. II, return of shareholders 21.11.82, holding of Lord Aberdare.
[2] D. N. B. Bruce, Henry Austen, First Baron Aberdare, 1815–95.
[3] R.J.S.C. 17049, Vol. I, return of shareholders 21.11.82, holding of C. W. Mills. See also Fulford, R., *Glyn's*, London, 1952, for a discussion of the part played by Glyn's bank in imperial finance in the nineteenth century.
[4] R.J.S.C. 17049, Vol. I, return of shareholders 21.11.82, holding of James F. Hutton.
[5] *Ibid.* Holding of J. Chamberlain.

threat was not seen. In January 1880 a Colonial Office official could express a rather simple-minded elation that the spread of French colonies and administration would only provide more opportunites for British traders.[1] This idea was dispelled by the publication of the French treaty with Segou on the upper Niger in May 1881; its protectionist clauses, establishing all kinds of privileges for French merchants, caused the British Colonial Secretary to lose his temper in contemplation of such ignorance of the elementary principles of political economy.[2] When, in 1882, French expansion took on a new impetus, there was no further illusion in Britain that French expansion would serve any other than French commercial interests. This new French vigour was largely due to the influence now wielded by Jules Ferry, a firm believer in the economic usefulness of colonies to metropolitan industry and commerce. As Minister of Education Jules Ferry had subsidized the Italian explorer de Brazza to allow him to undertake treaty-making expeditions which by March 1882 had laid the foundations of the new French colony of the Gaboon, south of the Cameroons. It was de Brazza's activities which first began seriously to alarm the British authorities, and to suggest to them that the time had perhaps come for counter-measures. James Hutton told the Colonial Office that he had heard in Paris, whilst trying to negotiate an amalgamation with the French Niger companies, that de Brazza had originally been instructed to go to the Niger to make treaties, and that his plans had been changed at the last minute.[3] There was an obvious danger that de Brazza, who scorned the coasts, would move round behind the British traders on the Oil Rivers to link up with the French Niger traders, thus taking over not only the British Niger trade, but also the markets behind the Oil Rivers from which the coastal traders obtained their palm oil. This was what particularly worried the British consul in the Oil Rivers, Edward Hewett. He therefore urged the Foreign Office to intervene in the Cameroons region between the French

---

[1] CO 87/114 Minute by Hemming 1.1.80.
[2] CO 96/136 Minute by Kimberley, n.d.
[3] F.O. Conf. Print 4825, no. 2, p. 2, enc. in C.O. to F.O. 6.1.83.

Gaboon and the Oil Rivers. The local chiefs had petitioned Gladstone and Queen Victoria for 'an English Government' in 1879, but the request had been politely answered and shelved.[1] It ought now to be accepted, and supplemented by treaties with the African rulers in the Niger and Oil Rivers. To control the area Hewett suggested the establishment of a protectorate, Crown colony, or a 'Chartered Company of British Merchants'. This latter he favoured most. It would relieve the British Government of all 'pecuniary liabilities . . . as well as the trouble of governing the country'. His idea was that all the forty-five firms in the Oil Rivers should amalgamate like those on the Niger and stop their 'useless competition'.[2]

The Foreign Office now began slowly and cautiously to decide on policy. The French threat to British trade, brought constantly to notice by the consul and the traders, mounting in intensity as the months passed, convinced the Foreign Office of the need for some action. But action was not decided by the Foreign Office alone. If a colony were to be established the Colonial Office was entitled to its say, and if money was to be spent in establishing and running a British administration then the Treasury must also be heard. Hostility from the Colonial Office, taken to extreme lengths, eventually prevented the establishment of a colony. The only alternative was a 'protectorate', a minimum form of control leaving the internal administration under the African rulers, but excluding foreign interference, the system to be run as cheaply as possible by the Foreign Office through a local consular staff. But even this, once decided, was almost wrecked by the fantastic niggardliness of the Treasury in refusing to sanction either the sums necessary to implement the policy, or means whereby such moneys could be raised. It was this lack of money which forced the Foreign Office to turn more and more to the traders for succour; and an organic connexion began to be formed between the two. Goldie, realizing the acute need for funds, exploited the situation in a masterly way, refusing any assistance which might weaken the

[1] F.O. Conf. Print 4824, no. 1, p. 1.
[2] F.O. Conf. Print 4824, no. 9, p. 20, Hewett to Granville 14.1.82.

dependence of the Foreign Office on the assistance of the
National African Company or give the Government a permanent source of revenue, but offering other kinds of help in
such a way that the Foreign Office came more and more to rely
on the company. When the Foreign Office, through lack of
funds, was forced finally to rely on the National African Company's employees and organization to assist in establishing the
British protectorate, the basic relationships involved in rule by
chartered company were already in operation, though Goldie
had not yet suggested the grant of a charter to his company.

If the final outcome of the lengthy discussions between the
Government departments be called a decision, it was a decision
by process of elimination, in which the alternative possibilities of
Crown colony, and real protectorate under the Foreign Office
with a settled revenue and proper staff, were each wrecked by
Colonial Office and Treasury hostility, until there remained
only the policy of a 'paper protectorate', without staff or
revenue. The idea of a Crown colony was the one which the
Colonial Office resisted most fiercely, for this department
would have had to assume the burden of responsibility for a new
Colony. Lord Kimberley,[1] the Colonial Secretary, was strongest
of all in his opposition to assuming any responsibility for the
region by his own department, in fact he suspected that the
Foreign Office was intriguing to get rid of a burden which he
thought of as rightly their own. The region itself was pestilential,
the people unmanageable, and the problems raised by the question of slavery (illegal in British territories since 1834) enough of
themselves 'to deter any prudent government'. British occupation would bring wars with the local peoples and heavy demands on the British taxpayer. Kimberley rejected all Hewett's
suggestions; British responsibilities in West Africa were already
'very heavy', and nothing more should be done.[2]

[1] Wodehouse, John, 1826–1902, succeeded as Baron Wodehouse 1846, Under-
Secretary of State for Foreign Affairs 1852–6, 1859–61, British Minister at St.
Petersburg 1856–8, Lord Lieutenant of Ireland 1864–6, created Earl 1866, Lord
Privy Seal 1868–70, Colonial Secretary 1880–2, India Office 1882–5 and 1886,
Leader of the Liberal Party in the House of Lords from 1891, India Office and Lord
President of the Council 1892–4, Foreign Secretary 1894–5.
[2] F.O. Conf. Print 4824, no. 22, p. 28.

E

What part was Goldie taking at this time? His eye was firmly fixed on the plan to obtain powers of rule by a charter or some other means; hence he could not press for a Crown colony, or even a protectorate, as both these systems would have meant the establishment of official forms of administration. He was thus a natural ally of the Colonial Office in opposing the schemes of the Foreign Office. In yet another way his ideas at this time fitted in perfectly with Colonial Office thinking. If Goldie could not advocate the establishment of a direct British authority, nevertheless French pressure on the Niger worried him greatly, and he had to have some alternative policy if only to help him in the negotiations for the purchase of the French companies which were still taking place. Goldie thought, and rightly so, that the reluctance of the French traders to come to a settlement was caused by their uncertainty as to the attitude of their Government;[1] was the Niger to be French or not? They would not sell, despite heavy losses in face of Goldie's fierce competition, if at some not too distant date the British Niger traders were to be driven from the Niger by French tariffs. One way to decide the French traders was to persuade the British Foreign Office to make a diplomatic settlement with the French, marking out 'spheres of influence' in which each agreed not to interfere with the other, the Niger to be in the British sphere. This would have the added advantage that after such a settlement there would remain the problem of how to administer the 'sphere', and the National African Company might well seem to be the cheapest and least troublesome way. James Hutton was deputed to put forward such a scheme to the Colonial Office, where he was well known. He there argued that French activity on the Niger was really a feint, and that its object was to force Britain to make concessions in other areas, particularly in the Gambia. Why not accept such a settlement, and give the French the Gambia in return for their abstention from the Niger

---

[1] Though their chief agent on the Niger, Mattei, was an *agent consulaire*, he never received any written instructions from his Government. It seems very likely that the French Government was playing a cat and mouse game with French traders, ready to abandon them if necessary for concessions elsewhere. See Masson, *op. cit.*, p. 408 for a discussion of Mattei's position.

and Oil Rivers? The idea could not have been better calculated to appeal to the Colonial Office, which had on several previous occasions tried to get rid of the Gambia, which they regarded as a costly white elephant.[1] They therefore urged the scheme on the Foreign Office most strongly.[2] At the same time the National African Company began to exploit its new connexions with the Foreign Office to add to the pressure for a diplomatic settlement. The new chairman, Lord Aberdare, sending his new year greetings for 1883 to his friend Lord Granville, the Foreign Secretary, took the opportunity to point out the dangers to the company's position in the present situation, and asked for negotiations with France to secure a delimitation of spheres.[3] Later in January Aberdare and five of the directors had an interview with Granville and asked specifically for an arrangement marking off the British and French spheres on either side of a line drawn through Timbuktu.[4] But it was not to be. Lord Lyons,[5] the British ambassador in Paris, argued that the scheme had no hope of success; it had been difficult enough to negotiate a minor frontier settlement in Sierra Leone, which was now before the Chambers; to put such a suggestion forward would be merely provocative.[6]

It was now March 1883. In that month Jules Ferry became Premier, and events in France took a turn which was to transform the vague fears of the British into actualities. The first manifestation of his new expansionist colonial policy in West Africa was a series of annexations (Cootenoo, Aghwey, Great and Little Popo, and Porto Novo) which laid the basis of the future French colony of Dahomey, driving a wedge between the existing British colonies of the Gold Coast and Lagos. In May

[1] Gray, J. M., *History of the Gambia*, Cambridge, 1940, contains a full discussion of schemes for the cession of the Gambia to France from 1866–76.
[2] F.O. Conf. Print 4825, no. 1, p. 1. C.O. to F.O. 6.1.83.
[3] FO 84/1654 Aberdare to Granville 1.1.85.
[4] *Ibid.* Aberdare to Granville 28.2.83.
[5] Richard B. P. Lyons, 1817–87, K.C.B. 1860, G.C.B. 1862, created Viscount Lyons of Christchurch 1881 and Earl Lyons 1887. British Minister in Washington 1858–65, ambassador in Constantinople and Privy Councillor 1865–7, ambassador in Paris 1867–87.
[6] F.O. Conf. Print 4825, F.O. to C.O. 5.3.83.

the French took direct action on the Niger. Hitherto the French
threat on the river had been purely commercial; Mattei it is
true, had made 'treaties' with some of the chiefs, but these were
monopolistic trade pacts, and gave no political authority to
France.[1] Now a French gunboat appeared off the Oil Rivers,
sailed into Bonny, still the largest middleman state, and tried to
make a treaty giving France a protectorate. Fortunately for the
British, the Bonny chiefs refused.[2] Mattei now prepared to make
use of his consular powers. In August 1883 he was ready to make
a determined bid to establish French political rights on the
Niger. At the mouth of the river he sought out the Achilles heel
of the British position, and attempted to make a treaty with the
Brassmen, still smarting under the competition of the National
Company. This he exploited to the full, promising the Brassmen
that the French traders would not 'interfere or establish a factory in their markets'. At first the Brassmen were impressed, and
eager to get even with Goldie's company, and they agreed to the
terms. But the next day, when the treaty was to be signed, they
refused, perhaps reflecting that their existing, if depleted trade,
depended on the shipping and marketing facilities of the Liverpool traders.[3] Nevertheless Mattei persisted in his efforts, and
tried to make political treaties throughout the lower Niger; his
agents 'avowed they were going to annex Onitsha'[4] and a
French gunboat entered the Niger to support them.[5]

These French moves naturally stiffened the British attitude.
It was clearly not now possible for the Colonial Office to argue
that there was no real threat to British trade, or to urge that
negotiations with France would produce a settlement. By May
of 1883 both departments of state were agreed that some action
would have to be taken to acquire political rights which could
exclude the French from the Niger and Oil Rivers. The
Colonial Office, however, was still adamantly opposed to any

[1] F.O. Conf. Print 4825 C.O. to F.O. 6.1.83 enc. interview with James Hutton.
[2] *Ibid.* Sec. of Admiralty to T. V. Lister 7.5.83.
[3] F.O. Conf. Print 4869 Johnson to Fern and Ellis 14.8.83.
[4] FO 84/1655 N.A.C. (National African Company) to F.O. 26.9.83, enc.
McIntosh to N.A.C. 14.3.83.
[5] *Ibid.* N.A.C. to F.O. 14.8.83, and same to same 26.9.83.

idea of setting up a Crown colony. Any action would have to be taken by the Foreign Office, and as such, it would be quasi-diplomatic action. Thus was born the concept of the protectorate as applied by Britain to the partition of Africa. Today African protectorates are almost indistinguishable from Crown colonies and their precise differentiation is a matter for the skilled craft of the lawyer;[1] cynics have seen no vital distinction between the one, open and direct, and the other, the mailed fist inside the velvet glove. The fact is that the protectorate system emerged not as a consciously thought-out policy, but as an expedient within the limitations which history had placed upon the free action of British politicians and officials. These limitations operated so widely that of all the vast areas acquired by Britain in Africa between 1880 and 1900, only one, British Bechuanaland, was given Crown colony status. All the rest were protectorates administered initially not by the Colonial Office but by the Foreign Office, and of these territories by far the greatest area was administered under the Foreign Office by chartered companies.

By April and May of 1883 officials in the Foreign Office were beginning to consider the forms which action might take. The minimum possibility, costing very little and involving no actual administration, was that the African rulers might be asked to sign treaties in which they agreed not to cede any land or political rights to a foreign power without British consent, but this was ruled out as insufficient, even by the Colonial Office.[2] The Foreign Office librarian, Edward Hertslet, prepared a learned memorandum on protectorates.[3] In June, Consul Hewett, once again attacked by illness, returned home to add his support to the pressure for action, bringing with him a petition from the chiefs of Akassa, the headquarters of the National African Company, asking for a treaty of protection,

---

[1] See Lindley, M. F., *The Acquisition and Government of Backward Territories in International Law*, etc., London, 1926, and O'Connall, D. P., *The Law of State Succession*, Cambridge, 1956, pp. 28 ff.

[2] F.O. Conf. Print 4825, F.O. to C.O. conf. 22.5.83 and CO 806/203 African 259, Appendix III, mem. by A.W.L.H. 24.3.83.

[3] F.O. Conf. Print 4824 mem. on protectorates by E.H. 24.4.83.

and strongly supported by the company,[1] who were now seriously worried by Mattei's activities.

But the months passed, the discussions continued, and no decision was made; all this against a background of increasing French activity. In October Lord Granville decided that the time had come for a policy to be settled. One can understand his attitude. There existed a department of state, the Colonial Office, apparently charged with the responsibility for running and establishing colonies, which now appeared obviously to be shirking those responsibilities. In this spirit he conveyed a broad hint to the Colonial Office that the natural method of dealing with the problem of French activity in the Niger and Oil Rivers, which was now acute and dangerous, was to establish a colony. In view of its large trade, the area could be developed into a more profitable possession than any of the existing British West African colonies.[2] But the Colonial Office were prepared for this move, and countered it by suggesting that the whole matter be referred to the Cabinet for a decision.[3] To this Lord Granville agreed. There then followed a veritable battle of memoranda, in which the officials of the two offices fought each other, circularizing members of the Cabinet to try to convert them to their views; the Colonial Office resurrecting the idea of ceding the Gambia in return for a French promise to keep out of the Niger; the Foreign Office suggesting that this was a policy of weakness which could only encourage the French, and arguing instead that Britain must acquire sufficient authority to exclude foreign powers.[4]

The question went before the colonial committee of the Cabinet in November 1883. On the whole the Foreign Office view prevailed. A protectorate was to be established over the Cameroons, the Oil Rivers, and the Niger mouths. However, it was laid down particularly that there should be no attempt to

1 F.O. Conf. Print 4825, Hewett to Granville 11.6.83.

2 F.O. Conf. Print 4869, F.O. to C.O. 5.10.83.

3 *Ibid.* C.O. to F.O. 25.10.83.

4 CO 806/214 African Print 27, mem. by R.M. 29.9.83, and other mema. FO 84/1655 conf. mem. by T.V.L. 27.10.83, mem. by T.V.L. 16.11.83, printed and circulated to the Cabinet.

create a British colony 'with all the necessary expensive machinery of government'. British control must be asserted by means of periodic visits from the consul.[1] Above all there was to be no charge on imperial funds incurred in establishing the protectorate.[2] These decisions were endorsed by the full Cabinet the next day.[3]

The policy laid down by the Cabinet did more than anything else to pave the way for Goldie's plan to achieve political power for his company on the Niger. It was an impossible policy to fulfil, for the establishment of a protectorate, however cheaply it was effected, was bound to cost *something*, and the Cabinet ruled that it must not be charged to imperial funds. The sum involved was a mere trifle. Consul Hewett would need vice-consuls to assist him in establishing and maintaining the protectorate, and it was calculated that this would cost £5,000 per annum.[4] There would also be some initial and non-recurrent cost in negotiating the treaties, presents for chiefs, and the like. Yet discussion on how to raise this money was to occupy six months, a delay which almost wrecked the scheme, and did, in the event, result in the loss of the Cameroons area. This obsession with petty expenditure merits some analysis, for it was this factor, operating at a time when the danger of foreign annexation was at its height, which provided the typical situation out of which the late-Victorian chartered companies emerged, and in no region is this more aptly illustrated than on the Niger. By systematically taking advantage of the Government's financial embarrassment Goldie was able gradually to attract to the National African Company an official status as an agent of the British Government.

How was the money to be raised? Had the Cabinet decided for a Crown colony the problem would have been simple, for the area would then have become British territory, and its administration entitled to levy taxes on people and things within its borders. But what were the rights of the protector within a

[1] FO 84/1681 R. Meade to J. Pauncefote 5.1.84.
[2] PRO 30/29/122 Granville to Dilke 24.9.84 reveals this limitation.
[3] FO 84/1655 F.O. to J. Pauncefote 29.11.83.
[4] *Ibid.* mem. by T.V.L. 23.12.83.

protectorate? The land was not British territory, the people not
subjects of Queen Victoria. Consul Hewett was not a man for
such fine distinctions, and would have financed his government
by a simple *ad valorem* duty on exports, estimated to yield
£7,500 per annum, but Lister thought that the consul had no
power to do such a thing, and that the tax should be disguised
as a fee paid by British subjects for services rendered to them by
the consul.[1] Other suggestions were that the consul should consult the traders to find out what they considered to be the most
convenient method of payment, or that there should be a ton-
nage tax on produce shipped.[2] Finally it was decided to consult
the Treasury and see if some assistance could be obtained. It
was hoped that the Treasury would agree to provide the initial
non-recurrent expenditure need as presents for the chiefs, and
also agree in principle to the idea of taxing the British traders to
pay for recurrent expenditure. So as to preserve secrecy, the
traders would not be consulted until the protectorate had
actually been established. Then they would be consulted as to
methods of payment.[3] But Childers, the Chancellor of the
Exchequer, refused to agree to provide any expenditure until it
was proved to him that the traders agreed to be taxed for recurrent expenses. Some method of consulting them without the
secret of the British preparations leaking to the French would
have to be found.[4] Was there anyone who could represent the
British traders in the Niger and Oil Rivers who would be
absolutely dependable and above suspicion, and whose public
discretion was beyond doubt? One man stood out as the obvious
choice, the friend and ex-colleague of the Prime Minister and
Foreign Secretary—Lord Aberdare, the chairman of the
National African Company. Early in February 1884 Lord
Granville wrote to Aberdare and told him of the plan to keep
the French out of the Oil Rivers and Niger. There was no

[1] FO 84/1634 mem. by Hewett 22.12.83 with minute by T.V.L.
[2] FO 84/1681 mem. by P. Currie 5.1.84. F.O. Conf. Print 5004, Sir Thos. Farrer
(Board of Trade) to P. Currie 28.12.83.
[3] *Ibid.* mem. by P.C. 5.1.84, mema. by H.P.A. (Sir Percy Anderson) 7.1.84 and
15.1.84.
[4] FO 84/1682 P. Currie to Granville 22.1.84.

possibility that Parliament would agree to throw the costs on imperial funds. 'In order to get the scheme going at all it is necessary that the traders will pay.' Could Lord Aberdare consult them discreetly and obtain assurances upon which the Government could rely?[1]

In asking Aberdare to consult the other traders Granville had thrown the question into Goldie's lap, for Aberdare ignored the Liverpool interests in the Oil Rivers, and 'consulted' only Goldie and James Hutton, both directors of the National Company.[2] Their reaction was decisive, for if they had accepted the proposal that they should agree to pay taxes to the consul they would have provided the Foreign Office with a basis from which to build up a regular financial system to administer not only the Oil Rivers but also the Niger. With finances to administer the Niger region, there would have been little incentive for the Foreign Office to transfer the administration at a later date to a company which would itself have been one of the chief taxpayers. If the charter was still the goal then Goldie and his fellow directors must see to it that the Foreign Office remain without funds. Hence they rejected outright any idea that they were willing to be taxed, arguing that the trade was already seriously hampered by French competition, and declared that the merchants were 'unanimous' in the opinion that the Treasury must bear the cost of any protectorate. Hutton went so far as to promise to mobilize his fellow Members of Parliament from Lancashire to support a vote of funds in the Commons,[3] the last thing that Lord Granville wanted!

Thus the Foreign Office emerged with nothing to reassure the Chancellor of the Exchequer. There was now a 'deadlock for want of funds'.[4] Almost immediately Goldie's tactics began to pay dividends. Early in 1883 the National Company had asked that their chief agent, David McIntosh, might be given consular status, so that he could resist Mattei more effectively. The

[1] *Ibid.* Granville to Aberdare, private, 6.2.84.
[2] *Ibid.* Aberdare to Granville 25.2.84, enc. Hutton to Aberdare 24.2.84.
[3] *Ibid.*, *loc. cit.*
[4] FO 84/1692 mem. by H.P.A. 27.2.84.

request was several times pressed by Aberdare, but was ignored.[1] In December 1883, before Goldie's refusal to agree to submit to taxation, the supervising under-secretary of the African department of the Foreign Office, T. V. Lister, had reconsidered the idea of giving McIntosh consular powers, so as to save the Foreign Office money in the new protectorate, but once again he rejected the idea, on the ground that the company 'want him in an official position in order to strengthen his hands, and to get them a monopoly of the Niger trade'.[2] After Goldie's refusal to agree to be taxed, however, Lister reconsidered his attitude. He had no illusions as to the motive behind the request, but he was now quietly resigned to the fact that money must be saved by all possible means. McIntosh, he realized,

would of course be much more the servant of the company than of the government and would use his power to establish a monopoly for his company. This would hardly do much for securing freedom of trade for all the world, but it would answer the purpose of preventing a French monopoly and encouraging at least one large British company—as we shall have to limit our desires for vice-consuls it might be as well to take advantage of the N.A.C. as regards the Niger, more especially as they will not tolerate the presence of any independent vice-consuls.[3]

McIntosh was soon afterwards appointed British vice-consul on the Niger.[4] Thus, the British official charged with negotiating the treaties of British protection on the Niger was an employee of Goldie's company, receiving no salary from the Foreign Office, and in a unique position to turn the situation to the advantage of his employers. This was to have profound consequences for the company.

The appointment of McIntosh eased, but by no means solved, the financial difficulties of the Foreign Office. There still remained a sum to be provided for vice-consuls in the Cameroons and Oil Rivers. The Treasury refused to pay initial

[1] FO 84/1654 Aberdare to Granville 3.6.83, and 5.6.83 and 13.6.83. The original request was made in February, see F.O. Conf. Print 4825 N.A.C. to F.O. 28.2.83.

[2] FO 84/1655 mem. by T.V.L. 23.12.83.

[3] FO 84/1682 mem. by T.V.L. 27.2.84.

[4] FO 84/1687 Goldie Taubman to Anderson 25.7.84 with minute by H.P.A. 31.7.84.

expenses unless it could be shown that the British traders agreed to be taxed, and further efforts to get the Treasury to modify its attitude were fruitless.[1] Short of abandoning the plan, the Foreign Office was left with but one resource, to make economies within the Office. This was now done; three consulates were closed, saving £1,680; others were reduced in staff, making a total saving of £3,640 per annum, £15 a year more than the now diminished estimate of running costs. The Treasury was told, and was asked for £8,000 for initial expenditure for outfits and presents to chiefs. At last, in May 1884, the Treasury agreed, and the initial expenditure, characteristically whittled down to £5,790, was granted.[2] The British taxpayer could indeed sleep sound in the sure conviction that no bureaucracy, drunk with the sight of millions, wasted his substance in profligate expenditure.

Consul Hewett was now able to return to Africa to try to secure a British protectorate over the Cameroons, the Oil Rivers, and the Niger. He carried with him a model treaty of nine articles, securing British protection, British control of relations with foreign powers, and full consular jurisdiction over British subjects and foreigners. Other articles promised the Africans progress and civilization, freedom of religion and freedom of trade, bound them to assist in salvaging shipwrecks, and, lest the protected demand too much of their new protectors, ensured that the treaty operate only 'so far as may be practicable from the date of signature'.[3] In the Oil Rivers the chiefs were suspicious, and feared (rightly) that the free trade clause was a trick to undermine their position as middlemen, but Hewett persuaded them to sign treaties with the offending clauses removed. At Brass the chiefs refused even this, and would only sign a treaty for six months on condition that Hewett promise to try to obtain 'the exclusive use of the Ase market' from the National Company.[4]

[1] FO 84/1683 mem. by H.P.A. 10.3.84.

[2] FO 84/1685 F.O. to Treasury 6.5.84. F.O. Conf. Print 5004, L. Courtney (Treasury) to Fitzmaurice (F.O.) 26.5.84.

[3] F.O. Conf. Print 5004, instructions to Consul Hewett, with enclosures 16.5.84.

[4] FO 84/1660 Hewett to F.O. 30.7.84. For texts of treaties see Hertslet, E., *Commercial Treaties*, Vol. XVII, pp. 158–258.

On the Niger Hewett appointed several of the National Company's employees to help him negotiate similar treaties.[1] The
company's chief agent, David McIntosh, though he was now
vice-consul and had been appointed to do this very work, was
occupied in another task. Since April 1884 he had been making
treaties in the name of the company. After Hewett's arrival
McIntosh speeded up the work and completed a set of treaties
which covered the Niger on both banks up to its confluence with
the Benue. The treaties conceded complete sovereignty to the
company, the chiefs ceded 'the whole of their territories' to the
company, granted rights to land, powers to settle disputes, 'to
exclude foreign settlers', and to exclude all persons not native to
the territory.[2] So Lister's prophecy that McIntosh would use his
position to create a monopoly materialized. When Consul
Hewett arrived on the Niger to make treaties on behalf of the
British Government he found himself forestalled by a prior set of
treaties in the name of the National African Company. He felt
therefore bound to alter the model treaty which he had been
given by the Foreign Office, and the treaties which he negotiated
on the Niger all contained an additional article:

Permission to trade in the territory of the King, Queen, and chiefs
shall be regulated according to the agreement entered into on . . .
(date inserted) between the said King, Queen and chiefs and the
National African Company, Limited.[3]

In the two years since its formation in 1882 the National
African Company had come most of the way towards acquiring
that political power which Goldie had planned to obtain. Its
name was now becoming known in the departments of state,
thanks largely to Aberdare and James Hutton, and Goldie himself was now known personally to the Foreign Secretary and his
officials. More important, the British Government was now
obligated to the company; it had placed its local staff at the dis-

[1] See the treaties negotiated by Bedford, Sergeant and Flint in Hertslet, *op. cit.*,
pp. 158–258 *passim*.
[2] These treaties are reproduced in Hertslet, E., *Map of Africa by Treaty*, Vol. I,
pp. 131–54.
[3] Hertslet, *Commercial Treaties*, Vol. XVII, pp. 158–258, *passim*, article VI of
appropriate treaties.

posal of the consul, and it had earned the gratitude of imperially-minded Englishmen. It had secured by its own treaties, recognized as valid by the British consul, powers which were so extensive as to transcend the sphere of purely commercial activity. Under powers delegated by the African rulers it could, in legal theory, set up courts to try British subjects and foreigners, arbitrate in local disputes and dispose of land. Indeed, the chiefs having 'ceded' the 'whole of their territories' it could be argued that the company now possessed full sovereignty. At the same time the British Government's treaties secured British protection to the area, and therefore the company, as a corporate British subject, was also entitled to protection. The basic relationships between a chartered company which governed its territories under concessions from local rulers, and the protecting power of the Imperial Government, existed already, in theory, in every particular except the instrument of the Royal Charter itself.

4

Berlin and the Charter

CONSUL HEWETT had rightly directed his attentions primarily to establishing the British protectorate over the Niger and Oil Rivers. By mid-July he had completed this work, and sailed eastward to the Cameroons. This last mission was perhaps the pleasantest part of his task. The chiefs of the Oil Rivers were suspicious, wary of their independence, jealous of their exclusive trading position, and difficult to handle. The kings of the Cameroons coast, however, had asked for protection, and there would be no difficulty. In other ways the task was a pleasant one, for immediately behind the Cameroons coast the steep hills offered the prospect of a refuge from the humid heat of the pestilential Oil Rivers, and Hewett intended to build himself a consular house, and run the affairs of the new protectorate from these new headquarters. On 19 July 1884 the British consul sailed into the Cameroons River. There a strange sight confronted him—the flag of Imperial Germany fluttering in the wind. It had been hoisted a few days previously by Dr. Nachtigal,[1] supposedly on a 'trade mission'. A few weeks earlier Nachtigal had done the same thing at Bageida in Togoland. Germany was now a colonial power in West Africa.

The sudden and totally unsuspected entry of Germany on to the West African scene did not at first unduly worry the British Foreign Office. The main purposes of the British plan had been achieved, and Hewett had concluded enough treaties to establish a good British title from Benin to the frontier of the new German Cameroons. Nor was there anything to suggest that the

[1] FO 84/1660 Hewett to Granville 30.7.84.

Germans would exclude British traders from their new colony. The object of the British plan had been to keep out the French, with their prohibitory tariffs, and this appeared to have been achieved. In fact, however, this facile optimism would not stand close analysis. Locally, the loss of the Cameroons had exposed the weakness of the British position; reluctance to assume responsibility and the delays imposed by the Treasury had alone caused the fiasco; had Hewett been able to leave for Africa as soon as the Cabinet had decided the issue in November 1883 he would have forestalled Nachtigal by half a year. The wider implications of the German intervention were even more serious, and were destined to take the Niger question into the sphere of international politics. If Britain had been dealing only with the traditional European powers in Africa, France and Portugal, she might have been justified in assuming that Hewett's scraps of paper unsupported as yet by an effective administration would have been sufficient to keep other powers away, for they too held territory on these terms, and would not wish to establish precedents which might be turned against themselves later. But Germany had no such incentive. As a new colonial power it was in her interest to define as wide an area as possible as 'unoccupied', and therefore open to annexation. The method of doing so was the time-honoured expedient of insisting on 'effective occupation'.[1]

At whose expense would these claims be asserted? It seems clear that Germany's entry into the colonial field was not motivated by the desire for colonies for their own sake. Bismarck[2] held the theory that colonies were useless and costly liabilities. His main interest was European politics and diplomacy, and his object in conceding to the clamour for colonies from the German maritime towns was mainly to further his diplomatic policies. Disputes caused by German colonial acquisitions could do this in either of two ways. The more feasible was that the British could be brought to realize how

---

[1] A device as old as colonial disputes themselves. James I of England argued thus in 1604 when resisting Spanish claims to the whole of the American continent.

[2] Aydelotte, W. O., *Bismarck and Colonial Policy*, Philadelphia, 1937, pp. 18–21; Dawson, W. H., *The German Empire*, Vol. II, p. 176.

dependent they were on German support against French colonial designs, and how dangerous it would be if France and Germany co-operated in the colonial sphere. Britain might then be drawn into Bismarck's system of alliances. The alternative, if Britain remained unmoved, was that colonial questions might draw France and Germany closer together, for French hostility would always be the focus for any anti-German alliance. This was a more ambitious policy, and more difficult to achieve, for France remained totally unreconciled to the loss of Alsace-Lorraine, taken by Germany after the Franco-Prussian war of 1870. Bismarck had always hoped that France might find a substitute for these territories in colonial expansion.[1]

In the event, the German entry into Africa caused more friction with Britain than with France, largely due to the clumsy and hesitant way in which Lord Granville reacted. Trying to avoid responsibilities for Britain, yet resisting German attempts to set up colonies, Granville appeared almost to be proclaiming a kind of British Monroe Doctrine for Africa.[2] In reply to German inquiries about Angra Pequena, the British asserted that a German protectorate in South-West Africa would infringe British rights, yet refused to establish a British protectorate. In April 1884, tired of British evasions, Bismarck set up the first of the German protectorates in Africa at Angra Pequena. A month later the British Cape Colony decided to annex South West Africa up to Walfisch Bay.[3] This was the sort of ineptitude that Bismarck had been waiting for. He sent his son Herbert to London to warn Granville that Germany would cause trouble for Britain elsewhere if Britain would not co-operate. Britain was encumbered in her administration of Egypt by the rights of the European powers to be represented in Egyptian finance, and Herbert Bismarck warned that Germany would oppose Britain

[1] Brandenburg, E., *From Bismarck to the World War, 1870–1914*, London, 1927, pp. 9–10.
[2] The phrase used by Count Hatzfelt; see G.P., Vol. IV, no. 742, note by him 24.5.84, referring to the policy declared by President Monroe of the U.S.A. which warned European powers against establishing any new colonies in the continent of America.
[3] Langer, W., *European Alliances and Alignments 1871–90*, New York, 1931, pp. 292–293.

at the forthcoming conference designed to ease the British position in Egypt.[1] At the same time the German Chancellor announced that he refused to recognize the recent Anglo-Portuguese treaty,[2] in which Britain had attempted to secure her commercial position on the Congo in face of French pressure by recognizing Portuguese claims, and obtaining favourable commercial concessions from Portugal. Lord Granville now began to see a glimmer of what Bismarck was about. He quickly accepted the German protectorate over Angra Pequena, and four days later, on 26 June, abandoned the Anglo-Portuguese treaty.[3] But in the very act of submission Granville outraged the Germans by allowing the Cape Colony to annex part of Bechuanaland and all of South-West Africa where British settlements were established. Germany refused to recognize these annexations, and retaliated by declaring a wider protectorate.[4] Bismarck followed this up by carrying out his earlier threat to wreck the London Conference on Egyptian affairs, which broke up inconclusively in August.[5]

It was clear to Bismarck that the German colonial adventure was not producing the required reaction from Britain, by drawing her more closely into the German system of alliances. He now attempted to put the second alternative into effect, that is, to try to use the German colonial policy to bring about some kind of agreement with France on the basis of their common hostility to Britain in Africa.

Hitherto Germany had not been concerned with the Niger. Bismarck's initial approach to the French stressed British ambitions in the Congo, and spoke of laying down rules for effective occupation and guarantees for free trade.[6] But Jules Ferry was not interested in free trade, and felt that the French position on the Congo was now secure, thanks to de Brazza. If he was to take

---

[1] G.P., IV, no. 745, Herbert Bismarck to Bismarck 16.6.84.

[2] FO 84/1811 Bismarck to Munster 7.6.84, communicated 14.6.84.

[3] G.P. IV, no. 749, H. Bismarck to Bismarck 22.6.84. Crowe, S. E., *The Berlin West African Conference*, London, 1942, pp. 16–20.

[4] Crowe, *op. cit.*, p. 60.

[5] Langer, *op. cit.*, p. 299; Crowe, *op. cit.*, p. 60; G.P. IV, no. 749, Bismarck to Munster 12.8.84.

[6] G.P. III, no. 680, Bismarck to Hatzfelt 7.8.84.

F

the risk of an unpopular co-operation with the hated Germans, it would have to be on French terms. Britain must be permanently encumbered with an international commission in Egypt, and Germany must help France to undermine the British position on the Niger, perhaps by entramelling her there, as in Egypt, with some kind of international control.[1] Bismarck could afford to co-operate on these terms, and the Franco-German negotiations began. By October 1884 all was agreed; and the British Government received its invitation to attend an international conference in Berlin to discuss freedom of commerce in the Congo, the setting up of international commissions to secure free navigation on the Niger and Congo, and 'formalities to be observed in order that new occupations on the coasts of Africa may be considered as effective'.[2]

The proposed conference at Berlin was seen by officials at the Foreign Office as directed against Britain in order to upset the gains already made on the Niger and Oil Rivers, and to make British policy vulnerable to all kinds of international interference.[3] For Goldie's plans the conference promised utter disaster. To get a charter and powers of administration from the British Government was a difficult enough task, but to hope to establish a monopoly on the river whilst the French traders were still there, with an international commission to protect them, was clearly impossible. His inquiries soon revealed that Lord Granville was in no position to exclude the Niger question from the deliberations of the conference. Goldie had to be content with impressing on the Government, through Lord Aberdare, the grave danger implied by the plan to establish an international commission.[4]

There was, however, another side to the picture. If the situation was desperately serious for Goldie's company, it was also one in which the company could further strengthen its ties with

---

[1] Ferry's thoughts are set out clearly in D.D.F., 1st series, Vol. 5, no. 376, mem. by J. Ferry on the German propositions, n.d., and *ibid.*, no. 252, Ferry to Ambassadors at Brussels and Lisbon 28.4.84.

[2] FO 84/1813 Dft. to Scott, Afn. 30, 7.10.84; Crowe, *op. cit.*, p. 67.

[3] See FO 84/1813 mem. by T.V.L. 14.10.84, and by H.P.A. same date.

[4] *Ibid.* Aberdare to Granville 16.10.84.

the British Government. There was no British administration on the Niger, and the Foreign Office, assailed by charges of ineffective occupation from the Germans, might be forced to use the company's resources on the Niger more and more in an attempt to create an impression of British authority. As this process continued, the word 'charter' might be whispered more and more frequently into the ear of Lord Granville, and might gradually take on the appearance of an obvious and inevitable solution. Such hints were begun as early as October 1884.[1] In addition there was one spectacular feat which the National Company might achieve. If Goldie could succeed in buying out the French traders before the Berlin Conference began, then the British position would be transformed. With only one British company actually trading on the Niger the British delegates could then argue that the plan for an international commission was totally irrelevant.

The commercial war against the French traders had been going on since the end of 1882. During the first six months of 1884 it was further intensified, and Goldie lent his private fortune to the company in an attempt to break the French by trading at a loss. By June the two smaller French firms had had enough, and sold out.[2] Meanwhile the weary negotiations continued with the largest and remaining group, the *Compagnie française de l'Afrique equatoriale*. Finally, a fortnight before the first meeting of the conference in Berlin, Goldie was able to announce that the French company had capitulated. The National Company was 'now alone on the Niger'.[3] The French, broken by competition, and demoralized by the failure of their government to give them support, were induced to amalgamate with the National Company in a similar way to that in which the original firms had formed the United Company in 1879. In return for its assets on the Niger, the *Compagnie française* received £60,000 in the form of shares in the National Company,

---

[1] In the letter referred to in the previous footnote, where Aberdare, in an aside, remarked that 'none but a commercial company would care to pay sufficiently for the best class of official' to administer the Niger.

[2] *The Times* 23.6.84. Report of N.A.C.'s Fourth General Meeting.

[3] FO 84/1814 Goldie Taubman to Anderson, private, 1.11.84.

considered as fully paid shares. Two of the French directors were raised to the Board of the National Company.[1] This deal was the best bargain Goldie ever made.

Having performed a service which immeasurably strengthened the hands of the British negotiators, Goldie was able to demand and be granted a further recognition of the National Company's status as the quasi-official representative of the British Government on the Niger. Goldie was well aware that the Foreign Office was particularly worried at the German charges of ineffective occupation.[2] At Angra Pequena the Germans had established their authority by declaring a protectorate over the settlements of the German merchant Herr Luderitz, to whom authority had subsequently been delegated. Germany could scarcely accuse Britain of ineffective occupation on the Niger if she were to do the same. Early in November Aberdare, pointing out the analogy with Luderitz, asked Lord Granville to declare that the field of operations of the National African Company had been taken under British protection.[3] His motive was to allow the National Company to hoist the Union Jack.[4] Three days before the conference began its sessions in Berlin the colonial committee of the Cabinet, whilst rejecting the idea of an automatic protectorate over the company's entire field of operations, gave permission for the company to hoist the Union Jack at all places where they held 'independent title'.[5]

Thus the company, besides being the sole trader on the Niger, was now recognized by Britain to be in some sense the representative of British authority on the river. It was fitting therefore that Goldie should accompany the British delegation to Berlin, to advise on Niger matters behind the scenes.[6] The conference began on 15 November, but was occupied first with the Congo

[1] R.J.S.C. 17049, Vol. I, Agreement between N.A.C. Ltd., and C.F.A.C. 31.10.84.

[2] See FO 84/1691 minute by T.V.L. 18.10.84, for an illustration of this anxiety.

[3] FO 84/1814 Aberdare to Granville 6.11.84.

[4] *Ibid.* minute by H.P.A. 6.11.84.   [5] *Ibid.* T. V. Lister to Aberdare 12.11.84.

[6] He was not the only unofficial representative. F. W. Bond and A. L. Jones represented the West African steamship lines; E. S. Cookson, T. S. Rogerson and John Holt represented the coastal traders of Liverpool. FO 84/1814 F.O. to Malet 12.11.84; and J. Bright to Fitzmaurice 11.11.84.

question. In December the discussions on the Niger began with the submission of a Franco-German draft declaration providing for free navigation on the Niger and the establishment of an international commission to administer a navigation fund and enforce the principles of free navigation.[1]

This was the expected attack on the British position. The entire British delegation saw it as such and insisted on Britain's right to administer the Niger without the supervision of an international commission. Fortunately for them, the general diplomatic situation had now taken a turn which favoured the British position. Franco-German relations had cooled, and Bismarck was anxious that Britain recognize the rights of King Leopold of the Belgians' Congo Association. In return for this recognition, Bismarck saw fit to drop the Franco-German draft, and support a new Niger Navigation Act, drafted and proposed by the British delegation. On 18 December this was accepted by the whole conference.[2]

On paper, the Niger Navigation Act contained a formidable list of obligations. It began by declaring that 'The navigation of the Niger, without excepting any of its branches and outlets, is and shall remain entirely free for the merchant ships of all nations equally.' There was to be no discrimination against any persons, no restrictions based merely on the fact of navigation, nor 'any obligation with regard to landing station or depot, or for breaking bulk, or for compulsory entry into port'. It was not permitted to concede 'exclusive privileges of navigation' to any company, transit dues were forbidden, and the only taxes permitted were those 'equivalent for services rendered for navigation itself'. These limitations applied not only to the Niger and its affluents, but to any roads, railways, or canals built to facilitate river navigation. The Niger was also to be neutral in time of war.

There was no reference to an international commission. The Act would be administered by Great Britain in those parts of the river under her influence and she undertook to 'protect foreign

---

[1] P.P. 1884–5, LV, MS p. 289, Protocol V, Annex 5.
[2] Crowe, *op. cit.*, p. 120 and pp. 126–7.

merchants and all trading nationalities . . . as if they were her own subjects'.[1] Here lay the triumph for the British delegation. Without the international commission the Act was so much waste paper; imposing though its restrictions appeared, each was to be broken with impunity. Without the international commission there was no outside body to which a competing foreign merchant could appeal. It was an even greater triumph for Goldie. Not only had he helped to conjure away a scheme which would have meant the end to all his plans of monopoly on the Niger; in addition the British Government, still penny-pinching and reluctant to pay for colonial administration, had incurred, on paper at least, heavy responsibilities, and now had to find an inexpensive method of fulfilling them.

It seemed almost inevitable that the new British obligations would be fulfilled by granting Goldie's company a royal charter. Such a solution logically concluded the process by which the company had attracted to itself more and more the character of Britain's representative on the Niger. The Foreign Office officials, and the Liberal politicians in the Cabinet, were well aware of Goldie's commercial ambitions and his monopolizing spirit; they could not approve of such ambitions—but what was the alternative? The Foreign Office could not expect the Colonial Office to set up a colonial regime, still less could they expect the Treasury to agree to pay for a protectorate regime run by consular staff. These two fundamental limitations had been clearly revealed by the discussions of 1882 to 1884. Thus the decision to grant a charter scarcely provoked controversy; the Foreign Office almost drifted into the assumption that the charter must be granted. In fact before the Berlin Conference began Sir Percy Anderson was arguing that Goldie's company should take on any new British responsibilities incurred.[2] When the terms of the Niger Navigation Act were known, Villiers Lister was for granting a charter 'without delay'.[3] When, at

[1] Full text in P.P. 1886, XLVII, p. 115, Chap. V of the General Act of the Berlin Conference, arts. 26 to 33.

[2] FO 84/1813 mem. by H.P.A. 14.10.84. Anderson was Senior Clerk of the African Department at this time.

[3] FO 84/1819 mem. by T.V.L. on Hewett's no. 33 of 1884, n.d., and *ibid.*, F.O. to C.O. 6.1.85.

the end of January 1885, after the delegates had returned from Berlin, Lister circulated a memorandum to the Cabinet setting out the arguments for the charter, he made it seem the only thing to do. If the new obligations incurred at Berlin were 'undertaken directly', he argued, this would entail 'a colonial government and a river fleet'. Yet British trade on the Niger was entirely in the hands of the National Company, who held cessions from the chiefs. The company was 'perfectly able and willing' to discharge British responsibilities. Unless the Cabinet thought it necessary to 'go to the great expense of setting up the machinery of government upon the two rivers (Niger and Benue) where the company now rules supreme' there was no other course, 'and certainly no better one', than that of 'legalising and affirming the position of the company' and 'placing the administration into its hands'. Lister appended a memorandum by the British ambassador in Berlin on the German policy of ruling through chartered companies. Since it was with Germany that trouble was likely to arise, it seemed to Lister that the ideal solution was to follow the course which that country had adopted.[1]

It was an easy matter to decide to grant a charter in principle. Then came the details. Discussion over the precise form of the charter was to occupy another eighteen months, a delay which was caused as much by Goldie's intransigence as by official red tape. It was natural that conflict should occur over details. The Government and the company were agreed on the principle of granting a charter. But when discussions began on the kind of charter to be granted, the basic dilemma of chartered company administration came to the fore. Agreed upon the means, the Government and the company worked for different ends. Goldie wanted a charter to allow him to exclude commercial rivals; the Government looked for a cheap way to fulfil British obligations on the Niger. Naturally each side tried to make the charter conform to its own ends. The essential problem therefore was one of control. Was the company to receive a charter which would allow it to be virtually independent, or would the Government

[1] FO 84/1879 mem. by T.V.L. 30.1.85.

be able to frame a charter which would give substantial authority to the Foreign Office over the day-to-day administration of the Niger?

Before Goldie had submitted any official request for a charter, Sir Julian Pauncefote, the Permanent Under-Secretary of the Foreign Office,[1] had seized upon this issue of control. Pauncefote disliked the way in which the company had established its own independent titles by treaties in the company's name with the African rulers. If Britain was to hold her own internationally and politically on the Niger, British rule must be imperial and direct. The company must first transfer all its political rights to the Crown, thus establishing a clear, direct title in the Crown. All jurisdiction would then appertain to the Queen, and the territories could be governed through Orders in Council. Then a charter could be granted to the company, vesting some of these powers in the company's officials, who would thus become officers of the Crown.[2]

Six days later Goldie sent, through Lord Aberdare, his first official request for a charter. His proposed charter was entirely opposed in spirit to the scheme which Pauncefote wanted. Goldie's draft was practically identical with the charter granted in 1881 to the British North Borneo Company. It was based on the assumption that the company already possessed the right to rule its territories by virtue of its treaties with native chiefs. Its territories would remain outside the Queen's jurisdiction or sovereignty. The Government merely recognized the validity of these rights, and in return the company agreed to submit to a measure of Government control.[3]

Goldie's scheme was now circulated to members of the Cabinet. Lord Granville and the Foreign Office officials sped it on its way with general approval, though with some reservations on the question of imperial control. Lord Derby, now Colonial

---

[1] 1828–1902, born at Munich, called to the Bar 1852, attorney-general of Hong-Kong 1865–72, knighted 1872, Chief Justice of the Leeward Isles 1874, legal under-secretary in Foreign Office 1876, Permanent Under-Secretary 1882, Envoy-Extraordinary to the U.S.A. 1889, ambassador in Washington 1893, peerage as Lord Pauncefote 1899.

[2] FO 84/1879 mem. by J.P. 7.2.85.   [3] *Ibid.* Aberdare to Granville 13.2.85.

Secretary, gave his approval, though he admitted that he was unable to understand the legal implications of granting such a charter. Lord Kimberley gave his blessing from the India Office. The papers now passed out of the circle of ministers with colonial experience and began to get a rougher handling. Childers, the Chancellor of the Exchequer, failed to see the need for any charter at all. The company could obtain all the necessary power by making an agreement with the Government. Childers confessed that he disliked charters, and would grant them only when their political advantages were very clearly apparent. Lord Selborne, the Lord Chancellor, was even more hostile, and his opinion on what was, after all, essentially a legal question, naturally carried much weight. He suspected that the company's treaties were fraudulent, and could not believe that the African kings and chiefs, even if they had known what they were signing away, had the power to do so. He deplored the idea that the British Government should give moral sanction to trickery of this kind, and firmly advised against the grant of any charter. The First Lord, Northbrooke, was equally opposed to the idea, and suspected that the whole thing was a plot to get the company a monopoly.[1]

This was not an auspicious beginning. Sir Julian Pauncefote, however, attempted to profit by it in order to press the need for a stricter control over the company. He asked that Lord Selborne should be shown his previous memorandum on the subject, and suggested that the British Government should now make a series of treaties of its own with the African rulers inside the company's sphere. This would overcome Selborne's objections about fraud, and would at the same time give the Queen a direct title. Any idea of granting a charter like that granted to the Borneo Company should be dropped forthwith.[2] This view gained immediate support from the Cabinet. All, except the arch-supporter of the 'Little England' theory, Sir William Harcourt, were convinced of the need for direct British authority.

[1] *Ibid.* minutes by Granville, n.d.; Fitzmaurice 16.2.85; T.V.L. 16.2.85; Herbert 19.2.85; Ashley 19.2.85; Lord Derby 19.2.85; Lord Selborne 3.3.85; Mr. Childers 21.2.85; Lord Northbrooke 4.3.85.
[2] *Ibid.* mem. by J.P. 5.3.85.

Lord Kimberley, now relieved of the cares of the Colonial Office, was prepared to argue that the Colonial Office should assume responsibility and directly control the officers of the company, who could be invested with administrative powers without there being any need to grant a charter. Lord Selborne went some way to meet Pauncefote's view. He agreed on the need for direct royal authority, but the grant of a charter needed long and serious consideration. Childers was fully converted, a protectorate or sovereignty must be established, after which an amended charter could be issued to the company.[1]

Having won his point, Pauncefote was now able to work out a plan of action. A notice would be inserted in the *London Gazette* declaring a British protectorate over the Niger region, after which an Order in Council would be prepared authorizing the Foreign Secretary to entrust powers of administration to any persons, and those need not necessarily be consular officials. Another Order in Council would appoint a High Commissioner with controlling power, including that of summoning a Legislative Council. The National Company would then be granted a charter, not on the model of the North Borneo charter, but of 'a much more limited and appropriate character'. The company's principal officers would then be appointed members of the High Commissioner's Legislative Council and entrusted with other powers under the first of the Orders in Council. A notice of what had been done could then be circulated to all the signatories of the Berlin Act as the fulfilment of Britain's obligations under it.[2] This plan was now circulated to the colonial committee of the Cabinet and obtained unanimous acceptance.[3]

There was now a delay. Talks had begun with Germany to define the boundary between the German Cameroons and the British Oil Rivers, and these talks soon broadened in scope to take in commercial matters. It was therefore necessary to await the result of these talks so that any changes could be taken

[1] *Ibid.* minutes by Kimberley 7.3.85; Harcourt 8.3.85; Childers, n.d.; Selborne, n.d.

[2] *Ibid.* J.P. to Granville 10.3.85.

[3] *Ibid.* mem. by Selborne 11.3.85; Kimberley 14.3.85; Fitzmaurice 14.3.85; and Childers 15.3.85.

account of in drafting the charter. The final agreement further strengthened the impression that the British Government intended to make its authority on the Niger a reality, and to curb monopoly. The two powers agreed to levy in their new territories 'duties solely for the purpose of meeting the expenses necessary to carry out the obligations imposed on them by the protectorates', and that there should be 'no differential treatment of foreigners or foreign goods' particularly 'as to settlement or access to markets'. Four months' notice would be given of any changes in tariffs, no monopolies would be allowed, and foreigners would be scrupulously protected. In a phrase which was later to be of crucial importance to Goldie's company the powers agreed that customs duties would 'only be raised to such an amount as may be considered sufficient to cover the expenses arising from the taking over of the protectorate'.[1]

The talks completed, Pauncefote set in motion the first steps in his plan. The notification of a British protectorate over the Niger region, and a new West African Order in Council enabling the Queen to vest authority in any persons, were published in the *London Gazette*.[2]

Meanwhile Goldie had heard privately of the rejection of his own draft charter and the plans for a more direct control. Pauncefote's scheme seemed worse than no charter at all, for it saddled the company with the responsibility and cost of administration, and gave nothing in return. Now that Britain, without consulting Goldie, had agreed with Germany to levy only such revenue as would cover the costs of administration, a monopoly was even more essential, for the National Company would not be able, like the Borneo Company, to make profits from the surpluses of revenue. Goldie therefore had to insist on a Borneo-type charter, even though the Niger was now, unlike North Borneo, a British protectorate. If this was impossible he asked for a tentative charter, on the model of that granted to the German East Africa Company, for ten years' duration. At the same time Goldie let it be known that this was a serious matter for the National Company; if the Government intended to 'abandon'

[1] P.P. 1886, LV, MS. p. 555 *et seq.*   [2] *London Gazette* 5.6.85.

the Niger, then the company would have 'to make terms with some foreign power'.[1] Sir Percy Anderson was shocked, and remonstrated with Goldie. He 'repeatedly told him that the only scheme which would have any chance of success would be one in which the Government's control would be in some shape definite'; but to no avail. Goldie wished to be independent; Anderson found him 'body and soul devoted to the interests of the company' and unable to appreciate 'questions of policy'.[2] Anderson therefore tried to sidestep Goldie by talking to Lord Aberdare. His Lordship seemed much more amenable, and promised that he would try to calm Goldie down and reach a compromise.[3] On the strength of this Granville ordered the preparation of a Niger charter 'as secretly and rapidly as possible,[4] but he had overestimated Aberdare's real power in the company. Goldie refused to yield, and the position was now one of stalemate.

Goldie's intransigence may have been stiffened by the political crisis brewing in England. Gladstone's Liberal Government was in difficulties, and it was known that an election could not follow its defeat, for the new electoral register made necessary by Gladstone's recent introduction of near-universal male suffrage was not yet ready. When the Liberals were defeated on a vote in the Commons in June 1885, Lord Salisbury formed a Conservative ministry which had to rely on Liberal passivity until the elections could be held. For Goldie, however, this was an important change. The legal advisor to the National Company, the man who had helped to frame the company's draft charter, became Salisbury's Lord Chancellor. Sir Hardinge Giffard's influence might now be decisive. The head of the African department in the Foreign Office certainly thought so,[5] as did Goldie himself.[6]

[1] FO 84/1879 enclosure in Goldie Taubman to F.O. 15.5.85.
[2] *Ibid.* mem. by H.P.A., n.d., filed at 17.5.85.
[3] *Ibid.* mem. by H.P.A. 27.5.85.   [4] *Ibid.* note by Granville, n.d., May 1885.
[5] FO 84/1739 mem. by H.P.A. on pending questions in the African Dept. for the information of Lord Salisbury 13.6.85.
[6] FO 84/1879 Goldie Taubman to F.O. 15.8.85 asking for the question of the charter to be referred to Giffard for decision.

To think in this way was to underestimate the integrity of Salisbury. No sinister influence displayed itself. Salisbury accepted Pauncefote's view that the company must submit to direct control, and allowed him to procede with his plans. The company's draft charter was sent for a legal opinion to the Law Officers, and not to Sir Hardinge Giffard. Unfortunately for Pauncefote, the Law Officers at first reported favourably on Goldie's scheme,[1] but after prompting from the Foreign Office they sent an additional opinion that such a charter 'would not be desirable'.[2] Meanwhile Pauncefote was quietly attempting to manœuvre Goldie into a position where he would appear to have accepted the Government scheme. Goldie was told that the Law Officers' opinion was likely to be 'doubtful', and that he ought therefore to ask that certain of his company's officers be given administrative powers by Order in Council. This Goldie did, but he took care to stress that this was a 'purely interim measure', and that the officials concerned must receive and carry out orders only from the company.[3] When the Law Officers' report and addendum were received, Goldie was told that his draft charter was now out of the question and that the Government was preparing 'another proposal' which would achieve the same ends.[4]

Goldie now saw why he had been manœuvred into asking for powers to be delegated to the company's employees—this was to be the basis for the 'other proposal' and he would find his powers shackled by all kinds of interference from the Government. The prospect made him lose both his temper and his sense of proportion. He descended on the Foreign Office in person and had a stormy interview with one of the officials. He wished it to be plainly understood that his request for powers for his employees was a temporary measure, lasting for only two or three months, 'pending the issue of a charter'. If the charter were not granted the Foreign Office could not rely on any

[1] *Ibid*. Law Officers to F.O. 8.8.85.
[2] *Ibid*. addendum to Law Officers' reply 20.8.85.
[3] *Ibid*. N.A.C. to F.O. 15.8.85, with minute by J.P.; and Goldie Taubman to J.P. 15.8.85.
[4] *Ibid*. F.O. to N.A.C., n.d., August 1885.

patriotic sentimentality on his part; this was a commercial business and 'it might be necessary in the interests of the shareholders to hand over the Company's treaties to the French'.[1] To show that he meant his threat to be taken seriously, Goldie followed it up by calling a special meeting of the shareholders at which the directors were given power to begin negotiations with the French.[2] At the same time he began an organized agitation in the British Chambers of Commerce, suggesting vague resolutions which called attention to the 'defenceless state of the Niger and Benue' and demanded that the Government set up an administration.[3]

It was all bluff. If Goldie had been really serious in his intention to sell out to France, he would scarcely have been so naïve as to tell the Foreign Office about his almost treasonable intentions in advance. Julian Pauncefote refused to take the threat seriously, and proceeded with his scheme. It was now set out in detail, and sent to the Law Officers and to Sir Hardinge Giffard for a legal opinion. The effect of the Lord Chancellor's opinion, if favourable, would be to show Goldie that this was the best he could hope for. Pauncefote's detailed scheme continued to emphasize royal control. The company would receive a charter of incorporation (even though it was already incorporated under the Companies Acts) and the charter would provide for the formation of a Council from the board of directors. This Council was to be 'under the control and authority of Her Majesty's Government with respect to all matters relating to the exercise of the Queen's jurisdiction'. Certain of the company's employees would be appointed by the Crown as commissioners to administer the Niger territories 'in accordance with instructions from the Crown'. Instructions from the Crown might be given directly to these officials, though 'usually' they would pass through the Council of the company. The Crown reserved the

---

[1] *Ibid.* mem. of interview with Goldie Taubman by J.W.W. 26.8.85.

[2] FO 84/1742 enc. in Goldie Taubman to F.O. 18.9.85, see also R.J.S.C. 17049, Vol. 1, 23.9.85.

[3] FO 84/1742 Manchester Chamber to F.O. 17.9.85; London Chamber to F.O. 17.9.85. The Liverpool Chamber, dominated by the Oil Rivers interests, naturally remained aloof.

right to exercise any of the delegated powers directly if the need arose, and the charter could be revoked at will whenever the Crown wished to do so.[1] At the same time Pauncefote said that he was prepared, if the scheme was rejected on legal grounds, to govern the area directly through consular officials.[2] However, there was no need for such extremes; both the Lord Chancellor and the Law Officers reported favourably, and Pauncefote was able to reopen negotiations with the company.[3]

The time had come for Goldie to acknowledge defeat. His 'Borneo' scheme had found no support at all in Government circles, and none seemed likely in the future. Worse still was the talk of establishing direct rule by consular officials, with its implications of free trade for all on the Niger. Goldie's problem now was to salvage as much as possible from the wreck of his plans. He tried to do so by getting back to first principles. The object of the 'Borneo' charter had been to leave the company practically uncontrolled so that its officials could exclude competitors by administrative discrimination and sanctions. If this was now impossible, and the officials were to be strictly controlled, then the monopoly would have to be found by other and more open means. Goldie therefore put forward new proposals which gave ground on the political issue, and brought his commercial ambitions into the light. He argued that the company had lost £300,000 in its fight to keep the Niger British— £100,000 in buying out the French firms, £100,000 spent in concluding its treaties, and £100,000 lost by the delay in granting the charter. In compensation for these losses he asked that the company be granted a complete monopoly of the imports of war materials and alcoholic liquors into the Niger.[4]

The move was a clever one. The demand for a monopoly of war materials could be justified on perfectly valid and obvious political grounds. The trade in alcoholic liquors aroused missionary and humanitarian sentiment which was prepared to justify its restriction and control by the administration in the

---

[1] FO 84/1879 F.O. to Law Officers 7.9.85.　　[2] *Ibid.* mem. by J.P. 7.9.85.
[3] FO 84/1745 J.P. to Goldie Taubman 8.12.85.
[4] FO 84/1879 Goldie Taubman to J.P. 8.12.86.

interests of the African population. Yet at the same time a monopoly of these articles would effectively capture the whole of the Niger trade, both imports and exports. Spirits, especially gin and rum, were the standard barter goods offered in exchange for palm oil and kernels. Liquor was practically a currency in this trade, without which it was impossible to obtain palm oil in any quantity. Above the palm oil region the Emirs would not allow trade in shea-butter or ivory unless arms and ammunition were given as barter goods, or at least presented to the rulers as 'dash' for permission to trade. Any trader who tried to break into the Niger without liquor or arms to offer the African in exchange for his produce would make little headway. A little salt, some tobacco, and minute quantities of Manchester cotton goods were the only other European imports of any significance.

In making these demands, Goldie showed that he was willing to meet Pauncefote on the political issue. His main wish, he confided, was that the company 'is to drive the coach (of course under the orders of the government) instead of holding the reins as a dummy in the box', but he was prepared to drop the idea of basing the charter upon the claim to independent sovereignty. He asked for a new and separate Order in Council for the Niger which would vest its administration in a Council composed of the directors of the company and one official member with a veto power appointed by the Crown. Goldie still insisted that the company's officials on the Niger should be subordinate to the company alone, and not permitted to communicate directly with the Foreign Office.[1]

Goldie's new proposals were felt to be sufficiently close to the Foreign Office view for a beginning to be made in the actual process of drafting the charter. For this purpose the Treasury was asked to lend the services of their expert on charters and Orders in Council, Mr. R. S. Wright. Normally Wright's task would have been purely technical and formal, without influence on questions of policy. In this case it was to be decisive, and to reverse the whole previous trend of policy towards Goldie's

[1] *Ibid.* Goldie Taubman to J.P. 9.12.85.

PLATE I

The Nunnery, Isle of Man

Reproduced by permission of Captain J. W. L. Fry-Goldie-Taubman

company. Wright's legalistic way of looking at the question
threw a harsh light on Pauncefote's plan which exposed it as
threadbare, makeshift, and above all, impossible to achieve in
the present framework of the law. Pauncefote's plan of delegating royal authority to the company could not be legally
achieved through the device of the charter and Orders in Council. The only legal means of expressing such a relationship was
by altering the law itself, and this would need a special Act of
Parliament.[1]

Parliamentary legislation was not possible. To put the question before Parliament was to throw away the very advantages
which the device of the chartered company was intended to
convey; the chartered company was a method of expanding
and administering territory at a time when public opinion, and
both the political parties in the House of Commons, were
opposed to ventures of this kind. To expose the project to
parliamentary debate would, besides risking the defeat of the
Government while the electoral registers were still not yet
ready, be particularly awkward in this instance. The Liverpool
merchants were unaware of the plan, and would whip up an
agitation against the National Company as soon as they heard of
it. They would be assured of the support of the Liverpool members, and there would be all kinds of revelations about the company's monopolistic tendencies. Wright was aware of all these
objections, and in general the avoidance of Parliamentary
legislation was an unwritten law of colonial administration. He
therefore concluded that the wisest course would be to issue 'a
vague and indefinite charter' which could be revoked at will by
the Queen. The charter should 'expressly exclude' any idea
that the Crown was sovereign on the Niger. So the wheel turned
full circle. Wright resurrected Goldie's original draft charter,
and adapted it to form the final draft. The idea of delegated
authority from the Crown was reduced to a minimum, the company being vested merely with the Queen's powers over British
subjects and foreigners under the Foreign Jurisdiction Acts. All
other powers, as in North Borneo, derived from the African

[1] FO 84/1879 Wright to J.P. 26.12.85.

G

rulers who had surrendered their authority by treaty with the company. These powers were now recognized in the charter by the British Government, in return for which the company agreed to submit to 'control' in the exercise of them. The plan to issue an Order in Council in conjunction with the charter was not immediately jettisoned, but it was never issued; presumably it proved unnecessary.[1]

All seemed now complete, save the final formalities. It was now January 1886, and after a year of wearisome disputes and bargaining, Goldie had achieved all that he had asked for. This is how it appears to the historian. To Goldie himself the picture was very different. He was by now suspicious, and above all, confused. He failed to see that Wright's new draft, though based on his own original proposal, was in fact a complete abandonment of Pauncefote's scheme, and naturally the Foreign Office were not prepared to admit that they had been chasing shadows for a twelve-month. The spectre of Government control had not been exorcized, and Goldie still feared that the company's monopoly was insecure. He therefore continued to press for specific monopolies to be written into the charter. Pauncefote put up numerous objections; the Crown was prohibited from granting monopolies under British law; monopolies were illegal under the Berlin Act and the Anglo-German agreement of 1885; and additional claims made by Goldie for monopolies of salt and tobacco amounted to a claim for purely commercial privileges and could not be justified on humanitarian grounds. But Goldie had an answer for each of these objections. The Crown was not in this case bound by British law, for the company at present held a complete monopoly by virtue of its treaties with African rulers under local law. The Crown had merely to recognize a part of these rights by conferring specific monopolies. Goldie also introduced a theory, which he was later to insist upon tenaciously, that the Berlin Act contained no prohibition of monopoly on the Niger, but merely gave the right to free transit on the water for vessels voyaging to countries outside the

[1] FO 84/1880 Wright to J.P. 7 or 11.1.86; Goldie Taubman to J.P., private, 7.1.86; List of papers sent to Lord Chancellor 26.2.86; F.O. to Law Officers 13.3.86.

company's sphere. As for the Anglo-German Agreement, there was nothing to fear from Germany; German firms were the main suppliers of the company and a large number of the company's shares were held by Germans.[1] When Pauncefote sent Wright's final draft of the charter for acceptance or rejection, Goldie still refused to commit the company to a final yea or nay. He noted that the draft charter, unlike that granted to the North Borneo Company, was revokable at will. The company was thus at the mercy of future Governments. He merely asked for monopolies like those written in to the Borneo Company's charter. If the British Government was bent on confiscating all the company's commercial privileges legally obtained by treaties with the African rulers, then 'reluctantly', and as a last resort, the directors asked for 'direct compensation for their shareholders'.[2]

Such was the position when in February 1886 Lord Salisbury's Government fell, and Gladstone returned to power with Lord Rosebery as his Foreign Secretary. The change made no difference to policy on the Niger, and Pauncefote was able to go ahead in search of a way out of these latest difficulties. He could not accept the idea of specific monopolies being written into the charter, but he was prepared to give the company some privilege in a concealed and roundabout way. Pauncefote began to read through the documents which imposed limits on the commercial policy to be pursued on the Niger, particularly the Anglo-German Agreement of 1885. Here he spotted a loophole. Though taxes levied were supposed to balance expenditure, the duties leviable had been defined as sufficient 'to cover the expenses arising out of the taking over of the protectorate'. The 'taking over' of the protectorate could be interpreted as covering the cost of the original treaties made by the National Company. It

---

[1] Most of the gin and rum imported to the Niger did come from Hamburg, or was German produce shipped through Rotterdam. However, there were no German shareholders in the Niger Company according to R.J.S.C. 17049, Vol. I. Returns of shareholders, 1882–9.

[2] These exchanges are in FO 84/1879 N.A.C. to Salisbury 28.12.85, and supplementary mem. by G.D.G.T., same date; FO 84/1880, mem. by J.P. 10.1.86; F.O. to Goldie Taubman 23.1.86 with note from J.P. to Salisbury 20.1.86; N.A.C. to F.O. 27.1.86 (asking for financial compensation).

might be possible therefore for the Government to allow the company to retain for its profit and loss account some of the taxes which it levied as compensation for this initial expenditure in establishing the protectorate. Early in February Pauncefote held a meeting with Goldie at which he put this idea forward as one he 'would submit for consideration'. Goldie seized on it, and then proposed it to the head of the African department, Sir Percy Anderson, from whom he obtained a sympathetic hearing. Goldie then asked officially that the company be authorized to levy in taxes £15,000 a year in perpetuity, or £24,000 a year for twenty years. These figures represented five per cent and eight per cent respectively on a sum of £300,000 which Goldie claimed had been spent on 'taking over' the protectorate. On the other hand the company would accept a direct cash payment of £150,000.[1]

Despite the utterly fantastic nature of the amount claimed, the principle of Goldie's proposal was accepted. Article 14 of the draft charter, which forbade monopoly, was modified 'so that it permits the levying of duties, with the sanction of the Secretary of State, for the repayment of expenses connected with the acquisition of treaty rights'. A further sentence was added to this clause obliging the company to submit its accounts of revenue and expenditure to the Secretary of State 'to secure efficient control over them'.[2] The final draft was officially accepted by the company on 4 March 1886; in doing so Goldie tried to make it understood that the company would be permitted to levy taxes to cover not £300,000 as at first demanded, but £250,000, though this, he declared, was grossly inadequate. But the Foreign Office refused to be committed; first the charter must be accepted as it stood, the question of compensation could be dealt with at a later date 'if necessary'.[3]

Having gained the principle, Goldie yielded. The charter now made its last formal journey, past the Law Officers, the Lord

[1] FO 84/1880 minutes by H.P.A. 8.2.86 and 10.2.86; by J.P. 10.2.86; H.P.A. to J.P. 10.2.86; and FO 84/1781 N.A.C. to J.P. 9.2.86.
[2] FO 84/1880 F.O. to Goldie Taubman 2.3.86.
[3] *Ibid.* N.A.C. to Rosebery 4.3.86; F.O. to Goldie Taubman 13.3.86. The sequel to the affair may be found in Chap. 6, p 113.

Chancellor, the Colonial Office, Mr. Gladstone (who could find no time to read it!), to its official midwife the Privy Council, where it received the Great Seal on 10 July 1886.[1] More by good luck than judgement, the long months of wrangling had brought nothing but gain to Goldie and his company. His conception of the company holding independent title by virtue of its treaties had been upheld, the idea of a strict Government control through a High Commissioner or official director had been rejected, and the right to transfer revenue from the administrative to the commercial account was to prove an important factor in allowing the company to shape its taxation policy to exclude competitors from the Niger.

Let us now examine the document itself. It began with a Preamble, into which was incorporated the Petition of the National Company, expressing the public motives of late-Victorian colonial expansion. The company claimed to have fulfilled all the necessary preliminaries for the receipt of a charter; it had acquired the territory by acts of cession from the native authorities, it was the sole European trader in the area, and it possessed in its present form as a limited company the power to accept a charter. By virtue of the grant of the charter the condition of the natives would be improved and the company would be enabled 'to render to Our Dominions services of much value' and to 'promote the Commercial Prosperity of many of Our Subjects'.

The charter was not a charter of incorporation, but an act of recognition of the company's rights and powers, in return for which the company submitted to control in certain matters. In this respect the company emerged with an even stronger position than that held by the North Borneo Company, which, though it held its powers by independent title by virtue of cessions from local rulers, nevertheless achieved its corporate

[1] *Ibid.* F.O. to L.O. 13.3.86; F.O. to Lord Chancellor 24.5.86; F.O. to C.O. 1.4.86; C.O. to F.O. 5.4.86; mem. by W. E. Gladstone 31.3.86; F.O. to Clerk of the Council 13.4.86; and P.P. 1899, LXIII (C. 9372), MS. p. 425 *et seq.* for full text of charter.

identity through its charter, and would lose that identity if the charter lapsed, or was revoked. By article 1 of the National African Company's charter the company was simply 'authorised and empowered to hold and retain the full benefit of the several cessions' to enable it to govern the territory 'for the purposes of the company, and on the terms of this our charter'. Expansion of territory was to follow the same principle, that is, through legitimate cessions from the local rulers (art. 12). It followed that the company must honour the promises made to Africans in these treaties (art. 2). The only British authority delegated to the company was the exercise 'for the time being' of the Queen's jurisdiction over British subjects and foreigners under the Foreign Jurisdiction Acts, the company to set up courts and appoint officers for this purpose at its own expense (art. 16).

The control to which the company submitted was imperial, humanitarian, and commercial. The company was to be British in character and domicile, with its principal office in England. Its chief officer on the Niger, and all its directors must henceforth be British subjects[1] (art. 5). The company must give facilities to ships of the Royal Navy (art. 10) and adopt a distinctive flag to show its British character (art. 11). The consent of the Secretary of State was required in all cases where the company wished to transfer any of its cessions or rights under its treaties (art. 4) and the company must act in accordance with any dissenting suggestions made by the Secretary of State on questions affecting its relations with foreign powers (art. 5). By the General Provision of the charter the company received recognition throughout the British Empire.

In fulfilling its humanitarian role the company must endeavour to the best of its power to 'discourage and, as far as may be practicable, abolish by degrees any system of domestic servitude'; foreigners were forbidden to hold slaves of any kind (art. 6). Its officers must not interfere with the religion of any class or tribe 'except insofar as may be necessary in the interests of humanity'; all forms of religious worship were to be free (art. 7). Local laws and customs, especially those dealing with

[1] This obliged the French directors to resign from the Board.

land, marriage, divorce, and the legitimacy of offspring, were to be respected (art. 8). The company must act in accordance with any dissenting suggestions made by the Secretary of State in matters of policy concerning the local peoples (art. 9).

Commercial control was in the interests of freedom of trade. Nothing in the charter was to be deemed to authorize any monopoly of trade, and differential treatment of the subjects of foreign powers 'as to settlement or access to markets' was expressly forbidden. But customs duties could be levied 'solely for the purpose of defraying the necessary expenses of government', accounts of which must be submitted, and the Secretary of State could modify them if he so wished (art. 14). The Company was to 'perform, observe, and undertake' all the stipulations and obligations incurred by Great Britain at the Berlin Conference, and respect all present and future international agreements and treaties affecting its territories (art. 15). The charter could be revoked at will (General Provisions).

As a legal document, conceived as it was with deliberate ambiguity, the charter had its amusing aspects. 'The rights which (it) professes to confer', wrote the Lord Chancellor, 'are not really conferred by it, but are possessed already ... the only penalty for violation of the restrictions imposed being a revocation of the charter, that revocation would not I think have any effect. The corporation would still exist if the charter were revoked, and would possess substantially all its property and rights'![1] But the realists had the last word—'the position is an awkward one', wrote one official, 'but having regard to the position of the country, and to our position under the Berlin arrangement, this is probably the best thing that can be done'.[2]

[1] FO 84/1880 mem. by Lord Chancellor 24.5.86.
[2] Ibid. mem. by Herschell 24.5.86.

5

Administration and the Liverpool Opposition

DURING the long months of negotiations for the charter the National Company had not been inactive on the Niger. As the representative of Great Britain on the river, authorized to hoist the British flag where it could show valid title, the company made the most of its rather anomalous position and tried to 'administer' the Niger and Benue without a charter. Its claims to do so rested on its treaties with African rulers, so that during the months between the end of the Berlin Conference early in 1885 and the issue of the charter in July 1886, most of the company's efforts were concentrated on making treaties. The treaties were not made haphazardly but according to a definite plan, the object of which was to control the banks of the Niger and Benue as far as they were navigable, so as to exclude all competitors from the rivers. By the end of 1884 most of the lower Niger below Onitsha had been fairly thoroughly covered with treaties. During the next eighteen months efforts were concentrated on the middle Niger where it flowed through Nupe, and on the Benue up to Yola. In these areas the company had great difficulty in making valid treaties. For the most part the river banks were ruled by powerful Muslim Emirs, not at all inclined to sign away their rights to a group of infidel traders. This was particularly the case in Nupe, where the Emir had, since the days of Masaba, regarded himself as the 'protector' of the traders, and could see no reason why the roles should now be reversed. When asked to sign a treaty he refused, and the company's chief agent McIntosh had to be content with concluding, in March 1885, an 'agreement' which was little more than a commercial arrangement, giving the company 'entire charge of all trading interests in the country', insisting that all foreigners obtain the company's permission to trade, and granting a monopoly of the working of mineral deposits. But even the control of trade was not clearly established, for the company had to promise 'to allow anyone who wishes to trade full liberty, always provided it shall be on equitable terms, and according to British law'.[1] The failure to obtain political rights was emphasized by the fact that the company continued to pay 'comey' (a tribute analogous to customs duties) to the Emir. Moreover the company obtained no rights to the banks of the river.

Similar difficulties were encountered in attempts to make treaties with Emirs on the Benue. But Goldie had a trump card to play. The Sultan of Sokoto, and the Emir of Gandu were the spiritual and political fountainheads of the Fulani social and political system, and it was convenient, and perhaps not inaccurate, to argue that this headship was analogous to that of a feudal monarch in medieval Europe, possessing ultimate sovereignty over the whole area. What the vassal would not cede, the lord might, especially if the cost was borne by the vassal and the tribute paid to the lord. Consequently, before McIntosh visited Nupe, Goldie had secured the services of one of the most eminent African explorers, Joseph Thomson. In June 1885 Thomson managed to obtain treaties with both the Sultan of Sokoto and the Emir of Gandu, which granted the company 'entire rights to the country on both sides of the River Benue (Niger in the Gandu treaty) and rivers flowing into it through my dominions for such distance from its and their banks as they may desire'.[2] The rulers also agreed to have no

[1] FO 84/1917 Mem. of Agreement between N.A.C. Ltd. and the King and chiefs of Nupe 19.3.85, sent in by R.N.C. 19.3.88.

[2] The wording of the Gandu treaty was slightly different: rights were granted over the river banks 'for a distance of ten hours journey inland, or such other distance as they may desire, from each bank. . . .' Thompson wrote an account of his mission in *Good Words*, Vol. 27, 1886, pp. 26 ff. For texts of treaties see Hertslet, *Map of Africa*, Vol. I, pp. 122-4.

communication with foreigners coming up the rivers except
through the company, and declared the treaties binding upon
their successors, and irrevocable.

Thus, by the middle of 1885, the company could claim to
have established a watertight system of treaties,[1] controlling the
lower Niger palm oil region by absolute cessions, and the Benue
and middle Niger by treaties with some of the Emirs, commercial arrangements with others, and the land grants from the Sultan of Sokoto and the Emir of Gandu. The time had now come
to exercise the claim to 'administer', despite the fact that the
charter was still in the balance. In June 1885, by virtue of its
treaties, the company issued a prohibition of all trade, except its
own, on the Niger and Benue. Competitors who had recently
come to the Niger were roughly dealt with; John Lander and
Company of Liverpool saw fit to ignore the prohibition and ask
the Foreign Office for protection. When Landers attempted
to trade at Onitsha, the National Company tried to prevent
them mooring or trading by insisting that the river banks now
belonged exclusively to the company. When the King of Onitsha
disputed this claim and allowed Landers to trade, the company
replied by closing Onitsha wharf and blockading the town with
armed steamers. When Landers' agent moved up into Nupe and
was welcomed by the Emir and allowed to trade, the company
was forced to descend to strong-arm methods. The agent was
seized by the National Company's men, who kicked him and
beat him up before allowing him to make a hasty retreat.[2] Even
then the poor fellow's troubles were not at an end, for he and
his launch were seized by the M'Blama people, on the mistaken
assumption that he was an employee of the National Company,
in retaliation for the seizure of three of their children by the
company. Though the agent escaped, Landers' launch was left
behind, and the National Company were in no hurry to return

[1] The important question as to how far these treaties were genuinely understood
by the African rulers who signed them, and how far these rulers possessed the
powers which they signed away, will be discussed later. See Chap. 7. p. 137 ff.

[2] FO 84/1740 Lander and Co. to F.O. 25.7.85; FO 84/1741 Goldie Taubman to
F.O. 8.8.85; FO 84/1780 Hatton and Cookson to F.O. 11.12.85 (filed at 1.1.86)
enclosing N.A.C. 20.11.85; FO 84/1785 Landers to F.O. 25.5.86; FO 84/1786
N.A.C. to Rosebery 4.6.86.

the children to get it back.[1] The affair was the subject of some publicity, and was taken up by W. F. Lawrence, one of the Liverpool Members of Parliament,[2] but fortunately for Goldie the charter had by this time been issued and the administration could be put on a more regular footing.

The Foreign Office had tried to hold aloof from the affair of Lander and Company. When the National Company prohibited the German traveller Herr Flegel from trading in Nupe, and later threatened to remove him by force from the Benue, pressure from the German Government forced Rosebery to insist that the National Company allow Flegel free passage.[3] This was a serious check, for Flegel had been commissioned by the *Gesellschaft für Deutsche Kolonization* to survey the possibilities for German trade on the Niger, and had the charter not been issued soon afterwards, it might have been impossible to prevent the establishment of German firms.

The charter was issued on 12 July 1886. Goldie and his fellow-directors lost no time thereafter in setting up a regular administrative system. During the next few days the Board sat regularly and poured forth an elaborate series of regulations, which had been prepared beforehand, dealing with every detail of the new administration. The Foreign Office was neither consulted nor informed of these measures—Goldie was determined to 'drive the coach'.

On paper the new regulations set up a most elaborate system of government; with its own body of law, a civil service, a judiciary, and a central government. In practice the regulations merely adopted the existing commercial organization of the company and grafted on to it political powers which, as we have

---

[1] *The Times* 20.6.86; FO 84/1786 R. Cliff to F.O. 20.6.86; *ibid.* Landers to F.O. 29.6.86; FO 84/1787 N.A.C. to Rosebery 23.7.86.

[2] FO 84/1789 notice of question by Lawrence for 31.8.86. *Hansard*, 3rd series, CCCVIII, cols. 875–6.

[3] Flegel wrote a fairly full account of his exploits in *Vom Niger Benue*, Leipzig, 1890. See also FO 84/1743 mem. by H.P.A. on German firms in the Niger district 10.10.85; FO 84/1781 Rosebery to Goldie Taubman 27.2.86.

seen, were already being exercised. There was nothing very remarkable about this, nor was it a technique confined to the company. The British Foreign Office did exactly the same when it
used its consuls and vice-consuls, supposedly diplomatic agents,
to 'rule' the new African protectorates. 'Paper administration'
was the inevitable result of the British policy of minimum
responsibility and minimum cost. As part of that policy a charter had been given to a trading company to rule the Niger. It is
not surprising that the company remained a trading company.

The source of command in the new administration remained
the Board of Directors in London, and Goldie in particular. By
changing names the company took on a political flavour. The
National African Company, as soon as was possible, became the
Royal Niger Company, Chartered and Limited. The Board of
Directors became 'The Council'; directors became 'Members
of the Council'; and shareholders attained the dignity of
'Members'. The Chairman, Lord Aberdare, was now 'Governor'; and Goldie was promoted from Deputy Chairman to
'Deputy Governor'.[1] Goldie was also given a new post as
'Political Administrator' in charge of all political and administrative matters.[2] The Council was the supreme executive,
legislative and judicial authority. It could pass legislation which
constituted the law of the 'Niger Territories', and could override or confirm emergency legislation made in the company's
territories. It alone could appoint administrative officers, whose
appointments were revokable at will, who derived all their
powers from it, and whose task was to execute its wishes. As a
judicial authority the Council was the final court of appeal in
all cases from the Niger Territories.[3]

In Africa supreme local authority was divided. As head of the
executive the old post of chief trading agent, held by McIntosh,
was now called 'Agent-General'. Two new posts were created,
each independent of the Agent-General and responsible to the
Council alone. These were the 'Senior Judicial Officer' and the

[1] FO 84/1880 N.A.C. to F.O. 13.7.86 enclosing notice of extra-ordinary general
meeting.
[2] FO 84/1872 R.N.C. to F.O. 22.10.87.
[3] FO 84/1793 Goldie Taubman to Iddesleigh 8.11.86, enclosing list of regulations.

'Commandant of Constabulary'. The Agent-General had control of the company's men and materials, and was responsible for executing orders from the Council; he could suspend all officials not directly subordinate to the Senior Judicial Officer or the Commandant of Constabulary, pending confirmation of his action by the Council. He could give orders to the Commandant of Constabulary to execute particular tasks, but he must not interfere in the discipline of the force. The Agent-General was assisted by a small staff of deputies, called Senior Executive Officers, who had authority to act with the full powers of the Agent-General when deputizing for him, or when cut off from contact with him.[1] The Senior Judicial Officer was, in effect, Chief Justice of the Niger Territories, though the Council of the company remained the final court of appeal and could override his decisions. He could hear all appeals from lower courts, and also acted as a court of first instance in major cases not justiciable in the minor courts. He could order the Commandant of Constabulary to take steps to secure the attendance of witnesses, or the enforcement of punishments. He could delegate his powers, and suspend minor courts. Sir James Marshall, a director of the company, and an ex-Chief Justice of the Gold Coast, became the company's first Senior Judicial Officer.[2] The Commandant of Constabulary was in command of, and directly responsible to, the Council for the discipline of the company's newly formed military force. This was a body of three European officers and 150 African men.[3]

The foundation of the administration was the District Agent. The District Agents were in fact merely the company's European trading agents under a new name. They held local powers under all three of the senior branches of the administration. The District Agent was responsible for executing orders from the Agent General; he was in command of local military forces not under the discipline of the constabulary (these would normally be

[1] *Ibid.*, *loc. cit.*, R.N.C. Regulation, no. VII (July 86/4), Powers of the Agent-General.
[2] *Ibid.*, *loc. cit.*, R.N.C. Regulation, no. VI (July 86/3), Powers of the Senior Judicial Officer.
[3] *Ibid.* R.N.C. Regulation, no. XVI (August 86/8).

ad hoc levies or African allies); and he was also a court of first instance, empowered to hear all cases except those involving foreigners or sums over fifty pounds, which were reserved for the Senior Judicial Officer.[1]

This pattern of administration remained basically unchanged throughout the Royal Niger Company's period of rule. It was the first British administration of what is now Northern Nigeria. Its shape, and the spirit behind it were to affect not only Nigeria, but ultimately the whole of British administrative policy in the tropics in the early twentieth century. Perhaps Goldie's most significant historical contribution was in the sphere of administration; through the administrative system of the Royal Niger Company he laid down the theoretical basis for what was later to become known as indirect rule—the system of administration based on using the existing legitimate African rulers. It is true that Goldie's work was in the main, though not entirely, theoretical. The great practical task of establishing a really effective system fell to Lord Lugard. Nevertheless, if Goldie's contribution is not placed in perspective the entire history of indirect rule goes out of focus. It will be the task of later chapters to show how Goldie played a direct part not only in beginning effective indirect rule in the Emirates, but also in actually laying down the policy which Lugard was instructed to follow.[2] At this point it is necessary to emphasize that Goldie's theories were not evolved at the end of the company's tenure of power, they were developed as early as 1886 on the basis of the trading company's experience since 1879. Indirect rule was not dreamed up in a historical vacuum, it was the logical consequence of British policy in the 1880's and of the protectorate system. The inspiration for the idea of ruling through the African chiefs and Emirs lay in the company's poverty both in men and money. Goldie's genius lay in fitting these limitations, which in other areas could lead to administrative chaos and nullity, into a consistent theory of administration.

These ideas were put on paper in a letter which Goldie wrote

---

[1] *Ibid.* R.N.C. Regulation, no. IX (July 86/6), Warrants for District Agents.
[2] See Chap. 11, pp. 258–ff.

to the Foreign Secretary in November 1886.[1] In effect Goldie was attempting to justify the sketchy nature of the administration, but in doing so he was putting forward positive and general principles. He insisted that the company's duty was not to establish a comprehensive government of the lives of the African inhabitants of the Niger Territories. Its main task was to regulate the actions of foreigners to the Territories, and hence the company would directly govern only foreigners. The African inhabitants would only be drawn into the sphere of the company's government by reason of their intercourse with foreigners, or because their customs were particularly barbarous or repugnant to civilized values. Goldie went on to state that no attempt would be made to set up or codify a system of law; cases involving Africans which came before the company's courts would be judged on the basis of local laws and customs, and the judicial officer would follow such procedure as he felt to be appropriate. Nor would there be any attempt to interfere with the politics of African states or tribes. They would continue to be ruled by their legitimate tribal or feudal authorities. Even slavery would not be suppressed by force, the company had not the power and already had enough on its hands. Everywhere, said Goldie, the company would follow a policy of 'interfering as little as possible in the internal laws of each native state or tribe'.

The Royal Niger Company's administration, then, was to concern itself almost entirely with foreigners to the territory, 'foreigners' comprising not only Europeans, including Britons, but all persons not born in the company's territories—Africans from the Oil Rivers, from Lagos or Sierra Leone, and even the company itself when acting as a trading corporation.[2] Almost all foreigners in the Niger Territories would be traders of one kind or another. The task of the administration was to exclude them. To exclude other traders would not only solve the perennial problem of competition, but would also cut down the cost of

[1] FO 84/1793 Goldie Taubman to Iddesleigh 8.11.86. See esp. the Judicial Regulation (no. X, July 86/7) enclosed with this letter.
[2] FO 84/1876 R.N.C. to F.O. 13.12.87 gives the company's legal definition of foreigners.

administration, reduce the risk of disputes with the local rulers, prevent intrigues by nationals of other European governments, seal off the inhabitants from disruptive influences, and at the same time place them in a commercial dependence on the company almost as effective as political control. This was the real basis of the Royal Niger Company's administration, a system of control through a monopoly, a system which exerted pressures upon the Niger peoples through exclusive commercial influence.

The true pattern of the company's administration is seen not in the elaborate network of agents and officers, courts and judges, but in the commercial regulations. Characteristically, the first regulations issued by the company, on the day after the charter received its seal, were the tariff and licensing regulations. These were the only regulations to which the foreigner had to submit. Throughout the company's history no regulations, apart from those establishing the framework of the administration, were ever issued which were not purely commercial. Their effect was to lay down the greatest possible impediments to the trade of competitors within the interpretation which Goldie had placed upon the limitations of the Berlin Act.

The tariff regulations ordered any 'vessel, boat, canoe, or other craft' coming from outside the Niger Territories to enter and clear at Akassa, at the mouth of the Niger, and obtain a certificate from the customs authorities there. Vessels could only trade at listed ports of entry and export, and not at other places. At Akassa import duties must be paid at the rate of two shillings a gallon on spirits, sixpence a pound on tobacco, a shilling a hundredweight on salt and 100 per cent *ad valorem* on war materials. The declaration of value by the importer must be not less than those shown on his invoices, three copies of which, written in English with prices given in British currency, were to be produced for inspection. If the officials suspected fraud they were empowered forcibly to purchase the goods at cost price plus two per cent. But this was not all. If the importer intended to trade above Lokoja, then he had to go through a second procedure, and pay a second set of duties, either at Akassa when he entered, or at the customs house at Lokoja. These duties were

PLATE 2

(*a*) West African Trading Hulks, 1862
From *Merchant Adventure*, John Holt and Company

(*b*) John Holt
From *Merchant Adventure*,
John Holt and Company

the same again as those at Akassa, except that all other merchandise except coal paid ten per cent *ad valorem*. Exports were
also taxed, but only once. All vessels taking produce on board at
the ports of export had to pass through the customs house there
and obtain clearance certificates. Duties were then levied at the
rate of twopence a hundredweight on palm kernels, a penny
per old wine gallon on palm oil and shea-butter, and a shilling a
pound on ivory; all other native produce paid twenty per cent
ad valorem, either in goods or produce. For attempting to defraud
the revenue the culprit was liable to a fine of £500 or, at the
option of the court, a penalty not exceeding five times the
amount lost to the revenue, and both his vessel and goods could
be seized and made forfeit. These duties were to come into
operation in October 1886, thus giving three months notice as
required by the charter and the Anglo-German Agreement.[1]

On the same day as the tariff regulations were issued the
company established a system of licences for trade. Every
foreigner wishing to engage in barter or retail selling was
obliged to obtain a retail trade licence costing £100; if in addition he wished to trade in spirits, he must take out an additional
spirits trading licence costing a further £100.[2]

These regulations excluded competitors by combining two
methods; by making them pay, and by using the administrative
machinery to create difficult conditions for trade. Worst hit
were the African traders, whether petty traders from Lagos or
Sierra Leone, or middlemen from the Oil Rivers. Most of these
were not literate enough to complete even the simplest of customs formalities without assistance from the officials, nor could
they produce invoices in English. They were barter traders,
unused to expressing values in currency, and possessing no
English coin with which to pay duties. Even if they had been
able to surmount these obstacles, the system of licences, needing
a cash outlay of £200, was quite beyond their means. The
licensing system was created with the deliberate intention of

---

[1] FO 84/1792 Goldie Taubman to Iddesleigh 21.10.86, Tariff **Regulations**
enclosed, made 13.7.86.
[2] *Ibid., loc. cit.*, Regulation, July 86/9 (later called R.N.C. Regulation no. XII).

H

excluding the African traders, who almost always caused Goldie to lose his sense of proportion. 'The effect of the licence,' he wrote,

will be to enforce some contribution to the revenue from—or else to exclude from the Territories—a class of men, happily now extinct, who were formerly the worst enemies of civilisation in Central Africa. These were disreputable coloured men (in the past they were generally inferior clerks, dismissed for peculation) who . . . lived by surreptitious dealing in slaves . . . stirring up the natives to discontent and bloodshed . . . under a mask of ardent piety.[1]

For the European firms the licence system and the customs duties were not impossible obstacles, though the duty on spirits, essential to the palm oil trade, was almost 100 per cent; and the double duties above Lokoja, added to the 100 per cent duty on war materials without which trade in the north was not possible, virtually excluded them from this region. Much more serious was the restriction on ports of entry and export. These places were naturally those at which the Royal Niger Company already possessed stations and a flourishing trade, and the battle for trade would thus be fought on the Niger Company's terms. Moreover the company claimed property rights in all these places to the land on both banks of the river, and would not sell land for wharves or warehouses. It was thus impossible to land, moor, set up market, or erect stores, without the company's assistance.

Naturally enough these measures provoked opposition. The exclusion of the Africans of the Oil Rivers struck at the heart of the Liverpool palm oil trade, and restricted it to the area immediately behind the coastal towns. Opposition from Liverpool might have been a formidable affair. The West African traders were well organized in their African Association, which in turn controlled the African Trade Section of the Chamber of Commerce. The Chamber as a whole would normally support its African section on African matters. The Liverpool Members of Parliament, whatever their party affiliations, were always

[1] FO 84/1796 Goldie Taubman to Iddesleigh 31.12.86.

sensitive to the city's commercial interests by which it lived, and were prepared to work together in agitating for Liverpool interests. The African Association could amass more capital than the Niger Company, its trade was larger, and it could wield great influence through its connexions with traders in other towns. In addition to the traders, the Liverpool West Africa shipowners, now amalgamated as the Elder Dempster Line, were a power to be reckoned with. They were largely dependent for their freight on the palm oil trade, and natural enemies of any monopoly which gave greater bargaining power to the traders to reduce freight charges. Elder Dempster had connexions with the larger British steamship companies and, through them, could mobilize the shipowners' lobby in Parliament.

Nevertheless the initial opposition from Liverpool was uncertain and hesitant. The explanation of this paradox lies in the ambitions of the Liverpool traders. They were filled with a grudging admiration for all that Goldie and his group had done on the Niger, and they now wished to do the same in the Oil Rivers. They were ready to abandon their uneasy alliance with the African middlemen and push up the rivers to trade directly with the producers, and they now saw that the best way to do this was to obtain a charter for themselves on the model of Goldie's Niger charter. This being so, the basic ground of their opposition to the Niger Company was cut from under their feet. Their real grievance was that a trading company had been given the political power to discriminate against its competitors, but they could not argue thus and at the same time ask for similar privileges for themselves in the Oil Rivers. They could not oppose the *principle* of chartered company administration. All their complaints thus took on the appearance of petty grievances and quibbles. The company's boundaries were undefined; the restriction of trade to certain ports was contrary to the Berlin Act; the customs duties and licences were excessive and had been promulgated without the Government's knowledge;[1] and so forth.

---

[1] The last section of FO 84/1880 of 1886 is full of such complaints from the African Association and from individual firms.

Such an approach could make very little impression on the Foreign Office. True, when it was discovered in September 1886 that the Niger Company had issued its tariff regulations without so much as a by-your-leave from the Government, the officials were angry, and Goldie was summoned to the Office and told that in future he must submit all regulations for approval in advance.[1] The tariff and licensing regulations were then considered in detail by both the Foreign Office and the Board of Trade, and after several months of correspondence Goldie was forced to make some minor changes in the judicial regulations; reduce the trade licence fee from £100 to £50, with an additional fee of £10 for additional stations; and to pay five per cent above invoice price for goods compulsorily purchased by the customs administration, instead of the two per cent originally fixed.[2] But these were trifling changes, of little practical importance, made by the Foreign Office in a spirit deliberately opposed to meddling in the company's internal affairs. The ardour for chartered company administration remained undiminished. The Niger Company was expected to fulfil Britain's imperial destiny in West Africa, to engage France 'in the contest for the middle Niger',[3] pressing up the waterways into the heart of the Sudan. The War Office Intelligence Department began corresponding with the company on the grand strategy of the European advance into West Africa.[4] To give the company a free hand the Colonial Office was told to order the Governor of Lagos to cease corresponding with Nupe, which must now be regarded as in the company's sphere, and outside the interest of Lagos.[5] Faced with such a spirit the opposition could make no

[1] FO 84/1792 minutes by H.P.A. and J.P. 25.10.86 and 27.10.86 on Goldie Taubman to Iddesleigh 21.10.86.

[2] FO 84/1793 F.O. to Board of Trade 25.11.86 and mem. of 9.11.86 by W.E.D.; FO 84/1862 Goldie Taubman to Salisbury 2.5.87; FO 84/1865 F.O. to R.N.C. 11.7.87; FO 84/1866 Sir George Goldie to Salisbury 25.7.87; FO 84/1875 F.O. to R.N.C. 5.12.87; FO 84/1876 R.N.C. to F.O. 13.12.87; FO 84/1889 filed at 21.3.87 mem. by H.P.A. 21.2.87 and 21.3.87, by J.P. 22.2.87, and mem. by W.E.D. on Niger Company, n.d.

[3] FO 84/1787 minutes by H.P.A. on W.O.I.D. to F.O. 21.7.86.   [4] *Ibid., loc. cit.*

[5] FO 84/1791 C.O. to F.O. 18.10.86 enclosing correspondence between Lagos and Nupe; FO 84/1792 Goldie Taubman to Iddesleigh 25.10.86; FO 84/1793 C.O. to F.O. 16.11.86.

headway. Only when the Liverpool Members of Parliament began to mobilize was any uneasiness shown, and promises were made that the working of the charter would be carefully watched.[1]

The attacks on the Niger Company mounted to a crescendo in March and April 1887, when the Liverpool merchants at last agreed upon an attempt at constructive criticism which did not attack the basic principle of chartered company rule. A petition was compiled, signed by all the member firms in the African Association, and presented to W. F. Lawrence, M.P., who had been leading the agitation in Parliament. The petition complained against the Company's tariffs, alleged that their object was 'to grind down the natives to most iniquitously low prices', and proposed that the Niger Company's charter should be restricted to the region north of Onitsha so as to leave the palm oil trade of the lower river open to the African traders of Brass and New Calabar.[2] At the same time other Liverpool Members of Parliament began to ask questions in the House with increasing frequency.[3] Sir Percy Anderson's comments on this opposition show that he understood perfectly the economics which lay behind it, and that in supporting the Niger Company the Foreign Office officials believed themselves to be on the side of progress:

Till recently trade in this part of Africa was carried on in a sort of fashion by houses doing individually no large trade. They worked through the coast middlemen who barred them from the interior markets. . . .

The rush for Africa has broken up the little family party. The rich and powerful Niger Company on the one hand, the Germans on the other, have broken through the middleman coast and freed their way to the interior markets. The Liverpool men are fighting the battle of the middlemen. . . .

They . . . injure themselves by their suggestion that the charter

[1] FO 84/1857 H.P.A. to Sir Jas. Ferguson (the Parliamentary Under-Secretary) 27.1.87, seen by Salisbury (draft of a general answer to complaints about the R.N.C.).

[2] FO 84/1880 African Association to Lawrence enc. in note by J. Ferguson 3.3.87.

[3] *Ibid.* F.O. to MacArthur 8.3.57, notice of question by Dillwyn for 21.3.87; FO 84/1861 Williamson to Ferguson 20.4.87. *Hansard*, 3rd series, CCCXII, col. 831, 21.3.87.

should not be allowed to apply to the Lower Niger. Their object is to reform the broken coast. Were they to succeed they might benefit till it was broken again, which would not be long delayed, and would stifle the prospect for trade generally, and free access to the comparatively civilised Mohammedan tribes of the interior. The demand is now as complete an anachronism as would be a petition for the restoration of medieval guilds.[1]

In April the attacks on the Niger Company began to take on a new bitterness. Attempts were made through another Liverpool M.P., Williamson, to make capital out of the Niger Company's shipments of gin, to discredit its judicial system, and in particular to publicize the execution of a West Indian named John Shaw, whose request to say a prayer before dying was alleged to have been refused. Particularly ominous was the interest which radical and Irish Members, financially unconnected with the West African trade, now began to take in the 'Niger scandal'.[2]

Then, quite suddenly, the letters and complaints from Liverpool ceased to come into the Foreign Office. All was silence. For the rest of 1887 there were no more complaints against the Niger Company from firms in the African Association. In August 1887, in reply to criticisms by 'low class newspapers', Goldie insisted that rival firms were not opposed to the company, and announced that he had a written statement from the African Association assuring him that it had never opposed the company's charter in any way, nor authorized any M.P. to put forward allegations hostile to the Niger Company.[3] This, though hardly accurate, was Goldie's way of announcing that the opposition was at an end.

The explanation for this silent revolution of alliances was that the two groups had begun to negotiate with each other. The object of these negotiations was to bring about a total or partial amalgamation of the Niger and Oil Rivers interests, an agree-

[1] FO 84/1880 minute by H.P.A. 15.3.87 on note by J. Ferguson 3.3.87.
[2] FO 84/1861 Williamson to Ferguson 20.4.87 inc. *Lagos Observer* 19.2.87 and R.N.C. to F.O. 22.4.87. *Hansard*, 3rd series, CCCXIII, cols. 1787–9, question by Williamson with supplementaries by Childers, Williamson, and Labouchere, and answers by Ferguson 25.4.87.
[3] FO 84/1880 Goldie to Salisbury 12.8.87.

ment to fix prices, and give the Oil Rivers merchants control of their region by persuading the British Government to extend the Niger Company's charter over that region.

The idea was far from fantastic. In fact the possibility of chartered company rule had been implicit in all the legal arrangements which the British Government had made for the Oil Rivers. Despite the fact that the Rivers had been ruled by Consular officials since 1884, the Government had been careful not to establish any legal separation between the Oil Rivers and Niger—legally they were one protectorate, the 'British Protectorate of the Niger Districts'.[1] The boundaries between the two administrations had never been laid down, and no map was ever published to indicate that there were two administrations. In October 1887, when further areas in the Niger Company's treaty sphere were placed under British protection, the fiction of one protectorate was maintained, and it was announced that the measures in preparation 'for the maintenance of peace and good order in the Niger Districts' would be published in due course;[2] a clear hint to the negotiating parties that charter extension was a possibility. The way was thus carefully left open for a simple extension of the Niger Company's charter to the whole of the 'Niger Districts', without recourse to Acts of Parliament or even the issue of a new Order in Council.

The Foreign Office was prepared to go even further in encouraging the scheme. At first the Liverpool merchants were none too eager for amalgamation. The *status quo* in the Oil Rivers, though far from perfect, had its advantages. The merchants paid no taxation, and Acting-Consul Harry Johnston[3] was reasonably amenable to their wishes. Goldie's proposals for amalgamation were not sufficiently attractive for them to sacrifice their independence and amalgamate.[4] In October 1887 the negotia-

[1] Notification of British Protectorate of the Niger Districts 5.6.85 to be found in Hertslet, *Map of Africa*, Vol. 1. p. 123.

[2] *Ibid.*, p. 127.

[3] For the full story of Johnston's career see Oliver, R., *Sir Harry Johnston and the Scramble for Africa*, London, 1957. Chapter 4 deals with his vice-consulship in the Oil Rivers.

[4] FO 84/1916 minute by H.P.A. 20.2.88 correctly analyses the attitude of the Liverpool men in Oct. 1887.

tions foundered, and complaints against Goldie's company were renewed.[1] The Foreign Office now proceeded to give the Liverpool interests a further inducement to amalgamate. A correspondence was begun with the Colonial Office asking them to consider establishing a Crown colony for the Oil Rivers.[2]

This was the peril which Goldie could now hold over the Liverpool traders. A Crown colony would mean high taxation, red tape, and control by civil servants. Goldie did not at first act directly. His intermediary was his fellow-director George Miller, a brother and partner of Alexander Miller. Millers were not only the largest single shareholding group in the Niger Company, but also the largest independent firm outside the African Association in the Oil Rivers, greatly feared by their rivals both for their unorthodox trading methods and the position which they had built up through their friendship and influence with the ambitious King Ja Ja of Opobo. George Miller had begun to urge amalgamation on the Liverpool men in August 1887, through correspondence with John Holt, the self-made man who had by this time built up one of the largest of the British West African firms.[3]

'My object,' George Miller declared, 'is just to stop . . . competition now, by a fusion of interests, second to secure the administration and control of the country by which we can secure a monopoly. . . . If we could carry through our arrangements we could deal together with the Africans and secure a profit no matter what happened.'[4]

Now, when the plan for a Crown colony was mooted at the end of the year, George Miller passed on to Holt a letter from Goldie, in which the latter strongly insisted on the dangers of colonial rule, which, he said, was 'maturing rapidly'. The danger was not simply the obvious one of higher taxation.

[1] FO 84/1874 Holt and Cotterell to F.O. 16.11.87.
[2] FO 84/1838 mema. by T.V.L. and H.P.A. on Hewett to F.O. 15.10.87 and FO 84/1916 C.O. to F.O. 18.2.88.
[3] A firm which survives today as the only sizeable British West African trading firm outside the Unilever combine. For Holt's career, and the subsequent history of the firm see *Merchant Adventure*, John Holt and Co. (Liverpool) Ltd., n.d.
[4] John Holt Papers, J.H.P. Box 4/1 Geo. Miller to John Holt 10 or 11.8.87. I am greatly indebted to Mr. Cecil Holt and John Holt and Co. (Liverpool) Ltd., for permission to see and use this invaluable collection of private papers.

Colonial rule would mean the wholesale admission of African petty traders from Sierra Leone; the Liverpool men would be plagued by a host of regulations and taxes; and their activities would be upset by constant military activities by officials wanting to 'make a name'. The area would be riddled with 'fictitious and premature development'. At the same time Goldie warned Liverpool against trying to get an independent charter for themselves; it was a 'legal and constitutional impossibility' to do so except by Act of Parliament or Royal Charter, and either of these was politically not feasible. If they wanted administrative power they would have to work through the Niger Company's charter, using the company's name, but in fact forming a new company to share the profits of the whole trade by mutual agreement. He concluded with an exhortation to sink all differences:

We are not so black (in the Niger) as they have painted us. They say that we have been aggressive and pushing! I do not admit 'aggression'; but, if true, so much the better for them when they become our partners, our Co-Directors, and our co-rulers. They will then re-christen 'aggression'; they will call it 'laudable energy', and they will emulate us in its display.[1]

John Holt was full of enthusiasm. He calculated that the rise in the price of palm oil alone, if in the hands of an amalgamated firm, would be enough to pay the entire cost of administration, and £10,000 a year could be made out of minor products which were not at present exploited because of 'mad competition'. He foresaw a splendid future:

Who can tell or limit the possibilities of that wondrously fertile region? Undeveloped! Even unexplored! Enterprise in opening up the country is dead because of the initial cost to the pioneer who has no chance of obtaining a reward for his courage, labour and risk because of the encroaching competitors who would assuredly dog his heels. Our policy is not rest and be thankful, but sit still and fight one another. Yet we know that the natural products of this district are boundless and that coffee, cocoa, etc., could all be more profitably grown than palm oil, or palm kernels.[2]

[1] *Ibid.* Goldie to Geo. Miller 13.11.87.
[2] J.H.P. Box 3/6 John Holt to Goldie 26.11.87.

It was one thing to analyse the evils of competition, but quite another to resolve them. The jealousies of the past few years were intense, and constantly the temptation was to revive old sores. When Goldie tried to speed matters in December 1887 by threatening to go on alone and 'press seaward as fast as possible,'[1] Holt replied in kind, welcoming a spell of fierce competition to ensure 'the survival of the fittest' and warning Goldie that threats would not drive anyone into amalgamation. If Goldie tried to force his way into the Oil Rivers, then Liverpool would force its way on to the Niger, compelling the Niger Company to set up a real administration, and constantly worrying the British Government to see that its revenue was properly accounted for.[2] Holt and Goldie understood one another, and this kind of recrimination was not serious. Much more difficult to resolve was the long-standing feud between Miller Brothers and the Liverpool firms, largely caused by Millers' relations with Ja Ja. In September 1887 this antagonism had flared up with a new intensity when the Liverpool firms succeeded in persuading the acting-consul, Harry Johnston, to exile Ja Ja to the West Indies. Johnston's action had taken place on a wharf belonging to Thos. Harrison and Company of Liverpool, the largest firm in the African Association. This produced a bitter quarrel between Harrisons and Millers. Millers began a campaign to secure Ja Ja's return, and this in turn made Millers hated in Liverpool.[3] But if the amalgamation scheme were to succeed Millers and Harrisons would have to be brought together, for the absence of either was enough to wreck it. Each could have been a dangerous competitor if left outside the amalgam, and their political opposition was dangerous to a scheme that had to be put into effect quietly and without fuss. Goldie's task, therefore, was to use his influence with Millers to relax the tension, and to win over the chairman of Harrisons, Stanley Rogerson. Though Millers refused to modify their support for Ja Ja, Goldie succeeded in flattering Rogerson into the

[1] *Ibid.* Box 3/7 Goldie to John Holt 19.12.87.
[2] *Ibid.* Box 3/6 John Holt to Goldie 13.1.88.
[3] For a more detailed treatment of Ja Ja's exile see Oliver, *Sir Harry Johnston* pp. 107–21.

belief that the idea had been his from the first, and that he was a potential empire-builder.[1] By February 1888 agreement was within sight.

In all these intrigues the shipping interests were conspicuous by their absence. This is not surprising. The shipowners had a vital interest in preventing any amalgamation between the traders; they disliked Goldie's control of the Niger trade—the prospect of his controlling virtually all the British trade of the Bight of Benin was a disastrous one to contemplate. The traders would be in a position practically to dictate freight charges, they would exclude the traders of Lagos and Freetown from whom the shippers collected passage money and freight charges, and they might even start a rival line of their own, assured of the constant freight of their own trade. It is no exaggeration to say that Elder Dempster faced ruin if the amalgamation plan were to succeed. Goldie and the Liverpool merchants therefore made every effort to keep their plans secret.

To hope that the shippers would remain in the dark was to underestimate the intelligence service operated by Alfred Jones, the Liverpool Welshman who had worked his way from cabin boy to shipping clerk and was now in control of the West African steamship lines.[2] Jones seems to have been acquainted with every move in the negotiations. As early as May 1887 he was protesting to the Foreign Office against any move to turn the Oil Rivers over to chartered company administration, and demanding instead that the administration be put under Government officials.[3] In February 1888, realizing that agreement was in sight, Jones began a fierce campaign of opposition.

Moreover, it was a kind of opposition which the Foreign Office could not brush off as easily as that of other opponents of the Niger Company. The shippers of Britain have always been

---

[1] J.H.P. Box 4/2 letters from Rogerson *passim*. Box 3/7 letters from Goldie *passim* describing his meetings with Rogerson.

[2] See Milne, A. H., *Sir Alfred Lewis Jones*, Liverpool, 1914.

[3] FO 84/1863 African Steamship Co. and British and African Steam Navigation Co. to F.O. 24.5.87.

clannish, and well-organized. Elder Dempster were financially linked with the Peninsular and Oriental and the Pacific Steam Navigation Companies, and they had friends in Parliament such as befitted their status in a nation which prided itself on its mercantile marine. When the Parliamentary under-secretary, Sir James Fergusson, received a deputation from the shippers in February 1888, he was so alarmed by its strength that he went out of his way to urge the Foreign Office to treat their complaints seriously. As a result the shippers were asked to send in a detailed statement of the injuries which they feared from the proposed amalgamation.[1] No other complainants had been treated so reasonably.

The shipowners' reply was nothing like the list of petty trifles, confusedly put together, that had hitherto passed for opposition. For the first time a powerful group was able to argue against chartered company administration from basic principles. The root cause of their fears was the very essence of administration by a trading company. Whatever restrictions were imposed by the Government, a chartered company which traded for its own benefit would use every method to impede and harass its rivals. No amount of paper safeguards could prevent this. The Royal Niger Company had no need to establish differential duties to exclude rivals, for its rivals must pay customs in cash, whilst the company merely credited itself with the duties on its own trade. It was outside the Government's power to find out exactly which expenses were administrative, and to balance them exactly against customs receipts. If the Niger and Oil Rivers firms amalgamated, and were allowed to rule the whole region, the profits of the new company would be so enormous that they would soon be running their own shipping line 'against which no one could compete'.[2] This last point was of course, the real kernel of the shippers' fears, and they insisted upon it. The chairman of one of the shipping companies, F. W. Bond, avowed that if he were the head of a trading company which also ruled its

[1] FO 84/1916 mem. by J.F. 23.2.88; draft by Anderson to shipping companies sent 15.3.88.
[2] FO 84/1917 Steamship Co's to F.O. 23.3.88.

territories, he 'would never rest until he had got a monopoly of all the trade and all the shipping', and, he said, every man in the business felt the same.[1]

The fight was now on. John Holt warned Goldie that the opposition of the shippers would not be 'the milk-and-water thing' that Goldie had hitherto had to face. 'They have energy, ideas, and unity.' But he was for fighting back; there were 'several ways' in which the shippers could be silenced. They were too rich. 'It takes a poor man to fight hard,' was Holt's characteristic comment. Goldie agreed, and urged Holt that they begin to organize a freight boycott.[2] The Foreign Office officials were equally worried. Alfred Jones had now begun to manipulate the big names. Thomas Sutherland, M.P., chairman of the Peninsular and Oriental, announced that he would press to the full his opposition to any scheme to extend the charter, and the lesser lights of the shipping lobby followed suit.[3] To show Goldie how serious the opposition was becoming, Villiers Lister sent him 'in strictest confidence', a copy of their protests. Lister probably hoped that this would induce Goldie to try to conciliate the shippers. Instead it provoked him to a violent attack in which he alleged that their motive was their vested interest in the liquor trade.[4] At the same time this gratuitous information convinced Goldie that the time had come to fight back. On the day he received Lister's note, Goldie terminated all the Niger Company's agreements with the shipping companies, and threatened that if their opposition did not cease, the Niger and Oil Rivers interests would establish a new shipping line.[5]

This was hardly what the Foreign Office wanted, particularly as the officials had tried to assure Alfred Jones that his fears of a rival shipping line were groundless. The Government therefore had to try direct conciliation. In April 1888 Lord Salisbury

[1] *Ibid.* minutes by H.P.A. and T.V.L. 26.3.88.

[2] J.H.P. Box 3/6 John Holt to Goldie 6.4.88, and 10.4.88, and 13.4.88, and 16.4.88. J.H.P. Box 5/7 Goldie to John Holt, 12.4.88.

[3] FO 84/1917 T. Sutherland to Pauncefote 23.3.88, and Baird to F.O. 9.3.88.

[4] FO 84/1918 Goldie to Lister 4.4.88.

[5] FO 84/1919 Steamship companies to F.O. 17.4.88, enclosing correspondence with R.N.C. 3–11.4.88.

personally received a deputation, and although Alfred Jones
could find little that was definite in the Prime Minister's replies,
he returned to Liverpool in high spirits, spread about the
impression that he had received some kind of promise that the
scheme would not go through without his consent, and began to
organize the smaller firms in Liverpool and Manchester which
were not members of the African Association.[1] Behind the scenes
things were going badly for Goldie's plans. Lord Salisbury was
alarmed by the hostility of the shippers, and asked his officials to
show him how the amalgamated company could be effectively
restrained from coercing its rivals. Sir Percy Anderson was
forced to admit that it was impossible. The objections put forward by the shippers were valid; whatever was written into the
charter could be evaded. The only way to ensure a just administration would be to obtain a direct control over the Agent-
General and the Company's Chief Justice, by giving them Royal
Commissions, and making them report directly to the Foreign
Office on all matters involving foreigners to the territories. He
realized that this was an admission which turned upside down
the basis of previous policy, with its emphasis on refusing to
accept responsibility for the acts of the company. But the escape
from responsibility had proved illusory, the Government was
regarded as responsible both by domestic critics, and foreign
governments. The position was very awkward, at the moment
there was responsibility without control, yet the Government
was not prepared to take over the administration of the Niger
and Oil Rivers directly and was thus at the mercy of the traders.
He doubted whether Goldie would accept a real control.[2]

But Sir Julian Pauncefote, who, it will be remembered, had
tried to obtain a close control over the company in the original
charter, pooh-poohed Anderson's fears, and argued that because
the charter was revocable at will Goldie was at the mercy of the
Crown. The history of other chartered companies, the Hudson's
Bay and East India Companies in particular, had shown that
the Government quickly found need to establish control. The

---

[1] J.H.P. Box 3/6 John Holt to Goldie 23.4.88 and 24.4.88.
[2] FO 84/1918 mem. by H.P.A. 11.4.88.

opposition of the shippers would be satisfied with the appointment of an official High Commissioner and Director of Customs. As a preliminary Pauncefote advocated the appointment of a Crown official to take charge of the company's administration on the Niger, and the transference of the judiciary to persons solely responsible to the Crown.[1]

The opposition of the shippers thus forced a real consideration among the officials of the problem of responsibility and control, and a determination to establish a real supervision if the charter were extended to the Oil Rivers. This resolve was immeasurably strengthened by another kind of opposition which must now be examined, the opposition of the German Government.

[1] *Ibid*. mem. by J.P. 11.4.88.

6

German Opposition—and a Setback

THE strongest guarantees against monopoly on the Niger were contained in the international agreements which Britain had concluded with the powers of Europe, particularly with Germany. Germany had held a peculiarly dominant position at the conference which had resulted in the Berlin Act of 1885, and the limitations incurred in that instrument had been further reinforced in detail by the Anglo-German Agreement of April–June 1885.[1]

The way in which Goldie escaped from these obligations forms in itself a fascinating study of political manœuvre; it provided his apprenticeship to the art of private diplomacy in which he was to excel in later years. The Niger Clauses of the Berlin Act were so simply overcome that it may even be possible that Goldie, who was present at their drafting by the British delegation, wrote them himself. Soon after the signature of the Act Goldie made known his interpretation of it, which thereafter he held to tenaciously. The Act made no mention of 'trade' on the Niger; it referred only to 'navigation'. Navigation, argued Goldie, simply meant moving on water. This all ships were free to do, without hindrance. But let them once touch the banks of the river, they then ceased to be pure navigators; they had entered the company's territories and must submit to its laws and pay its taxes. 'Navigation', on Goldie's definition, thus amounted merely to transit; only vessels sailing through the

[1] For detail of both these instruments see Chap. 4, pp. 69 and 74–5.

Niger Territories to places outside could claim free passage.[1] Even this freedom was in reality illusory, for vessels sailing the length of the Niger and Benue would be forced to obtain fuel and provisions on the river, and as soon as they did so they became traders, and thus subject to local laws and taxes. Goldie's case was ingenious, well-argued, and entirely consistent with the letter, if not the spirit, of the Berlin Act.

The Anglo-German Agreement of 1885 was a more difficult obstacle. Goldie had played no part in its negotiation, and its wording was apparently clear and unambiguous, particularly the stipulation that taxes should only be levied sufficient to cover actual administrative costs, and no more. But once again Goldie was able to find loopholes, partly by obtaining a concession which permitted him to transfer part of the administrative revenue to the commercial profit-and-loss account, partly by using an accounting system which made any accurate division between administrative and commercial expenses impossible.

The first concession had been inspired by the Foreign Office. It will be remembered that Sir Julian Pauncefote, in rejecting Goldie's request in 1886 for specific monopolies to be written into the charter, had suggested instead that the company might recoup itself, out of administrative revenue, for 'expenses incurred in the taking over of the protectorate'.[2] In October 1887 Goldie returned to this theme, claiming that the company had spent £388,309 in treaty-making and that these were legitimately 'expenses incurred in the taking over of the protectorate'. The company would settle for £250,000, this sum to constitute a debt on the Niger Territories, upon which interest at five per cent per annum totalling £12,500, could be paid to the company out of the administrative receipts. Despite the fantastic amount claimed, the request was granted.[3]

---

[1] FO 84/1742 Goldie to Anderson 18.9.86, enclosing *The Niger Benue and the Berlin Conference* (a pamphlet by Goldie).

[2] See Chap. 4, pp. 83–84.

[3] The Board of Trade made some protest, failing to see how such sums could have been expended whilst the company's capital remained intact. However, the Crown Agents certified (without inspecting the company's books) that the sums had in fact

I

But the greatest loophole for circumventing the Anglo-German Agreement was the system of accounting to be followed when assessing whether in fact administrative costs were to balance taxation revenue. What was an administrative cost? Under the Niger Company's system of administration it was impossible to separate administrative from commercial expenditure. The political agents also organized the company's trade; the trading steamers carried constabulary on punitive expeditions; the stations on the rivers were both administrative and commercial outposts; even a treaty-making expedition would naturally try to do good business on its journey. Goldie was thus able to fix administrative expenditure at any convenient figure, and the accounts he submitted to the Foreign Office always showed an excess of administrative expenses over revenue, except for the year 1893.[1]

All these matters might have remained purely academic, so far as Germany was concerned, had not a German trader decided to compete on the Niger. Jacob Hoenigsberg may well have been an *agent provocateur*, at least it is true to say that shifts in German policy closely followed his fortunes on the Niger. It may also be more than coincidence which led Hoenigsberg to try his fortune in Nupe, the weakest link in the Niger Company's system of treaties.

At first the relationship with Hoenigsberg was peaceful and friendly; the German obeyed all the regulations and paid his customs duties, and the Niger Company rented him accommodation at its stations, and even transported goods for him when his launch needed repairs. In June 1887, however, the company's officials provoked an incident which abruptly ended this friendliness. After the German had cleared at Akassa his launch and a cargo of salt intended for Nupe, he was stopped up river and ordered to return to obtain fresh clearance for two canoes

been expended. FO 84/1872 Goldie to Salisbury 24.10.87 with enclosures; FO 84/1876 R.N.C. to F.O. 22.12.87; FO 84/1914 Board of Trade to F.O. 26.1.88; FO 84/1917 C.O. to F.O. 7.3.88.

[1] For complete accounts see P.P. 1899, LXIII (c. 9372).

which he was towing, even though the salt which they carried had been cleared, and duty paid. Without more ado Hoenigsberg abandoned the voyage, suspecting that even if he obtained fresh clearance he would only be presented with more obstacles.[1] Instead he returned to Nupe in November 1887 and plunged into politics. He proceeded to provoke a major quarrel between the Emir and the Niger Company by telling the Emir that the company claimed that he had ceded his country to them, and that they held a monopoly of trade. The Emir Maliki was filled with wrath at these pretensions, and summoned William Wallace, the Senior Executive Officer in Nupe, to ask him 'what was in the Proclamations and Notices outside the Egga factory, what the flag meant, as he had heard that it signified the taking of his country . . . why duties were collected . . . and if Robinson (the District Agent) were king of his country'. To placate the Emir, Wallace was forced to raise the company's subsidy from £400 to £2,000 a year.[2] Even this did not satisfy Maliki, who drew up a written statement witnessed by Hoenigsberg and the African traders in Egga in the presence of Wallace and the District Agent, in which Maliki declared that he had never ceded any territory to the Niger Company, that he alone had the power to levy taxes in Nupe, and that all comers could be assured of free trade.[3]

Goldie was naturally not anxious to let the Foreign Office know of this setback, and they remained in ignorance of what had happened for six months more. This allowed the German Foreign Office to put through a clever little diplomatic tactic. The British were asked to persuade the Niger Company to issue a regulation declaring that no vessel in transit on the Niger would be obliged to stop in its course, or pay duties of any kind.[4] The request was perfectly reasonable and accorded even with Goldie's interpretation of the Berlin Act. Goldie at first refused, and

[1] FO 84/1871 mem. by German F.O. 26.9.87 and R.N.C. to F.O. 20.10.87. Both accounts agree as to the facts.

[2] FO 84/2109 Macdonald Report, Chap. 4, based on Wallace's diary.

[3] FO 84/1874 Assembly of Undersigned at Bida with King Moliki of Nupe 17.11.87. Received 14.5.88.

[4] FO 84/1872 F.O. to R.N.C. 21.10.87, quoting note from von Plessen 21.9.87.

then, under pressure, sent in drafts which first defined the company's territories so as to include all the navigable waterways of the Niger up to the rapids at Bussa and of the Benue as far as the limit of navigation. Transit was free to ships which passed these barriers! At the end of their patience, the Foreign Office finally produced its own draft regulation, sent it to Goldie, and ordered him to promulgate it. The final form declared that transit was free to all vessels whatever their starting place or destination, and that only vessels which touched, loaded, or discharged from or into the Niger Territories became subject to the company's revenue system.[1] The German Government now proceeded to correlate this declaration of free transit with the Emir's statement that he was independent. If the Emir was independent then Nupe was not inside the company's territories, and trade with Nupe must be transit trade. The German *chargé d'affaires* therefore asked that the company be prevented from levying any more duties on the Nupe trade, and be asked to refund those already paid.[2] Goldie could only reply by dropping the pretence to hold Nupe by treaty with its Emir; instead to claim it by virtue of Joseph Thomson's treaty with Gandu in 1885, arguing that Gandu was politically sovereign over Nupe.[3]

By now Goldie was sure that Hoenigsberg was behind the German agitation, and resolved to get rid of him. In January 1888 a circular was sent to all the company's officials dropping the hint that Hoenigsberg should be deported at the first opportunity.[4] The circular arrived just after Hoenigsberg had been found guilty of attempting to trade in Nupe without paying duties, for which offence his goods had been seized and confiscated. The German was promptly re-arrested and taken to Asaba, where, in the Supreme Court, he was charged with 'promoting and attempting to promote strife and disorder'. He was found guilty and sentenced to be deported. If he attempted to

[1] FO 84/1873 Goldie to F.O. 2.11.87; FO 84/1874 Goldie to Lister 23.11.87 enclosing Regn. 28; FO 84/1876 R.N.C. to F.O. 16.12.87 with minutes; *ibid.* Goldie to Lister 23.12.87.

[2] FO 84/1894 Hatzfeldt to Salisbury 27.1.88.

[3] FO 84/1916 R.N.C. to F.O. 21.2.88.

[4] *Ibid., loc. cit.*, mem. by Goldie enclosed.

return to the Niger Territories he would be liable to three months' imprisonment.[1]

Once more the German Government forced the Foreign Office to intervene. When Goldie refused to accept the suggestion that Hoenigsberg be allowed to return on condition that he abstain from political intrigues in Nupe, he was told that the British and German Governments had agreed on this formula, and ordered to comply with it.[2] Thus, in this affair, and also on the matter of the transit regulation, the Germans had forced the Foreign Office to exercise direct authority on the Niger. The doctrine that the British Government escaped responsibility by delegating power to the Niger Company was wearing rather thin. Goldie took pains to point out that if the Foreign Office wished to give orders, it must be prepared also to take responsibility for the results, and perhaps to pay a financial price. The return of Hoenigsberg, he argued, would be regarded by Emir Maliki as a defeat for the company. It was to be hoped that Britain would not refuse assistance if trouble should result from further intrigues by Hoenigsberg.[3] The Foreign Office neither denied nor admitted the claim, but it was logical enough.

Whilst pressing the case of Herr Hoenigsberg, the German Government had not limited themselves to detailed complaints. His deportation crystallized German hostility, and led them to formulate more general demands, using the affair to persuade the British, in the most reasonable way possible, to establish some kind of state-control over the Niger administration. The matter of transit was one of the chief complaints. If the company were allowed to claim all the navigable water on the Niger and Benue, then free transit was a farce. The test should be the familiar one of effective occupation—a clerk and a warehouse did not constitute a true administration. Where African states were not really administered the trade with them should be treated as transit trade, and allowed to pass freely up and down the rivers. The high level of duties was also objected to, and the

---

[1] FO 84/1894 mem. by Hatzfeldt 5.3.88 with 10 enclosures and *ibid*. Leyden to Barrington 19.5.88.

[2] FO 84/1935 F.O. to R.N.C. 20.12.88.   [3] *Ibid*. R.N.C. to F.O. 22.12.88.

Germans claimed that the revenue from customs did not balance administrative expenditure. In the north, where traders paid double duties, there was no administration at all. The duties on spirits were alleged to be discriminatory against Germany, whose main exports to West Africa were gin and rum. The records of the Hamburg distillers showed that the Niger Company traded extensively in spirits, duties on which were paid simply by transferring a figure from one side of a balance sheet to another. The Germans also alleged that the Niger Company imported spirits to the north where others were prohibited from doing so. The system of ports of entry was also attacked, on the ground that it was discriminatory. No town ever became a port of entry until the company itself had established its trading position thoroughly. The basis of all these grievances, argued Germany, was administration by a company which itself traded. No trader would cheerfully pay money to a commercial rival, on the other hand no German trader had ever complained of British customs administration in Crown colonies. The remedy was therefore simple, and need not entail even the disappearance of the Niger Company's administration. All that was needed was 'for Her Majesty's Government to undertake the collection of duties in the Niger Company's territories by Government officials who would be responsible for the strict observance of international engagements'.[1]

The Foreign Office officials were uneasy at the entire trend of such arguments: 'academic discussion' was not their *forte*, and they would have liked to reply with a general denial of the allegations, and confine discussion to details. However, the German complaints made an impression on Lord Salisbury. 'Any denial *from us*,' he wrote, 'as we have not got any representative of our own in the country, would be, so to speak, mere hearsay evidence, and would carry little weight.'[2] It was this comment which inspired the officials when in April 1888 they once more began to stress the need for an imperial official to

[1] FO 84/1892 Malet to Salisbury, Conf. Af., no. 16, 7.3.88 inc. mem. by Scott of interview with Herr Steinrich. FO 84/1894 Hatzfeldt to Salisbury 10.3.88.
[2] FO 84/1894 minutes on Hatzfeldt to Salisbury 10.3.88.

control the company on the spot, and began to treat the plan for extending the charter to the Oil Rivers with more caution.

In July the Germans succeeded in bringing matters to a head. Announcing that further discussion was fruitless, they informed Britain that Germany would appoint a consul on the Niger with power to settle disputes as they arose. For its part Britain was asked to send out an independent official to inquire into the Niger Company's administration. If Britain refused, Germany might find it necessary to call together the signatories of the Berlin Act to see that its clauses were respected.[1] Lord Salisbury did not resist, but accepted the request at once. Though the river was now too low for an investigation to take place in 1888, he promised that an imperial officer would be appointed to inquire into the Niger Company's administration at the earliest possible time in 1889.[2]

The decision to appoint a Special Commissioner was a real check to Goldie's ambitions. Once the decision had been made, it was natural that all complaints against the Niger Company, most of which a year ago would have been ignored or dismissed as frivolous, should be given to the Commissioner for investigation. Thus, as each charge was passed over to him, the subjects of the inquiry piled up until it became a comprehensive examination of all the problems of the Niger and Oil Rivers.

A problem which presented itself almost immediately was that which had been at the back of all the German arguments— did the company's receipts from taxation balance its administrative expenditure as provided for in the Anglo-German Agreement of 1885? There was no way of telling from the budget sent in by Goldie in July 1888. This was all he saw fit to present:

[1] FO 84/1892 Malet to Salisbury 43 Af. 14.7.88. In 1889 the Germans did send von Puttkamer, a nephew of Bismarck who was also consul at Lagos, to 'investigate' the Niger Company. His report was much as might be expected, and occasioned some controversy in the press of both countries. See *The Times* 23.12.89.

[2] FO 84/1890 draft to Scott 28.8.88.

NIGER GOVERNMENT

Revenue and Expenditure Account 1887[1]

Revenue	£	Expenditure	£
Import Duties	24,037	Staff (proportion for administration)	22,727
Export Duties	16,781		
Licences	1,280	Steamers, Launches, etc. (proportion for administration)	13,636
Misc.	298		
		Stations (proportion for administration)	5,217
		Misc. (proportion for administration)	5,908
	42,396		47,488

This would hardly provide an answer to German complaints, and Goldie was asked to give details of how these figures had been reached. His reply posed the problem in an insoluble form. The company's 'purely commercial' expenditure for 1887, said Goldie, had amounted to £38,595; its 'purely administrative' expenditure was £8,369, but £78,238 had been expended in ways which were both commercial and administrative. This sum had simply been divided into two equal parts, one to the commercial, the other to the administrative balance sheet. Goldie went on to claim that this method was in reality 'very disadvantageous' for the company. If government were carried on by some other authority the company would be able to conduct its trade with a third of its steamers, a third of its stations, and a tenth of its staff. The division, he claimed, was thus nearer 30–70 than 50–50, but he had put forward the equal division to 'disarm criticism'. In any case, the Niger Company itself paid fourteen-fifteenths of the taxation, so what was the point of making too nice distinctions?[2]

These explanations did not convince either Sir Percy Anderson or Lord Salisbury, and Goldie was told that he would have to divide much more clearly; he could not charge stations to the administrative account if they were trading stations, the fact that agents had to keep friendly with local rulers did not make them administrators. Similarly staff must be clearly divided by

[1] FO 84/1925 R.N.C. to F.O. 31.7.88.   [2] FO 84/1926 R.N.C. to F.O. 20.8.88.

function, where this was impossible they must be paid a separate salary for administrative work. Goldie was also informed that these items would be checked in detail by the Special Commissioner who was to visit the Niger in 1889.[1]

Goldie was not disposed to accept this without protest; his detailed replies to each of the Foreign Office suggestions were elaborations on a single theme—the Niger Company was not a normal administration, it was an organism of government which had grown up naturally in the soil of African trade. Its authority largely derived from the commercial pressure which a trading company could exert on the African peoples. As such it was cheap, effective, and humane. The alternative was a clear-cut division between trade and administration which would transform the administration from one based on economic pressure to one based on force. This would entail the recruitment of a large army, a host of officials, and would have to be financed by greatly increased taxation. For administration the Niger Company needed eighty to a hundred stations, but for trade alone ten or twelve would do. If for the sake of clear accounts the company ceased trading at most of its outlying stations and charged their cost to the administration, the cost would be enormous, and the agents at them, who now ruled partly through commercial pressures, would need bodies of African troops to assist them. The same was true of the company's steamers. Normally traders used high draught vessels and went up the river at flood water, but the company's fleet, used both for trade and administration, had to be able to ascend at any time, and was therefore especially constructed with a very shallow draught, much more costly than the normal trading vessel.[2]

Goldie's arguments were unanswerable. Anderson was disposed to agree that as the Niger Company paid most of the taxation anyway, there was little point in making a fuss, but Julian Pauncefote could see the fallacy in the argument:

It is idle for the Company to argue that as they contribute (by

[1] *Ibid., loc. cit.*, minutes by H.P.A. 25.8.88 and Salisbury 20.9.88 and FO 84/1928 F.O. to R.N.C. 20.9.88.
[2] FO 84/1931 R.N.C. to F.O. 31.10.88.

their own trade) the main part of the revenue foreigners have no right to complain of high duties. It is precisely the high taxation which shuts out the foreigner. . . .

Pauncefote wanted to fix the revenue at a certain sum, to be revised every three years, but this was if anything more arbitrary than Goldie's 50–50 division, and it is difficult to see how it would convince critics that expenses and revenue balanced. There was little that could be done except to pass the whole problem over to the Special Commissioner. Goldie was told that the existing duties, except that on palm kernels, were provisionally sanctioned, and on no account to be increased.[1]

The affair of the palm kernels export duty was the reverse side of the problem. The kernel of the palm fruit had at first been thrown away, but in the 1880's its uses were beginning to be realized, and a small trade had begun. In 1886 the company had fixed the export duty on kernels at twopence a hundredweight. In the next two years the demand for kernels raised the price in Yorubaland and the Oil Rivers to £6 a ton, but on the Niger, where the trade was undeveloped, the price stayed at £4 a ton. What Goldie feared was a rush of specialist traders, creaming off this one product in the high-water season, whilst the company trading all the year and carrying the administrative costs, would be forced out of the most profitable commodity.[2] The solution was provided by the permission granted to transfer £12,500 a year from administrative to commercial balance sheet to cover 'expenses incurred in the taking over of the protectorate'.[3] Ostensibly to cover this charge Goldie increased the duty on kernels from twopence a hundredweight to two shillings. This was exactly the amount (£2 a ton) needed to equalize the cost price of Niger kernels (£4 a ton) with the price elsewhere in West Africa (£6 a ton). In a moment of indiscretion Goldie admitted to Sir Percy Anderson that 'the Company plays a sort of game of backgammon with the duties, clapping a duty in front of each article of export as the demand for it arises'.[4]

---

[1] *Ibid., loc. cit.*, minutes by H.P.A. 13.11.88, J.P. 10.11.88 and 14.11.88 and FO 84/1934 F.O. to R.N.C. 4.12.88.

[2] FO 84/1986 mem. by H.P.A. on interview with Goldie 7.1.89.   [3] See p. 113.

[4] FO 84/1931 minute by H.P.A. on R.N.C. to F.O. 31.10.88.

In July 1888 the German Government formally protested against the company's duty on palm kernels. Lord Salisbury was once more quick to respond, and Goldie was told that the duty must be reduced to conform to the spirit of the agreement with Germany. Once more the Germans had forced responsibility on the Foreign Office, once more the company had been disciplined. The move angered Goldie very much; he regarded it as a breach of the charter 'which—no more and no less— conferred the right to levy duties on the Company and others to cover administrative expenditure'. Responsibility for balancing the budget now lay with the Foreign Office. He therefore asked for financial assistance. 'A small subsidy of (say) fifty thousand pounds (£50,000) per annum would enable the Company to abolish all its export duties.'[1]

In attempting to place financial responsibility on the Government Goldie had invaded the holy of holies. Anderson was incredulous, it must be a joke, 'not a particularly good one'. 'The request for a subsidy is a piece of impertinence,' snapped Salisbury in school-masterly fashion, 'and should not be noticed.'[2] Further discussions failed to produce an agreed solution, though Goldie offered to reduce the kernels duty in return for compensating increases on palm oil. Finally the company was told that the duty could stay at two shillings a hundredweight until the Special Commissioner had made a report on the whole question of the company's taxation system.[3]

The German opposition was beginning to have its effect on Goldie's plans for expanding the area of chartered company rule into the Oil Rivers. This influence was not direct; the Germans were careful not to interfere in the internal affairs of a British protectorate; this might have led to awkward British counter-moves in German East Africa and elsewhere. But by constantly proving that a chartered company did not absolve

[1] FO 84/1928 R.N.C. to F.O. 24.9.88.
[2] *Ibid.*, *loc. cit.*, minutes by H.P.A. and Salisbury.
[3] FO 84/1987 F.O. to R.N.C. 31.1.89.

Britain from ultimate responsibility, the Germans succeeded in producing a much more cautious approach to the charter extension scheme. Once the British Government had determined that rival interests would have to be satisfied before the scheme could be accepted, the plan was ruined.

This is not to say that the British Government had lost faith in chartered company rule. British public opinion and the political parties were not yet prepared for imperial adventures, and the chartered company was still a heaven-sent method of establishing colonies at no cost to the taxpayer. In 1888 the Imperial British East Africa Company had received a charter, and Cecil Rhodes was to receive another for the British South Africa Company in the following year. The desire to extend the Niger Company's charter to the Oil Rivers was but a part of this general trend, though the Government was determined that in extending the charter reforms should be carried out which would give the Foreign Office sufficient control to balance its responsibility.

Such an attitude must have been something of a shock for the merchants. When they asked that if the charter were extended they be permitted to levy £25,000 a year from the administrative revenues to cover interest on £500,000 they claimed to have spent in 'expenses arising out of the taking over of the protectorate', the request was turned down without discussion[1]—a marked contrast to the way in which Goldie had obtained a similar privilege for the Niger. In September 1888 Rogerson, the chairman of the African Association, came to the Foreign Office, told Sir Clement Hill[2] that the amalgamation had been agreed, and asked if it was now necessary to make treaties with the Oil Rivers chiefs ceding their rights to the new company. Hill was ready to send an official letter saying that this was not necessary, but the under-secretary, Villiers Lister, brought him

[1] FO 84/1924 African Association to F.O. 4.7.88 and FO 84/1925 F.O. to African Association 27.7.88.
[2] Hill had been appointed assistant clerk in March 1886, and knighted in June 1887, and was virtually deputy to Sir Percy Anderson (the senior clerk in the African dept.). Hill became senior clerk in 1894 when Anderson was promoted to be supervising under-secretary on Lister's retirement.

up sharply, indicating that the old era of conversational back-
stairs intrigue had ended. In future every communication from
the traders must be in writing, no official request had ever
actually been received from the Niger Company for their charter to be extended, and in any case the Government had not yet
decided its policy.[1] Even so Lister was prepared to go ahead
with the plan, he merely wished to see it done with proper
protocol. He assumed that if the Crown obtained control of the
appointment of judicial officers in the new company then critics
of the scheme, in particular the steamship companies, would be
satisfied. But Salisbury would have none of this; the whole question should be investigated by the Special Commissioner, and
nothing should be done until his report was received.[2]

This was an important decision in itself. But upon what
grounds was the Special Commissioner to decide whether to
recommend extension of the charter or not? The permanent
head of the Foreign Office was responsible for asserting a principle which was to be a new and interesting departure in British
policy in West Africa. Before the charter could be extended, he
insisted, the African chiefs must first agree to hand over their
powers to the Niger Company. This was not to be a mere for-
mality, and Pauncefote insisted on safeguards against fraud.
Even if the amalgamated company were given a new name, the
chiefs must be told that it was really the Niger Company. To
make sure of fair play the treaties must be made with the assistance and co-operation of Consul Hewett.[3] Thus Pauncefote
had introduced, albeit in crude form, the principle of 'consultation'. A second condition which Pauncefote declared
essential to the scheme was that the shipping interests must also
receive satisfaction. This was a matter which the traders would
have to settle by private negotiation. Once the shippers had
been appeased, and treaties obtained by the free consent of the
African chiefs, then the charter could be extended.

[1] FO 84/1928 mema. by C.H.H. and T.V.L. 15.9.88.
[2] *Ibid.* minutes by T.V.L. 17.9.88 and Salisbury, n.d.
[3] Pauncefote consistently rejected the suggestions put to him that the name of the
Niger Company be kept out of the treaty-making. See FO 84/1929 minute by J.P.
on Af. Association to F.O. 6.10.88 and FO 84/1930 minute by J.P. on R.N.C. to
F.O. 12.10.88.

These were in reality impossible conditions. The Oil Rivers chiefs would never have agreed to submit to the authority which had driven the Brassmen and the New Calabar people from the Niger markets. Likewise the shipping interests adopted a rigid attitude; they preferred a divided trading community to any promises which an amalgam could make, they even refused to share in the administration under the charter.[1]

Faced with these difficulties the alliance between Goldie and the Liverpool traders began to show signs of strain. A few of the smaller Liverpool firms began to drift away. Rumours began to leak out that the Government was planning to hand over the Oil Rivers to Goldie, and there were letters to *The Times* demanding a Parliamentary committee of inquiry. Goldie was provoked by one of these into a reply, in which he insisted that the plan for extension had been demanded by the Liverpool trade, not the Niger Company, as a better system of administration than a Crown colony, as a source of civilization to the 'barbarous' peoples, and a benefit to 'the overcrowded working classes of Great Britain'.[2] The letter was a blunder on Goldie's part. The circulation of *The Times* in the Oil Rivers was admittedly small, but if Goldie imagined that a sophisticated chief like George Pepple of Bonny, who was particularly addicted to reading theatrical news, would miss such a titbit, he was sadly mistaken. The secret was out. John Holt saw this immediately, and abruptly changed sides. The chiefs would now know that the Niger Company was behind the charter scheme and would oppose it with all their might. The only way to salvage something from the wreck was for the Liverpool merchants to break with Goldie and go on alone. They could make treaties with the chiefs inserting a clause 'that the Royal Niger Company shall in no wise participate therein or be a party thereto'. Even so it would be difficult to remove their suspicions.[3] Holt's defection was followed by that of Miller Brothers and three other firms. Even the four which remained were wavering. In April they prepared draft articles for amalgama-

[1] FO 84/1930 mem. by C.H.H. of interview with F. W. Bond 12.10.88.
[2] *The Times*, 4.1.89.
[3] FO 84/1940 Macdonald to Salisbury 12.6.89 contains Holt to Hewett 5.2.89 in the text.

ting the Liverpool firms only, and although fusion with the Niger Company was provided for in another agreement, stress was laid on the idea of a separate charter, the Government to act as arbitrator in drawing up a boundary between the two chartered territories.[1] In June the African Association Limited was incorporated under the Companies Acts and although the articles allowed for amalgamation, this was little more than a matter of form. The main purpose of the new company was the obtaining of a separate charter.[2]

This was, however, a forlorn hope. Goldie's letter to *The Times* had not only helped to disintegrate the allies, it had forewarned their enemies. The opposition was somewhat slow to mobilize, but when it did it was the most formidable agitation yet seen on a Niger issue. Its organizers were, of course, the steamship companies. In June 1889 they achieved a real triumph by winning over the Liverpool Chamber itself, and presented a monster petition signed by twenty-one West African companies, including Holt's and Stuart and Douglas, both parties to the original charter plan.[3] Even this was surpassed when Lord Hartington, the great Whig peer, endorsed the shippers' views, and promised to force a debate in Parliament if a charter for the Oil Rivers were contemplated.[4] It seemed almost as if the Niger Company itself was disintegrating when James Pinnock, a founder-director of the United African Company in 1879, resigned from the board and joined his protests to the rest,[5] henceforth to become one of Goldie's implacable enemies. Soon the Foreign Office was inundated with protests at the plan to extend the charter, the shippers had at last mobilized the Chambers of Commerce all over the country; from Liverpool, Manchester, Glasgow, Belfast and Middlesborough the resolutions came flowing in. But by now they were wasting their energies, for in July 1889, unknown to them, the first report of the Special Commissioner to the Niger had been received.

[1] FO 84/1992 papers given by Rogerson 5.4.89.
[2] FO 84/1997 mem. by J.F. on interview with Rogerson 20.6.89 with Mema. and Arts. of Association enclosed dated 3.6.89.
[3] FO 84/1998 Liverpool Chamber to F.O. 28.6.89.
[4] FO 84/1999 Hartington to Ferguson 18.7.89.
[5] FO 84/2000 Pinnock to F.O. 30.7.89.

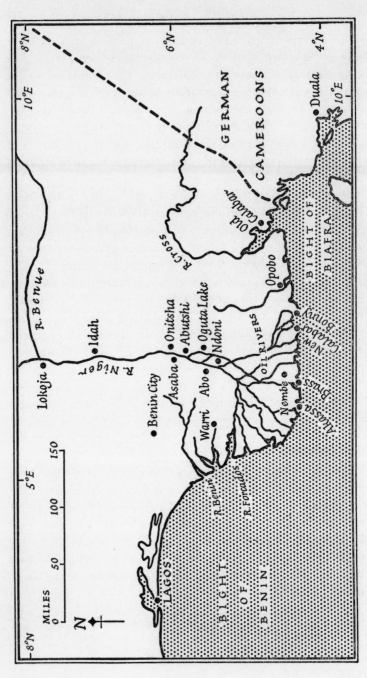

2. The Niger and the Oil Rivers 1889

7

Major Macdonald Investigates

THE man selected to 'inquire into certain questions affecting Imperial and Colonial interests in the West Coast of Africa, and into the position of the Royal Niger Company'[1] was Major Claude Maxwell Macdonald. An army man from an army family, he had fought with Highland regiments in the Egyptian campaign of 1882, and as a volunteer in the Suakin campaign of 1884 where he had won promotion and been decorated by both the Khedive of Egypt and the Sultan of Turkey. He had then embarked upon an administrative career, first as military attaché to the British embassy in Cairo, and then to the difficult position of Acting Agent and Consul General at Zanzibar.[2] His experience therefore gave him some claim to knowledge of Islamic African peoples. Though he was ambitious for a colonial or diplomatic career, Macdonald was scrupulously honest, and not afraid to speak out. Moreover, he came to the Niger with certain fixed ideas which were to prove important when seen in the perspective of developing British attitudes to the West African peoples. He assumed without question that the wishes, ideas and opinions of the African, whether he were chief or slave, were of great, if not paramount, importance in making administrative decisions; and he also took it for granted that the purpose of British control in West Africa was to achieve social reform by means of dynamic economic development.

Macdonald wrote two reports; one on the problem of the

[1] FO 84/1881 F.O. to Macdonald 15.12.88.
[2] *Who was Who 1897–1916* (1920), p. 449. There is no article on Macdonald in the *Dictionary of National Biography*, a surprising omission in view of his later career on the Niger Coast, in China at the time of the 'Boxer' rebellion, and in Japan.

K

future administration of the Oil Rivers, and one on the Niger Company's administration. Neither of these was ever published, despite great agitation at the time that this should be done. The secrecy which has enveloped these documents until they were allowed to be seen in 1952 has condemned them to an obscurity which has been a serious loss for historians of the late-Victorian colonial empire. Macdonald's report on the Niger Company is the only source in existence which can show us what Goldie's company really did on the Niger, and what its presence meant to the people who lived there. The report on the Oil Rivers is perhaps of even greater significance, not only for the way in which it approaches the problem from the African's point of view, but also because of the way in which Macdonald went about his inquiries, and the assumptions which lay behind his methods. The problem of the future of the Oil Rivers had originally been posed in the Foreign Office as one primarily of imperial finance, of saving money by turning the region over to Goldie. It had been complicated by the opposition of the shippers, so that their assent had to be won. The wishes of the Africans had been the last factor to be taken into account when Pauncefote insisted that the chiefs must be told openly that they would, in signing treaties, in effect be going under the Niger Company's administration. There was nothing in his instructions to indicate to Macdonald which of these factors should be given priority. Normally it was to be expected that recommendations of this kind of inquiry would be based on 'Imperial interests'—a phrase which meant 'expediency'.

These sort of considerations never seem to have occurred to Macdonald. He simply assumed, without any discussion or attempt to justify his method, that his task was to find out the wishes of the Africans, and implement them. For him 'Imperial interests' were the interests of the Africans. He therefore went from town to town, and in the most thorough fashion open to him, proceeded to conduct what was in effect a rudimentary kind of plebiscite. In each place he tried to collect together a cross section of the local society, chiefs, influential traders, elders, literate Africans, European managers, even those who could give some idea of the wishes and aspirations of the poor and the slaves. They were then asked to indicate which form of rule they preferred; chartered company, colony, or Foreign Office protectorate. A full, and often lengthy, discussion followed, Macdonald explaining the implications of each system in a factual way. The results of all these meetings were then correlated, and Macdonald put forward the general view as his own recommendations. This was indeed government by consent. Though the acquisition of territory by treaty was in a sense a form of 'consultation' this was probably the first example of African opinion being allowed to determine the *form* of colonial government.

Perhaps even more surprising was the reception given to the Oil Rivers report by the Foreign Office officials and the politicians. Macdonald's method was neither questioned nor discussed, there was not a hint of apprehension at his trust of African opinion. Far from meeting opposition for his novel approach, Macdonald found himself entrusted with the task of implementing his own recommendations. All this is so contrary to what have generally been assumed to be the contemporary British attitudes that the procedure is open to suspicion. Ulterior motives behind the appeal to African opinion are not difficult to find. The Foreign Office was already having doubts about the plan to extend the charter—would not a genuine appeal to African opinion ruin all chances of extending the charter without endangering personal and official relations with Goldie and the traders? Was Macdonald given the impression that if he were to reach certain conclusions it would be highly convenient? However, to put this forward as a serious historical interpretation would be unjust. There is, of course, no denying that Macdonald's liberal attitude was in the circumstances both convenient and practicable, and that in other conditions it might have met with a very different reception. But there is no hint in the documents that Macdonald was 'got at' in any way; they rather indicate the reverse; the Foreign Office were discussing the charter extension plan with Goldie and his allies whilst Macdonald was still conducting his inquiries, and so, in

a sense, prejudicing his case. Moreover, Macdonald's subsequent career belies this interpretation; he preserved his liberal
attitude throughout his later career in the Oil Rivers, and this
was often far from 'convenient'.

Macdonald arrived in Bonny, the port of call for the mail
steamers, on 1 March 1889. Here he began his inquiry, staying
three weeks, afterwards going on to Opobo, New Calabar, the
Sombrero River, Old Calabar, the Forcados River, and the
Benin country, staying several days at each place. His object, in
his own words, was 'to make myself thoroughly acquainted with
the wishes, feelings and ideas of all classes of the community'.
He pointed out clearly to all those who gave him their views
'that what I required to know was their own ideas and wishes
with regard to the form of government' which they desired for
the future. He promised to treat their replies as confidential if
they wished. Though pointing out that the British Government
would not be bound by individual views, he promised that it
'would be guided by the wishes of the community generally'.
The question of extending the charter was always 'brought
forward prominently'. In asking his questions Macdonald tried
to make a simple kind of social analysis by 'classes'. He sought
out the European trading agents and got their personal views, as
opposed to those of the firms they represented. These answers
reflected the views of the European residents, and to some
extent the views of the African middlemen with whom they
were closely associated commercially. The answers of the kings
and chiefs gave a voice to the wealthy trading aristocracy. The
missionaries, both European and African, were much influenced
by the petty African traders of Lagos and Sierra Leone, and in
Macdonald's opinion 'may be said to represent the wishes and
sentiments of the bulk of the poorer classes of slaves and free
men'.

Bonny was the centre of the river system and the headquarters
of the Church Missionary Society. It was ruled by King George
Pepple, a sophisticated aristocrat who had been educated in

England. Pepple and his chiefs strongly objected to chartered company rule, whether by the Niger Company or any other traders. Whilst insisting on the security of their lands and slaves, or fair compensation for them, the Bonny rulers 'decided to become a British colony'.[1] Bishop Crowther, though he scarcely echoed their views on slavery, likewise pressed for a colonial regime, citing Lagos as a virtuous example.[2] Most surprising was the attitude of 'Captain' Boler, the local agent of Harrison and Company, whose chairman, T. S. Rogerson, was a principal advocate of the charter extension plan. Boler, though he had been told by his firm to press for the charter, attacked it strongly when consulted in confidence by Macdonald. The Bonny chiefs, he said, 'would never submit to be governed in any way by a trading association'.[3] This attitude among the Europeans was one which Macdonald was to encounter again and again. It does little to support the generally held view that West African trading agents were on the whole a ruffianly lot, of poor moral fibre.

Opobo, Ja Ja's town, was still in tumult as a result of his exile, and under blockade by British gunboats. Nevertheless Macdonald managed to get in touch with the 'rebels' and Cookie Gam and five other chiefs answered that 'they would rather be under the immediate rule of the British government as a colony', but were willing to be guided by the wishes of the Bonny people.[4] The European agents were divided, Miller Brothers' agents said that the chiefs would never accept rule by the Niger Company, but would accept a separate chartered company administration run by the local merchants, but Macdonald felt that his views were not frank, and were 'influenced by orders from home'. Messrs. Mitchell and Zeller, both with fifteen years' experience in the rivers, 'in opposition to orders received from their employers', stressed that the chiefs would never agree to be ruled by a chartered company of any kind.

[1] FO 84/1940 Macdonald to Salisbury 12.6.89 (his report on the Oil Rivers) Inc. 1, H. A. Allison, secretary to King George, to Macdonald 4.4.89.
[2] *Ibid*. enc. 2 mem. by S. A. Crowther.   [3] *Ibid*. text of report.
[4] *Ibid*. enc. 3. Chiefs of Opobo to Macdonald 29.3.89.

At New Calabar 'the feeling against the Royal Niger Company was most marked and bitter, even to a desire to enter into hostilities.' The chiefs demanded colonial administration 'or rather . . . a more direct government by Her Majesty'.[1] At Old Calabar, the seat of consular rule where Hewett had his residence, Macdonald was struck by 'the more advanced state of the native chiefs and the absence of any sort of feeling good or bad with regard to the Niger Company'. At a meeting with a very large number of chiefs Macdonald felt that the general feeling was for a more direct government, though some of the chiefs could not see why any change at all was necessary. They were all rather uneasy at the prospect of social changes, they knew of the humanitarian sentiments of Britain, but could not share them, and insisted on the preservation of their systems of slavery, poligamy and land tenure, the people ought to be 'gradually prepared' for any changes.[2] The Europeans in Old Calabar 'the most intelligent and straightforward in the whole delta' according to Macdonald, were unanimous that consular rule should be continued as the best form of government for the rivers.

Macdonald finished his task by visiting Brass and the Benin country. At Brass, as was to be expected, he found the Africans very bitter against the Niger Company, and the European agents 'violently' opposed to the charter plan. King Frederick William Koko asked for colonial rule 'and not extension of charter—not wishing to be ruled by *its* powers'. The Brassmen too, were worried at possible attacks on domestic slavery, assuring Macdonald that they did 'not buy and *use* them as *slaves* but as *brethren* and *children*'. Nana, the 'Governor' of Benin, echoed these sentiments, and asked for 'Queen's Government'.[3]

[1] *Ibid.* enc. 4. New Calabar chiefs to Macdonald 4.4.89.
[2] *Ibid.* enc. 8. Eyo Honesty to Macdonald 16.4.89, also encs. 6 and 7, and unnumbered encs. Henshaw III to Macdonald 16.4.89, Duke IX to Macdonald 17.4.89, Ikorpong and Ikornetu to Macdonald 16.4.89 and Cobham V to Macdonald 16.4.89.
[3] *Ibid.* enc. 7. Koko to Macdonald, and Inc. 8, Nana to Macdonald. N.B. Macdonald made a clerical error in numbering these enclosures, there are thus two encs. 7 and 8.

Macdonald's inquiries were completed by the end of April, and he returned to London to write his Oil Rivers report whilst waiting to go up the Niger in July. He confessed that he himself could see 'some advantage' in the plan to extend the Niger Company's charter. Though he had not yet visited the company's territories, independent witnesses, most of them hostile to the company, had been forced to admit that Goldie and his associates had done wonders on the Niger, law and order existed where a few years ago there had been chaos. It was clear that extension would make the company richer, and thereby enable it to employ a better class of official, administer the greater area more cheaply, and reduce taxation. But though all this was true, 'the opposition which the extension would meet both in public and secretly from the chiefs and native traders—the number of quarrels and disturbances which would ensue would more than counterbalance any advantages to be derived.' Thus, though he was not impressed by the state of the Crown colonies in West Africa, he found it difficult 'in the face of such a unanimous opinion' to suggest any other scheme than the establishment of a separate colony of the Oil Rivers, bounded in the west by the Niger Territories, and on the east by the German Cameroons. The problem of slavery, illegal in British colonies since 1834, could be handled with tact, and it was agreed that the area was rich enough to support itself by its own taxation.

As soon as this report was received Villiers Lister wanted to issue an announcement setting out the future regime in detail, but Salisbury vetoed this. He was not convinced that the slavery problem was as simple as Macdonald claimed. However, Macdonald's main point was immediately taken, and in July the Government let it be known that there was no foundation for any report that Her Majesty's Government intended to grant a charter for the Oil Rivers to any group or association.[1]

· · · ·

[1] FO 84/1997 T.V.L. to Salisbury 18.6.89; FO 84/1998 T.V.L. to Salisbury 28.6.89; FO 84/1999 minute by H.P.A. on G. A. Moore and Co. to F.O. 15.7.89; FO 84/2000 F.O. to G. A. Moore 22.7.89.

On 28 June 1889 Macdonald once more took ship for West Africa, this time to ascend the Niger and Benue. By August he had reached Lokoja, and spent just over a month inspecting the company's stations on the Benue, after which he spent most of September and half of October on the upper Niger visiting Nupe and Ilorin. By the end of October he had finished his work after travelling in the Oguta and Forcados regions. After a short holiday in England (at Margate in December!) to recover from a fever he had contracted, Macdonald sent in his report on the Niger in January 1890.[1]

His methods of inquiry were as thorough as could be expected; the visit had to be organized by the Niger Company, travelling on its steamers and boarding at its stations, so that the company's point of view was constantly before him. Sometimes this led to false impressions, particularly when Macdonald interviewed minor chiefs in the presence of company officials, but these misjudgements were few. There was also one grave omission, Macdonald's failure to visit Gandu and Sokoto, which he does not explain. Perhaps time was short, or possibly he was told by the company that the situation in the north was too dangerous to travel with safety. With these exceptions, and that of the Emir of Yola, who refused to see him, Macdonald interviewed almost all the chiefs in the Niger Territories and was given an account of how they had negotiated and signed their treaties with the company. He was able to look at the company's administration as an outsider and assess its effectiveness. He took great pains to collect a mass of detail about the company's monopolistic activities and analysed the evidence impartially. Everywhere he was careful to consult independent or hostile opinion, missionaries and rival traders both African and European. His final report gives as good a picture of the workings of the administration which Goldie had built up as could reasonably be expected. As such it is a unique document.

Macdonald began with a detailed analysis of the company's

---

[1] FO 84/2109 *Report on the Administration of the Niger Territories* by Major Macdonald, handed in 9.1.90. Where sources are not referred to in the remainder of this chapter they are taken from this report.

treaties—were they genuine or fraudulent? Here his evidence must be treated with caution; Macdonald was well aware that wider issues might be at stake than the simple rights of the Niger Company to rule this or that strip of country. The company's claims were also British claims, and to reject them here or there might leave awkward gaps to be filled by foreigners, and have effects on British interests in years to come when the company's administration might be but a memory. Generally therefore, Macdonald took pains to put the best construction possible on every claim. When Macdonald found a treaty fraudulent we can be fairly sure that he was convinced.

The most extensive system of treaties covered the Niger south of Onitsha, the palm oil region. Many of these treaties had been concluded in 1884 and 1885 before the charter had been issued. The terms of the treaties varied, but in most of them the chiefs ceded their territories absolutely; gave the company the right to exclude foreigners; a monopoly of all mining, farming and building; the right to acquire land subject to a fair payment to owners; and in some cases the control of relations with other tribes or states. In return the company promised 'not to interfere with any native laws', and in some cases promised also 'to protect the said chiefs from the attacks of any neighbouring aggressive tribes'. Usually the company paid the chiefs a subsidy.[1] By 1889 the company had concluded 209 treaties from Akassa to Lokoja, and paid out £1,284 7s. a year in subsidies. Macdonald found that most of the chiefs agreed that they had signed the treaties, and seemed to understand what they had done. The exception was the important town of Onitsha, where the king denied that he had ever signed a treaty, and insisted on his right to trade with all comers. Since 1885 the company had maintained a blockade of the town, and there had been some fighting. One can only speculate as to the motives which led chiefs to sign away their rights in this fashion. The subsidies must have been an inducement, and the promise to protect them against aggressive neighbours would be an attraction to the weaker states. In some cases it is clear that the motive was

[1] For details of each treaty see Hertslet, *Map of Africa*, etc., Vol. I, pp. 122–56.

economic, and the chiefs looked upon the treaty as establishing a new middleman, the Niger Company, who would pay better prices than the coastal Africans. The Attah of Idah admitted as much to Macdonald when he said that he had hoped to 'become fat' as a result of his treaty, instead, he complained, he had 'shrunk up and become dry'. The further question arises as to whether these chiefs in fact possessed the powers they so glibly signed away. Reputable authorities are agreed that by local law the chiefs did not own their territories like a European sovereign, and that ultimate rights lay with the tribe or clan as a whole. The Niger Company has been castigated for sharp practice on this score.[1] This is perhaps unrealistic and unfair. Goldie and his colleagues could not be expected to be conversant with the intricacies of the political and legal theory of the Niger delta peoples in 1885. Moreover a real attempt was made to consult any groups which might have a claim to a voice in the tribe. In some villages as many as fifty treaties were made with small groups of people, all of whom claimed independence from the rest. Finally those who argue that treaty making was immoral must recognize that the alternative, if rule is to be acquired, is conquest by force. Macdonald, at any rate, concluded that the treaties had been fairly made, and gave the Niger Company complete sovereign rights over the lower Niger.

On the Benue the position was very different. Here, instead of the tribal communities of the lower Niger, were larger territorial states, each ruled by an Emir, and linked together by a system of quasi-feudal relationships under the twin heads of the Fulani empire, the Sultan of Sokoto and the Emir of Gandu. All these states were monarchical in character, with the nucleus of a central administration in the Emir's household, and were used to conducting a taxation system which bore both on agriculture and trade. Correspondence, either in Arabic, or in Fulani or Hausa, using Arabic letters, was used both in internal govern-

[1] E.g. by Elias, T. K. in his *Nigerian Land Law and Custom*, London, 1951. The whole process of treaty-making is attacked also in Lugard, F. D., *The Dual Mandate in British Tropical Africa*, London, 1923, pp. 14–17. Lugard was himself an accomplished treaty maker, and worked for the Niger Company in the 1890's. He concluded that the main function of treaties was to salve the European conscience.

ment and in communicating with other Emirs or even foreigners like the Niger Company or the states of North Africa. Each state had a small standing army of cavalry, and was able to call out a kind of feudal host in an emergency. The Muslim religion dominated intellectual, social and political life. It was not to be expected that the Emir of such a state would easily be persuaded to cede his territory to a group of contemptible infidel traders.

In fact none did. Only the non-Muslim peoples, keeping a precarious footing on the Benue against the Fulani hosts, had genuinely accepted the company's treaties, and these now complained that the company refused to protect them. The Emir of Yola had always refused to sign a treaty, as he now refused to see Macdonald, and a trip to his capital was a dangerous mission. The Emir of Nassarawa had merely sold to the company a strip of land covering the banks of the river throughout his country; he admitted the transaction, but disputed the amount of land which the company claimed. Treaties had also been signed with the Emirs of Muri and Keffi, but these gave no political rights to the company, indeed the Muri treaty promised 'protection' to the company. Where the company claimed political rights, these had in every case been improperly obtained. Macdonald laid most of the blame on the African interpreters, responsible for swearing that the Emirs had fully understood the negotiations. Many of these now admitted that they had perjured themselves in so doing. The position of these African diplomats was a difficult one, for they had to steer a course between a demanding European employer and an arbitrary African despot. One of these interpreters, W. N. Thomas, exposed their dilemma to Macdonald:

I cannot say that I made the king (i.e. the Emir of Bakundi) understand that he ceded his country to the Company. I made him understand that he gave his country to the Company for trading purposes, that nobody else could trade in the country without the permission of the Company, that all Europeans should be under the jurisdiction of the Company, but I was not aware that 'ceding' meant giving over the rights of government and I dare not have made this suggestion to him. . . .

In one case the blame could not be laid on Africans. The treaty with the Emir of Bauchi had been signed by the company's chief agent McIntosh, now the Agent-General, assisted by a deputy and interpreted by a Whydah man. The Emir strongly denied ceding any political rights, and Macdonald thought it 'not at all probable that a powerful Mohammedan Emir would hand over the whole of his territories to two white men, Christians, for bags of salt amounting to £100; the revenue of his territories would come to a sum which, put at a low figure, would be more than five times the yearly subsidy he receives from the Company'. Macdonald therefore challenged the interpreter, only to find that McIntosh strenuously upheld the treaty. McIntosh spoke Hausa, and insisted that the Emir had fully understood what was taking place. His motive for accepting the treaty was that he had seen Nupe grow so powerful through its intercourse with the company that he wished to do the same. From his survey of the Benue as a whole, Macdonald was forced to conclude that the company possessed little but commercial rights, and practically no jurisdiction.

The thorniest of all these treaty problems was that of the relationship between Nupe and the company, for behind it lay the German claim that Nupe was independent, and that trade with Nupe was transit trade, and therefore not subject to the company's taxes. In September 1889 Macdonald, accompanied by a Hausa-speaking missionary as his interpreter, succeeded in discussing the question with Emir Maliki and his *Ndegi*, or Prime Minister. No Niger Company officials were allowed to be present. The interpreter first read out, clause by clause, the 'treaty' made with McIntosh in 1885.[1] After a 'long oration' the Emir agreed that this was truly what he had signed. Macdonald had thus established that the Emir agreed that he had ceded 'the entire charge of all trading rights' to the company. He now tried to establish whether the company possessed any political jurisdiction. Did the Emir regard himself as tributary to Gandu or not? Maliki was immediately suspicious, why did Macdonald wish to know this? Macdonald replied that he would explain later.

[1] See Chap. 5, pp. 88–89.

'The Emir then asked me,' Macdonald continues, 'whether I knew or had heard of the Sultan of Stamboul (i.e. Istanbul)—I said yes, and if they would come to Wanangi I would show them a letter I had from that Sovereign (I alluded to my firman as an officer of the fourth class of the Osimanieh Order). . . . The Emir said—"It is well" (I could see however that he did not believe about the firman). "The Sultan of Stamboul is the head of the Mohamedan religion." I said I knew it.—"After him is the Sultan of Sokoto"; not wishing to raise a theological discussion I bowed assent, "next to him though nearly equal was the Sultan of Gandu, and after him the Emir of Nupe himself." He acknowledged the Sultan of Gandu to be his spiritual head.'[1]

Macdonald now explained the reason for his question, reading the Emir the preamble to the company's treaty with Gandu, made by Joseph Thomson in 1885[2] which granted the company the land on both banks of the Niger throughout Nupe country. This put the Emir in a real flurry, and the *Ndegi* rushed over to inspect the document. The Emir was indignant; the whole thing was absurd. The Emir of Gandu would never hand over Nupe territory without at least informing him—why, would Queen Victoria hand over Lagos to the French without so much as telling the inhabitants? Macdonald now returned to the Nupe agreement itself. What was the company supposed to receive for its £2,000 a year subsidy? At last, 'after much beating about the bush' both the Emir and the *Ndegi* admitted that the company had a right to levy duties on the Nupe trade. Macdonald therefore concluded that the Nupe agreement of 1885 was enough to justify the company's claim that Nupe was within the chartered sphere. The Gandu treaty, which he believed was *bona fide*, made the company the legal rulers of Nupe. Having made this judgement, Macdonald naturally rejected the claims of Herr Hoenigsberg. He had been assured by many British merchants hostile to the Niger Company that Hoenigsberg was really a trouble maker. By his actions Hoenigsberg had put the lives of all Europeans in Nupe in peril; his sentence of deportation was entirely just, and he had no claim to receive compensation from the company.

---

[1] There was of course no 'Sultan' of Gandu, merely the Emir.
[2] See Chap. 5, p. 89.

Having discussed the theoretical rights of the company, Mac-donald went on to examine the actual state of the administra-tion. His main purpose here was to estimate whether the cost of the administration did in fact balance receipts from taxation as Goldie claimed, but Macdonald incidentally gives enough information to assess how far, and at what places, the company had established an effective rule. The system of administration was essentially based on the river, and depended on the com-pany's steamers to link its stations together, and to transport constabulary to places where force had to be used. Macdonald found that the company had twenty-three vessels in all. Eight of these were large screw-propelled steamships, many of them capable of carrying 6,000 tons of cargo, and costing initially anything from £3,000 to £19,000 to build, of these five had been employed administratively. There were also two large paddle-steamers, and eleven smaller vessels, many of which were in bad condition, and some positively unsafe. All of these had been used as dispatch vessels to carry the officials, or as revenue boats. There were also two hulks, permanently moored as customs posts. The total cost of all these vessels Macdonald quoted as £124,000. Goldie had claimed £26,000 as the proportion of steamer costs for administration, out of a total cost, according to the company's books, of £39,000. Macdonald thought this much too high. Whilst he had been on the river only the smaller vessels had done any administrative work, the big ships had been entirely occupied in carrying cargo for trade. Moreover, he felt that Goldie could have prepared a much more accurate estimate by separating the accounts of each ship into adminis-trative and commercial divisions. The administrative account could quite easily be based on a detailed analysis of all the punitive expeditions, which were the main administrative burden placed on the steamers, when the larger ships had to act as transports and gunboats to assist the constabulary.

The constabulary itself was an item about which there could be little dispute, its purpose was clearly administrative, and it had no direct commercial function. Macdonald judged it to be far the most impressive administrative achievement of the company.[1] Goldie's own military training and his own theories about Africans as soldiers played no small part in establishing this force. It consisted by now of 424 men, of whom only five were Europeans. The Africans were recruited deliberately from three regions. Fanti from the Gold Coast Colony predominated, there were about 250 of them, and they were found to make the best non-commissioned officers. The Hausa numbered about a hundred, and were regarded as the best fighters, but as they were Muslims their loyalty was rather suspect in the event of any conflict with the Emirs. The rest were Yoruba. Two of the Africans ranked as commissioned officers, but their pay, though generous by African labour standards (£3 to £3 17s. 6d. per month with rations and uniform) was much less than that of the Europeans. The Africans in the ranks were relatively well-paid; the two sergeants-major received fifty shillings a month, fifteen sergeants forty shillings, sixteen corporals thirty-five shillings, and privates thirty shillings, all with free rations and uniforms. There were also two Muslim *mallams* serving as chaplains to the Hausa troops. The European officers were extremely well-paid; so much so that whilst the pay of the Africans cost the company £7,700 a year that of the five Europeans cost £10,000.

Goldie's military training gave him an interest in artillery, reflected in the armament of the constabulary. Each man was armed with a Snider rifle and bayonet, and the company maintained arsenals at dispersed posts throughout the Niger Territories where larger weapons were kept, ranging from Gardiner machine guns and five-pounder mortar cannon to a twelve-pounder Whitworth. Macdonald, after watching an extensive parade and drilling exhibition at Asaba, judged that the artillery had performed outstandingly well. Discipline was excellent; since the force had been formed there had only been

---

[1] It was later to be the model for the constabulary which Macdonald himself organized in the Niger Coast Protectorate, and had a great influence on the methods which Lugard employed in raising the West African Frontier Force. The Royal Niger Constabulary is thus the true prototype of Nigeria's armed forces. The uniform which Nigerian troops wear today is practically the same as that worn by the Niger Company's constabulary.

eight courts-martial, all for minor offences, and no man had
ever deserted. The constabulary was not used like a police force.
Its purpose was not to patrol the rivers or constantly keep order,
but to act as a reserve of force concentrated at Asaba to be used
where administration was in danger of collapsing or had already
broken down. These expeditions were fairly frequent, taking
place about once a month. They were usually made in reply to
some act of defiance on the lower Niger; attacking a station,
refusing to pay fines, or attacking steamers on the river. Three
or four officers and fifty to a hundred men would take part, often
assisted by local 'native allies'. They were not bloody affairs,
the number of killed and wounded on both sides could usually
be counted on one hand. Sometimes a fine would be imposed on
the miscreants, failing this the offending town would be burned
down, and any animals which the inhabitants had been fool-
hardy enough to leave behind as they fled into the bush would
be destroyed.

But these were extraordinary measures. The normal day-to-
day administration was conducted from the Niger Company's
stations, and the effectiveness of the administration is really to
be judged on the power exercised through these posts. It was
here that Macdonald's attempt to separate administrative and
commercial expenditure broke down; he was forced to admit
that any division must be an arbitrary one, and that Goldie's
arguments were justified. It was clear, for instance, that when
the 'pagans' on the Benue asked the company to set up a trading
post, their prime reason for doing so was not commercial, but so
that they could be strengthened in their struggle against the
Fulani. He therefore concluded that Goldie's estimate of the
administrative cost of the stations was far from excessive.

If its stations were the real basis of the company's power,
their distribution also reveals the wide differences in the company's effective authority within its territories. There were forty
stations in all, ranging from small stores kept by an African and
his family to embryo cities of fifty acres. On the lower Niger
below Lokoja there were twenty-three stations, on the upper
Niger only seven, and along the whole length of the Benue only

ten. The company was thus still concentrating its activity in the palm oil region. Moreover, the southern stations were closer together, and contained all the really large establishments. The company's buildings at Akassa, the depot station at the mouth of the Niger, covered thirty-five acres, including customs houses, wharves, engineering shops, offices and houses for the employees. The commercial headquarters at Abutshi covered fifty acres. The administrative headquarters at Asaba was almost as large; and included the only prison in the Niger Territories, the best house in the country (the residence of the Chief Justice, a pre-fabricated building of wood and iron), the barracks of the constabulary, and a botanical research station covering eight acres. The whole area of the lower Niger was covered with a network of smaller stations centred on these three, and this net-work controlled the creeks and tributaries leading into the Niger so that a revenue frontier could be established.

The northern stations were much less impressive. The oldest of them at Egga still flourished, exporting a great variety of Nupe produce, especially ivory, shea-butter, and groundnuts. It had always been the policy of the Emirs of Nupe to try to chan-nel the trade of the north through Egga, and this seems to have been effective even in 1889. The company's station at Lokoja was a sorry contrast, its trade a poor trickle of local produce, the only stone building that of the C.M.S. missionaries, 'with no barracks or administrative buildings of any kind and not a single soldier'. And this was supposed to be the headquarters of the northern region. The five other stations on the Niger above Lokoja were small trading posts administered by Africans of junior status.

On the Benue the company had made a real effort to expand its trade, as a counterweight to the increasing hostility of the Emir of Nupe. Two of the stations were of some size; Loko was a starting point for caravans for Sokoto, and an African agent of the first rank had a busy time organizing the post; Ibi was the headquarters for the Benue region, where the Senior Executive Officer and a District Agent lived, supported by a sergeant and fifty men of the constabulary. There was also a small experimental

L

rubber plantation at Koonini, four more minor posts under second class African agents, and two hulks moored near to Yola. Macdonald was not impressed with the Benue administration; he criticized the company for failing to honour its promises to protect the 'pagan' peoples against the Fulani, and felt that by working through the non-Muslim peoples the company could have built up a rich trade and a much more solid administration. What Macdonald failed to see was that the company might thus have provoked a unified resistance from Sokoto and the subordinate emirates on the Benue, a combination which the small constabulary, efficient though it was, could not have overcome. In the Muslim regions, both on the Benue and in Nupe, it must be admitted that there was no real administration. The company was there on sufferance, and any pressure which it could exert on the Emirs was purely commercial. Such evidence as exists from African sources bears out this judgement. Baba, the grandmother from Karo, makes no mention of the Niger Company in her delightful and moving story of the last years of Fulani rule in Hausaland.[1] Nor does the anonymous Arab chronicler of Kano, writing at the end of the nineteenth century.[2] Though the company is well known in Nupe oral traditions, it is seen as an outside force, only capable of intervention by reason of its power on the water.

On the lower Niger the position was undoubtedly different. Few of the Africans living near to the river banks could have been unaware of the company's power. If they had a surplus to trade, they found their outlets narrowed down to the company's posts, and the visits of other traders, African or European, less and less frequent. If the chiefs and elders intrigued against the company, attacked the company's stations, formed alliances with other tribes, or invited other traders in, they would feel the company's power. Their lookouts would spy the approaching steamers, see the guns mounted on the decks and the uniformed African soldiers with their British officers shouting orders. The

---

[1] Smith, M. F., *Baba of Karo. A Woman of the Muslim Hausa*, with an introduction by M. G. Smith, London, 1954.

[2] Palmer, H. R., *Sudanese Memoirs*, Vol. III, p. 92 ff.

women and children, and if possible, the animals, would be hastily shepherded into the surrounding bush. Perhaps some of the men, with their antiquated guns, would make a show of resistance, but the guns from the ships were so noisy and the smoke and fire so terrifying that they would soon break and run in face of the fearful imperturbability of the disciplined ranks before them. At a safe distance they would watch the smoke rising from the burning houses. Later they would return, to rebuild them in a few days. The chief would hold palaver with the company's man. There would be a fine to pay, much trade without goods in return, and soon the steamers would be churning the water once more. The gods were indeed against any African whose relationship with the company was more formal than this. If he had a dispute with a foreigner or with the company, he might find himself on a charge before the company's courts. But the chance was remote. Remoter still was the possibility that he might find himself, like sixteen other Africans in 1889, locked in the prison at Asaba.

Like the constabulary, the judiciary could be classified as purely administrative, but it did not receive the same praise from Macdonald. From the first the Niger Company's courts had been characterized by irregularities of the gravest kind. The worst of these was the so-called 'Zweifel case'. Zweifel was an employee of the company who, together with William Wallace, then the acting Agent-General, had taken a party of Sierra Leonean labourers up the river to explore the possibilities of gathering rubber. When the party arrived at Lokoja the labourers refused to go any farther, saying that they had come to cut rubber, not to 'walk in the bush for nothing'. Zweifel then singled out the man whom he thought to be the ringleader and shot him dead. A general skirmish followed in which Wallace gave the order to the soldiers and local allies surrounding the labourers to fire upon them. Six were killed and twenty-eight wounded as a result. Several of the labourers managed to escape, and after an epic journey three hundred miles across country made their way to Lagos, where, being British subjects, they complained to the Governor. Meanwhile the Niger

Company's Chief Justice, Sir James Marshall, a director of the company and a former colonial judge, conducted an inquiry into the affair, at which, according to Goldie, he exonerated Wallace and Zweifel. Shortly afterwards, however, Marshall resigned his post, and calling at Lagos on his way home, gave an account of the affair which corroborated the story put forward by the escaped labourers. Goldie accused Marshall of changing his attitude after a quarrel with the company on a totally different question. Whatever the cause, Marshall's resignation exposed the myth that the company's courts were in some sense independent of administrative pressure. The Governors of Sierra Leone and Lagos pressed for a prosecution of Wallace and Zweifel for murder, and the Colonial Office supported them. Lord Salisbury overrode his officials at the Foreign Office and agreed. An official dispatch was sent to Goldie complaining against the fact that Wallace and Zweifel both continued to be employed by the company, and pointing out that the affair argued 'an indifference for African life which is the worst possible recommendation for an extension of their power over new and more populous regions'. Goldie was also told that Wallace, being a British subject (Zweifel was a German and not amenable to British courts) would be charged with murder. Nevertheless Goldie succeeded, in some mysterious way, in hushing the whole thing up. After an interview with Salisbury and the Colonial Secretary at which Goldie urged 'the serious disadvantages' of reopening the case, the affair vanishes from the official records. Neither Wallace nor Zweifel ever faced a trial. Both continued in their employment with the company. William Wallace went on to become head of the administration on the Niger, and later obtained a knighthood and entered the Colonial Office administration to become Acting High Commissioner of Northern Nigeria.[1]

Macdonald kept silent on the Zweifel affair, though he knew of it, and in fact inspected a rubber collecting station at which

[1] FO 84/1922 C.O. to F.O. with encs. 16.6.88; FO 84/1923 R.N.C. to F.O. 23.6.88; FO 84/1925 C.O. to F.O. 26.7.88; FO 84/1933 C.O. to F.O. 26.11.88 enc. R.N.C. to Knutsford; FO 84/2000 typed memo. by Salisbury on the Zweifel case, n.d.; *ibid.* F.O. to R.N.C. 26.7.89; FO 84/2002 R.N.C. to F.O. 29.8.89.

Zweifel was in charge. Nevertheless in discussing the judiciary as a whole, Macdonald made it clear that all was not well. Irregularities had occurred, and more would occur if reforms were not carried through. One of the company's employees had been tried and sentenced to death by a Senior Executive Officer on the Benue for murdering a young girl 'under circumstances of the most dreadful brutality', but the Council of the Company had reducedthe sentence to ten years' penal servitude, and later ordered that the man be released after he had served only two years in prison. Two other convicted murderers had received only a year in prison, whilst an employee convicted of man-slaughter had received only three months. These were indi-vidual cases, but Macdonald regarded the fundamentals of the system as faulty. The powers of young and inexperienced officials, none of whom had any legal training, over the lives of Africans were far too sweeping; they should not have the right to impose death sentences, and the accused should have the right to appeal to a higher court against the decisions of administrative officers. In general the company, thought Mac-donald, ought to try to separate the judiciary much more clearly from the administration, and it should employ more men whose whole time would be employed as judges only.

The main work of the judiciary was the enforcement of the company's regulations, and these, as we have seen, were entirely concerned with the regulation of commerce conducted by foreigners to the Niger Territories. The judicial and administra-tive system was thus, basically, a system of enforcing the monopoly. This fact produced serious anomalies in the ad-ministration of justice. In criminal cases which might involve imprisonment or the death penalty, the company naturally had to take great care where foreigners protected by their respective governments were involved; and therefore the local officials were severely limited in their power to pass sentences on foreigners, and these had to be confirmed by the Council in London. On the other hand all traders from outside had to be classified as 'foreigners', for natives by their treaties, and by virtue of their protectorate status, could not be taxed on their trade. What of the middlemen from the Oil Rivers? If they were classed as natives they could trade freely. But if they were classed as foreigners the sentences which could be imposed on them in the courts were too light to have any real deterrent effect. Macdonald found that the company played a double game here; the coastal Africans were treated as natives in criminal cases, and severely sentenced, but commercially they were treated as foreigners so that they were obliged to pay all the duties and take out trading licences. In Macdonald's view this was unjust. The Oil Rivers peoples were, like the peoples in the Niger Company's territories, subject to the one 'British Protectorate of the Niger Districts', there was no legal division between the two spheres. The fact that the Niger Company administered a part of the protectorate did not entitle it to define those natives outside its sphere as foreigners. Macdonald therefore ruled that all the coastal Africans were natives of the whole protectorate, and were not under any obligation to pay licence fees or customs duties to the company, or be obliged to trade at special ports of entry or export.

This recommendation was revolutionary in its implications. The chief energies of the company had hitherto been concentrated on excluding the middlemen, and of late the revenue system had been expanded to cut off all the creeks through which the Brass and New Calabar people shipped palm oil to the coast. The struggle against the middleman had been the main factor behind the struggle with the Liverpool traders. To allow duty-free trade by coastal Africans amounted to a complete abolition of the company's monopoly, which Goldie regarded as essential for a chartered company which was not allowed to make profits from its administrative revenues. Further recommendations were of the same character. European rivals of the company had long complained of the company's insistence that the purchase from natives of land for wharves and stores needed prior permission from the company. Macdonald thought that this rule was illegal by Article 14 of the charter, which forbade monopoly. On the other hand if the company claimed that the land was its property, such a claim should only be accepted if the land in question was actually in use. Other recommendations would have given easier entry to the petty traders from Lagos and Sierra Leone, excluded both by the £50 licence fee, and the twenty per cent duty on the export of all native produce which annihilated their prospect of profit. Macdonald urged that the latter should be cut to five per cent, or abolished, and that a system of hawkers' licences should be set up, costing only £5 a year, permitting the holder to trade in certain scheduled articles.

Nevertheless Macdonald did not condemn the Niger Company outright as a monopolistic organization. The crucial test of this was the company's administrative budget; had the company in fact expended the sums which it claimed to have spent on administration? If so then it was entitled to recoup the money from taxes. If not, the level of duties, which incidentally had the effect of excluding competitors, was too high. On this point, one of the main objects of the inquiry, Macdonald was unable to give a satisfactory assessment. In all, he concluded that the estimate of expenditure claimed by Goldie was not excessive, but argued that in future the company should be made to put forward a detailed budget, which would separate commercial and administrative costs much more clearly, and which could be checked, item by item, against the company's books. Macdonald could only comment on the individual items on the basis of his own observations and impressions. The amount claimed for constabulary expenditure he regarded as very fair, and thought that Goldie might legitimately have asked double the amount. Nor could he quarrel with the amount claimed as the cost of the stations.[1] Goldie's claim for the administrative cost of the steamers Macdonald found quite excessive. Goldie had claimed that a third or a quarter of the fleet would have sufficed for trade alone, but Macdonald observed that the entire fleet had been constantly engaged in carrying cargo the

[1] Macdonald's reasoning here is, however, difficult to follow, for he went on to disagree with Goldie's claim that only ten or twelve stations were needed for trade alone. Macdonald felt that the forty stations of the company were not fully exploiting the trade. This rather destroyed Goldie's figures, for they were based on the difference between the cost of stations needed merely for trade, and the full cost, which was supposed to include uneconomic trading posts, established mainly for political reasons.

whole time he was there. The costs of salaries and staff he felt to be reasonable.

If the administrative costs were in general fairly estimated, then Macdonald could not complain that the level of duties was too high, for their yield did not, according to Goldie's figures, balance the administrative costs. But it was possible that the incidence of the duties on certain commodities was unfair. Here the greatest cause of complaint was the controversial export duty on palm kernels, against which the Germans had protested so fiercely. Macdonald, after analysing the profitability of kernels, ruled that the duty was unfair, and recommended that it be reduced, and replaced by a tax on imported Manchester cottons (which bore no duty) or by increasing the export duty on palm oil.

The general tone of Macdonald's report appears at first sight to favour the company. Many of the worst charges against it were dismissed or made to look less significant. The Commissioner had found much to praise, the constabulary in particular. His criticisms appeared to be minor ones, and his recommendations small adjustments to the existing pattern of administration—a few changes in the customs duties and licences, and some reform of the judiciary. Yet, had they been enforced, they would have ruined Goldie's carefully constructed monopoly. European traders could once more have come into the Niger and bought land for wharves and warehouses, and perhaps creamed off the kernel trade. Worse still, the system of trade through the African middlemen could have been introduced once more, with the Brass and New Calabar men paying no taxes whatsoever. In addition the small individual traders from Lagos and Freetown would have been able to return. At the same time the Niger Company, saddled with the costs of the administration and debarred from profiting from the revenues, would have been placed in an unenviable position.

Macdonald's report on the Niger Company's administration was received at the Foreign Office in the middle of January

1890. The time had now arrived to make decisions both on this report, and on his first report on the future administration of the Oil Rivers, which had been put by to await the final completion of Macdonald's missions. The new regime in the Oil Rivers was the most urgent question, and it was tackled first. Progress was slow, partly because Macdonald spent much of the year in Berlin discussing the delimitation of the Oil Rivers–Cameroons boundary, and partly because his recommendation for a Crown colony raised the problem of Colonial Office acceptance of the scheme, and the even more difficult question of the abolishment of African slaveholding, opposed by all the Oil Rivers chiefs. The once-favoured charter was scarcely discussed; Lister thought it 'hardly worthy of consideration' now.[1] Macdonald finally modified his original proposal. A Crown colony could be established 'when the way has been prepared by an administration resembling that of a colony in that all the officials shall be directly servants of the Crown, but without the cumbersome machinery.' His idea was to establish a vigorous administration, under the control of the Foreign Office, whose task would be one of pioneer development. He cast aside with contempt the previous attitudes of reluctance to accept responsibility. The new regime, by taxing the liquor trade, would have a large revenue, and could really govern and administer. It should establish a capital in the interior, and set about achieving the social reforms necessary if the place was to become a colony. He dismissed Goldie's view that the administration should interfere as little as possible in the internal affairs of the African states as absurd; human sacrifice and the murder of twins were 'native institutions'. Such barbarities needed 'more or less despotic' interference to put an end to them. Macdonald's willingness to extend the sphere of administration to bear directly on African social life marks a new departure and a new view of the purpose of British rule in West Africa. The concept of development, social as well as economic, was one which was to have increasing influence in the succeeding decades. Macdonald's view was

[1] FO 84/2083 conf. mema. by Lister and Macdonald, printed and filed at 1.7.90, but probably written in March 1890.

accepted, and he began to draw up detailed plans for a constabulary modelled on that of the Niger Company, for a revenue system, public works, marine and public health departments.[1] Finally, on 1 January 1891, Macdonald was appointed 'Her Majesty's Commissioner and Consul-General' for what was soon to become the Niger Coast Protectorate. He could not have achieved a more thorough acceptance of his recommendations than to be asked personally to implement them.

His appointment marks a turning point not only in the history of the Niger Company, but in the whole story of the late-Victorian chartered companies in Africa. Until now the Government, limited by its inability to obtain money from Parliament for colonial ventures, and reluctant itself to accept responsibilities, had looked on the chartered company almost as a panacea for all ills. For the first time it had been found impossible, after a decision had been made provisionally to do so, to use the chartered company as a method of delegating authority. In the process the illusory nature of the theory that the Government somehow escaped responsibility by delegation of power to a company was demonstrated yet again. In the next few years this point was to be brought home forcibly by the bankruptcy of the Imperial British East Africa Company and by the ill-fated Jameson Raid conducted by the British South Africa Company. There would be no more charters in Africa.

For the Niger Company Macdonald's appointment was of even greater particular significance. Goldie had often argued the superiority of the chartered company form of administration, of running the administration by officials with a long experience of trade, of a commercial system of promotions more flexible than the seniority rules of government agencies, of uniting trade and government as a total system of economic and political pressures. He had attacked the idea of interference in the internal politics of African states. He had claimed a special insight into the problems of ruling Africans who were especially addicted to trade and commerce. The new Oil Rivers administration, ruling an area essentially similar to the palm oil region

[1] FO 84/2019 Macdonald to Salisbury 15.12.90.

of the company's territories, was now to provide a yardstick with which to measure the progress of the company's sphere. Two systems were to be tested in practice, monopoly or free trade, indirect or direct methods of government.

What of Macdonald's other recommendations, those which would have broken the monopolistic structure which Goldie had built up since the charter had been granted in 1886? Was not the company in danger of losing its very life-blood, without which it could scarcely continue to trade profitably, let alone compete with a rival administration? Of this the Government was aware. To destroy the monopoly was to destroy the charter, and the alternative was the establishment of another area of direct rule by the Foreign or Colonial Office. The Government was not yet ready for this. The lull in foreign activity on the Niger since 1886 had rather obscured basic reality, the Foreign Office was indulging its fancy in the belief that Goldie's company would obligingly perform its work of preserving the Niger for Britain, but could at the same time be reformed and controlled. In 1889 this illusion began to be dispelled by renewed pressure, this time from France, which Goldie was able to utilize to make it clear that the price of his fulfilment of imperial designs was the continuance of the monopoly. Macdonald's recommendations were shelved and forgotten, the company remained unreformed. Goldie was left, as before, in absolute control, unhampered, to fulfil the company's imperial mission. To leave the monopoly intact was also to leave many basic problems unsolved, and to allow old grievances to fester. Opposition to Goldie mounted in intensity, uniting, now that the idea of a charter for the Oil Rivers was abandoned, all the economic interests in the region, from the meanest Lagos hawker who could scribble out a letter to Whitehall to the wealthiest Liverpool merchant or shipowner. And behind the scenes the men of Brass and New Calabar, their trade dwindling month by month until their very food supply was in danger, were storing up anger and hatred, collecting weapons, and plotting for the day of revenge against the company that had ruined them by taking away their markets.

8

'Giving away Mountains and Rivers and Lakes . . .'

UNTIL about 1889 or 1890 almost all the energies of Goldie's company had been concentrated on warding off the attacks of foreign and domestic critics of the company's monopolistic regime. There had been no direct attempt by a foreign power to obtain territory inside the company's sphere, or even in regions near by, since the issue of the charter. In this respect the Niger region had been somewhat exceptional, for the European powers had already begun their scramble to divide up the African continent. Britain and Germany had established chartered companies in East Africa, each trying to forestall the other in controlling the great lakes of the interior. France and King Leopold's Congo State had been similarly engaged in the regions around the Congo and its tributaries. By 1888 a serious struggle was taking place between the Portuguese and Rhodes' British South Africa Company on the borders of Mozambique. Even in West Africa there were minor scrambles along the short boundaries where French and British territories touched each other. Yet Goldie had little to fear from foreigners in these early years. He controlled the mouth of the Niger and could prevent all access to the interior through it. Expansion along the coast would be at the expense of Lagos or the Oil Rivers, which protected the flanks each side of the Niger mouth. Aggression from the interior was not likely, for the French advancing from Senegal had scarcely reached Timbuktu, those in Porto Novo were pinned to the coast by the powerful independent African kingdom of Dahomey, and Algeria was a far-away colony with no real influence on the Sahara. Nor were the Germans in the Cameroons much to be feared, for all their attempts to move inland had been forced back by disease or difficult terrain, or hostility from the fierce peoples of the interior.

Nevertheless intelligent British observers, Goldie included, could discern by 1889 that the era of tranquillity was passing. In most of South, Central, and East Africa rough frontiers had already been drawn and would soon be defined in international agreements. Diplomatically the most striking fact about the carving up of these regions had been the total exclusion of France from the mainland; only on the island of Madagascar did she maintain a foothold. The growing body of French opinion which favoured expansion in Africa, and whose members had already begun to occupy responsible posts in the Foreign and Colonial ministries, did not fail to notice this fact, and to resent it. The French were also aware that once the boundary lines had been drawn south of the Equator, international rivalry would inevitably gravitate northwards. For this, the expansionists argued, France must be prepared. She must seize her opportunity to dominate the northern half of the continent before the Germans and British elbowed her out of this, the last great tract of Africa as yet unexpropriated by Europe. From her existing bases France must strike boldly to the heart of the Sahara, joining Algeria, Senegal, the Ivory Coast, Porto Novo and Gabun into one vast extension of France in Africa, soon to be covered with a network of railways. The 'trans-Saharan dream' soon became a basic axiom of the French colonial group's thinking. The greatest obstacle to the dream appeared to be the somewhat enigmatic Englishman Sir George Goldie. It was he who had bought out the struggling French Niger companies in 1884; he who had prevented international control of the Niger at Berlin; he who had been entrusted by a British Government, which appeared to support him against all critics, with the extension of British influence in West Africa. His company already claimed to control countries on the edge of the Sahara, farther inland than any other British West African colony.

The French Government and Foreign Ministry could sympathize with the strategic thinking which lay behind the trans-Saharan plans of the expansionists. But like their British counterparts they had to think of the cost. Already expenditure on the Senegal railway had been appallingly high, and the idea of a rapid link-up with Algeria was too grandiose to be entertained seriously. If the plan was to be achieved it must be done gradually, and the English advance prevented by diplomatic means. The obvious answer was to begin negotiations to fix a limit to British expansion, particularly by the Niger Company.

In reality the British were very willing to come to such an agreement. It had been the aim of British policy since the 1870's to prevent a scramble for territory in West Africa by drawing a line north of which the French could be left free to develop Senegal and the upper Niger, and south of which British trade would reign supreme on the 'open door' principle. An agreement now could prevent the approaching struggle for the interior of the Niger and Benue basins, where the Niger Company was in fact very weakly established, besides saving a good deal of expense for the colonies of the Gold Coast, Sierra Leone and the Gambia, and even Lagos, which might have to look to her western frontiers.

The prospects for such an agreement were particularly hopeful in that neither power held any effective authority in the interior itself. If a line could be drawn some way between the regions where each power held sway, then each side could claim it as a diplomatic triumph which secured several thousand square miles of 'unoccupied' territory. The task of each side was thus to establish a claim on paper to as much of the Sudanic region as possible, so that the delimiting line could be drawn as far away from the areas already under effective rule as possible. It is clear that here, the British, who might at first seem to have been under a disadvantage in their dependence on a chartered company to secure their claims, showed much greater skill than the French, whom they completely misled. This triumph was in large measure the result of brilliant tactical manœuvres by Goldie, who was able to produce, on paper, such an account of the Niger Company's authority that Lord Salisbury was able to persuade the French to accept with alacrity an agreement which, they were soon to discover, was based on a complete misunderstanding of the effective power of the company.

The process of misleading the French had begun in 1889, when the British negotiators in Paris had offered to draw a line running from the sea up the tenth parallel of latitude to longitude four degrees west, then turning north-east in a straight line to Burrum on the Niger. Such a line would not only have excluded the French from the hinterlands of Sierra Leone and the Gold Coast, but would have prevented their advance beyond Timbuktu, and extended the Niger Company's sphere a good five hundred miles north-west of Nupe. The interesting thing is that this claim, though not accepted, was not dismissed by the French as utterly absurd. The myth of the Niger Company's extensive authority had been established. The French, however, were cautious, and the final agreement of 10 August 1889 was confined to the settlement of outstanding commercial and boundary questions near the coast, in particular defining the frontier between Lagos and Porto Novo up to the ninth degree of latitude.[1] The Niger Company's sphere was thus left open. 'The Niger Company will have to protect the Central Niger and the rear of Lagos,' Sir Percy Anderson wrote on the draft agreement. 'They are aware of this.'[2] The company had emerged once more as an agent for imperial defence and expansion.

In the breathing space which was now available before negotiations with France on a more comprehensive agreement could begin, Sir Percy Anderson began to put pressure on Goldie to expand the company's treaty area in order to forestall the French. The central portion of the Niger, across which the line would be drawn, was controlled by two groups of African

[1] The full negotiations can be followed in FO 84/1950 and FO 84/1951 (despatches from Lytton and Egerton in Paris). For the final text see Hertslet, *Map of Africa*, Vol. II, pp. 728–36.
[2] FO 84/1951 minute by H.P.A. on Egerton's, no. 88, Af. 27.6.89.

states; one subject to the Emirate of Gandu, and the other loosely known as the Borgu empire, about which practically nothing was known. Anderson was worried at the vagueness of the Niger Company's rights in this area, and pressed Goldie in the strongest terms to take action to reinforce such treaties as were already in existence, and to make more if necessary.[1] Goldie was quick to see that here was an opportunity to point out the renewed dependence of the Government on his company, and to resist the demand for reforms made by Macdonald. In a subtle way Goldie pointed out that if the company was to perform its imperial work properly, it must be given freedom to control its revenues and expenditure. The company's present weakness in Borgu, Goldie argued, was due to the fact that he had postponed action there to save administrative expenditure because of the 'grudging way' the Foreign Office had dealt with the company's budget. He had not intended to take action until signs of aggression from another power made it necessary. He presumed from Anderson's notes that the time had now come, and promised to telegraph instructions at once to the Niger.[2] Thus he made it clear that if the Foreign Office wanted co-operation, then it must be prepared to pay the price by allowing the company to increase taxes. Anderson seems not to have dissented from this view.

Goldie now proceeded to act on Anderson's warnings. His theory was that the south-western banks of the central Niger were ruled by Borgu, and the north-eastern by states subject to Gandu. With each of these the company already possessed treaties, but Goldie admitted that they conferred only commercial rights of monopoly, and would provide a poor basis for a claim to political jurisdiction.[3] What Goldie called Borgu was a particularly important place. Goldie was under the mistaken impression that Bussa, which controlled the famous rapids where Mungo Park had lost his life, was in fact the capital of Borgu. This was a mistake which was later to cause him a great deal of

---

[1] Anderson's notes to Goldie were written privately, and not filed in the Foreign Office archives. Fortunately, however, Goldie's replies were. See FO 84/1997 Goldie to Anderson 17.6.89, from which the gist of Anderson's letter is deduced.

[2] *Ibid.* Goldie to Anderson 18.6.89.   [3] *Ibid.* same to same 17.6.89.

difficulty,[1] for Bussa was actually merely one of the states which made up the curious Borguan federation. Nevertheless, in 1889, Goldie was right to stress its importance, for if Bussa could be controlled then French expeditions could not sail up the Niger into the interior claiming transit rights under the Berlin Act, for they would have to land here, and tranship cargo and passengers, thereby making themselves subject to the company's laws and regulations. An expedition was therefore sent out to negotiate a new treaty with the King of Bussa. This was accomplished by Will Lister, a European, assisted by an African interpreter, in January 1890. The new treaty was clearly political in its content, and gave the company the right to establish a protectorate. The King granted the company full and complete jurisdiction over all persons not born in Bussa, including the right to tax them, and agreed to place his country 'if and when called upon to do so by the Company, under the protection of the flag of Great Britain'. In return the company promised to admit foreigners to trade, providing they paid such taxation as was necessary. The King was to receive annually a subsidy of fifty bags of cowries in goods at local prices. The treaty was signed by Lister and the African interpreter, but the King, his eldest son, and two officials, the *Eyusu* and the *Sarkin Ruwa* merely made crosses. There was also an Arabic signature of a witness.[2] The treaty has some strange features. Would the King sign away these rights for fifty bags of cowries? It is scarcely conceivable that neither the King, his son, or the two court officials, were incapable at least of scrawling out an Arabic signature. If so the pedagogic talents of the local *mallams* must have been sadly inadequate. Nevertheless, with this document the company had a claim to Bussa. The French had nothing, true or false.

Having established a claim to the south-western banks of the

---

[1] See Chap. 10, p. 220.

[2] FO 2/167 treaties between the R.N.C. and native chiefs, Pt. 1, 1891–8, p. 53. Treaty with Borgu. Printed in Hertslet, *Map of Africa*, Vol. I, pp. 128–9. Note that Hertslet's printing gives the Arabic signature of the witness as *Gila*. The copy in the F.O. archives gives an imitation of the Arabic letters, which somewhat resemble GILA in Roman letters!

central Niger, Goldie now had to reinforce the company's
claims to the north-eastern banks, supposedly under the sway of
Gandu. If a treaty was to be made with the Emir of Gandu, then
one must also be made with the Sultan of Sokoto, his religious
superior. Early in 1890 the company dispatched David Ashford
King, an African from Sierra Leone, to visit these rulers. This
in itself was peculiar. In 1885 the company had found it
necessary to employ one of the most famous living explorers,
Joseph Thomson, fitted out with a large expedition and expensive presents, to accomplish this same task. Now the company
was to be represented at the court of the *Sarkin Musulmi* (Commander of the Faithful) by a 'black kafir'.[1] The documents
which King brought back after his journey were equally
curious. They purported to be treaties made in April with both
Gandu and Sokoto. Each was identically worded, and claimed
to be a 'literal translation' of originals in Arabic:

> Be it known that I, Malike, King of Gandu ['Umoru, King of the
> Mussulmans' in the Sokoto treaty] am desirous of introducing Euro-
> pean trade in all parts of my dominions, so as to increase the pros-
> perity of my people, and knowing that this cannot be effected except
> by securing to foreigners the protection of European government,
> with power of exercising jurisdiction over foreigners, as is the custom
> with them; also with the power of levying taxes upon foreigners as
> may be necessary for the exercise and support of this jurisdiction: I,
> Malike, King of Gandu [Umoru, King of the Mussulmans of the Sou-
> dan] with the consent and advice of my council, agree and grant to
> the Royal Niger Company (Chartered and Limited), formerly
> known as the 'National African Company (Limited)', full and com-
> plete power and jurisdiction over all foreigners visiting and residing
> in any part of my dominions. I also grant to you jurisdiction and full
> rights of protection over all foreigners, also power of raising taxes of
> any kind whatsoever from such foreigners.
>
> No person shall exercise any jurisdiction over such foreigners nor
> levy any tax whatsoever on such foreigners than the Royal Niger
> Company (Chartered and Limited).
>
> These grants I make for myself, my heirs, and successors, and
> declare them to be unchangeable and irrevocable for ever.
>
> I further confirm the treaty made with me with the National

---

[1] Religious intolerance against 'kafirs' (infidels) in the Fulani Empire was tem-
pered only by racial snobbery and a sense of kinship with 'white' men.

African Company (Limited)—now known as the 'Royal Niger Company (Chartered and Limited)'—in the month of June, according to European reckoning, 1885.

Dated at Gandu [Wurnu] this 7th [15th] day of April 1890.[1]

These 'treaties' bore no signatures of the rulers, who were both literate, nor did David King sign for the company. The Sokoto document was not sealed with the Imperial Seal of the Chancery, as was normal in such cases. The rulers were to be paid no subsidy in return for their concessions. At first sight one might believe that these were simple forgeries, concocted in the London office. Yet to postulate this only deepens the mystery, for if Goldie had wanted to forge treaties, he would surely have done the job properly, with signatures, the Sokoto seal, and all. In any case this was a dangerous expedient, for had the French later succeeded in obtaining genuine treaties with real signatures the fraud would be exposed, doubt would be cast on all the company's treaties, and a scramble might begin in what had hitherto been accepted as the company's treaty area. It seems likely therefore that the company deliberately chose to send an African like King, who could simply be told to get the treaties as best he could. If the treaties were later proved forgeries, then the blame could be laid at the door of a 'disreputable coloured agent', as had been done with the Benue treaties investigated by Macdonald. Yet here too, if the company's treaties were open to suspicion, those of the French were non-existent. It was in the public exploitation of these claims, not in the exercise of the rights conferred by them, that Goldie was to display the value of his company as an imperial agent.

New negotiations with France were precipitated by the conclusion of the Anglo-German Agreement of July 1890—the famous Heligoland Treaty. In return for the British cession of the North Sea island of Heligoland, which controlled the approaches to the Kiel Canal, Germany willingly settled all

[1] FO 84/2171 R.N.C. to F.O. 20.7.91 with encs. Printed in Herslet, *Map of Africa*, Vol. I, pp. 129–30.

outstanding disputes with Britain in East Africa. British claims to Uganda were recognized, Germany ceded the Witu enclave which had lain awkwardly inside the British East Africa Company's sphere, and allowed Britain to establish a protectorate over Zanzibar. This in itself was enough to arouse French hostility, for in 1862 Britain and France had solemnly agreed to maintain the independence of the Sultan of Zanzibar. All the resentments of the French colonial party at their exclusion from East Africa could thus focus on this issue. What really alarmed them, however, were the clauses of the Heligoland Treaty which referred to West Africa. After settling the frontiers of German Togoland, and the boundary between the Cameroons and the British protectorate of the Niger Districts up to the Benue River, the treaty went on to establish free transit of each other's goods between the Benue and Lake Chad, and provided for the notification of all treaties made by either power in this region to the other.[1] These stipulations seemed to imply a clear intention to partition the Bornu and Chad regions, where lay the focus for any linking of French colonies in North, Equatorial and West Africa. The French colonial party threw itself into a panic, the press was full of complaints of an Anglo-German plot to squeeze France out of the rest of Africa, and Goldie was credited with the most wildly expansionist plans; Francois Deloncle writing in the *Siècle* gloomily prophesied a huge British territory extending from the Niger to Abyssinia. There must be no more betrayals like that of 1884 which had allowed this aggressive Englishman to buy out the French Niger companies. The French Government must force the British to come to some agreement which would allow France to achieve the trans-Saharan dream.[2] All this was of course a complete over-estimate of the Niger Company's power, but one which Goldie deliberately fostered. At the annual general meeting of the company in July, Lord Aberdare's speech was calculated to alarm the French further. He announced the conclusion of the new treaties with Bussa, Gandu and Sokoto, claiming that they

[1] Hertslet, *Map of Africa*, Vol. III, pp. 899–906.
[2] *République Française* 10.7.90; *Le Siècle* 10.7.90.

gave the company complete jurisdiction up to the Sahara. Aberdare advised France to accept defeat, and to turn her energies to the development of Senegal and the western Sudan, not wasting her energies in a futile attempt to prevent the inevitable expansion of the company over Bornu, Wadai, and Darfur to its eventual goal, the Nile.[1] This was language calculated to rush the French into negotiations. A few days before, on the evening of 24 July, the French ambassador, M. Waddington, had called on Lord Salisbury and asked him to accept a straight line drawn from Say on the Niger to Lake Chad as the southern boundary of the Algerian hinterland, France was in return to recognize the lands to the south of it as part of the British protectorate. But Salisbury denied that Say was the limit of the company's authority on the Niger, and asked for time to consult Goldie. Actually Waddington had come so ill-prepared that he mistook the line on his map which represented Mungo Park's last journey as the Niger Company's boundary, but Salisbury was too polite to say so.[2] When Goldie was consulted the next day, he insisted that any line should clearly assign all the countries dependent on Sokoto to the company, that the line should not start at Say in the Niger, but at Gogo or Burrum, three hundred miles farther up the river. France should 'positively engage not to interfere politically in any way south of that line.'[3] When Lord Salisbury saw Waddington again on 28 July he pressed all these claims. The ambassador protested energetically, alleging that this left France 'nothing but the desert', a phrase which was to have an unhappy sequel for him. He urged the British Prime Minister to sign an agreement at once 'without paying attention to these pretensions', and straightway produced drafts in which Britain recognized a French protectorate over Madagascar and accepted the Say–Chad line. But Salisbury would not be hurried, and insisted that he would have to consult the Niger Company again, arguing that he was 'bound by their charter'. On 30 July

[1] Speech of Lord Aberdare at the A.G.M. of the R.N.C. 29.7.90; see also FO 84/2087 Goldie to F.O. 22.7.90, and same to same 24.7.90.
[2] FO 84/2029 Salisbury to Lytton, no. 5, Af. telegraphic, 24.7.90.
[3] FO 84/2087 Goldie to Anderson, private, 25.7.90.

Waddington and Salisbury met again. Salisbury now said that the company was willing to accept Say as the starting point of the line provided that the line was deflected to include all the Sokoto empire in the company's sphere. After 'some discussion' Waddington agreed to deflect the Say–Chad line 'as to include in the zone of the Niger Company all that fairly belongs to the Kingdom of Sokoto', the precise line to be left to a boundary commission to work out in detail, it being understood that the line would curve to the north to include Sokoto. This understanding was embodied in a formal declaration which also recognized the French protectorate over Madagascar, and was signed on 5 August 1890.[1]

The declaration was quite a triumph of diplomatic skill for Salisbury. The French had been completely outwitted. In their haste to prevent further 'expansion' by the Niger Company they had failed to make the challenge of which they were capable. Waddington did not even ask to see the texts of the company's new 'treaties' with Gandu and Sokoto, which neither he nor Salisbury had ever seen, still less realized to be unsigned. No Frenchman had visited the Niger since 1884, so the ambassador was naturally unaware of the weak state of the company's rule in the north. The struggle for the line was meaningless from the British point of view; Say or Gogo, both were miles outside any territory over which the company had the remotest influence. Salisbury was aware of all this, and found it amusing. At a Mansion House dinner the day after the signing of the declaration he could not resist letting the cat out of the bag:

We have been engaged in drawing lines upon maps where no white man's foot has ever trod; we have been giving away mountains and rivers and lakes to each other, only hindered by the small impediment that we never knew exactly where the mountains and rivers and lakes were.[2]

As for the English imperialists who had the effrontery to reproach him with conceding too much, he asked them to

[1] FO 84/2029 telegrams to Lytton, nos. 6 and 7, 28.7.90 and 30.7.90. Full text in Hertslet, *Map of Africa*, Vol. II, pp. 738–9.
[2] Quoted in Lady G. Cecil, *Life of Robert, Marquis of Salisbury*, Vol. IV, p. 323.

remember that what he had given away was 'what agricul-
turalists would call "light" land'. Poor Waddington now began
to see that he had been bamboozled:

'No doubt the Sahara is not a garden,' he wrote to Salisbury a few
days later, 'and contains, as you say, much "light" land; but your
public reminder of the fact was, perhaps you will allow, hardly
necessary. You might well have left us to find it out.'[1]

Had Salisbury restrained himself, the French colonial group
would not have had long to wait to 'find it out'. In fact the
Anglo-French Declaration caught them on the wrong foot,
cutting right across plans which they had already set in motion
to force their Government's hand in extending French influence
on the Niger and Benue. Dissatisfied with official policy, the
French expansionists had concluded that the only way to obtain
results was to imitate Goldie's tactics, and to reconstitute the
vague 'colonial party' as more than just a political and jour-
nalistic pressure group. The organizer was Percher, the editor of
the *Journal des Débats*, better known by his pen name, Harry Alis.
Its object was the achievement of the trans-Saharan link-up by
securing the Sokoto-Chad-Bornu region by means of privately
organized and financed missions, which could later be legalized
by the setting up of chartered companies on the model of
Goldie's company.[2] As early as March, 1890, this group of merchants, journalists and humanitarians had raised enough money
to send off Crampel to Brazzaville with orders to ascend the
Ubangi River to Lake Chad, so as to cut off the Niger Company's
approach from the Benue. Crampel arrived on the coast five
days after the signature of the declaration. At the same time it
had been decided to send an expedition up the Niger and Benue

[1] *Ibid.* quoted p. 324.
[2] By a law of 1854 chartered companies were illegal in France, and this was a
serious impediment to this policy. In 1891 the colonial group managed to obtain a
full investigation of the legal questions involved, and after reports which singled out
the Niger Company as the greatest of the English chartered companies by reason of
its territorial expansion and financial profitability, a *projet de loi* was introduced to
repeal the law of 1854, and allow chartered companies under certain conditions.
Nevertheless the French never found it necessary to resort to this technique of
administration, presumably because the state was always willing to establish direct
machinery of government.

claiming the transit privileges of the Berlin Act, so as to see whether the 'free' waterway could be used to obtain access to Lake Chad, and this task was entrusted to an experienced explorer of the Congo, Lieutenant Mizon. A special company was formed to finance this expedition; the *Syndicat française du Haut Benito*. A third arm of this triple assault on Lake Chad was entrusted to the famous explorer Monteil, who left Senegal in October 1890, intending to reach Chad via Say on the Niger, Sokoto, and Kano. In November the metropolitan organization of the movement was completed with the establishment of the *Comité de l'Afrique française*, with Harry Alis as its secretary, and a membership including the explorer Binger, the under-secretary of state for the colonies Etienne, and numerous merchants, journalists, geographical societies and members of the *Société Antiesclavagiste*.[1]

Each of these expeditions was clearly aimed against the Niger Company, but the Anglo-French Declaration of August 1890 tied the hands of the French explorers. Monteil could not now make treaties after he left Say, for he would then be south of the Say–Barruwa line. Similarly Mizon, if he was to respect the Declaration, could not play politics on the Benue, and Crampel would have to keep away from the southern shores of Lake Chad. Thus the French, in their anxiety to protect 'the hinterland of Algeria' from the 'aggressive' Niger Company had only succeeded in limiting their own capabilities for expansion at Goldie's expense.

On the other hand the Mizon expedition remained a formidable challenge to the Niger Company. Who could say what a well-armed band of Frenchmen would do if, once inside the company's sphere, they began to think in terms of 'effective occupation' or to intrigue with discontented Africans? Moreover Mizon, by claiming rights under the Berlin Act, resurrected the ghost of economic competition and threatened the monopoly itself. If he could establish himself in those Benue emirates which Macdonald had judged to be independent, than all the prob-

---

[1] Hanotaux and Martineau, *Histoire des Colonies françaises*, Tome IV, pp. 437–53. See also *Le Siècle* 28.8.90; *Débats* 28.8.90; *Le Temps* 11.9.90.

lems which Herr Hoenigsberg had presented in Nupe would be recreated on a greater scale.

Mizon was a bold and direct fellow. He knew that by the Berlin Act navigation of the Niger was free, and he wished to know no more. He sailed straight up the Forcados entrance to the Niger with twenty-five armed men, in the steam launch *René Caillé*, a Hotchkiss cannon mounted in the bows. He saw no reason to inform the Niger Company of his arrival. Unfortunately the Patani tribes resented his presence even more than did Sir George Goldie, and they fell upon the Frenchmen on the night of 15 October 1890, wounding Mizon, his interpreter, and most of the Africans in the expedition. When an official of the Niger Company arrived next day the Frenchmen were forced to permit him to take them in tow to Akassa to get medical help. Agent-General Flint was there to admonish them for entering by the wrong mouth of the Niger, failing to obtain clearance at Akassa, and failing to obtain the company's permission to enter the Niger Territories. When Goldie received the news in a cable from Flint he immediately telegraphed in reply:

Foreign explorers (evidently dangerous order) cannot penetrate territory without previous consent council. You must leave navigation free but prevent touching anywhere territory.[1]

Flint thereupon told Mizon that the expedition could only continue on condition that it did not land or touch at any of the river banks.[2] This was of course practically a prohibition, for if the party could not land to buy food and fuel then they would not get far. Mizon therefore telegraphed to Paris, asking that the French Government intervene. The Foreign Ministry protested to Britain that the Niger Company's action was contrary to the

[1] FO 84/2093 R.N.C. to F.O. 21.10.90 inc. Flint to R.N.C. tel., n.d.
[2] There are numerous accounts of the Mizon mission written from the French point of view. Hanotaux and Martineau, *Histoire des Colonies françaises*, etc., Tome IV, pp. 486–92 treats the subject in some detail. There is a useful article, unfortunately based entirely on French sources, by M. J. Chauveau, entitled 'Mizon à Yola', in *Revue d'histoire des colonies*, Vol. XLI (1954), pp. 227–44. A valuable French source, overlooked by Chauveau, is Mizon's own account, published as a special supplement to *Le Temps* of 10.8.92. I have also used *Débats* 9.4.91 and *Débats* 27.12.90 both of which print correspondence between Mizon and Harry Alis, the editor.

Berlin Act, and Salisbury was assured that Mizon was engaged
on a 'purely scientific mission'.[1] Goldie was then told that he
must allow the expedition to proceed.[2] This he did grudgingly,
on condition that Mizon undertook to conform to the regulations; promised not to use his armaments until he had passed
Yola; and promised not to re-enter the Niger Territories without prior permission from the company. Mizon, when confronted with these terms, tried to quibble, but to all his questions
Agent-General Flint merely replied that he had better inquire at
the company's offices in Ludgate Hill, London, E.C. Faced with
such urbane stoicism, Mizon gave in, and signed the conditions.[3]

The expedition had already been delayed two months, ill-
luck now added more months of waiting, all but two of the
Europeans fell ill, one died and the rest were sent home. Then
an eccentric in the launch's engine broke and had to be sent to
Akassa to be repaired. Naturally the company's workmen did
not hurry over the job. Mizon used the time to look closer at the
company's administration, and began sending long reports to
Harry Alis which must have made the colonial group writhe at
their folly in overestimating the company's powers. Mizon also
struck up a friendship with El Hadj M'Ahmed, an influential
man from Khartoum employed by the Emir of Nupe in maintaining friendly relations with the Sultan of Sokoto. El Hadj was
soon entertaining the Frenchman with the story of the strained
relationships between the company and Nupe and discussing
the 'pretended' treaty with Sokoto. Realizing the man's value
as a witness, Mizon took him on as a member of the expedition.[4]

But Goldie also took the chance of profiting by the delay. He
had not been misled for one moment by the assurances that
Mizon's objects were 'scientific and commercial'. He had
immediately diagnosed a threat to Bornu, and leakages in the
French press in November confirmed this guess.[5] As soon as the

[1] FO 84/2028 Lytton to Salisbury, 158 Af. 16.11.90 inc. Ribot to Sutton 15.11.90.
[2] FO 84/2095 F.O. to R.N.C. 20.11.90 and 26.11.90.
[3] Ibid. R.N.C. to F.O. 27.11.90; FO 84/2096 Currie to Goldie, private, 5.12.90;
Chauveau, op. cit., pp. 231–2 and Temps supplement of 10.8.92.
[4] Temps supplement of 10.8.92.
[5] See the denial of this intention in Le Siècle 14.11.90, which reprints in full a
story from the Tablettes des deux Charentes.

news of Mizon's arrival in the Niger had been received, an
expedition had been organized under the Senior Executive
Officer for the Benue, Charles MacIntosh. It was the most formidable party which the company had yet dispatched on a
mission of this kind; two or three Europeans, with a strong
detachment of constabulary, fully armed, comprising a total
strength, with porters, of three hundred men. Within three
weeks of their departure from the Benue the expedition arrived
at Kukuwa, the capital of Bornu. At first they were well-
received by the Sheikh, who accepted their gifts, but MacIntosh
could make no headway in his attempts to negotiate a treaty.
Bornu, controlling the approaches to the Niger Territories from
the east, was a country with a long history which had been
dominated by the struggle to maintain the independence of the
country against the inroads of other Muslim powers both to the
east and westward. This tradition could be turned against the
European visitors by the Arab merchants who dominated Bornu
commerce, who had long been afraid that Europeans might by-
pass North Africa by using the Benue for trade with Bornu.
MacIntosh was met by 'two months of oriental dilly-dally',
after which the Sheikh breathed defiance. The presents were
returned, the treaty proposal rejected, and the Turkish flag
hoisted as a sign of his submission to that conveniently remote
power. If the Europeans wanted his country he invited them to
come and take it by force. Finally the Sheikh 'kindly conveyed
to Mr. MacIntosh a hint that a prolongation of his stay there
would be dangerous'—to quote Goldie's rather quaint description of the scene.[1] MacIntosh had failed, Goldie could only hope
that the Sultan's tender regard for his sovereignty would prevent the French from succeeding. Salisbury was not so optimis-
tic; 'They ought to have got a bit of writing promising that
the Sultan would not ally himself with any Western powers,'
he grumbled.[2]

Meanwhile MacIntosh returned to his post on the Benue.
Mizon was now ready to move on, his launch repaired and

[1] See *Morning Post* 9.6.91; *The Times* 14.9.91; FO 84/2252 Goldie to F.O. 8.6.91.
[2] FO 84/2174 minute by Salisbury on *The Times* cutting of 14.9.91.

sickness under control. MacIntosh took the precaution of escorting him through Muri country, so that the Frenchman would be kept clear of its recalcitrant Emir. Reaching Yola, Mizon at first was given a cool reception by the Emir, but later the potentate relaxed somewhat, gave houses to the French party, and allowed them to trade. They stayed four months, and in December 1891 left to join up with French posts recently established in the Sangha region to the south-east.

Goldie could be reasonably content with the way things had gone. Mizon, he knew from his district agent in Yola, had failed to make a treaty with the Emir, whatever he might claim later. Above all, the troublesome Frenchman had failed to get to Bornu or Lake Chad. In fact the ostentatious French pincer-movement seemed to be fizzling out by the end of 1891. In August it was confirmed that the Crampel mission, trying to reach Chad from the Gabun, had been wiped out by allies of a new adventurer from the east, Rabeh Zobeir. Monteil was in the Sokoto empire somewhere, but it seemed that he was merely collecting information; awkward perhaps, but not dangerous. There was time to relax.

If it seemed so, the illusion was shattered with Mizon's return to France. The Frenchman was ambitious, and made the most of his meagre achievements. The French expansionists were naturally not anxious to question his claim to have established a French protectorate over Yola and the surrounding country of Adamawa too closely. Mizon could count on the support of a large section of the press, and an influential social group, to publicize his exploits to the full. His return to France was accompanied by so much pomp and ceremony that the average Frenchman might have been forgiven for imagining that Mizon had conquered the whole continent of Africa single-handed. When he landed at Bordeaux he was met by a crowd of wildly excited people, and the great names of the colonial group, including Prince d'Arenberg, Admiral Vallon, Delcassé, and others, with representatives of all the Geographical and Colonial

Societies, paid their tribute as the explorer received the Officer-ship of the *Legion d'Honneur*. Etienne, in a speech of welcome, declared that Mizon had returned to add a new country, Adamawa, to the Fatherland, and publicly embraced the now famous Lieutenant. Arriving at the *Gare d'Orleans* in Paris Mizon was received with flags and bunting, and the crowd sang patriotic songs. He was now to be lionized by Parisian society, and Mizon, always accompanied by the devoted little African girl S'Nabou whom he was supposed to have rescued from her wicked parents, was the great catch for any hostess worthy of the name. There was a ceremonial banquet attended by the per-sonal representative of the President of the Republic, by Jules Ferry, Jamais the colonial under-secretary, Gabriel Hanotaux, and a host of others. In the course of the speeches, all of them hostile to Goldie and the Niger Company, Etienne let it be known that Mizon would shortly return to the Niger to develop the new French province of Adamawa.[1]

By August 1892 the preparations for his return were com-pleted. The Chamber had voted 100,000 francs, Baron de Rothschild subscribed 20,000 francs, and the *Comité de l'Afrique française* another 15,000 francs. Mizon also collected a quarter of a million francs worth of goods and merchandise for export to Adamawa from French commercial firms. The organization was completed by the floatation of the *Compagnie française de l'Afrique centrale*, the embryonic chartered company for Adama-wa, a body which was practically identical with the *Comité de l'Afrique française*.[2] The party was to consist of about a hundred men, all armed, to be carried in two vessels of twenty and eighty tons, each of which was armed with a four-pounder quick-firing cannon.[3]

Goldie may be forgiven for regarding the claim that this was a 'scientific and commercial' expedition as laughable. In his opinion it was a military and political expedition, and the ships could not therefore claim free transit as merchant vessels under

[1] *Le Temps* 23.6.92; *Débats* 24.6.92; *République Française* 6.7.92.
[2] *Politique Coloniale* 23.7.92; *Figaro* 7.8.92; *Débats* 8.8.92.
[3] FO 84/2209 Phipps to Anderson, private, 29.7.92.

the Berlin Act. Would the British Government support him in prohibiting access?[1] Unfortunately for him, it was an awkward time to ask. Salisbury could see Goldie's point, and found it difficult to imagine why Mizon required 'such apparatus of travel' as quick-firing cannon, but his Government was falling. The new Liberal Foreign Secretary, Lord Rosebery, was immediately involved in a fight with his little-Englander colleagues on the question of Uganda and the bankruptcy of the Imperial British East Africa Company, and could not afford to involve himself in another crisis concerning a chartered company. The Foreign Office dithered, Mizon was interviewed by the embassy in Paris, and the French Government gave solemn assurances that the mission was 'essentially commercial and scientific', and that Mizon would adhere scrupulously to the letter of the law.[2] To Goldie this was pure sophistry:

> If Mizon's own evidence has made one thing clear it is that no word that he says, no asservation however solemn, is worthy of any credence whatsoever, that he is one of those witnesses against whom no competent counsel would think it necessary to bring rebutting evidence but would be content to let him 'stand down' self-convicted as a contemptible liar. It is a waste of time even to consider what such a man asserts.[3]

Goldie disclaimed responsibility for 'the bloodshed and disorders which may only too probably result' if Mizon were allowed to proceed.[4] His fulminations were of no avail, Rosebery insisted that Mizon be allowed to proceed, and that the company's officials give him 'every facility'.[5] Goldie, it is true, interpreted this in a somewhat restricted sense. The officials were told that Mizon was a dangerous man, ready to destroy life and property and to incite the chiefs to murder and violence. The laws were to be coldly and rigidly enforced, and if he were to resist, force should be used against him. If Mizon, resisting, caused 'the death of the lowest Kruboy in the Company's

---

[1] FO 84/2253 Goldie to F.O. 12.7.92.

[2] FO 84/2209 Phipps to Anderson, private, 29.7.92; FO 84/2213 Waddington to Salisbury 10.8.92.

[3] FO 84/2209 Goldie to Hill, private, 16.8.92.

[4] FO 84/2257 Goldie to F.O. 15.8.92.   [5] *Ibid.* F.O. to R.N.C. 2 4.8.92.

service', he should be 'tried, convicted and executed for murder'. No official should 'permit any fear of making a mistake' to
paralyse his energy. Coal and wood, medical attention and
'bread alone' could be supplied if absolutely necessary.[1]

All this seemed a little extreme and ridiculous to the officials
in the Foreign Office. Yet for once Goldie's characteristic
extremism was nearer the truth than even he could have
imagined. At first all went well, Mizon cleared his vessels
properly at Akassa, was given fuel on his way up the Niger, and
went up the Benue in December. Then there was silence. It was
not until May 1893 that the truth of what Mizon had been doing
on the Benue broke sensationally in the French press. Goldie
had known what was afoot, but wisely kept silent, leaving Mizon
rope enough to hang himself.[2] The scandal broke when the
surgeon of the expedition, Dr. Henri Ward, five months after he
had returned to France through ill-health, gave an interview to
the journal *l'Intransigeant*. The story he told was perhaps the
most disgusting in the annals of European exploration of Africa,
surpassing the worst brutalities of Stanley or Karl Peters. Mizon
in Africa, said Ward, was a man that Paris knew nothing about
—'a vulgar careerist, without talent, without energy, who can
only make his way by trickery'. His sole aim was an official
appointment. In reality he had bungled the first mission, the
Emir of Yola had refused to sign a treaty, and given him forty-
eight hours to clear out of his town. Mizon dared not return.
Therefore he had deliberately run his ship aground in the Emir
of Muri's country, where he knew that the Emir was hostile to
the Niger Company. So that he could get a treaty from the
Emir of Muri, Mizon agreed to use his party to help the Emir
catch slaves. Three weeks after signing a treaty with the Emir in
1892, Mizon had agreed, on Christmas Day of all days, to
attack the pagan village of Kwana. From three hundred yards
Mizon had personally directed a barrage of thirty salvoes from
his quick-firing cannon against the walls of the village. The
French party then stormed the village, after which the Muri

[1] FO 84/2257 circular to agents and instructions to Wallace, the Agent-
General, enc. in R.N.C. to F.O. 25.8.92.
[2] This is revealed by FO 84/2266 R.N.C. to F.O. 16.12.92.

army joined them in putting it to the sack and destroying all the huts and houses. Those who could fled to the hills, leaving fifty dead and a hundred wounded. Two hundred and fifty women and children were rounded up and given as slaves to the Emir. More were forced by hunger to come down from the hills and give themselves up about a week later. These too were enslaved. The Emir was so pleased that he offered Mizon his choice of the women; he accepted two girls aged twelve and thirteen for his Arab servant, and a little girl of eight for the amusement of S'Nabou.

'You will remember perhaps,' said Ward, 'that at the Mizon banquet Prince d'Arenberg, alluding to the candidature of Stanley in England, said these words: "If our compatriot Mizon were to take it into his head to present himself as a candidate—for Adamawa" (added he smiling), "one would not have to ask him as they asked Stanley: How many niggers have you killed in Africa?"'

'One may ask him that now.'

Dr. Ward went on to say that he had decided to make all this public to deliver the other Europeans in the party from Mizon's power. Nebout, the second in command, had written begging him to do so, if not he had determined to commit suicide.[1]

The colonial group did its best to hush the whole thing up; the French Colonial Office asked all newspapers to suppress the story, but the radical press refused to be muzzled. The imperialist papers kept an angry silence, but the editor of *La Libre Parole* could not restrain himself, forsook his pen for a pistol, and in a duel with Ward shot him in the knee—'a curious commentary on the title of the newspaper', as Goldie drily remarked.[2]

Goldie's dark warnings had thus been amply justified. Mizon could hardly have found another crime to commit; he had made treaties in the British sphere contrary to the Anglo-French Declaration of 1890; he had disobeyed his instructions, broken

[1] *L'Intransigeant* 5.5.93. See also *Memorandum on French Slave-Raiding in British Territory*, June 1893 by Goldie, enclosed in FO 83/1240 R.N.C. to F.O. 25.5.93. Articles written later in defence of Mizon, both by the explorer himself and by Harry Alis, agree on the facts of this account, but argue that Mizon's assistance of the Emir was merely aid in fulfilment of the protectorate treaty, and that the enslavement of captives could not be avoided under local customs.

[2] FO 83/1240 Goldie to F.O. 25.5.93 with enclosures.

solemn pledges given by the French Government, made war inside a British protectorate, sold arms to Africans, and murdered, maimed and sold into slavery hundreds of British protected persons. Goldie assumed, rather naïvely, that Mizon would now be recalled, and claimed £100,000 as compensation for the victims.[1]

But the French political system was not as simple as he imagined. Though the Foreign Affairs Bureau admitted that Mizon's conduct was 'outrageous',[2] it took weeks of quibbling before he was officially recalled, and even when the Niger Company delivered to Mizon the letters recalling him, he refused to obey, alleging that they were forgeries.

Mizon's very ruthlessness also played into Goldie's hand on the Niger itself. The company's system of non-interference was calculated to demonstrate to the Emirs that they lost no real power by placing themselves under protection by a treaty with the Niger Company. Mizon's military way of doing things seemed to display French rule as a much more serious danger to their independence. Was it not preferable to place one's country under the rule of a trading company which excluded all foreigners, yet left the substance of power over Africans, before it was too late? Such was the Emir of Yola's reasoning. Early in February 1893 he wrote to William Wallace, at that time Senior Executive officer on the Benue:

There are some now in Muri country coming up here, we do not want them. None of the people in my country want to see them, and therefore I send you this letter. You can forward it to the Governor of your company and the Queen of all England. . . . From and after this, you are to know that I deliver to your sole protection all that portion of land belonging to Adamawa, upper and lower, in the River Benue, of my boundary. You are to see it protected from all quarrel that may come in to cause by any powers, not allowing any foreigners to come in without your consent.[3]

[1] *Ibid.* R.N.C. to F.O. 25.5.93.
[2] FO 27/3134 Phipps to Rosebery, 137 Af., 28,6.93.
[3] FO 27/3160 R.N.C. to F.O. 15.6.93 inc. Zubiru to Mai Gashi (i.e. Wallace, so nicknamed because of his generous moustachios) 20.2.93.

N

The time had obviously come for a treaty to be negotiated, a thing which the company had tried to do many times in the past, and always failed to achieve. District-Agent Spink arrived at Yola in May 1893. At first the Emir saw no reason to sign any 'book', having recently written to Wallace. When Spink insisted, the Emir, who appears to have regarded the act of composition as a sore duty, tried to give him a document already written. No, said Spink, he must sign a proper treaty form. The Emir then consulted his councillors and agreed to 'sign', sending for his *mallam* to do so. 'I asked him,' Spink reported, 'if he would not do the Company the honour of his own autograph.' The Emir, flattered, then signed. The treaty was on the standard printed 'Form Number 10 (Moslems)'. The Emir ceded 'for ever . . . the whole of my territory' giving 'full jurisdiction of every kind'. He promised to make no war, or have any relations, with any foreign state or tribe. The company promised to maintain free trade 'subject, however, to administrative dispositions in the interests of commerce and of order'. Nor would the company interfere with local laws or customs 'consistently with the maintenance of order and good government, and for the progress of civilisation'. The Emir would be protected from the attacks of neighbouring tribes, and was paid goods valued at one thousand bags of cowries, at once.[1] After signing the forms, the Emir made a speech which gives an indication of how he regarded what he had just done.

'Briefly it was this,' the District Agent reported: 'that we [the Company] would not permit our people to interfere with native women; that we would punish them if found stealing; that we would not employ runaway slaves; that we would not interfere in any way with the religious principles of himself and subjects; and that if any white man were to come and preach Christianity we would not permit him to remain in our stations. He had heard such men were in Nupe kingdom, and he would not permit them to remain in Adamawa country.'[2]

A month later Mizon and his party moved in to Yola, and a complicated struggle began between William Wallace and

[1] FO 27/3161 R.N.C. to F.O. 14.8.93 enc. Adamawa Treaty 7.5.93.
[2] *Ibid.* R.N.C. to F.O. 7.9.93 enc. report of Spink 30.5.93.

Mizon for the favour of the Emir, played out against a tense background of latent violence and threats. When the Frenchman arrived Wallace slipped quietly back to Muri, where he closed down two stations set up by the French, and confiscated the produce and goods left in them. Meanwhile Mizon succeeded in meeting the Emir several times, and presented him with two hundred pieces of silk, selling him forty rifles and two brass cannon, and set one of his servants to work drilling and instructing the Emir's troops. Such generosity did not go unrewarded, and on 25 August the Emir obligingly signed a treaty placing himself under French protection. An attempt by the Niger Company's men to arrest one of Mizon's ships for illegal trading was repulsed with armed resistance. Finally, on 22 September, Mizon sailed back down the Benue in one of his ships. The other, left as the French base in Yola, was promptly seized by Wallace, who quickly intimidated the agent in charge by threatening to hang him if he resisted. Mizon himself was allowed to go unmolested, he was even granted a safe conduct to visit Onitsha where he placed little S'Nabou, his child companion of three years, so beloved of the Paris salons, in the hands of the Catholic fathers. A few weeks later she gave birth to a son, remarkably light in complexion.[1]

The Emir of Yola was not the only interest to be alarmed at Mizon's activities in Adamawa. The Germans had long coveted the south-eastern part of that country, in fact the Heligoland Treaty gave them British recognition of their claims, though the frontier line did not pass beyond the Benue. But the Germans had no posts in the region, nor any treaties with African rulers. Numerous expeditions from the Cameroons coast since 1890 had all failed to penetrate the region, stopped either by hostile Africans, or disease. How easy the task would have been if only

[1] The above account of Mizon's second visit to Yola and his return is based on a very large number of press reports and official documents too numerous to specify individually. The largest single sources may be found in FO 27/3162, especially R.N.C. to F.O. 21.10.93 enc. Wallace's reports and 21 enclosures, and R.N.C. to F.O. 16.11.93 continuing this correspondence.

the Niger Company had co-operated and allowed German expeditions to sail up the Benue River and reach the heart of Adamawa in a few days!

This was the trump card which Goldie now prepared to play. It is no exaggeration to say that in doing so he assumed complete control of the negotiations with Germany on the Adamawa question; the British Foreign Office did his bidding down to the last detail, so that the Anglo-German Agreement which resulted in 1893 was in reality a treaty between Goldie and Germany. The experience profoundly affected Goldie himself. It took him into a new dimension, and made him aware of ambitions that had hitherto lain dormant. After this taste of diplomacy and statecraft Goldie was to find it difficult to fix his eye firmly on the company's balance sheets. He began to realize that he was making history, and to wonder what the historians would have to say about him. His policy began to change, and more and more he turned his mind to administration, rather than monopoly.

But this is to anticipate. In May 1893 Mizon was still on the Benue, there was every prospect of an international incident of the gravest kind occurring (if indeed worse could happen), and the British Foreign Office was somewhat abashed at the way Goldie's prophesies had materialized. Perhaps this had taught them to treat Goldie's advice with more respect. Consequently, when overtures came from Germany, Goldie was left alone to deal with them in his own way. Goldie's position was made easier by the emergence of a similar free-lance diplomat on the German side. Mizon's advance on Adamawa had alarmed the commercial and financial groups in Hamburg and elsewhere who had interests in the Cameroons, and who had already financed unsuccessful expeditions to Adamawa. They formed a committee for the protection of German interests in the Cameroons, and elected Herr Ernst Vohsen as its chairman. In April 1893 Vohsen wrote to Goldie asking him to allow a German expedition to pass up the Benue to Yola, and on to Ngaundere. Its purpose was to make treaties south of Yola to check the French, and particularly Mizon.[1] Goldie refused to arrange

[1] FO 64/1316 R.N.C. to F.O. 6.5.93 enc. Vohsen to Goldie 21.4.93.

anything by letter and asked Vohsen to come to London. In discussion the two men agreed on the conditions whereby German expeditions could ascend the Benue, and by September 1892, when Mizon arrived in Yola, Baron von Uechtritz and Dr. Passarge were in the town to provide valuable confirmatory evidence of the Frenchman's proceedings. In the meantime the Niger Company was able to save the life of Lieutenant von Stettin, who had succeeded after great privations in making his way overland from the Cameroons to Yola. In return Vohsen began to work up an agitation against Mizon in the German press.[1]

But Goldie took the discussions further. Could they not use their influence with their respective governments to bring about a partition of the region between Lake Chad and the Benue to the exclusion of France? He suggested a division giving Germany most of Adamawa and the territories east of Bornu as far as the Shari watershed. Thus the Niger Company would have no French territory on its borders between Lake Chad and the sea, though Goldie was not so naïve as to point this out to Vohsen. The German enthusiastically rushed off and put the scheme to the German Foreign Office. In July 1893 the negotiations began officially. The Germans admitted that they were in a great hurry, they were afraid of Mizon, and wanted to get orders out to the German expedition in Yola to make treaties in the sphere which might be allotted to Germany under any agreement.

There followed a certain amount of quibbling from the British side. The real trouble with the German offer, although it left Yola in the British sphere, was that the proposed boundary came too close to the town, on a part of the river which was fully navigable. It had always been a studied part of Goldie's policy never to allow foreigners to establish such a foothold. Such enclaves could be reached by river navigation and implied the prospect of foreign ships sailing freely up and down the rivers as they had a right to do under the Berlin Act. Goldie was also worried at what the Emir of Yola might think when he saw a frontier drawn 'almost within sight of his walls' so soon after the company had promised to protect him against foreign

[1] *Ibid.*, *loc. cit.* enclosures 2 and 3, correspondence with Vohsen.

aggression. Goldie therefore suggested Faro as the point on the Benue where the line up to Lake Chad should begin. The Germans, however, were intent on getting some of the navigable waterway, but they were willing to allay Goldie's fears of the Emir's wrath by leaving more land around Yola. Goldie on his side finally agreed to German access to the navigable waterway. The final solution was an intricate piece of armchair geography. With a fine disregard for natural features or ethnic considerations the point of a pair of compasses was placed on Yola, and with a radius five kilometres less than the distance from Yola to Faro, an arc was described to intersect the old Anglo-German boundary south of Yola and the Benue River to the east. Germany recognized that Yola and Bornu were British, and Britain recognized that the region east of Bornu as far as the watershed of the Shari River was German. After some hesitation Goldie also agreed to a clause in which both powers agreed to apply the relevant sections of the Berlin Act to the portions of the Benue under their control. In an exchange of notes the two powers agreed to use their influence with the chiefs in their respective spheres to restrain them from interference in the other's sphere; the Niger Company was to persuade the Emir of Yola to accept the boundary, whilst the Germans promised to maintain the allegiance of the chiefs in their sphere to the Emir of Yola, their suzerain.[1]

The real significance of this agreement, and the real triumph for Goldie, lay in the boundary arrangements. German recognition of the Niger Company's right to Yola and Bornu was in itself a considerable achievement, but the British *quid pro quo*, the recognition of Germany's claim to the region between Bornu and the Shari basin, was no sacrifice, it merely established a region claimed by Germany which the French would have to violate if they wished to challenge the Niger Company's position in the east. A convenient buffer had been set up. No doubt the Germans recognized this. They too had sacrificed nothing. Neither

[1] For full text see Hertslet, *Map of Africa*, Vol. III, no. 275, pp. 914 ff. Full documentation of each item on which the above account is based would be enormous. All are to be found in FO 64/1301–4 inclusive, and FO 64/1316–19 inclusive.

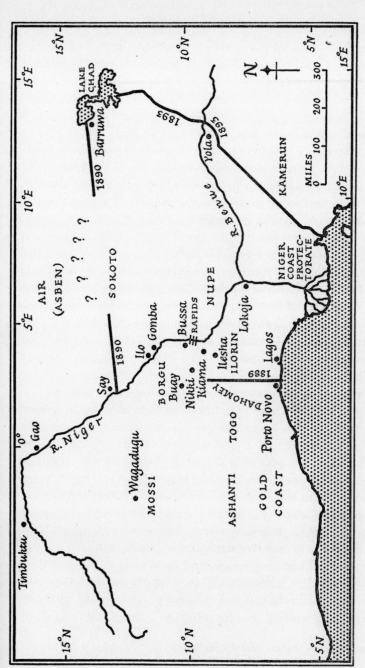

3. Frontiers of the Royal Niger Company's Territories 1893

power had the slightest claim to political rights, whether in Bornu or the Shari basin. Spoils are easy to divide if they have not yet been captured.

The Germans were not so foolish as to assume that France would accept the Anglo-German Agreement without protest. Indeed, it is perhaps no exaggeration to say that the object of the German Government in agreeing to Goldie's proposals had been to force France to negotiate with them. Within a week a French delegation was in Berlin, and soon the British intelligence system was reporting that the Germans were about to give France a part of their navigable stretch of the Benue, just what the Anglo-German Agreement had been designed to avoid. The British ambassador in Berlin, Sir Evelyn Malet, tried his utmost to prevent such a cession, but the final agreement concluded early in 1894 gave Bifara, on a navigable tributary of the Benue, to France. German claims east of Bornu were severely reduced, but she retained her access to Lake Chad and most of her claim to Adamawa.[1]

The grant of a French enclave on the navigable Benue was a hint that the French and Germans together intended to mount an attack on the Niger Company's monopolistic navigation rules. Dr. Kayser of the German Foreign Office practically told the British ambassador that this would be so. He declared that the way Goldie had been allowed practically to close the Niger and Benue was an affront to international law, and now that France and Germany had sunk their differences they would want to develop their new territories by river transport, and would unite to secure free navigation. This would be the 'next great African question'. Kayser and his colleagues continued to stress this theme, complaining particularly at the system of ports of entry and the company's monopoly of fuel supplies, until Malet was so worried that he asked the Foreign Office to force

---

[1] For full text see Hertslet, *Map of Africa*, Vol. II, no. 198, pp. 657 ff. For how the British viewed the progress of the negotiations see FO 64/1333; FO 64/1335 and FO 64/1346 *passim*.

the Niger Company to liberalize the regime. When ordered to protest at Kayser's language, and to point out the recent services of the company to German explorers, Malet said that the Germans were so touchy he dared not do so, and asked to be excused the duty. The protest was never delivered.[1]

Instead, at the very moment when Goldie might have imagined himself to be at the high point of his independence after successfully concluding an important piece of British colonial diplomacy, he found himself once more subject to Foreign Office control, and, it may be noted, once more in response to foreign pressure. He was told that now both France and Germany were riverain powers it would be 'prudent' to frame new navigation regulations which left no doubt that the company intended to respect the Berlin Act.[2] He made no protest, nor did he try, as he had on previous occasions, to send in draft regulations which nullified themselves. Regulation XL 1894 was a clear and generous measure. Vessels had still to call for clearance papers when entering the Niger Territory, and arms and ammunition were restricted as they had to be by the Brussels Act,[3] but the regulations expressly permitted the purchase of wood, other fuel, and provisions, which, 'as heretofore' were not counted as cargo. Wooding stations were also added to the list of 'ports of entry' so that the longest distance between places where fuel could be bought did not exceed ninety miles. Even the smallest fuel bunkers could take sufficient fuel for two hundred miles.[4]

The navigation question proved to be the last flicker of the frontier disputes in the east, engendered more by a desire to oppose than any real grievance. It was characteristic of the company's opponents that they imagined trade and transport on the rivers to be an easy matter once the restraints were removed.

[1] FO 64/1332 Kimberley to Malet, 38 Af., 11.4.94 and same to same, 48 Af. Conf. 21.4.94; FO 64/1333 Malet to Rosebery, 28 Af. Conf. 7.3.94. enc. mem. by Gosselin on conversation with Kayser 6.3.94; *ibid.* Malet to Kimberley, 37 Af. Conf. and 38 Af. Conf. both of 24.3.94 and same to same, 47 Af. 14.4.94.

[2] FO 83/1310 F.O. to R.N.C. 19.3.94.

[3] An Act of the International Conference held in Brussels in 1890 and directed against the slave trade.

[4] FO 83/1310 R.N.C. to F.O. 3.4.94 with enclosures.

In fact it was many years before the French or the Germans were able to exploit the more liberal regulations. In effect therefore, the Franco-German Agreement of 1894 did little to whittle away the security which Goldie had bought in the Anglo-German Agreement of 1893. The eastern frontier of Nigeria was settled broadly as it was to remain until the war of 1914. Hundreds of miles of the Benue waterway, the Fulani emirates from Lokoja to Yola, and the ancient country of Bornu were henceforth to be British.

9

The Revenge of the Brassmen

DURING the years in which Goldie had faced, and triumphed over, the threat from Mizon and the French, he had also been confronted by the fiercest campaign of opposition from Liverpool. Once the scheme for a chartered administration in the Oil Rivers had been scouted, the Liverpool interests, both large and small, shippers and traders, were able to build up a substantial unity, and to ground their complaints on the basic injustice of entrusting rule to a corporation which itself traded. Though this campaign could muster a considerable number of Members of Parliament, and could mount a formidable press campaign, it was able to do little more than force through one or two comparatively minor reforms, which did nothing to alter the basic monopolistic structure of the company's administration. Goldie fought back in his own way, and, as we shall see, eventually silenced his European critics in 1893. The Africans of the Oil Rivers thereafter had no one to voice their grievances, and the stage was set for violence.

Paradoxically it was Goldie's very success in resisting the pressure from France, and his brilliant defence of the eastern frontier, which permitted the situation in the Niger delta to slide downhill towards what now appears to the historian as an inevitable tragedy. Whilst Goldie could effectively protect British strategic interests on the Niger and Benue, the Government, though recognizing the truth of many of the criticisms levelled against the Niger Company, had no incentive to hamstring Goldie, and could not contemplate taking on the direct responsibility for ruling the Niger Territories when there appeared to be no urgent need to do so.

The crucial question for the Liverpool men was that of the boundary between the new Niger Coast Protectorate, now under the rule of Sir Claude Macdonald, and the Niger Company's territories. This boundary had never been defined, nor had a map been issued. As soon as he realized that the plan for extending the charter over the Oil Rivers had fallen through, Goldie took the opportunity to advance as rapidly as possible into the coastal region before the new administration under Macdonald had time to settle down and define its frontiers. The crucial areas were the Oguta Lake, which provided an inlet to the Niger for the men of Brass and New Calabar, and the Forcados River, now realized to be a much better entrance to the Niger than the Nun River, on which the company's headquarters at Akassa were situated. The company therefore made treaties in both these areas, some of them deliberate forgeries,[1] despite the fact that Consul Hewett had made prior treaties in the name of the Oil Rivers Protectorate some years before. As soon as possible an effective revenue system was established in both these areas, so as to prevent the entry of Brass and New Calabar men through Oguta Lake, to prevent illicit entry through Forcados on the main Niger, and to control the port of Warri, which tapped the trade of Benin. The boundary question came to a head in 1891, when Macdonald had begun to draw together the reins of his new administration. When Macdonald came home on leave he conducted some rather acrimonious negotiations with Goldie, and after much bickering a kind of standstill arrangement was made for the Oguta Lake; an arrangement which accepted the gains already made by the Niger Company, but limited any further expansion southwards.[2] As rumours of this agreement leaked out, the Liverpool

[1] The treaties made in the Forcados region are the only original treaties made by the Niger Company which can be seen in the F.O. files. They were confiscated by Consul Hewett in 1888. They are clearly forgeries, the chiefs alleged to have 'signed' them were supposed to have been illiterate and so made crosses or marks. The crosses on these originals are neat and unsmudged, and each cross is identical, obviously and unmistakably the work of a literate hand. They can be seen enclosed in FO 84/1881 Hewett to Salisbury 10.11.88.

[2] FO 84/2168 F.O. to R.N.C. 18.6.91, with minutes giving an account of the discussions.

merchants began to realize that if the Niger Company established a really effective revenue post on the Oguta Lake this
would eventually lead to destitution along the coast, particularly
at Brass. As they had constantly restrained the Brassmen, holding out hopes of redress only to see further territories now
handed over to the Niger Company, they prophesied real
trouble.[1] But the Foreign Office rejected these arguments; the
doctrine of progress was involved. The 'new commercial
system' of dispensing with the services of the middlemen was
bound to cause 'some discontent' among the coastal Africans.
British traders need not be affected, but should 'find fresh
openings which will compensate them for the loss of trade
diverted by rivalry into fresh outlets'.[2] In the very next month,
however, when the Liverpool men succeeded in getting a detailed statement of the boundary, it appeared that the most
important of these very 'fresh openings' had been handed over
to the company with the acceptance of their claim to the left
bank of the Forcados. At Warri the African Association, and
many smaller firms, had built up a thriving new trade with local
middlemen working the interior back to Benin.[3]

It was this concession, more than any other single factor,
which was responsible for the fierce attacks made on the company during 1892. Firms from every part of Britain were
mobilized, and poured in a veritable stream of correspondence
to the Foreign Office. For the first time Members of Parliament
outside Liverpool began to get interested in the question, particularly the Radicals, already uneasy at the way things were
going with chartered company administration in East Africa.
By February 1892 the Foreign Office began to get seriously
worried; Cross, one of the Liverpool Members of Parliament,
openly told Villiers Lister that 'a tremendous onslaught upon
the Niger Company was being prepared'. Sir Percy Anderson
was even allowed to prepare a long 'address', in the form of a

[1] See esp. FO 84/2176 African Association to F.O. 3.10.91 and *ibid*. G. A. Moore
to F.O. 5.10.91.
[2] FO 84/2177 F.O. to African Association 24.10.91.
[3] FO 84/2180 African Association to F.O. 5.12.91, which mentions F.O. to
African Association of 28.11.90, which appears to have been lost.

reasoned defence of the Niger Company, which was sent to the
Liverpool Chamber of Commerce to try to spike the guns of the
campaign before it got under way.[1] The address was so naïvely
partisan that it only inflamed the opposition further. Nevertheless the Foreign Office held its ground, and fought the opposition
solidly. Questions in Parliament were evaded, requests for
details of the company's revenue and expenditure accounts put
off, demands for publication of its treaties rejected, and the constantly reiterated demand that the delta of the Niger be placed
under the administration of the Niger Coast Protectorate dismissed on the ground that it would be a 'breach of the Company's charter'.[2]

In July 1892 Parliament was dissolved, and the general election which ensued returned Gladstone to power once more,
resting his support on Irish votes. The Liverpool interests hoped
that the Liberals would now curb Goldie; they had begun to
think that he had some secret hold over the Conservatives, perhaps because they knew that Chamberlain was a shareholder.[3]
But they were mistaken; the 'conspiracy' was not the result of
intrigue or influence, but of fixed policy. The memorandum
which Anderson prepared for the new Foreign Minister, Lord
Rosebery, on the state of business in the African department
clearly reveals the real reasons for the strong support given to
Goldie. The Niger Company, argued Anderson, had 'secured to
England' incomparably the best of the newly opened African
rivers, more navigable to a greater depth to more civilized and
wealthy regions than any other. If the area were ruled directly
by the Crown 'a large initial expenditure and a higher annual
outlay' would be inevitable. He did not deny that monopoly
existed; in theory, and by the charter, monopoly was impossible,
'but there are ways by which rival traders can be discouraged
... it does not make newcomers welcome'. If the region became

[1] FO 84/2241 see the memoranda by Anderson, Lister and Salisbury attached to
F.O. to President of Liverpool Chamber 2.2.92.
[2] FO 84/2239–53 inclusive are literally packed with material illustrating this
campaign and the F.O. response to it.
[3] See the letter from G. A. Moore to Salisbury of 2.7.92 in FO 84/2253 which
attacks Goldie's 'intimate connexions' especially 'the large interest held in the
Company by a Liberal Unionist Leader', i.e. Chamberlain.

even more prosperous, then the opposition would intensify. 'This
is, however, a detail. The possession by England of this portion
of Africa . . . is secured'. The realization that monopoly was the
price which had to be paid for the fulfilment by the company of
its imperial mission could not have been more clearly stated.[1]

Lord Rosebery, who was in any case now thoroughly occupied by the internal crisis in his own party about Uganda and
East Africa, accepted this view, and the previous policy of
resisting the opposition continued. The policy of non-interven-
tion applied equally to the complaints of the department's own
officials in the Niger Coast Protectorate. Macdonald, now the
Commissioner and Consul-General, continued to press for the
reforms which he had urged in his report on the Company's
internal administration. He pressed for an end to the system
whereby all attempts to purchase land on the banks of the Niger
had to be conducted through the company's officials. His requests were shelved and forgotten.[2] Macdonald's attempts to
ameliorate the conditions of entry for the coastal middlemen
met with a stubborn resistance from Goldie. The Foreign
Office would do nothing without the company's consent, and
finally, when forced to choose, supported Goldie's existing
regulations on the curious ground that 'the Company had not
violated its charter'—a comment which strangely ignored the
power of the Secretary of State, by the charter, to regulate
matters of policy.[3]

On only one important matter did the newly elected Government establish a tighter control. The pressure in Parliament for
the production of accounts of the company's revenue and
expenditure led to the realization in the Foreign Office that no
such accounts had been submitted by Goldie for four years.
When Goldie was asked to send in accounts, they were as
obscure as those which he had submitted in 1888. Once more he
argued that it was in fact impossible to divide accurately the

[1] FO 84/2256 conf. printed mem. by H.P.A. August 1892.
[2] FO 84/2240 F.O. to R.N.C. 21.1.92 and reply 28.1.92, asking to defer action
until Goldie's return to England. The matter was never referred to again.
[3] FO 84/2266 R.N.C. to F.O. 19.12.92; FO 84/2259 mem. by H.P.A. 26.4.93
misfiled at 27.9.92.

administrative from the commercial expenditure. Once more there was a long wrangling correspondence in which the Foreign Office tried to obtain more detailed and reliable figures, but in vain. Finally, in a mood of exasperation, the Foreign Office decided to exert its authority and fix the total amount that the company could collect in revenue at £70,000 for any one year. This was slightly more than the amount raised in the accounts Goldie had just submitted. Goldie now immediately sent in the accounts for 1891, showing that revenue now exceeded £100,000 per annum. Finally a compromise was reached in which the company was limited to collecting £90,000 in each of the years 1894 and 1895, Goldie reserving his right to withdraw from the Niger and liquidate the company if the financial position proved untenable (an oblique reference to the East Africa Company's difficulties in Uganda). He could also ask for more if the company needed to make war on the Fulani empire, as it would one day have to do.[1] This restriction did nothing to relax the monopoly, for it did not limit the *rate* of taxation, if the yield from taxes approached the limit the company could, and later did, increase the rate of taxation so as to discourage trade and reduce the yield in revenue. The Foreign Office officials were well aware of this,[2] the chief value of the limitation was that it made unnecessary the tedious annual examination in detail of the company's budget,[3] whilst also providing a gesture of control with which to confront critics.

The Liverpool opposition had now begun to despair of any action from the Government. Nothing could be done by political pressure. The Victorian business man, however, had an acute sense of the power of money and commerce. If the state would not coerce Goldie, perhaps Liverpool could achieve its objects by private means. The time had come for a trade war.

This was now possible, for most of the Liverpool interests

[1] FO 83/1239 R.N.C. to F.O. 4.5.93, with minutes, and private note Goldie to Anderson 4.5.93.
[2] FO 83/1239 minutes by T.V.L. on R.N.C. to F.O. 4.5.93.
[3] *Ibid., loc. cit.*, minute by Anderson 9.3.93.

were amalgamated in the African Association Ltd., which had once hoped for a separate charter for the Oil Rivers. The African Association had already entered the Niger in 1890 in retaliation for Goldie's expansion into the Forcados and Oguta Lake areas. In 1891 the attack had been intensified. In 1892 it mounted to a crescendo. It was all done legally, the licences and customs duties were paid, and the vessels officially entered and cleared at Akassa. This, of course, was trading at a loss. But it was also siphoning off produce which normally went to the Niger Company's stations, and raising the prices which the company had to pay to Africans. The seriousness of this competition is clearly revealed by a table of customs duties paid to the Niger Company. These figures reveal a steady growth in the amounts paid by rival traders, a growth which the company did not share proportionately:

TABLE OF CUSTOMS DUTIES PAID 1890–1892[1]

| | Imports | | Exports | |
| | Royal Niger Company | Other Traders | Royal Niger Company | Others Traders |
	£	£	£	£
1890	33,833	2,935	22,477	2,179
1891	48,226	5,541	27,397	3,801
1892	39,753	11,895	42,839	7,433

The legal trade, however, was not the only way in which the African Association tried to carry the war to Goldie's territory. Every effort was made to assist the attempts of the African middlemen to break into the Niger, particularly those of the Brassmen. This was, of course, a clandestine support for what was in reality smuggling. The Brassmen now embarked on a brief revival of their fortunes. Imports into Brass rose from £40,500 in 1891–2 to £52,000 in 1892–3, and exports from £65,500 to £104,000, most of this increase coming from smuggling on the Niger.[2] Both types of competition began to affect

[1] Compiled from P.P. 1899, LXIII (c. 9372), pp. 52–4. The rise in yield from exports in 1892 can partly be explained by the increase in the palm oil duty (100 per cent) and the increased duty on kernels (33 per cent) effective from 31.12.91. Import duties remained unchanged. .

[2] FO 83/1382 Kirk to Salisbury, no. 2, 25.8.95, enc. 1. These figures would naturally include much trade which was local.

o

the Niger Company's balance-sheets. The normal profits 'by working account' had normally stood at about £60,000 until 1890. In 1891 working profits slumped to £51,891, and in 1892 they dropped even further to £43,167.[1]

Goldie did not hesitate to use the company's administration to fight back. In August 1890 the company passed a regulation prohibiting the import of spirituous liquors above Abutshi. The burden of proof that liquors had not been imported rested 'upon the person so selling or importing them'. Punishment for the first offence could include a fine of £100 and a month in prison, and for further offences £500 and six months in prison, and the forfeiture of the vessels engaged and their cargo.[2] This was a clever move, for it restricted the African Association's search for palm oil and kernels, which were usually bought with liquor, to the region south of Abutshi, and at the same time won over the Protestant missionaries to support the Niger Company, and stifle any criticism they may have been tempted to make. Henceforth the African Association could be pictured as wishing to debauch the Africans in a sea of alcohol, restrained only by the humanitarian policies of the Niger Company. Goldie aimed another blow at the African Association in July 1891 when the duty on palm oil was doubled (from a penny to twopence per old wine gallon) and that on kernels raised from one shilling and sixpence (to which it had been reduced in 1889) to two shillings a hundredweight. The measure was justified in a long preamble to the new regulation, where it was argued that the purpose of the duties was to provide funds to check the advance of the Fulani against the pagan peoples and to suppress the slave trade in accordance with the Brussels Act.[3] The Foreign Office, mindful of German sensitivities about the duty on kernels, thought it best to inform Goldie that the Brussels Act was not yet in force. Goldie replied that this could not absolve the company from its 'duty and policy' to check slave raiding.[4] If so he had found a convenient way of fulfilling it—taxing the com-

[1] P.P. 1899, LXIII (c. 9372), pp. 38–42.
[2] FO 84/2089 R.N.C. to F.O. 21.8.90.
[3] FO 84/2171 R.N.C. to F.O. 17.7.91 enc. Regulation XXXVI.
[4] *Ibid.* F.O. to R.N.C. 24.7.91 and reply 27.7.91.

pany's rivals on commodities produced only in the south to pay for administration in the north, where the company alone traded.

The trade war on the Niger nevertheless continued. By May 1892 the African Association felt that Goldie was ready to come to terms, and through the Liverpool Chamber of Commerce, asked him to begin discussions. As if to display his defiance, Goldie made them wait until December before beginning talks. The Liverpool delegates, representing the African Association, the shippers, and the independent firms, put forward a five-point plan for basic reform of the Niger Company.

1. That the Crown should be asked to appoint a Resident Commissioner to observe the working of the charter and receive complaints.

2. That the administrative accounts for 1886 to 1891 should be laid before Parliament, and thereafter annually, 'rendered in the fullest detail . . . verified by independent auditors, and be entirely separated from the trading accounts of the Company'.

3. That the administration should be entirely separated from the trading organization of the Niger Company, and contain representatives of the Crown, and of the rival traders, in what was in effect a kind of legislative council.

4. That the customs duties should be revised so that taxes fell on imports, export duties to be abolished.

5. The transfer to the Niger Coast Protectorate of all the company's territory south of, and including, Onitsha.

In return for this last concession the Liverpool traders offered to pay the Niger Company a 'rent' of six to seven thousand pounds a year.

These demands reflected a gross over-estimate of the African Association's coercive power through competition. For Goldie to have agreed to them would have been abject surrender. The 'rent' offered was in fact less than the company now drew from the Liverpool traders in taxation. It is not surprising that the conference broke down after only two hours of discussion. Goldie refused even to talk about the first two demands, on the ground that they were matters for the Government (though he

took care when reporting the negotiations to the Foreign Office
to insist that a Resident Commissioner would be 'intolerable',
and to stress that the chartered company system was essentially
one outside parliamentary control.) As for the other items, discussion scarcely attained a serious level.[1]

Until now Goldie had been on the defensive. Once he realized
the extent of the African Association's ambitions he began a
counter-attack. In the early months of 1893 he started a complicated series of manœuvres to divide the opposition. His chief
weapon was the offer of favourable contracts in order to
detach firms from the alliance. His great triumph came in
March 1893, when the steamship companies were won over by
the offer of advantageous freight rates, and Alfred Jones resigned
his chairmanship of the African Trade Section of the Liverpool
Chamber of Commerce.[2] Meanwhile the war on the Niger was
intensified until it was Goldie, not the African Association, who
was dictating terms.

Final agreement was reached in June 1893. It was clearly a
settlement imposed by Goldie, for it bears the same stamp as all
the amalgamation agreements since the formation of the United
African Company in 1879. The Niger Company bought up all
the African Association's assets on the Niger; plant, merchandise, produce, buildings and goodwill. Payment was made in
debentures to the value of £7,500 and 5,033 shares considered as
fully paid at £10 par value especially created for this purpose;
in other words a share equivalent to about one-tenth of the
future profits of the Niger Company. The two companies agreed
to cease all competition, the Niger Company would keep out of
the Oil Rivers and the African Association would stay away
from the Niger. The African Association would stop all its
public criticism of the Niger Company, in return it received the
right to appoint a director of the Niger Company.[3]

[1] FO 84/2266 R.N.C. to F.O. 19.12.92. John Holt Papers Box 4/8 Documents on
fusion with R.N.C. 1893-5.

[2] *Liverpool Daily Post* 8.3.93 gives an interesting report of this rather stormy
meeting.

[3] R.J.S.C. 17049, Vol. I, R.N.C. Agreement with African Association 2.3.94 in
fulfilment of agreement of 9.6.93.

This last stipulation is particularly interesting. To carry it out Goldie had only to see that a director from the African Association was voted in at the next annual meeting. Yet he chose to alter the articles of association of the Niger Company so that

The Company may from time to time appoint as additional Member or Members of the Council any persons whether shareholders or not whom they consider to be representative of the commercial interests in or connected with the Niger Territories or the region ajacent thereto . . .[1]

This wider power was never exercised, it remains nevertheless a fascinating climax to the struggle with Liverpool. The victory won, Goldie began to tire of the crude profit of his now perfect monopoly. He was beginning to look more critically at his company and to ponder its future; he was ready for change and reform. The new article left the way open for the transformation of the company's ruling council into an embryonic legislative council, representing diverse interests. The idea was not entirely his own; the third article of the demands made by the Liverpool negotiators in December 1892 had envisaged a much broader council, with the British Government represented. They in their turn were influenced by Mary Kingsley, who was later to advocate the idea of rule by merchants as an alternative to the Crown colony system in West Africa. The idea was an adaptation of the traditional British pattern of responsible government long established in the white settled colonies. Had Goldie proceeded with this experiment, and extended the representation on the council further than the single delegate from the African Association, the history of Nigeria might have been very different. Cecil Rhodes, grafting representation for white settler interests on the structure of the British South Africa Company, prolonged chartered company rule in Rhodesia until 1923.

The agreement with Liverpool must have been welcomed by Goldie with the greatest relief. The Niger Company's troubles, apparently, were now over. For seven long years the Liverpool

[1] FO 83/1241 R.N.C. to F.O. 13.7.93 with enclosures.

men had been behind the constant attacks on the company in Parliament and the press. Now Liverpool was silent. The secretary of the African Association even went to the length of personally delivering eulogistic lectures on the Niger Territories, illustrated by lantern slides. Such opposition as was left was feeble, ill-informed, and badly organized. Moreover the monopoly, the life-blood of the administrative system, was now absolutely secure. After 1894 the Niger Company was for all practical purposes the only trader on the Niger and Benue; the monopoly was literally one hundred per cent effective in exports from the rivers, and the company imported ninety-nine and a half per cent of all goods coming into the rivers.[1]

The very thoroughness of this success laid the basis for the catastrophe which was impending. The Brass people were now abandoned by their traditional allies. The short-lived boom in the Brass trade which had been a by-product of the trade war between Liverpool and the Niger Company came to an abrupt end. The few free-lance firms outside the African Association were too small to step into the breach. Worse still, Goldie's company was now able to set up an efficient system of defence against smuggling between the Brass villages and the Niger, and this system became excessively severe now that there was no organized body of criticism. Brass canoes, stealing through the creeks at night, were fired on from the customs posts, and lives were lost.[2] The Brassmen were prevented from collecting payment of debts due to them from the Ijo producers, and the company even threatened to take reprisals against any Ijo honest enough to try to pay the Brassmen.[3] The economic situation in

---

[1] P.P. 1899, LXIII (c. 9372), revenue and expenditure accounts 1894–8.

[2] FO 83/1382 Kirk to Salisbury, no. 1 of 25.8.94, Enc. 1.

[3] *Ibid.*, *loc. cit.* the so-called 'Debt Regulation' (Regulation XXVIII) forbad foreigners to the territories to collect debts due from Africans. Goldie justified it on the ground that the company was attempting to get rid of the 'trust' system (a system of giving credit in advance, starting with advances made by the European traders, and passed downwards through the middleman system) and substitute a cash trade. Goldie was forced to modify this regulation by the Foreign Office so that its final form (Regulation XXIX or 'The Protection of Natives Regulation') applied only to debts contracted in the course of commercial transactions. This hardly affected the position for the Brassmen. (FO 84/1917 F.O. to R.N.C. 6.3.88 and reply 9.3.88, with encs; FO 84/1918 R.N.C. to F.O. 5.4.88 with encs.)

the Brass villages became desperate when the company began seizing the 'chop' canoes bringing yams and cassava from the Niger Territories. The Brassmen were forced to turn more and more to fish and the few plantains which grew in their infertile swamps. By the end of 1894 the company's revenue system was so efficient that the European free-lance traders wrote home to ask that no more goods be sent out for barter, as trade was at a standstill.[1] Food was so short that some of the slave population were actually starving.[2]

Economic factors alone might have been enough to cause a revolutionary movement among the Brassmen, but what actually produced a temper of violence were considerations of a more psychological kind, especially a sense of frustration, and a feeling among the Brass people that they had been humbled and insulted. The sense of ignominy was produced by the poverty itself, and also by a series of incidents in which Niger Company employees had behaved in an arrogant and brutish way, offending local morals and customs. The wife of a prominent Brass freeman had been outraged on board one of the hulks by a Niger Company clerk, and presents were forced on her afterwards as if she were a common prostitute. Another less virtuous lady, mistress to one of the clerks at Akassa, had been seized by the company's beachmaster there—a man with the singularly inappropriate name of Captain Christian—stripped naked, and coated with tar. It seemed to the Brassmen that

The ill-treatments of the Niger Company is very bad. They said that the Brassmen should eat dust. According to their saying we see truly that we eat the dusts.[3]

Frustration arose from the repeated assurances which the Brassmen had received both from the Liverpool traders and the Oil Rivers Consular staff that their grievances would be looked into; the impression was sometimes given that Queen Victoria

[1] FO 83/1374 Steinberg and Co. to F.O. 4.2.95.

[2] Most of the evidence for conditions in Brass comes from Sir John Kirk's report, to be found in FO 83/1382, appended to correspondence from Kirk of 25.8.95. Where, in the account which follows, sources are not specified, their origin is from Kirk's letters or the report which follows.

[3] FO 2/83 Macdonald to F.O., no. 8, 4.2.95, Enc. 4, Kings and chiefs of Brass to Macdonald 4.2.95.

herself would personally attend to the matter. Breaking point
was reached in November 1894, when Macdonald, once more
urged by the Brassmen to do something, virtually admitted to
them that he was powerless.[1] This, coming just at the time when
the company's blockade had brought trade to a standstill, may
well have been the spark which set the Brassmen ablaze.

Internal politics also played their part. The Brassmen were
sharply divided into Christian and Animistic parties. The King,
Ebefa, was 'an old good-hearted drunkard' who supported the
British connexion and had several times restrained his chiefs
from attacking the company's headquarters at Akassa, only a
few miles away. He rested his power very largely on the support
of the Christian faction, led by Chief Warri. His great rival was
Chief Koko, a fanatical Animist entirely under the influence of
the ju-ju priests. One result of the loss of trade had been a return
to the traditional religion. At one time the Christian party had
dominated the state, and the local church had been well-
attended and self-supporting. Now the church could no longer
maintain its buildings or the clergyman, and more and more of
the influential men 'lost faith in the white man's God, who had
allowed them to be oppressed' and went over to Koko, himself a
lapsed Christian. The outbreak of a smallpox epidemic at the
end of 1894 was the signal for more relapses, and the demand for
human sacrifices and cannibal rituals which were supposed to
have stopped the last outbreak in 1884. In November 1894 the
smallpox laid its hand on King Ebefa, and carried him off.
Koko became King of Brass.[2]

It was not difficult for the new King to persuade all parties,
including the Christians, that the time had come for violence.
Poverty, injured pride, and now a dreadful disease, conspired to
this end. All resolved to join together in a desperate nihilistic
bid for revenge against the company. There was no intention to
rebel against the Niger Coast Protectorate, or against the British
Crown:

[1] *Ibid., loc. cit.*
[2] See, in addition to Kirk's report already cited, FO 83/1375 Capt. Macdonald
to F.O. 25.2.95. Capt. Macdonald was Vice-Consul at Brass, not to be confused
with Major, now Sir Claude, Macdonald, the Commissioner and Consul-General.

Our boys fired, killed and plundered, and even the innocent provisions sellers were captured and killed likewise. If the Queen of England was acting in like manner as the Niger Company the whole of Africa would have been dead through starvation . . . the Company is not the Queen's man; and instead if we Brass people die through hunger we had rather go to them and die on their sords.[1]

The place which the Brassmen had chosen to go and die on their swords was Akassa, where lay the company's trading headquarters and engineering workshops. If some would die on the enemy swords, others might live to bring back plunder beyond their dreams. Then the Niger Company could 'eat dirt'.

The conspirators disagreed over one problem, and it nearly prevented the attack. The fetish priests wanted it understood that any prisoners should be sacrificed with the usual cannibalistic rites, to stop the smallpox, but Chief Warri and his Christian minority threatened to withdraw from the attack if this were agreed upon. After a fierce argument the question was dropped, and the Christians agreed to continue with the scheme. Final preparations were completed in secrecy, helped by the fact that none of the Europeans near by could understand the Brass language. On Monday, 28 December, all was ready; the canoes, with big guns mounted on them, were manœuvred into position, and King Koko arrived to take command. He threw off his European dress, substituting a loin cloth, covered his body with chalk, and hung monkey skulls around his waist. Then he and his men sprinkled themselves with holy water at the ju-ju house, and the canoes moved down the creeks toward Akassa. Almost every able-bodied man from Nembe, the capital, was in the expedition—over one thousand warriors.[2]

In the meantime someone let out the secret. At nine o'clock on the night of Sunday, 27 December, the Acting Vice-Consul at Brass, who lived in the European town where the merchants lived, received an anonymous letter:

Brass people leaving tomorrow at noon to destroy Niger Company's

[1] FO 2/83 Macdonald to F.O., no. 9, 4.2.95, enc. 4, King and chiefs of Brass to Macdonald 4.2.95.
[2] FO 2/83 Macdonald to F.O., no. 9, 4.2.96, enc. 3, statement of Father Bubendorf (the only European witness in Nembe).

factories and lives at Akassa on Tuesday morning. Be sure you send
at once to stop them.

AN OBSERVER.[1]

The Vice-Consul immediately sent off the warning to Flint,
the Company's Agent-General at Akassa. But Flint pooh-
poohed the whole thing; rumours of this kind were always
evident during the high-water season. There was no constabulary at Akassa, but if attack came he would do his best.[2]
Consequently, though the warning came twenty-one hours
before the attack, nothing was done to defend Akassa, the company's people were unprepared, and only one of the six or seven
vessels in the harbour had steam up.

On Tuesday, 29 December, the Brass canoes slid into Akassa
at half past four in the morning. The attack had been brilliantly
planned and was a fearful success. The Kruboys[3] and other
African employees were slaughtered as they slept in their huts.
The Europeans only escaped with their lives through the provi-
dential appearance of a mail steamer, at which the Brassmen
drew back, because, they later claimed, this was the Queen's
ship and they had no quarrel with the Queen. This gave Flint
and the others time to board a launch which had steam up and
make their escape.[4] The Brassmen now put Akassa to the sack.
All the workshops and machinery were wrecked with hammers
and crowbars found lying about, and particular care was taken
to smash up the engines of the hated steamers. The stores and
warehouses were looted and torn down. The prisoners and
booty were loaded into forty or fifty war-canoes, and a triumphal
return to Nembe began, with drums beating and flags flying,
openly parading past the house of the amazed and impotent
Vice-Consul.

The prisoners caused the first rift among the attackers. King
Koko demanded that all the captives should be delivered up
for cannibalistic sacrifice to the fetish priests, but Warri and

---

[1] *Ibid.* enc. 2. Acting Vice-Consul Harrison to Macdonald 5.2.95.

[2] *Ibid.* enc. 1. Flint to Harrison 28.12.95.

[3] Men recruited from the 'Kru Coast' of Liberia, and well known for their skill
as sailors.

[4] FO 2/83 Macdonald to F.O., no. 10, 11.2.95.

eight other Christian chiefs defied the King and secretly
smuggled their twenty-five captives to the Consulate, where they
were released. The majority, under Koko, proceeded to slaughter
most of their captives, and ritually ate parts of their bodies to
stop the smallpox. Warri and the staunch Christians shut themselves away in their houses because they 'could not bear to look
upon the slaughter', but some of the lapsed Christians seem to
have been the most carried away by the orgy. Most ironical of
all perhaps, was the behaviour of Robert Apracassa, who had
been educated in Goldie's own Isle of Man. He was observed
'jumping about quite naked, painted white, with pieces of
human flesh hanging to him, shouting and singing'. Yet even in
the midst of cannibalism the Brassmen were not without a
peculiar code of morality. The fate of the prisoners was regarded
as a just retribution for their services to the iniquitous company,
and an effort was made to spare the innocent. King Koko himself decreed that Mrs. Price, wife of one of the steamer captains,
should not die, and against fierce opposition from the priests he
delivered her over to the Consulate.[1]

If the Brassmen had been subtly trained in the intricacies of
English politics they could hardly have chosen a better method
of focusing attention on their grievances, though they might
have conducted their slaughter with a more delicate air. In the
British Empire the stimulus of revolt has so often been the pre-
lude to major reforms of long-neglected colonial institutions.
There is something in the character of the Englishman which
makes him insist that violence must have a cause; an ingrained
belief in original virtue which makes him incapable of believing
that men can ever be wholly without justification when they
rebel. Within a few days of the news of the Brass attack reaching
England, the Niger Company's monopoly, and even its charter,
were in real danger. Goldie's first reaction to the news was one of

[1] This account of the aftermath of the attack is based on FO 2/83 Macdonald to
F.O., no. 9, 4.2.95, which enclosed several accounts, including those of the Vice-
Consul and Father Bubendorf.

blank amazement—'We always looked on Akassa as being as safe as Picadilly,' he confessed.[1] This mood soon turned to indignation as he realized that public sympathy was, paradoxically it seemed to him, turning to the Brassmen, who seemed likely to escape severe punishment. It was the Brassmen who had attacked the company, and the officials of the Niger Coast Protectorate, who ought to have prevented such a catastrophe, were now using the affair to try and get rid of the Niger Company. Macdonald, especially, did all he could to justify the Brassmen. He stressed the care which the Brassmen had shown to discriminate between the company's officials and those of the Crown, and laid responsibility at the door of the company for causing poverty and starvation among the Brassmen.[2] This infuriated Goldie. The Brass attack was prompted, in his opinion, by the simple desire for loot. Perhaps they had no quarrel with the British Government, but he could not doubt that the British Government had a quarrel with them, and that the British Navy, aided by Macdonald's constabulary and the company's men, would now 'exterminate Nembe'.[3]

The consensus of opinion was against him. Lord Kimberley was now Foreign Secretary, Rosebery having assumed the Premiership on Gladstone's retirement in March 1894. Kimberley was the first Foreign Secretary to look on the company with an unsympathetic eye. He could not accept Goldie's demand for severe reprisals, 'no doubt open outrage must be punished, but if a remedy is not at the same time applied . . . we should be liable for just and severe blame.'[4] Meanwhile Macdonald had been joined by Rear-Admiral Bedford, and the two of them were soon agreed that the company had in effect provoked the attack, and that they must do their best to prevent a severe punishment of the Brassmen. They tried negotiation with the chiefs, but the Brassmen were now desperate, and refused to surrender their arms unless they obtained guarantees that they would be allowed to trade on the Niger. Rather reluctantly the

[1] FO 83/1374 Goldie to Hill, private, 1.2.95.
[2] FO 2/86 Macdonald to F.O., tel., 5.2.95.
[3] FO 83/1374 Goldie to Kimberley 8.2.95.
[4] *Ibid.* minute by Kimberley on R.N.C. to F.O. 8.2.95.

Admiral mounted an expedition against Nembe, but the Brassmen put up a stiff resistance which could not be routed, and
after five of his officers had been killed Bedford concluded 'that
the punishment inflicted . . . was sufficient, and a retreat was
decided upon'.[1] In the next few days the expedition burned
some of the surrounding villages, and then the Admiral called a
halt. By contemporary standards the punishment inflicted was
extraordinarily light (though no doubt a Brassman might have
thought differently). Much more terrible than the efforts of the
navy were those of nature. In the succeeding weeks hunger
began to stalk the country, and hunger and smallpox are
terrible allies.

But the Brassmen had not surrendered their rifles. This, to
Goldie, was intolerable, and he succeeded in persuading the
Foreign Office to telegraph orders to Macdonald that the rifles
would have to be surrendered. Macdonald, however, did not
want to make this demand. The possession of a rifle was a mark
of social prestige, and the Africans in the protectorate had never
been forbidden to carry arms. The Brassmen would not surrender their arms without another expedition to compel them, and
Macdonald knew that the Admiral would hate such an idea.
Macdonald therefore neatly side-stepped, agreeing to disarm
the Brassmen and asking that the Admiralty give assistance. He
knew what Admiral Bedford's response would be. The Admiral
protested at the idea, arguing that it would only lead to fresh
attacks by the Brassmen if they were 'provoked as they were at
Akassa'. Macdonald followed this up with his own protest. In
reply he was asked how, if the rifles were not surrendered, the
Brassmen could be 'made to understand that the alleged
grievances can only be considered after reparation for the
massacre'? Perhaps Macdonald sensed that Lord Kimberley
was wavering, for his response was an impassioned telegram:

People of Brass understand thoroughly reparation has been and is
being made for past offences; canons, canoes, plunder and prisoners
have been surrendered, and the chiefs who took part in the atrocities

---

[1] FO 2/83 Macdonald to F.O., no. 11, 28.2.95; FO 83/1375 Admiralty to F.O.
25.2.95 enc. Bedford's account.

fined; towns are destroyed, trade almost ruined, women and children starving in the bush; hundreds have been killed; smallpox has been raging; the rainy season is beginning. I have seen all this and visited the towns destroyed. I most strongly deprecate further punishment in the name of humanity, and request a settlement of the question. Senior Naval Officer concurs in this entirely.[1]

Kimberley was almost ashamed to read this, and obviously deeply moved. For the first time Macdonald found support against the company from his own superiors. Kimberley replied immediately by telegraph, mildly chastising the Commissioner for failing to report the distress earlier, and ordering him to stop the blockade of trade, and do all that he could to alleviate the suffering. A Commissioner would be sent out as soon as possible to investigate the entire question.[2]

Kimberley's promise of an inquiry was in fact a concession to growing pressure in Parliament and the press. From the first Kimberley had made it plain that he would not resist the demand for an investigation. As question after question in Parliament received an answer, the proposed investigation transformed itself into a comprehensive inquiry into the Niger Company's administration, with the accent on the alleged illtreatment and provocation of the Brass people. It was perhaps inevitable that this should happen, for from the company's point of view there was nothing to investigate; the Brassmen had openly and patently attacked Akassa. What more could be said? On all sides opinion rallied to the attackers; the Liverpool Chamber of Commerce and the Aborigines Protection Society flew to their defence; Sir Charles Dilke, W. F. Lawrence, Thomas Bayley, Baden-Powell and others pressed their case in Parliament; the Liverpool newspapers fulminated against the company under headlines which accused the company of

---

[1] Quotation from FO 2/86 Macdonald to F.O., tel., 9.4.95. See also *ibid.* Macdonald to F.O., tel., 27.3.95; *ibid.* F.O. to Macdonald, tel., 5.4.95; FO 83/1377 Admiralty to F.O. 29.3.95 enc. Bedford to Admiralty 29.3.95.
[2] FO 2/86 Kimberley to Macdonald, tel., 10.4.95.

'murdering natives' and flooding its territories with gin.[1] In private the Niger Coast Protectorate officials endorsed these accusations. Sir Claude Macdonald was particularly bitter against the company. Goldie, in an article in *The Times*,[2] had practically accused Macdonald of hypocrisy for supporting the Brassmen in view of the way in which the Niger Coast officials had got rid of their own middlemen like Ja Ja. This was a restatement of the 'progress' argument: middlemen were a commercial anachronism. Macdonald, in a private note to Sir Clement Hill of the Foreign Office, turned the argument upside down, and practically demanded an end to the Niger Company's charter:

Ja Ja was deported . . . because he was a big monopolist . . . now we have wiped the floor with the Brassmen because they have endeavoured to go for the biggest monopolist of the crowd—the Royal Niger Company. As I daresay you are aware, in the vast territories of the Niger Company there is not one single outside trader, black, white, green or yellow. The markets are all theirs. They can open and shut any given market at will, which means subsistence or starvation to the native inhabitants of the place. They can offer any price they like to the Producers, and the latter must either take it or starve. And why, in heaven's name, why? Because they (the Company) must pay their 6 or 7 per cent to shareholders.

This was not progress, but a system which by excluding competitors left vast tracts of country where palm oil was not collected at all. The Niger Company was nothing but an overgrown European Ja Ja. Macdonald ended by asking Hill to show his letter to Lord Kimberley if he thought it would do any good, 'Goldie is on the spot, and had a ready and clever tongue, and I am a duffer at the best, and "far away".'[3] Macdonald was supported by his subordinates, and by Admiral Bedford.[4] At times their partisanship puzzled the officials—'It is strange that cannibalism is continually ignored,' remarked Hill, evidently concerned at its odd lack of propaganda value. He

[1] *Hansard*, 4th series, XXX, col. 1262, col. 1571; *ibid.* XXXI, col. 560, col. 781, cols. 1249–50. *Liverpool Daily Post* 5.3.95.
[2] *The Times* 4.2.95, p. 9.   [3] FO 2/83 Macdonald to Hill, private, 26.3.95.
[4] FO 83/1375 Capt. Macdonald to F.O. 25.2.95; FO 83/1377 Admiralty to F.O. Conf. 8.4.95 with enclosure.

was right, Macdonald dismissed it as 'a form of sacrifice which their forefathers have practised from time immemorial'.[1]

In March 1895 the Foreign Office began to look around for candidates for the commissionership. It was no easy task to find a suitably impartial person. Almost any retired Colonial official, to whom these posts were usually given, would inevitably be prejudiced against the chartered company system by his background—the Governor of Sierra Leone was turned down on the ground that he would need too much 'coaching'.[2] On the other hand the Foreign Office could hardly appoint a director of a chartered company. The choice fell on Sir John Kirk, who combined experience as British Consul-General at Zanzibar and representative at the Brussels Conference with a directorship of the now charterless Imperial British East Africa Company.

Kirk's instructions, drafted by Sir Percy Anderson in April, were evidently regarded as a matter of high Government policy, for they were not despatched until they had been seen not only by Kimberley but also by the Prime Minister and the Chancellor of the Exchequer. They took the form of a series of charges and counter-charges; accusations of smuggling, attacking Akassa, looting and cannibalism against the Brassmen; accusations of firing on canoes, ill-treating women, excluding the Brassmen from their food-supplies, against the Niger Company. Finally Kirk was asked to suggest ways to ameliorate the Brassmen's position. Anderson would have closed the draft here, but Kimberley personally wrote in an instruction that Kirk should devise methods which would permit the Brassmen to trade in the company's territories on the lower Niger, and examine particularly schemes for the joint collection of duties by the company and Coast Protectorate administrations. This could mean only one thing—the end of the company's monopoly, at least in the oil palm region.[3]

Kirk's investigation was one of the most rapidly concluded in

[1] FO 2/100 Macdonald to Kimberley 1.5.95.
[2] FO 83/1376 minutes by C.H.H. and H.P.A. on Baden-Powell's question for 7.3.95.
[3] FO 83/1378 minutes and draft instructions to Kirk, and fair draft of 6.5.95 with addition by Kimberley.

the annals of British colonial inquiries. He arrived at Lagos on
6 June, by 14 June he had finished his inquiries at Brass and
was on his way to Akassa. Two days later he had completed his
task, and after settling the boundary dispute between Macdonald and the company, was on his way home by 30 June.
Evidently he had no wish to abuse his allowance of five guineas
a day and expenses.

He took longer to compose his report, which was not submitted until August. In the meantime all kinds of rumours flew
about; particularly persistent was the notion that Kirk intended
to recommend the transference of the Brass district to the Niger
Company. Koko and the chiefs of Brass were so alarmed that
they composed a letter to the Prince of Wales, couched in a style
containing distinct echoes of that of the recipient's own mother.
Style and content combined to produce a macabre ludicrousness
which must have tickled the Prince's sense of humour. The
chiefs, thanking the Royal Family for sending Kirk, stressed the
fact that they had received their punishment, and begged not to
be placed under the company 'to be *oppressed* and *exterminated* in
revenge'. It was their

grievances and sufferances here under the *Royal Niger Company*, which
have driven us to take the laws into our own hands by way of
revenge in looting the Company's factories at Akassa and attacking
its officials for which we are now *very very sorry* indeed, *particularly* in
the *killing* and *eating* of parts of its employees.

They suspected that their other petitions had been 'no doubt
suppressed', but they knew that this one was '*in very safe hands*':

. . . we now throw ourselves entirely at the mercy of the *good old
Queen* knowing *her* to be a most kind, *tender hearted*, and sympathetic
old mother.[1]

They need not have worried, for Kirk had worked out much
more complicated schemes of reform than the simple handing
over of Brass to the company. His findings on the various questions he had been asked to investigate favoured the Brassmen's
case, but the Niger Company was not blamed. This piece of
mental gymnastic was achieved at the expense of the British

---

[1] FO 83/1380 Koko and chiefs of Brass to Prince of Wales, 28.6.95.

P

Government itself, which had after all, Kirk insisted, given approval to all the company's regulations. Responsibility had evidently come home to roost. In fact Kirk was not much concerned with the rights and wrongs of the whole question, or who was to blame. Most of the charges against both sides he found proven. The Brassmen were inveterate smugglers; the company had fired on Brassmen and killed them; it did exclude Brassmen from the Niger. But neither side could be blamed. The Niger Company, in shooting Brassmen, had a right to use force to make its customs regulations effective, and these regulations had been approved by the British Government. On the other hand the Brassmen were utterly dependent on trade for subsistence, if they were to live they had to smuggle. Kirk's main concern was for the final item of his instructions, amelioration of the Brassmen's position by giving them access to the Niger. He concluded that the chief problem was the existence of two separate systems of customs duties in the Niger Coast Protectorate and in the Niger Company's territory. The dual system made smuggling inevitable for any African who wished to trade through the Coast Protectorate into the Niger if he were to avoid paying two sets of duties. The 'one thing essential' to any scheme to ameliorate the Brassmen's condition and secure the Company's safety was 'a common tariff and a common arms law throughout the whole maritime zone (including therein the delta of the Niger) that will do away with all inland customs frontiers.' He therefore put forward two schemes of reform, the one partial, the other a general reorganization of the company's administration. The general scheme, if it could be implemented, Kirk advocated as the more effective. The Niger Company would have to agree to the implementation of any reforms:

The Royal Niger Company has done so much national work, first in securing and then in defending and extending British interests on the Niger, that it well deserves every consideration.

The first, or 'partial' scheme was an adaptation of the Liverpool plan to transfer the palm oil region of the lower Niger to the Coast Protectorate under Macdonald. Kirk's version saved the company from the ignominy of actual transfer. The delta region, though continuing to be administered by the company, would be united in a customs union with the Coast Protectorate, and the fiscal boundary on either side of the Niger abolished. The licence system would be abolished, and complete freedom of entry granted to all comers. The two administrations would divide the revenue of the whole maritime region into equal shares. Above the delta the company could continue to be solely in control of revenue, operate its licence system as before, and monopolize the trade. There were difficulties, however, for the company would lose profits through competition in the delta region, and although Kirk estimated that the company's share of the delta revenue would amount to twice its present revenue from the whole of its territories, this was no compensation because the charter forbad the transference of administrative surpluses to the commercial profit and loss account.

Kirk therefore argued that a much more fundamental reform might be easier to implement. The ultimate solution, revocation of the charter and the establishment of direct Government administration, he rejected:

Finality in the present conditions in the Niger Territories is not to be looked for in any arrangements come to now. There is still much preliminary work to be done (and that can best perhaps be done through a Company), that will require the use of means that in time will have to make way for a more complete form of government.

The scheme which Kirk was now advocating made use of experience with the old East India Company, whose trading activities had been abolished, remaining as a governing body only 'so as to prepare the way for what inevitably must come—a direct British administration'. If the Niger Company were allowed to concentrate all its capital exclusively on administration, then it would be forced, in the interests of revenue which could only be obtained from independent traders, to establish a tariff regime which would produce maximum competition and the maximum amount of trade. Under such a regime the advantages of the chartered company would be retained, there would be no burden on the Treasury; the disadvantage of monopoly would be removed.

Access for the Brassmen and other coastal traders was to be
secured by uniting the company's territories and the Niger
Coast Protectorate in a customs union, with a common tariff
and system of taxation, the rates to be fixed by Her Majesty's
Government. A common fund would receive all revenues, and
it would be divided by the Secretary of State according to the
needs of each regime. As soon as possible the company should
cease trading, sell off all its stocks and relinquish all its monopoly
rights over minerals, land and forests. Its authorized capital of
just over £1,000,000 should be reduced to the actual working
capital of £400,000, and this capital should then be used entirely
for administrative purposes. After paying its administrative
expenses out of revenue receipts, the company could use the
'surplus' to pay interest on its capital at the rate of five per cent
per annum. (Presumably 'interest' could now be regarded as
one of the expenses of administration, so that the international
obligation not to transfer administrative profits to the commercial balance sheet did not apply in this case.)[1]

Kirk's general scheme had one particular merit. It was
acceptable to Goldie, who seems to have been consulted by Kirk
as he drafted his report, and certainly knew of the proposal in
advance of the Foreign Office. Goldie may even have
invented the scheme himself.[2] Certainly he now became its
ardent advocate, so much so that Kirk was drafted on to the
Council of the Niger Company. Kirk and Goldie henceforth

[1] Kirk's report is filed at FO 83/1382 under the date 25.8.95. It takes the form of
two dispatches, the first narrating his journey and proceedings, the second the
recommendations for reform. The report was also published as a Parliamentary
Paper (P.P. 1896, LIX, MS. p. 361), but this published document was so cut and
altered that it is useless to the historian. It omits all reference to the schemes of
reform. I have therefore referred throughout to the manuscript version.

[2] A letter which Goldie wrote to Lord Scarbrough on 11.12.96 seems to imply
this, when he says, 'If we succeed in this campaign (against Nupe and Ilorin) . . .
we must not take the terms which I offered Lord Salisbury through Kirk. . . .' The
reference to Salisbury, who had not yet become Prime Minister when Kirk wrote
his report, may be a chronological slip, on the other hand it could refer to Goldie's
offer after the report was received to implement his own version of the Kirk
scheme.

worked together for its achievement. Both of them began to press the Foreign Office to begin the implementation of the scheme, and Goldie circulated the shareholders and the Liverpool men, including the shippers, with a memorandum setting out the plan in more detail, and promising to use the company's capital under the new establishment 'to push independent trade' and to supply steamer carriage, storage space and stations, to all alike on a fixed tariff.[1] It has been seen that Goldie had been moving away from the purely commercial considerations which had so dominated his earlier policy; since the Anglo-German Agreement of 1893 he had been increasingly concerned with politics and administration, and thinking of the future. He had made the agreement with Liverpool an opportunity to alter the company's constitution to open the way for a broader representation of interests. The Kirk scheme now seemed to be the answer to all his perplexities. He was heartily sick of the attacks from Liverpool, from the Radical Members of Parliament, from the press. He wanted not just a place in history, for he knew that he had that already, but an honoured place:

'I am not content', he informed his shareholders, 'that the sacrifice to a national object of all the best years of my life . . . should result in my name being remembered only as that of a monopolist, who blocked the road to civilisation and commerce in the Niger Basin.'[2]

The reader will do well to bear these words in mind both in contemplating the man's life hitherto, and in following the story to its end. It was not Goldie's fault that the monopoly persisted during the five years which remained of the chartered company's existence. Constantly he pressed the Kirk scheme on the British Government. Had Lord Kimberley remained Foreign Secretary the scheme might well have come to fulfilment, for Kimberley's object in sending Kirk had been to allow the Brassmen to trade without involving direct Government administration and expenditure—good Liberal colonial policy. In June

[1] FO 83/1383 Kirk to F.O. 12.9.95; FO 83/1384 Goldie to Clarke, private, 26.10.95 inc. *Note for Persons Acquainted with the Situation in the Niger Territories.*
[2] *Ibid., loc. cit.* this quotation is taken from the conclusion of the *Note* enclosed.

1895, however, the Liberal Government fell, and Salisbury led the Conservatives back into office with Joseph Chamberlain as Colonial Secretary. For the first time for many decades a true imperialist, ready to invest money, men and responsibility in Africa, held a position of real power in the Cabinet. This was not a good omen for private imperialists like Goldie, for their chartered regimes rested on the reluctance of the Government to assume the burdens of direct expansion and its costs. Chamberlain, bent on developing the 'Imperial estate', could look upon the chartered company as merely a temporary expedient pending the establishment of an efficient, direct, and progressive colonial regime.

Chamberlain was still a shareholder in the company, but Goldie knew this would not lead to any favours. He tried his best to get the question decided before the new Colonial Secretary had time to settle in. Salisbury put off a meeting, but Goldie succeeded in extracting a promise that the Prime Minister would see him privately in December. Meanwhile he continued to sound out the officials, but got nothing out of them. In desperation he even turned to the old idea of amalgamation with Liverpool and extension of the charter, hoping to persuade Sir Claude Macdonald to act as Governor, but Anderson told him that the idea was 'not worthy of discussion'. One cannot help sympathizing with Goldie's complaint that his position was 'intolerable'. With the Brass question unsettled, the company's forces were bottled up in the delta in fear of another attack, while the Government accused him of neglecting the interior and the frontiers.[1]

In December Goldie had his meeting with Salisbury, and pressed the Kirk scheme on him. But Salisbury was full of objections; it might need Parliamentary legislation, and the payment of dividends out of administration revenues could not be reconciled with the Anglo-German Agreement of 1885. Goldie took great pains to refute these objections, arguing that the existing charter would allow any reforms without the inter-

---

[1] FO 83/1385 R.N.C. to F.O. 5.11.95, with minutes by Salisbury and Barrington; *ibid.* Anderson to Salisbury 20.11.95 reporting interviews with Goldie.

vention of Parliament, and stressing that the capital of the company could be treated as a colonial loan, and the interest on it be therefore a 'necessary expense of government'.[1] In reality Salisbury was hedging, waiting for Chamberlain's verdict. In January 1896 the Prime Minister's secretary told Goldie that, after discussing the question with Chamberlain, Salisbury had come to the conclusion that the Kirk scheme would be 'absolutely unacceptable to parliament'.[2] Chamberlain was obviously in no mood to tinker with a regime that he regarded as an anachronism so as to prolong its life. Goldie must have realized that the charter had not long to run. No doubt Chamberlain was right, in principle, to make this decision. But once made, action ought to have followed quickly. As it was the company was left, completely unreformed, to continue its administration of the Niger Territories until Chamberlain could see his way to take action. Many people suffered as a result: the traders, itching to get into the Niger; Goldie, struggling, with an organization that he regarded as basically faulty, to maintain the fiction that the company provided an adequate administration with inadequate resources; and not least the Brassmen, who had started it all, betrayed now not by Goldie, but by the Queen's Government to which they had looked, in all their naïve trust, for an end to their troubles.

[1] There is no record of what passed at the meeting, the above account is inferred from Goldie's letters to the F.O. in December, especially FO 83/1387, Mem. *The Niger Company's Charter* communicated by Goldie 30.12.95.

[2] FO 83/1440 Barrington to Goldie 3.1.96.

The Burdens of Empire

To appreciate Goldie's position at the time of the Brassmen's attack on Akassa, we must now take a wider look at the Niger Company's position. It was a time of acute, almost catastrophic, danger, full of difficulties of a most formidable kind. For while the Brassmen had been making their preparations, a major threat from France had been developing in the north-western part of the Niger Territories, and in this same region the British Colonial Office was trying to force Goldie along a path which he did not wish to, and at this time could not, follow. As the Brassmen were looting Akassa, a French gunboat was openly defying the company's administration on the lower Niger, a French officer with a party of African troops was in occupation of a fortified position on the navigable Niger below Bussa, and French expeditions were wandering over what had hitherto been accepted as the company's treaty sphere. As if this were not enough, Goldie was being subjected to intense pressure from the Colonial Office to mount a formidable and costly military expedition for the conquest of the Muslim emirate of Ilorin.

Each of these dangers was symptomatic of a profound change which was affecting the policies of European governments in Africa; a change which was ultimately to bring about the fall of the chartered regime. While European governments were content to establish their claims to African territory on little more than dubious treaties and imaginary lines on the map, the Niger Company had found no difficulty, indeed had often had the advantage, in fulfilling its role as British representative on the

Niger. But if France or Germany once decided to spend a few thousand francs or marks on the training of African regiments for the establishment of posts in the interior garrisoned by troops, then the company would be hopelessly outplayed in the struggle for territory. Gradually, between about 1894 and 1897, this transition took place. And at the same time the British West African colonies, under the new regime inaugurated by Chamberlain, took the same road. 'Effective occupation' was coming to be the watchword of European diplomacy in Africa.

Goldie was well aware of this trend. His advocacy of the Kirk scheme was his response to it. If the era of military occupation and conquest had come, then the company must be allowed to reorganize its activities and concentrate on administration, leaving trade to others. It could then strengthen its military forces, build forts, and really occupy its territories. As we have seen, Goldie was not permitted to undertake this reorganization by Chamberlain. Yet Chamberlain expected Goldie to continue to fulfil the company's imperial role despite the intensification of the conditions of the struggle for territory, and even to fight a military campaign in Ilorin where there was no foreign threat. Little wonder that relations between the company and the British Government degenerated into a constant tug-of-war, punctuated by mutual bickering, pettiness, recriminations, insults and downright blackmail from each side.

Neither the French threat nor the pressure of the Colonial Office for the conquest of Ilorin were sudden in their appearance; both had been maturing for some years. Since the conclusion of the Say–Barruwa line in 1890, and the Anglo-German Agreement of 1893, international rivalry naturally centred on the undefined area between Say and the termination of the Anglo-French boundary between Lagos and Porto Novo. This region was dominated by the African state of Borgu, which Goldie claimed for the company by reason of the treaties with Bussa, one of the states in the Borguan system. Before 1893 there had been several attempts to draw a line across this region; on one occasion the French even offered a line connecting Say right across to Bunduku on the western frontier of the Gold Coast. But Salisbury, against the advice of his officials, rejected it. The French were planning a war against Dahomey, and feared that if a line were not agreed beforehand, Goldie would take his chance to expand into Borgu while they were busy with the war. Salisbury thought that after the enormous expense of the war the French would be 'very tired of West African negotiations'.[1] He was already slightly out of his depth. The Dahomey campaign was not a punitive expedition on a grand scale like the British wars with Ashanti in the Gold Coast. The French followed up their conquest by settling garrisons in the chief towns of Dahomey and really beginning the administration of the country.

After the Dahomey war the French attitude to the Niger Company radically altered. Both Mizon and Monteil, the latter now returned from his journey across the Fulani emirates to Lake Chad, exposed the myth of the 'powerful' Niger Company. The mistake made in conceding the Say–Barruwa line was now fully realized, and the French began to make efforts to get round the provisions of that awkward agreement. This was not too difficult. The agreement had many anomalies. In the first place it was simply a line drawn between two points, not one which enclosed an area, and the 1890 Declaration expressly mentioned that the Borgu region was left open. The French argued that this allowed them to make acquisitions in Borgu even though these might actually be south of the Say–Barruwa line. Moreover the wording of the declaration was seriously defective from the British point of view. Though Britain recognized that all the territory from Algeria up to the line was French, the French merely agreed to deflect the line 'so as to comprise in the sphere of action of the Niger Company all that fairly belongs to the Kingdom of Sokoto'. Technically the French did not, therefore, expressly recognize that territory south of the line was

---

[1] For the details of this remarkable blunder see FO 84/2208 Dufferin to Salisbury, 108 Af., 13.5.92 and enclosure; *ibid*. minutes by H.P.A., J. W. Lowther and Salisbury on same; and FO 84/2211 Phipps to Anderson, private, 30.11.92.

British. The French now began to argue that their action south of the line was only limited so far as Sokoto was concerned, elsewhere they were free.[1]

The continuing negotiations therefore foundered, this time through French intransigence. In mid-1894 Goldie almost pulled off a master stroke of diplomacy which would have out-done all his previous efforts. He was not really interested in Borgu for itself, but only in preventing French access to the navigable Niger. On the other hand the real motive, so he thought, behind French interest in the region, was to keep open a corridor to connect the new Dahomey colony with Algeria, Senegal, and the other French West African colonies. He there-fore suggested conceding Borgu, but not access to the Niger, in return for a French recognition of British claims to predomi-nance in the Nile basin. The security of the Nile basin was already emerging as the greatest preoccupation of British policy in tropical Africa; if Goldie could have bought it by apparently sacrificing the company's interests, it would have been an achievement surpassing even those of Cecil Rhodes. Securing fundamental British interests, without any gain to the company itself, who could then have argued that the Niger Company was little more than a monopolistic conspiracy? But it was not to be; though the French Foreign Ministry was probably prepared to accept the basic principle of the plan, it found itself outwitted by its own Colonial Office.[2]

The French Colonial Office, newly organized as an independ-dent department of state[3] and staffed very largely by nominees of the colonial group, could see no reason to allow the Foreign Office to repeat its mistake of 1890 when direct action against the now despised Niger Company could bring rapid gains; not only preserving an open corridor between Dahomey and the rest of French West Africa, but also gaining access to the navigable

---

[1] *Siècle* 8.11.93; FO 27/3134 Phipps to Hill, private, 25.8.93.

[2] Goldie's scheme can be found in FO 27/3208 Mem. by Goldie received 10.7.94; for Hanotaux's reaction see FO 27/3186 Phipps to Kimberley, 232 Af. Conf. 13.9.94 and FO 27/3187 Phipps to Kimberley, 260 Af. most conf. 4.10.94 which reveals that Hanotaux was prepared to go to the length of bribing members of the Colonial party to get an agreement.

[3] It had hitherto been attached to the Ministry of Marine.

Niger somewhere below the Bussa rapids so as to create an open highway for the development of the Dahomey hinterland. In concert with the Ministry of Marine the French Colonial Office now proceeded to organize a series of expeditions designed to secure Borgu, access to the Niger below Bussa, and the establishment of French rights to sail freely up and down the Niger through the company's territories. This ruined any chances of agreement by diplomacy.

Goldie, however, had not been slow to read the writing on the wall. Already in 1894 he had sent William Wallace to Gandu and Sokoto to conclude new treaties to reinforce the Thomson treaties of 1885 and the King treaties of 1890. Wallace returned with properly signed and sealed documents granting the company full power over foreigners, including the right to tax them, and agreeing not to recognize any other European powers.[1] After concluding these treaties Wallace had made an extensive investigation of the African political situation on the middle Niger around Bussa. His report was a disquieting one, for he found many areas which were not subject either to Gandu or Bussa, and therefore outside the company's treaty system and open to annexation by France.[2] Goldie had anticipated this, and before Wallace's return had taken steps to organize a treaty-making expedition not simply to Bussa, but to all the towns in Borgu. The importance attached to this expedition was shown in the appointment of Captain Frederick Lugard as its leader. Lugard was already famous in England and notorious in France for his intervention in the religious wars in Uganda while employed by the British East Africa Company, an intervention which the French alleged had been directed against the Catholic pro-French party. His appointment by Goldie was thus an open challenge to the French.[3]

[1] Texts in FO 2/167 Treaties between R.N.C. and native chiefs, Pt. I, 1891–8, nos. 137 and 139. Treaties with Sokoto 26.6.94 and Gandu 4.7.94.

[2] FO 27/3300 Lord Scarbrough to F.O. 26.2.96 enc. extracts from Wallace's diary made in 1894.

[3] For Lugard's earlier career see Perham, Margery, *Lugard: The Years of Adventure 1858–98*, London, 1956. Miss Perham discusses the details of Lugard's appointment on pp. 490–2. She makes it clear that the Foreign Office regarded Goldie's choice as a useful means of finding employment for an otherwise embarrassing agent. There

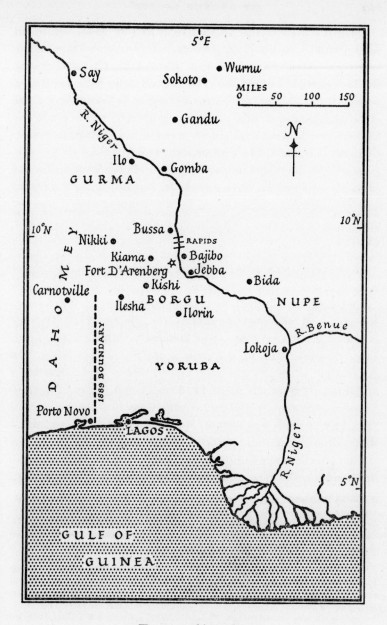

4. Treaty-making 1894–5

Lugard left Liverpool for the Niger in July 1894, and in the same month Captain H. A. Decœur left France for Dahomey to take the overland route for Borgu. There were contrasts between the two parties. Lugard had 280 porters, who were to be protected by forty soldiers, who turned out to be 'according to his standards the rawest of recruits, undisciplined and untrained'.[1] Decœur had 290 men, half of whom were well-trained Sengalese *tirailleurs*. Lugard's instructions from Goldie told him to make treaties from the Niger across to Nikki and then westward as far as the Gold Coast frontier if possible, but he was to remember

above all, that diplomacy and not conquest is *the* object of your expedition westwards . . . the exercise of force cannot further your objects. . . .

In contrast Decœur was ordered not simply to make treaties in Borgu, but to leave garrisons in occupation of the places he visited and to establish the rudiments of an administration. Lugard had only one advantage; the Niger. While Decœur laboured wearily on foot across Dahomey with his large party, Lugard could steam up the river to the frontiers of Borgu.[2] In September, when Decœur had reached Carnotville, Lugard was at Jebba, from which place he went farther up the Niger to Bussa to continue Wallace's investigations into the position of that state in the Borgu system. He came to the same conclusion that although in some respects Bussa was looked on as the 'father' of the other Borguan towns, to cover the area properly he would have to make treaties with the practically independent

is also an interesting note by Sir Percy Anderson in FO 83/1315 dated 19.9.94 reporting a conversation with Goldie in which he, Anderson, told him 'that the Secretary of State was not prepared to take the responsibility of stopping the expedition on which Capt. Lugard has been despatched', adding that 'I would not say more than this'. Goldie replied 'that he quite understood'.

[1] Perham, *op. cit.*, p. 504, paraphrasing Lugard's diary.

[2] Goldie to Lugard 24.7.94 quoted in Perham, *op. cit.*, p. 493 and *ibid.*, p. 504. For Decœur's mission see the interesting memorandum by the War Office Intelligence Dept. in FO 27/3258 enclosed in W.O.I.D. to F.O. 4.7.95. Even Lugard's advantage of the river access might have been denied him had the French succeeded in sending the mission under Capt. Toutée, which was planned to ascend the Niger claiming free navigation; but Goldie successfully resisted the scheme on the ground that free navigation did not extend to armed parties. Toutée's mission finally went overland.

rulers of Nikki and Kiama. Returning to Jebba, Lugard set out across country for Kiama, which he reached on 17 October.

We must now take a closer look at these Borguan people whom Lugard was about to ask to sign away their sovereignty. Though the country was miserably poor, the people were fierce and warlike, skilled in the use of poisoned arrows, qualities which enabled them, in contrast to some of their richer and more sophisticated neighbours, to preserve their independence from the Fulani. In religion they were 'pagan', or what today would be called Animistic, but there were Muslim quarters in most of the towns, and some Muslim influences had penetrated in debased and superstitious forms into Borguan life. Almost the only literate people were Muslim *mallams*, and these holy men were regarded with awe, particularly from their supposed magical powers conferred by writing. Texts from the Koran written on slips of wood, hide or paper, were assumed to work minor miracles. It was therefore particularly dangerous to write one's name, or even to have it written down, and to allow such writing to pass into other hands who might use it for evil magic. In most places there was also a superstitious fear of white men, possibly due to the fact that the dreaded Fulani were of lighter colour than the Borguans. If white men came, with an armed band to support them, and asked a king to put his name on pieces of paper, which they then took away, this could conjure up horrible prospects. The safest thing therefore, was, if possible, to evade the European's requests. If they were insistent, then the best man to deal with the business would be the local *mallam*, who could use his supernatural powers to prevent the worst effects of letting the Europeans take away writing, and could probably prevent the king's name from actually appearing on the treaty.

This made things very difficult from Lugard's point of view. He had little information on the area, and could not check whether the names given to him were correct. Even if he had his doubts, the only way to get accuracy was to force the information out of the rulers. This he was not strong enough to do, and his instructions from Goldie forbade it anyway. Decœur, on the other hand, was in a much stronger position. The garrisons left in each town could gather information, and the local rulers could be coerced by his strong force into signing with their true names.

Thus, at Kiama, the King and chiefs readily signed a treaty with Lugard granting the company full jurisdiction over foreigners and accepting 'the protection of the British' (though this protection was only granted 'as far as practicable'). The King and his advisers signed with crosses. Subsequently however, it was found that the name given in the treaty as that of the King (Musa Pobida) was in fact that of one of his Muslim clerks. When the French came later they were able to extract a proper Arabic signature from the King.[1]

Lugard then moved on to Nikki. On the way there he was approached by one Abdulla, an *Imam*, or *Leman* as he was known locally. Abdulla claimed that he had been deputed by the King of Nikki to negotiate with the English, for the King was blind, and had a superstitious dread of meeting Europeans. When he

[1] For text see FO 2/167, no. 176, Treaty with Keioma (Kiama) 22.10.94. The fact that Musa Pobida was not the King's name was disclosed by inquiries made later by the Governor of Lagos. His object was to prove the treaties valid in face of French claims so there can be little doubt that his verdict was a true one. See FO 27/3438 C.O. to F.O. 2.3.98 enc. McCallum to Chamberlain 28.2.98, tel., and FO 27/3439 C.O. to F.O. 15.4.98 secret enc. McCallum to Chamberlain 1.3.98 secret. For the King's superstitious dread of putting his name to paper see FO 27/3438 C.O. to F.O. 3.3.98 enc. Lugard's comments.

My interpretation of this, and the subsequent treaty at Nikki, is somewhat different to that put forward in my unpublished Ph.D. thesis, obtainable in the Library of the University of London, *British Policy and Chartered Company Administration in Nigeria, 1879–1900*, pp. 463–8, where the interpretation given in Perham, *op. cit.*, pp. 507–18, is challenged. Since my thesis was presented I have had the pleasure of discussing these treaties on several occasions with Miss Perham, and her arguments have forced me to alter my interpretation on several points. Miss Perham knew Lugard personally for many years, and has most thoroughly mastered his mountainous correspondence and documents. She has convinced me that Lugard was thoroughly honest and scrupulous in all that he did in Borgu, and that it is unfair to suggest as I implied on p. 466 of my thesis, that Lugard was not above using trickery to further his aims. I found also that Miss Perham was much more knowledgeable and accurate than I on the anthropology and sociology of Borgu; that I had underestimated the influence of the Muslims in this region I had described as 'purely' pagan, and that this, for me, provided a better explanation of Lugard's difficulties. However, as the reader who wishes for the pleasure of reading Miss Perham's fuller account of these negotiations will quickly realize my interpretation remains radically different from hers. Miss Perham thinks the treaties conferred valid title; I argue that Lugard was duped into taking away worthless documents.

arrived at Nikki Lugard failed in his attempts to see the King, though his African interpreter did manage to see him, and assured Lugard that the *Leman* had indeed been deputed to negotiate a treaty. On 10 November Lugard therefore made a treaty, in the name of the King, with the *Leman*, the *Sarkin Powa* (head butcher), and one 'Naimiu'. The *Leman* signed each of the names, and Lugard added a declaration, supported by another signed by the African interpreter, that these men were truly deputed to sign. The name given to the King in the treaty was Lafia. Lugard himself had doubts on this score, for he afterwards added 'also called Absalamu, son of Wurukura' to his copy of the treaty, hearing that this was another name given to the King. Once more the Borguan dread of committing the name to writing was to cause trouble. The use of the name Lafia was particularly unfortunate, for it was the name of a king who had been dead for six years. The King's real name was Sire Toru.[1]

Lugard left Nikki a few days after concluding the treaty. His instructions from Goldie, and the weakness of the force at his disposal, prevented him from leaving a garrison in the town. In fact on 16 November his party was attacked after it had left the town by Borguan marauders who nearly killed Lugard. After fighting his way out Lugard abandoned any idea of moving farther westward and made his way back through Yorubaland.[2]

The race for Borgu had been a close thing. Only five days after Lugard left Nikki, Captain Decœur and the French party arrived in the town. Decœur now did all he could to undo Lugard's advantage in arriving first. His force was strong, and it was not difficult to persuade the King to overcome his supersti-

[1] For text see FO 2/167, no. 194, Treaty with Nikki 10.11.94, with declarations by Lugard and Joseph; FO 27/3232 Enc. 5 in Dufferin to Salisbury, 202 Af. 19.7.95; FO 27/3274 Dufferin to Salisbury, 53 Af. 21.3.96 enc. a report on this and other Lugard treaties by Howard and Everett, with paraphrases from Lugard's diary; FO 27/3411 Monson to Salisbury, 63 Af. 14.2.98 enc. report by Gosselin and Everett on their examination of the original of this treaty; FO 27/3412 Monson to Salisbury, 111 Af. Conf. 18.3.98 enc. 'Observations, etc.' by Gosselin and Everett (highly critical of Lugard's action in adding 'Absalamu', etc. to the King's name); FO 27/3427 C.O. to F.O. 22.2.98 mema. by Lugard dated 6.2.98 and 12.2.98; FO 27/3439 C.O. to F.O. 15.4.98 secret, enc. McCallum to Chamberlain, secret, 1.3.98 (an investigation on the spot by the Governor of Lagos).
[2] For the full story of this exciting journey see Perham, *op. cit.*, pp. 519–30.

Q

tious dread of the Europeans; on 26 November the King personally signed a treaty placing himself 'under the exclusive Protectorate of France'.[1]

In January 1895, two months later, Governor Ballot of Dahomey arrived with a second expedition which had been following up the work of Decœur. Ballot now obtained a written repudiation of Lugard's Nikki treaty, in which the King denied delegating any powers, and accused the Muslim faction in Nikki, led by the *Leman*, of fraudently signing the treaty without authorization, and (what was perhaps a greater crime) keeping the presents given in return by Lugard for their own use.[2] But Ballot had not come to Borgu merely to settle the dispute over Lugard's treaty. With a rapidity hitherto unheard of, the French set about occupying their new acquisitions. Ballot had already left small detachments of African troops, usually with a European officer in command, in the towns between Carnotville and Nikki. From Nikki Ballot went onward to the Niger itself, where he began to make surveys of navigability and entered into relations with tribes which were technically in the Niger Company's treaty system.[3] Though Ballot returned to the coast in March 1895 these were ominous developments for Goldie, especially as they were conducted by the highest-ranking French official in the neighbourhood. The Niger Company could not afford a scramble with France conducted on the principle of effective occupation, yet if Goldie were to stand idle and allow the French to establish a footing on the navigable Niger the revenue system was in serious danger. It was now becoming clear that access to the navigable Niger, and not just the barren country of Borgu itself, was the aim of the French expeditions. A party of men detached from the Decœur mission soon established themselves at Say, and in February a mission under Toutée arrived at Kiama and made a treaty there, ignoring Lugard's prior treaty. This, and other treaties made by Toutée struck a new and alarming note, for they all contained

[1] FO 27/3232 Dufferin to Salisbury, 202 Af. 18.7.95 enc. copy of this treaty.
[2] *Ibid., loc. cit.* encs. of declarations dated 20.1.95 and 21.1.95 by Sire Toru.
[3] *Journal des Débats* 8.5.95; FO 27/3257 W.O.I.D. to F.O. 21.5.95 enc. mem. on French Posts in Borgu.

stipulations for effective occupation; the establishment of residents, provisions for public works and government building, and the stationing of a garrison in each town.[1] As Toutée moved towards the Niger this was the signal for Decœur's main party, and the detachment left at Say, to join up down-river at Leaba, where there was actually a Niger Company station. This did not deter them from making a treaty with the local ruler, after which they returned to Dahomey overland.[2] Meanwhile Toutée reached the Niger at Bajibo, in Nupe country, late in February 1895. Here he really showed his hand, setting to work to construct earthworks and fortifications around his settlement, which he named Fort D'Arenberg after the Prince who was the patron of the colonial party in France. From Fort D'Arenberg he then set out to continue Ballot's surveys of navigability, making treaties on his way upstream with Bussa and other towns where the company traded and had treaties. A garrison was left in the fort.[3]

Nor was this all. Apparently to synchronize with Toutée's activities on the river, a French naval gunboat, the *Ardent*, had sailed boldly up the Niger in December 1894, making no attempt to inform the company of its intentions. A hundred miles up the Niger the gunboat ran aground on a sandbank. One of the officers then succeeded in chartering a launch to bring supplies to the stranded vessel; and he also refused to inform the company of his actions, or to obtain any permission to clear the launch. When arrested by revenue officers, he broke free, declaring that 'the River Niger was as free as the British Channel'.[4]

This then, was the dangerous position which had materialized just at the time the Brassmen chose to mount their attack on Akassa. In the months that followed, with the Brassmen neither disarmed, nor placated by reform, the company's constabulary was pinned down in the delta to avert another attack. A French

[1] FO 27/3274 Dufferin to Salisbury, 27 Af. 21.2.96 enc. copies of Toutée's treaties with Kishi and Kiama.

[2] *Ibid.*, *loc. cit.*, enc. Treaty with Leaba 24.4.95; see also FO 27/3258 W.O.I.D. to F.O. 4.7.95 enc. mem. on Decoeur and Toutée.

[3] *Débats* 8.5.95; *L'Estafette* 5.6.95: FO 27/3257 mem. by Clement Hill on the position of the Niger Co. 6.5.95.

[4] FO 27/3257 R.N.C. to F.O. 22.5.95 with enclosures.

gunboat lay up the river, and its officers defied the company's officials. Toutée, with African soldiers, occupied Fort D'Arenberg. All over Borgu the French were establishing garrisons and setting up administrative machinery. The corridor to the navigable Niger and free transit up that river seemed to have been established by France as a *fait accompli*.

Goldie could not hope to eject the French by force, so he had to try diplomacy. He tried, in the early months of 1895, a rather wild fling designed to repeat the tactics successfully pursued in 1893. Contacts were resumed with Herr Vohsen, who at this moment had an expedition under Dr. Gruner wandering in the north which had actually concluded a treaty with Gandu. Goldie's plan was to establish Germany in western Borgu, joining this region to Togoland and thus creating a German barrier between the French in Dahomey and the Niger. The contacts between Goldie and Vohsen were taken up by the two governments, but the Germans were once more insistent on obtaining a navigable part of the Niger. Goldie feared that, as in 1894, the Germans might cede some of their gains to the French, and the scheme fell through.[1]

Meanwhile something had to be done about the French. The simplest problem was that of the warship in the lower Niger. The ship was easy to watch, and the Admiralty sent a gunboat to 'assist' in refloating the vessel, really to prevent her making for the upper river to assist Toutée. Meanwhile the British embassy in Paris secured a repudiation of the captain's action, stating that he had acted without orders and that he would be reprimanded and probably dismissed his ship. Even so, it was not until July 1895 that the vessel left the Niger, her officers witnesses of, and sufferers by, the Brass attack on Akassa.[2]

---

[1] This is a very bald summary of the negotiations. For details see FO 64/1372 Goldie to F.O. 11.1.95 enc. Vohsen to Goldie 9.1.95; FO 64/1367 Kimberley to Hatzfeldt 16.3.95 and 14.6.95 and *ibid*. Observations on the British Proposals communicated by Hatzfeldt 28.3.95. The German demands for the so-called 'Trans-Volta strip' in the Gold Coast were as much a stumbling block as the demand for Niger access.

[2] The Frenchmen lost some of their belongings, but none was injured in body. FO 27/3188 Dufferin to Kimberley 64, Af. tel., 13.12.94 and 65 Af. tel., 13.12.94; FO 27/3229 Salisbury to Dufferin, 207 Af. 5.7.95.

There remained the serious problem of Fort D'Arenberg, opposite Bajibo. The strongest pressure was brought on the French Government to evacuate the fort, but the French strongly asserted Toutée's right to be there, and even began to insinuate that they could not recognize that the Niger Company, being a mere trading concern, had any claim to administrative authority. It was even asserted that because France had never recognized explicitly any of the company's treaties, she was free to establish posts where she would.[1] Goldie thought that the delays were merely an excuse to give the French time to bring up reinforcements for Toutée from Dahomey, and was very worried.[2] Once more, however, as at the time of the Mizon affair, Goldie was to find surprising allies among the African rulers. The French policy of effective occupation was all very well, provided it was done thoroughly, if not it had serious drawbacks, especially when it was attempted, as Toutée was attempting it, with a small party of thirty or forty soldiers. The African rulers raised few objections to the pretensions of a company which scarcely ever interfered with their affairs. It was a different matter when bodies of troops appeared and dug themselves in. Why had they come? They had obviously not come to shake hands, give presents, ask for signatures on curious bits of paper, and make trade as the company men did. At D'Arenberg there were about thirty soldiers and twice as many porters and camp followers. Parties of soldiers had gone foraging for food, and looted villages in the process, and farther west in Borgu similar things were now happening; soldiers were even telling the kings how they should rule their own people. The local rulers began to think they would be a good deal better off with the Niger Company for a 'protector'. The King of Kiama wrote to Lugard complaining that the French 'came into this country as if it were a heathen country . . . they are too strong for me, and I pray that you will come between me and them.' Agent-General Wallace reported that the Kings of Kiama and Bussa

<hr />

[1] FO 27/3229 Kimberley to Dufferin, 111 Af. 28.3.95; FO 27/3231 Howard to Kimberley, 119 Af. 9.5.95.
[2] FO 27/3257 Goldie to F.O. 16.5.95 and 21.5.95.

were so incensed at the French that they might well join in alliance with the Emir of Nupe and expel the French by force. He was genuinely afraid that the Frenchmen would be slaughtered, and made arrangements with them so that they could find sanctuary in the company's station at Egga if need be.[1] Toutée's position soon became untenable, and he decided that discretion was the better part of valour, taking the somewhat ignominious course of allowing himself to be evacuated down-river by the company. Though he left a skeleton garrison in the fort, this too was evacuated in September 1895.[2]

With the withdrawal from Fort D'Arenberg the stage was set for the renewal of negotiations. The French, for the time being, sent no more expeditions into the Niger Company's sphere. As if to clear the air the French press adopted a remarkably conciliatory tone; the *Politique Coloniale* went so far as to define effective occupation as the establishment of regular and continuous commercial intercourse with the 'occupied' state. *Figaro* even printed an interview in which Goldie defended the company's claims.[3] In the winter of 1895 there was a brief flirtation with Germany to try to revive Goldie's plan for a German buffer colony in Borgu, but the Germans made inordinate demands and the talks petered out.[4] In January 1896 negotiations were recommenced with France. For several months more a tedious farce was played out in Paris, where the 'experts' of both sides, none of whom had ever visited the Niger or Borgu, and knowing not one word of any of the languages involved, wrangled incessantly over the rival treaties, taking days to examine the significance of a word here, a date there, a

[1] These were not propagandist reports, nor even written for F.O. eyes. See FO 27/3258 R.N.C. to F.O. 26.6.95 inc. Wallace to R.N.C. 18.5.95 and King of Kiama to Lugard 30.4.95.
[2] FO 27/3258 R.N.C. to F.O. 22.8.95; FO 27/3232 Dufferin to Salisbury, 244 Af. 10.9.95 enc. Hanotaux to Howard 9.9.95.
[3] *Politique Coloniale* 17.8.95; *Figaro* 19.8.95.
[4] FO 83/1386 mem. on the negotiations of Nov. 1895, etc., by H.P.A. 28.11.95. Once more the Trans-Volta strip, and the German demand for access to the Niger, were the stumbling-blocks.

signature or a name. When concrete proposals for a line were made by the French their demands were fantastic, including not only the cession of vast tracks of the navigable Niger down almost as far as Lokoja, but even the revision in France's favour, of the Lagos–Porto Novo boundary agreed upon and respected since 1889. When the British, in May 1896, informed the French that no access of any kind could be granted to the navigable Niger the negotiations were virtually broken off.[1]

It was clear that the failure of the talks would lead to another bout of direct action, probably more formidable than that of 1894–5. Goldie had already taken advantage of the lull caused by the renewed negotiations to visit the Niger and personally supervise the establishment of a chain of posts below the rapids at Bussa to control the upper section of the navigable river. Fort D'Arenberg had been occupied by the constabulary and renamed Fort Goldie.[2] But this kind of activity cost a great deal of money, and brought no return to the company in trading profits. With the company unreformed it was not possible to increase the funds available for such work by increasing taxation, for apart from the company itself, there were no traders to tax. How could the company, with its limited resources, face the competition of a European state like France with its vast resources of men and money? The burden of maintaining British interests on the Niger was now, for the first time, becoming unsupportable. Already there were mutterings in the lesser ranks of Government that the company had had its day. Howard, one of the negotiators in Paris, strongly urged the Foreign Office in August 1896 to watch carefully lest the Niger Company fail to guard its frontiers, which some day the British Government would inherit. His colleague Colonel Everett of the Intelligence Department went so far as to advocate that the Government should take over the administration, 'spend a little money—

---

[1] For French demands see FO 27/3275 Dufferin to Salisbury, 69 Af. 30.4.96 and enclosure, and same to same, 75 Af. 8.5.96 with enclosure. It was later modified slightly (see *ibid*. Dufferin to Salisbury, 88 Af. 23.5.96 with enclosure) and it was on this occasion that the British refused all access to the navigable river.

[2] FO 83/1387 Goldie to F.O. 23.12.95 in which Goldie gives details of his plans to do this.

which Goldie cannot afford to do', and concede access to the Niger to France, which would not matter if there could be free trade on the Niger.[1] This was a mood which was soon to find expression at higher levels in the months which followed. Yet, although the politicians and officials were well aware that this was a time of acute difficulty for Goldie, it was at precisely this moment that the Colonial Office pressure to begin a military campaign against Ilorin reached its climax, and forced Goldie to move. As if this were not enough, the Foreign Office not only tied Goldie's hands and prevented him from using the expedition to strengthen the company's position in Borgu, but obligingly informed the French of Goldie's precise movements. This gave France a heaven-sent opportunity to occupy in force a considerable stretch of the Niger below Bussa. The result was the Niger Crisis of 1897–8 which brought Britain and France to the verge of war—and incidentally destroyed the chartered Niger Company.

The Ilorin problem was one with deep roots in Nigerian history; yet its emergence at the end of 1896 as an acute crisis revealed how the trend towards effective occupation, in this case not in a French territory but in the colony of Lagos, could produce great difficulties for Goldie's unreformed company. The basis of the problem was the struggle between the Ilorins, as the southermost outpost of the Fulani *jihad*,[2] and the still unconquered Animistic Yoruba to the south-west. The Ilorin people were themselves Yoruba, but in the early nineteenth century the traditional state had been overthrown and a Muslim emirate set up in its stead.[3] For a time it seemed as if the conquest of Ilorin was but the preliminary to the collapse of the entire Yoruba power-system, indeed the near-by capital of the Yoruba empire, Old Oyo, had to be evacuated and a new city built

[1] FO 27/3276 Howard to Salisbury, 147 Af. Conf. 5.8.96; FO 27/3301 Everett to Hill 31.12.96.

[2] For the origins of the *jihad* see Chap. 2, pp. 15–17.

[3] Though many of the traditional forms of social and political life persisted, adapted to the needs of the new regime. This was particularly so in the military sphere, where the Yoruba system of 'baloguns' (generals who possessed a good deal of independent initiative) persisted.

farther south. The Yoruba were saved by the emergence of the new state of Ibadan on the northern frontiers facing Ilorin. The Ibadans first checked, then defied the Ilorins, in a permanent war punctuated only by periods of uneasy truce.[1]

In the 1880's this antagonism concerned the British authorities but little. Though Ilorin was recognized as part of the Niger Company's sphere, and Ibadan as within the protectorate ruled by the Governor of Lagos, the wars and rumours of wars were far away on remote borders. There was a certain amount of commercial rivalry as the company tried to channel Ilorin trade to the Niger, whilst Lagos fostered the overland route, but this was not serious. Neither side administered any territory near enough to the Ibadan-Ilorin frontier to be affected closely by the rivalry. But as the decade of the 1890's progressed, a contrast between the company's administrative progress and that of Lagos developed. Whilst the Niger Company stood still and made no attempt to interfere in Ilorin, the Lagos colony was creeping forward into the interior, becoming more and more involved with the Ibadans, building tracks and crude roads across country, planning railways and telegraph lines, and finally arriving, with detachments of the Lagos constabulary, at Ilorin border. There they found a state of affairs practically unchanged since the 1880's and the Emir of Ilorin raiding at will into Ibadan country, unchecked by the company.

The Ilorin problem was not one to be seen in isolation, though the Lagos authorities usually did so. Beside Ilorin lay its more powerful neighbour Nupe, bound by traditional ties of alliance and a natural sympathy for fellow-Muslims struggling against 'kafirs' on the borderlands of Islam. Interference, particularly military action, in Ilorin, was bound to have repercussions in Nupe. Basically Goldie was prepared to ignore Ilorin, the company had never been represented in that state except by African trading agents. Nupe was a different matter; it controlled a large section of the banks of the Niger, it was a centre for the caravan trade to the north, and it was a powerful

[1] For details see Johnson, S., *History of the Yorubas*, London, 1921; Hogben, S. J., *The Muhammadan Emirates of Nigeria*, London, 1930, pp. 151-6.

state in its own right. Since Simpson's visit in 1871[1] the Emir of
Nupe had regarded himself as the 'protector' of the British
Niger traders, so that to establish a real administration it was
necessary to turn completely upside down the traditional
relationship. Goldie always showed himself acutely aware of
Nupe susceptibilities, and trod warily. Nevertheless the company was inevitably forced, in order to maintain British claims
to Nupe and to keep its monopoly, to undermine year by year
Nupe's real power and independence. The expulsion of Hoenigsberg[2] had been a first stage in this process. In 1889 it had
assumed territorial aspects, for Lokoja, where the company now
stationed a detachment of constabulary, was regarded as part of
the Nupe sphere of influence. It was not thought of as directly
part of Nupe's territory, but as a kind of proving ground for
military manœuvres which were also slave raids, administered
as a fief by one of the great Nupe princes. In 1889 the company
challenged the claim of Prince Bunu to hold Lokoja, and the
garrison stopped his soldiers from collecting tribute and slaves.
The result was extremely unnerving to the Nupe aristocracy,
whose hold over the subject population had never been strong,
and at times was only preserved with the aid of the company's
steamers. Refugees and escaped slaves now began to find
sanctuary either in the company's stations, or in the mission
centres of the Church Missionary Society. The latter were
looked on with great suspicion, for in the Fulani *jihad* it had been
the *mallams* who had first entered the pagan countries, spying
out the land in preparation for revolution. It was natural that
Christian preachers should be regarded as analogous in their
function, particularly when they seemed more concerned for
the welfare of subversive elements in society, slaves and low-
born people. The Nupe aristocracy therefore made things as
difficult as possible, and the Emir had great difficulty in restrain-
ing his generals from attacking Lokoja. At times the station was
actually evacuated.[3]

[1] See Chap. 2, pp. 24–5.   [2] See Chap. 6, pp. 114 ff.

[3] Reconstructed from C.M.S. Papers, G3 A3/05 Sudan Mission leaflets nos. 13
and 15; *ibid.* no. 8, Annual Letter of J. J. Williams from Lokoja 12.11.91. I am
grateful to Dr. Jacob Ajayi for advice and assistance based on his very thorough
knowledge of the history of Christian missions in Nigeria.

The situation became so difficult by the end of 1891 that Goldie decided to go out to the Niger and try to reach some kind of a working arrangement with the Emir of Nupe. He took with him the Earl of Scarbrough, who had become interested in the territories after visiting them on big game hunting expeditions and had asked Goldie to put him on the board of directors.[1] Scarbrough was soon to be Goldie's greatest friend and confidant, and later his successor as chairman of the Niger Company after its charter was revoked. Goldie and Scarbrough had no intention of browbeating the Emir. They took with them a letter from Queen Victoria to the Emir, drafted by Sir Percy Anderson to cover 'our meaning that he is under our protection, yet . . . not incompatible with his possible assertion of independence'.[2] When he arrived at Lokoja Goldie felt that war with Nupe was a distinct possibility, and he blamed his own officials for interference with the institution of slavery, in his opinion not justified by the terms of the company's treaty with Nupe, which made no mention of slaves. When he and Scarbrough met the Emir and his *N'degi* (chief minister) at Bida he did all he could to reassure them. He promised that the company would respect the treaty and stop its men from interfering between master and slave in Nupe territory. He knew that the Princes were worried that the company intended to occupy Nupe as it had occupied the pagan states farther down the river, but he assured them that this was not the case. The pagans were disorderly, and trade was not secure under their system of government, and this was not so with the Nupe people. However, Nupe must promise for its part not to raid for slaves in the company's territories outside Nupe. If this happened Goldie threatened to declare war, blockade Nupe, and divert its trade to other emirates. The Emir was well satisfied with all this, and summed up their understanding as, 'You keep what you have and I will keep what I have.' The visit ended, Goldie concluded that war with Nupe was bound to come, but the longer it was delayed 'the stronger will be the position of the company'.[3]

[1] Scarbrough to Goldie 23.10.90, in the possession of the Earl of Scarbrough.
[2] FO 84/2179 minute by H.P.A. 3.12.91 on R.N.C. to F.O. 26.11.91.
[3] FO 84/2245 Goldie to Salisbury 24.3.92.

Since the early days of the charter the Colonial Office had prevented its officials in Lagos from interfering in Nupe. Attempts as late as 1891 on the part of the Governor of Lagos to open up relations with Nupe in the hope that pressure could thus be brought on Ilorin had met with sharp reprimands from the Foreign Office.[1] For Lagos to interfere in Nupe was regarded as frank meddling; but what of Ilorin? Here the Niger Company had no trade worth speaking of, and so the commercial pressures which Goldie could exercise over Nupe could not be applied. In 1892 a request by the Governor of Lagos to visit Ilorin and negotiate a peace with the Ibadans was allowed by Lord Rosebery against bitter opposition from Goldie.[2] The visit stirred up a good deal of bitterness between the two regimes; the Niger Company alleging that Governor Carter was bent on stirring up trouble, and Carter replying with a report on his visit alleging that not only was there no administration in Ilorin, but also that the Emir denied ever having made a treaty with the company.[3]

This pattern of events was repeated in 1894, but with more disturbing results, when Lagos was allowed to send Captain Bower as an emissary to Ilorin to try to settle boundary disputes between Ilorin and Ibadan. Bower was roughly treated by the Ilorins, and Governor Carter responded by demanding that if the company could do nothing to keep the Ilorins in check then Lagos should be allowed to 'destroy the headquarters of this band of robbers'.[4] This was the beginning of a long campaign by Lagos designed to show that the company was powerless to control Ilorin, and that Lagos would have to step in, afterwards of course, annexing the area and restoring it to Yoruba rule. The fact that the Niger Company forces were concentrated on the Niger delta after the Brass attack, or that the company was facing an acute threat from France in Borgu, was not seen as

[1] FO 84/2175 C.O. to F.O. 21.9.91 with enclosures and minute by C.H.H.
[2] FO 84/2263 fair draft corrected by Rosebery sent to Niger Company 9.11.92.
[3] FO 84/2264 R.N.C. to F.O. 21.11.92; *Morning Post* 22.2.93 (a Reuter's telegram from Lagos inspired by Carter) and FO 83/1239 C.O. to F.O. 5.5.93 enc. Carter to Ripon Conf. 28.3.93.
[4] FO 83/1374 C.O. to F.O. 2.1.95 enc. Carter to Ripon 24.11.94.

any impediment. Captain Bower even went so far as to criticize the sending of Lugard to Nikki on the ground that the company 'are unable or unwilling—both I fancy—to give protection or good government to what is already under them'.[1] In April 1895 Acting-Governor Denton reported that Irun and Oyibe, places which were once part of the *Ekite Parapo*,[2] but were now ruled by Ilorin, had asked if they could emigrate wholesale into the Lagos sphere. They had asked the Niger Company for protection against slave-raiding by the Ilorins, but had been refused. Denton asked to be allowed to grant the request;

at present it appears that the . . . (company) has only very limited power to protect even the villages which are situated close to the River Niger and that at a short distance inland the natives are able to carry out their own will as far as pillaging those weaker than themselves and slave raiding is concerned.

It was 'not to be wondered at' that these people wished to be ruled from Lagos.[3]

Up to this time Goldie, enjoying the confidence of the Foreign Office which was well aware of his difficulties in facing the French in Borgu, had managed to evade any action. 'Explanations' were duly provided by the Foreign Office in reply to the Lagos complaints, and the problem shelved. Joseph Chamberlain's appointment as Colonial Secretary altered the whole tone of these exchanges, injecting a definitely authoritarian tone into the Colonial Office letters. In November 1895 news came through that the Emir of Ilorin had threatened to kill any messengers sent from Lagos. The Colonial Office immediately sent a blunt note to the Foreign Office asking that the Niger Company compel the Emir to adopt a more friendly tone.[4] Goldie promised to do all he could through the local African

---

[1] FO 83/1376 C.O. to F.O. 21.3.95, enc. Bower to Col. Sec. 28.12.94. Bower enclosed also a letter from Bishop Tugwell complaining that since Goldie's Nupe visit of 1892 the company was countenancing slave raiding, which he thought a 'scandal'. Bower used this to argue that Yagba and Kabba, pagan areas under Nupe rule, ought to be ruled from Lagos.

[2] A confederation of smaller states formed to defend the frontiers of Yorubaland earlier in the century.

[3] FO 83/1377 C.O. to F.O. 5.4.95 enc. Denton to Ripon 1.3.95.

[4] FO 83/1385 C.O. to F.O. 3.11.95 Conf.

agent, but admitted that a military campaign was now necessary, pleading that this was impossible because of the continued threat from the Brassmen.[1] Things became worse early in 1896 when a detachment of Lagos constabulary was openly attacked at their station at Odo Otin by the Emir's forces. Chamberlain now asked that the company should co-operate with Lagos in a military campaign against Ilorin.[2] Goldie saw that he would have to move, for if he delayed any longer Chamberlain would allow Lagos to reduce Ilorin alone, and absorb the emirate. He therefore replied with a firm promise to crush Ilorin with the company's forces alone. It could not be done immediately, and he gave convincing reasons why not. The company's campaign would have to be based on its most powerful weapon, the river fleet, and the Niger at this time of year was too low for the effective manœuvre necessary to isolate Ilorin from her ally Nupe. On hearing the news from Lagos, Goldie had immediately ordered two specially designed stern-wheelers to operate as river patrol to cut off reinforcements to Ilorin from the north bank of the Niger. These would be ready in August, and the war could then begin. But he put in a plea for negotiation. Goldie was not convinced that virtue was all on the Lagos side. The Emir believed that Odo Otin was in his sphere, and had been taken from him by 'aggression'. He was under British protection and entitled to see his territorial integrity maintained.[3]

This did not satisfy Chamberlain, particularly when it was discovered that the Emir was not at all disposed to negotiate, even with the company.[4] In the meantime the situation had further deteriorated. The attacks on Odo Otin continued, and the Ilorins were having considerable success in conducting propaganda against Lagos inside Yorubaland. This propaganda

---

[1] *Ibid.* R.N.C. to F.O. 16.11.95.

[2] FO 83/1443 C.O. to F.O. 14.4.96 with enclosure.

[3] *Ibid.* R.N.C. to F.O. 17.4.96.

[4] Goldie said, in the letter referred to in the above footnote, that the Emir had written to the Queen through the company. When Chamberlain asked to see it Goldie had to admit that it was non-existent! Chamberlain therefore suspected that Goldie intended only delay. See FO 83/1444 C.O. to F.O. 27.5.96 for Chamberlain's reactions.

made great play of the contrast between the free and easy life of
the Ilorins under the Niger Company, and that of the Yoruba
suffering from the constant advance of Lagos power. It must
have been particularly galling to the Lagos officials. Governor
Carter asked to be allowed to move independently against
Ilorin, and to use the traditional hatred of the Ibadans to do so:

> Ten thousand Ibadans could be got at a week's notice to join such
> an expedition, and it would be a labour of love to them. In such a
> case my policy would be to repeople Ilorin with Yorubas, mainly
> from Ibadan, and drive the unruly foreign element back to their
> own countries. This would be no more than justice to the Yorubas,
> to whom Ilorin properly belongs.[1]

Chamberlain would not go as far as this, but almost as far,
and with consequences which might have been worse for Goldie.
He demanded that if the company would not 'at once' move
against Ilorin, Lagos should do so, and the company be charged
with the cost of the expedition.[2]

Goldie naturally resisted this suggestion with all his power;
once more promising to fight a war with Ilorin, he again stressed
that he could do nothing until the high water allowed the company's fleet to manoeuvre easily, and demanded some guarantee that the Brassmen would remain quiet. The idea that Lagos
be permitted to pursue a forward policy for which the company
must pay would ruin the company's finances, and was ridiculous.[3] (Just how ridiculous he pointed out obliquely three
weeks later when he asked to be allowed to attack Rabeh
Zobeir, who had marauded into the company's sphere from his
base in German territory, and to charge the cost to Germany.)[4]
His arguments were convincing, and the Foreign Office resisted
Chamberlain's demand. It did not matter who conquered
Ilorin, so long as it was controlled by someone. Chamberlain's
scheme was therefore vetoed and Goldie told to get on with the
preparations for the war. Sir Ralph Moor, the successor to

---

[1] FO 83/1444 C.O. to F.O. 4.5.96 enc. Carter to Chamberlain 9.1.96 and same
to same 11.1.96.
[2] *Ibid.* C.O. to F.O. 27.5.96.   [3] FO 84/1445 R.N.C. to F.O. 2.6.96.
[4] *Ibid.* R.N.C. to F.O. 25.6.96.

Macdonald as Commissioner for the Niger Coast Protectorate, was asked to keep the Brassmen quiet.[1]

Goldie now began to prepare for the war which he had promised to begin in the high-water season about October or November. But it was not to be quite the sort of campaign which Chamberlain had been demanding. For Goldie was planning to deal with Nupe, and Ilorin was only to be tackled if circumstances permitted.

Trouble in Nupe had come to a head just at the time when Chamberlain was forcing the pace in the summer of 1896. The old policy of 'diplomacy' was breaking down in Nupe. The constabulary officers, many of them seconded from the British army, were finding it difficult to obey their orders not to interfere with Nupe slave raiding. Early in 1896 Goldie had personally gone out to the Niger to try to re-establish discipline.[2] In June 1896 the Nupe raiders retaliated, capturing a patrol of forty-five constabulary commanded by two British officers. This in itself was a bad blow to the company's prestige, but much worse was the fact that the Nupe raiders also captured the forty-five rifles which the men carried, and a Gardiner machine gun with ample ammunition. Agent-General Wallace hoped that he could secure the men's release by withholding the Emir's subsidy, but he warned Goldie that if war came the stations on the upper river might be lost.[3] Though the officers and men were later released, Goldie now decided that the time had come to conquer Nupe.

Not a word of all these difficulties was allowed to reach the ears of the Foreign Office. In October, however, Goldie had to reveal something of his plan to Sir Clement Hill. The company had been meeting opposition from the War Office in its attempts to obtain the secondment of officers and other ranks for the campaign, and Goldie asked that the War Office be told that this

[1] *Ibid.* minute by H.P.A. on R.N.C. to F.O. 25.6.96.

[2] Goldie to Scarbrough 22.1.96 in the possession of Lord Scarbrough.

[3] From the same collection, Goldie to Scarbrough 2.8.96 enc. report from Wallace, and reports of subordinate officials to Wallace written in June.

was a campaign undertaken 'in response to strong representa-
tions' from the Government. Hill naturally wanted to know
some details, but he was not unduly surprised when Goldie told
him that he proposed to attack not Ilorin, but Nupe, for Goldie
argued that the defeat of Nupe would be the best way to 'relieve
the Colonial Office of the pressure of Ilorin'. His plea was
successful, and the officers and men were allowed to join the
expedition.[1]

Goldie's secrecy about his intentions may at first sight seem
strange. In the event he must have regretted the fact that he was
forced to give any information at all. Despite all the niggling
pressure that had been put on him to attack Ilorin, defend the
company's sphere from the French, and erect fortifications in
Borgu, the Government, when faced with actual plans for a
military campaign by the chartered company, immediately
became sensitive and touchy. Was this to be another Jameson
Raid, more perilous in its consequences because attacking
French territory? The French sensed this mood, and demanded
assurances. Lord Salisbury was only too anxious to give them.
France was assured that the expedition would on no account
move north of Bajibo into disputed territory. Bussa, claimed by
the company since 1885, was thus out of bounds to the expedition.[2] Salisbury might have been forgiven his trust of the French
had France given a similar undertaking to keep out of the disputed area whilst the Nupe war was unfinished. But they did
nothing of the kind: Hanotaux openly told Salisbury that as
Goldie was operating in Nupe, which lay north of the agreed
boundary between Lagos and Porto Novo, France would have
to take counter-measures. Undeterred, Salisbury extracted a
pledge from Goldie not to move out of Nupe or Ilorin, and
instructed the British ambassador in Paris to give precise details
of the destination of the expedition to the French press.[3]
Stupidity could hardly have been carried further. Within ten

[1] FO 83/1449 minute by C.H.H. on interview with Goldie 16.10.96.
[2] FO 27/3273 Salisbury to Gosselin, 273 Af. 1.12.96 reports assurances given to
the French ambassador in London.
[3] FO 27/3276 Monson to Salisbury, 236 Af. Conf. 27.12.96; FO 83/1519 F.O. to
R.N.C. 4.1.97; FO 27/3335 Salisbury to Monson, 9 Af. 12.1.97.

R

days the French newspapers announced the departure of no less than three 'exploring missions' for the 'Dahomey hinterland'; one under Lieutenant Baud, one commanded by Lieutenant Bretonnet, a companion of Mizon's voyages, and one under the Governor of Dahomey himself.[1] Lord Salisbury had, in effect, ensured that the middle Niger lay undefended; he had presented a long stretch of the navigable Niger obligingly upon a silver platter to France; and he himself had mixed the dangerous ingredients of a brew which was to be called the Niger Crisis, and might well have become the Anglo-French War of 1898. In view of the poor showing which the Niger Company made in that crisis, which cost it the charter, all this is worth remembering. Salisbury forbade Goldie to do what six months later Chamberlain was complaining had been left undone.

[1] *Politique Coloniale* 26.1.97.

The War against Nupe and Ilorin

AT the beginning of December 1896 Goldie began his voyage out to the Niger to lead the company's troops in the coming campaign. We know that in the weeks on board ship Goldie pondered a good deal on the significance of the war which was about to take place, and the effect which it would have on the future of the company. He was well aware that Salisbury had made a dreadful blunder which would inevitably lead to grave trouble with France, but he seems to have understood Salisbury's attitude in view of the disastrous conclusion to the abortive Jameson Raid. But there were other considerations no less fraught with danger. He had to take into account the risk of failure, though, to be sure, Goldie seems not to have entertained any real fear on this score. Nonetheless, victory was not certain, the Nupe people had a powerful military organization, were superior in manpower, and their weapons, though inferior, were not to be despised. Defeat would mean the end of the company both as a financial organization and as a political regime. If the British Government were forced to extricate the company, it would be too much to hope that the charter would remain intact, and the compensation paid would be as meagre as that paid to the ill-fated East Africa Company. Relations between the company and the Government were worse than they had ever been.

The chief cause of this friction was the long struggle with the Colonial Office which had led to this campaign, and the growing criticism that the company was weak and hesitant in facing the French (which Goldie was realist enough to know would not be affected by the present attack of cold feet). This coolness in the Government's attitude to the company had allowed the opposition to reform, and make considerable headway. In 1896 Goldie's carefully constructed system of alliance was breaking up. Alfred Jones' shipping companies, whilst assuring Goldie that they would fight for the Kirk scheme 'tooth and nail', were writing quietly to the Foreign Office attacking the company's monopoly and asking for the charter to be revoked and a direct administration established.[1] Even the African Association could not keep faith, but began to send in cautious protests at the continued exclusion of the Brassmen.[2] Goldie's ally and fellow-director James Hutton lost control of the hitherto faithful Manchester Chamber of Commerce, which now began to press for the unification of all the Niger regions under one colonial government.[3] Parliamentary critics, led by Sir Charles Dilke and supported by the Liverpool members, began to unearth damaging information, particularly when they showed that all the company's European employees were bound, by a bond of £1,000, not to disclose any information about the Niger Territories to any outside interests 'official or private'. This worried the Foreign Office officials, who were unaware of it hitherto, and it made the 'control' of the Secretary of State look pretty thin.[4]

The unresolved Brass question, and Goldie's use of it to agitate for the Kirk scheme, was also a source of irritation to the Foreign Office officials. Goldie resisted all attempts by the Niger Coast Protectorate administration to give the Brassmen any access to the Niger, insisting that a full-scale reform of the administration was necessary. In the early part of 1896, when Goldie had gone out to try to discipline the officers in Nupe and

[1] FO 83/1451 Elder Dempster to F.O. 16.11.96 and 1.12.96; Goldie tells of Jones's promise in a letter to Scarbrough 11.12.96, in the possession of Lord Scarbrough.

[2] FO 83/1448 African Association to F.O. 31.8.96.

[3] FO 83/1444 Manchester Chamber to F.O. 26.5.96.

[4] *Ibid.* question by Dilke for 4.5.96, *Letter of Honourable Understanding* enclosed in Goldie to Hill 1.5.95 appended.

to supervise the building of the chain of posts in Borgu, he had taken the opportunity of discussing the Brass question, over the head of the Foreign Office, with the new Commissioner of the Coast Protectorate, Sir Ralph Moor. He quickly won Moor over to the Kirk scheme and persuaded him to sign a 'scheme' which was simply a detailed adaptation of Kirk's reforms. Naturally Moor's signature could not bind the Foreign Office, but it was annoying to find that traditional opponents of the company were agreed with Goldie on the precise details of reform.[1]

This irritation displayed itself in a particularly spiteful way at the very time when Goldie was on board ship for the Niger and Nupe. Goldie had constantly argued that until the Brassmen were disarmed the company could not move against Ilorin. Now he had been forced to move he sent an urgent telegram back to Lord Scarbrough, who had been left in charge in London, asking him to persuade the Foreign Office to arrange for a naval gunboat to be stationed in the delta during the campaign, to protect Akassa from the Brassmen. The Foreign Office officials had no fear at all of the Brassmen, it was just 'one of Sir George Goldie's shots aimed to show the difficulties and expense we cause the Company', but in what can only be put down to a fit of mischievous spleen they decided to use the request to cause acute embarrassment to Scarbrough, forced to take decisions in Goldie's absence. The affair was treated as if it were a matter of high state policy, minutes and memoranda were circulated to Balfour, the Duke of Devonshire, Chamberlain, the Admiralty and the War Office, and as a result, instead of a gunboat on the river, the company found its delta region occupied by men of the West India Regiment.[2] Scarbrough was appalled, and immediately saw the significance of the move. Apart from the enormous cost of housing and provisioning these troops, which was to be paid by the company,[3] he had been deliberately

[1] FO 2/100 Moor to F.O., no. 18, 13.3.96 with enclosures.
[2] FO 83/1519 R.N.C. to F.O. 12.1.97 inc. cable from Goldie, Scarbrough to Hill 12.1.97, minute from C.H.H. *Ibid.* F.O. to War Office, Balfour, Devonshire, Chamberlain, Admiralty and Intelligence Division 14.1.97.
[3] *Ibid.* F.O. to R.N.C. 15.1.97.

manœuvred into a position in which imperial troops were in occupation of company territory, a powerful argument for getting rid of the company at some future date on the ground that in moments of crisis the company was incapable of defending itself. Scarbrough protested, pointing out that no request for troops had been made, and asking why the troops were not occupying Brass and the Niger Coast Protectorate, instead of the company's territory. The company, he insisted, 'have persistently refrained from soliciting Imperial aid . . . and they do not ask for it now. They recognize their full responsibility in this respect and are prepared to face it.' Sir Clement Hill could have told him the real reason for the presence of the troops; the company was not to be trusted, no one knew what Goldie was really up to on the Niger, and the troops would 'show that the Niger is within the scope of Imperial operations'. His view prevailed, and the Government refused to alter its decision.[1]

All these were depressing signs that the company's tenure of power was drawing slowly to a close. But Goldie was neither daunted nor depressed. He was now fifty years old, healthy in body and young enough in mind to view the approaching campaign with mounting excitement. Gradually the whole affair took on the appearance of a gambler's fling, but a gamble which involved more skill than chance. He calculated the 'odds' frequently, and with each stage of the journey he felt that they moved more and more in his favour. Similarly the stake involved increased in significance. The campaign was going to be given tremendous publicity; *The Times* had sent a correspondent to cover the war in detail on the spot, and other newspapers were organizing their contacts on the coast to get news through as quickly as possible. Soon the company would be famous, and its officers celebrated for deeds of valour in the defence of British interests. The motive of the war would be announced as the suppression of slavery and slave-raiding. With victory, the company would no longer be an obscure trading company which Englishmen only heard of by reading rather disturbing reports of allegations in Parliament. It would then not be so easy for

[1] FO 83/1520 Scarbrough to F.O. 18.1.97, with minute by C.H.H.

Chamberlain to revoke the charter and take over the administration of the Niger; public opinion would want to know why a company which had recently ventured so much should now be bought up ignominiously. Not only did Goldie think that the Government would be forced to implement the Kirk scheme, but he now felt that the company could put up the price for doing so:

'If we succeed in the campaign,' he confided to Scarbrough, '(and *of course* we shall succeed) we must not take the terms which I offered Lord Salisbury through Kirk and subsequently through Moor. We are now risking the whole existence of the Company, against immense odds and if we give up commerce we must have an equivalent for the risk. Besides, we shall have the public on our side if (no! *when*) we succeed. . . .'[1]

There can be no doubt, despite the efforts later made by the Colonial Office to play down the significance of the campaign, that the war against Nupe and Ilorin was brilliantly conceived and executed. Goldie had to work within serious limitations of finance; he had to destroy powerful military states without the use of more than a few European officers and sergeants, and with the company's African troops outnumbered by about fifty to one; and to do it as quickly as possible. To overcome these limitations Goldie exploited every possible advantage of European technical and military science, and wedded them to intrigue and diplomacy born of his own understanding of the local political situation in Nupe and Ilorin.[2]

The technical aids employed in the campaign were of a most

---

[1] Goldie to Scarbrough 11.12.96, written from Las Palmas, in the possession of the Earl of Scarbrough.

[2] It would not be possible to give footnote references in the narrative which follows for every detail of the campaign. The main source for the tactical fighting is Vandeleur, S., *Campaigning on the Upper Nile and Niger*, London, 1898, an account by one of the European officers, to which Goldie added an introduction. The main source for Goldie's strategical plans are the letters he wrote at the time to Lord Scarbrough, kindly loaned to me by the present Earl. In CO 147/124 may be found *Report by Sir George Goldie on the Niger-Soudan Campaign to the Earl of Scarbrough, Deputy-Governor R.N.C.*, printed by the Niger Company and distributed to shareholders in 1897. Other sources are referred to in footnotes.

varied kind. Tinned food was extensively used. Thousands of yards of wire were taken out to surround the camp at night to trip up enemy cavalry charges. The force also carried 'surprise lights', a kind of flare which could be attached high on the trees around a camp to be ignited by remote control and glare out over an attacking force at night. Goldie's army was one of the first to use electric searchlights in war. Special shells were manufactured to fire the thatch of the Nupe houses and buildings. The big guns were made in such a way that they could be quickly taken to pieces, each part small enough to be carried on the backs of porters. In the same way six Maxim guns had been made under the personal supervision of the inventor himself so that they could be easily dismantled.

The enemy was not an unorganized rabble of ill-equipped savages. The Nupe army could muster somewhere between ten and thirty thousand men, most of them equipped with fire-arms, many of which were of recent design. For the most part this army consisted of cavalry, whereas only the officers of the company's forces were mounted; if once the Nupe horsemen were allowed to get to close quarters with the company's African troops all was lost. The Nupe army was divided into regiments each under a commander, but its discipline could not compare with the steady calculated courage of the company's African rank and file, a courage produced only by training and practice.

But the real weakness of Nupe was political. The region around the capital at Bida was sound, but the outlying districts suffered from the greed of an aristocracy which was regarded as alien, and which used the local populations as a labour reserve with which to stock its slave farms. In most areas this did not greatly affect the military situation, for the people were power-less to rebel against the cavalry of the Emir. But Nupe was divided in two by the Niger, and the mobility of the Emir's forces depended on the non-Muslim tribes who controlled almost all the canoes and river transport. Since 1882, when the National Company's steamers had saved the Emir by suppress-ing the rebellion of the canoemen, these people had been waiting their chance to restore the ancient Nupe dynasty of pre-Fulani days, and a claimant to the throne was always somewhere in evidence. If the company should now reverse the policy of 1882 and throw its steamers on the side of the rebels, the Emir's army would be cut in two, and those now in the south would be unable to join up with the main force at Bida.

Even the aristocracy itself was not united. The long struggles between Masaba and his rivals in the middle of the century, though no longer conducted by open civil war, still had their effect, and parties still existed which supported the claims to the succession of various branches of the royal family. Moreover the army lying south of the Niger was led by the *Markum* Mohamedu, who himself held pretensions to the throne, and was next in line of succession. Goldie was to make sure that his loyalty to the Emir was severely tested.

Though the equipment and tactics of the campaign had been prepared beforehand down to the last detail, Goldie left himself free to decide the broad strategy at the last moment. In August Goldie felt that he would first attack the *Markum's* force south of the river, and then advance on Bida, thus securing the advantage of attacking a divided enemy. In December, however, hearing that the *Markum's* force was larger than expected Goldie was tempted to march on Bida first, leaving the destruction of the *Markum* to the consequent rebellion of the pagan tribes. It was not until January, when Goldie arrived at Lokoja and met the troops that he made his final plan:

1. Beat and disperse the Markum's forces which natives will then eat up. 2. Advance on Bida. 3. Dictate terms to Ilorin or smash them. 4. Smash Iddah and settle lower river palavers.

Agent-General Wallace had the task of patrolling the Niger with the river fleet to prevent the *Markum's* army recrossing the river. On 2 January the troops were reviewed and put to last-minute practice with the Maxims. Before Goldie, dog-tired, smoked a last cigar before going to bed he sent off the news to Scarbrough. 'It all makes me as fit as a twenty-year-old,' he exulted.[1]

The little army left Lokoja on 6 January 1897. It consisted of 513 African soldiers commanded by 30 European officers, with 900 porters as transport. As they marched out, Wallace with a flotilla of ten steamers went up-river to patrol the river between Egga and Jebba. The troops' first objective was the *Markum's* army. After arriving at Sura village on the twelfth, a detachment of four hundred soldiers and three hundred porters was sent off on a forced march to the *Markum's* camp near Kabba, but the *Markum* refused to engage and made off to the north to try to regain contact with Bida; Goldie was thus able to march into Kabba on the thirteenth unopposed. In the afternoon he gathered all the chiefs of Kabba and the neighbouring towns in the market-place and formally proclaimed the independence of the region from the Nupe yoke. Slavery was declared to be abolished. Goldie then addressed the people 'in the most inimitable pigeon English' (which was then translated by interpreters into Yoruba and Nupe) to the effect that henceforth the company would protect them.

The army now moved north to Egbom on the Niger, where contact with the river fleet could be resumed. Arriving there on the twenty-second, Goldie found that his plans were working out well. Wallace had raised the river people into revolt and had already seized several towns. The Emir was without canoes; the *Markum* had failed to cross the Niger and his army was now dispersing along the southern bank farther up the Niger.

By this time Goldie had gone down with fever; yet he continued to work, keeping the intelligence system entirely in his own hands. Prisoners were interrogated in his presence, and there was a constant flow of guides, spies and messengers. Nor did he allow his bad health to delay the crossing of the Niger and the march on Bida. With reinforced artillery from the steamers, the force crossed the Niger on the twenty-third and twenty-fourth, and the march on Bida began on the next day, when there was some skirmishing.

On the twenty-sixth Goldie led the van in the attack on Bida itself. Fighting began at half-past seven in the morning and continued throughout the advance over the four miles between the

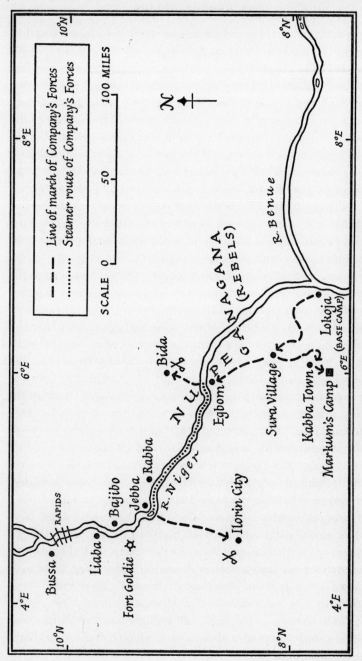

5. The War against Nupe and Ilorin 1897

camp and the city. There Goldie saw the Nupe army massed in strength, thousands of them in white robes, and nearly all mounted. They were drawn up on a ridge in front of the formidable walls of the city. Behind them the people of the town were congregating, confident of victory and looking forward to an interesting spectacle. The van now awaited the arrival of the main body with the artillery, and then advanced to within 2,000 yards of the city walls. This, however, was the signal for a mass charge by the Nupe cavalry, supported by rifle fire and charges by bodies of horsemen concealed in little woods which lay on either flank. The position of the force became desperate, and the order came through to retreat. This naturally elated the Nupe people, and a great shout went up from horsemen and spectators alike. Hurriedly the troops formed up into the classical square formation, and slowly fought their way back from the city to the base-camp. Superior discipline and training, together with the superb courage of the rank and file, now proved their value. The Nupe cavalry charged again and again, only to break under the regular volleys from the square. Many of the company's Yoruba troops had never faced cavalry in action, but they were as steady as the rest. By half-past two in the afternoon they reached the camp, and helped those left there to set up the heavy artillery, which did terrible slaughter among the thick concentrations of cavalry milling round the camp. The Nupe tried to retaliate by dragging up an old cannon, but this did little damage. As darkness fell the cavalry, disheartened by the shellfire, retired, dragging away their many dead and wounded. For Goldie it had been a near-disastrous day's fighting.

During the night the twelve-pounder Whitworth gun arrived. It had taken the porters twelve hours to drag it over the ten miles of difficult country between the camp and the river. It was then set up, and a shell was fired at Bida, using a compass bearing at maximum sighting. It landed three miles away within the city walls close to the *Markum's* palace. Throughout the night rockets were fired off to terrorize the Nupe, and another twelve-pounder shell was fired into Bida. The Nupe mounted no attack.

On the next day, 27 January, the troops again advanced towards Bida. This time the square formation was used from the first. Approaching the city the square was much harassed by Nupe snipers, concealed in the trees along the route. Goldie's personal servant fell mortally wounded at his side. An African private, badly wounded, calmly sat down, and to Goldie's amazement, took out a knife and removed the bullet. As the square approached the armies massed near the city, the Nupe again mounted massed cavalry charges, but they were met by co-ordinated volleys at 400 yards, and by Maxim fire. The Nupe began to hesitate in the charges, wondering what was to happen now. Within 2,500 yards of the city walls, the square halted.

Unknown to the Nupe, the battle was now decided. The square was at last within range to use the big guns against Bida. After firing a few salvoes to clear the defenders from outside the walls, the square moved to within 500 yards and the bombardment commenced. Shell after shell was sent hurtling into the town, the general target being the Emir's palace and the surrounding area. Soon the city was ablaze and the Nupe army scattered. The troops then entered the town, marched through it, and set fire to the outskirts as they left. For the loss of eight killed and nine wounded the company had achieved one of the most important military victories ever won south of the Sahara.

Yet the weakness of the company was emphasized in the political aftermath of the battle of Bida. The cost of the campaign was straining its resources to the limit, and there was little hope of profit as a result of victory. The company could not afford to follow up the victory with the establishment of a direct administration in Nupe. The best Goldie could hope for was to mould a new administrative system which, using checks and balances, would be amenable to his wishes, and cost nothing to run. From this situation was created a system which was in embryo the system of indirect rule which Lord Lugard was later to establish as the characteristic type of administration in Northern Nigeria, a system which in the twentieth century was to become the dominant trait of British policy in tropical Africa.[1]

After the fall of Bida there were several factors which, taken together, provided the basis for a new political settlement. The simplest problem was that of the rebels who had assisted the company. Their demands were granted, their territory split off and made independent of Nupe, and the shadow-king Idirisu brought out of hiding and made ruler. This weakened the rump of Nupe, and set up stout allies on its borders if there should again be war. A second factor was the disorganized but still un-conquered army of the *Markum*. Goldie had been trying to win him over since the march on Kabba, but without success. Several members of his family had been captured at Bida, however, including his mother and his children, and the mother wrote to her son urging him to surrender for the sake of his children. The *Markum* then began negotiations with Goldie in February, and quickly came to terms, for his life's ambition, the Emirate itself, was dangled before him as bait. On 5 February he signed a treaty in which the Emir Abu Bokhari was declared to be deposed and the *Markum* Mohamedu, as the 'next successor' made Emir. The new ruler recognized 'that all Nupe is entirely under the power of the company, and under the British Flag'; admitted the claims of the people in the south-west under Idirisu to be independent; and granted the company the right to any portions of land on the Niger banks for three miles inland which it might require. 'The Emir Mohammed will govern the rest of Nupe, but will conform to such directions in respect of his government as the representatives of the Com-

---

[1] I would not wish to suggest that Lugard merely copied Goldie's system. When Lugard set up his native administrations he was in a much stronger position than Goldie, and his system had many important features, particularly that of the native treasury, which Goldie's system did not possess. Moreover, Lugard had already, before he knew Goldie well, experienced and studied forms of indirect rule in Uganda and other parts of Africa, and in India. The point I wish to make is that indirect rule in Nigeria *evolved*, out of historical circumstances, of which one of the most important was the legacy of the Niger Company, and the limitations of Goldie's resources. There is a further discussion of Goldie as an 'indirect ruler' at the end of this chapter.

pany may give him from time to time.'[1] In this last and novel clause Goldie had injected his idea of ruling indirectly.

The troops rested a few days at Bida, and made their own amusements. The officers organized the first European-style race meeting in Nigeria, and Goldie presented the Bida Cup valued at twenty guineas. The wily old first minister of Nupe, for whose intellect Goldie had a hearty admiration, was immortalized in the 'N'degi Stakes'. Then Goldie had to hurry on to Jebba ahead of the troops, to prepare his plans against Ilorin.

It was here that he received the first piece of disturbing news in the form of a letter from the officer in charge at Fort Goldie. The letter reported that a foreign expedition had occupied Ilo, just north of Bussa. Its nationality was not certain, but it must be either French or German, for the natives reported that the flag which had been hoisted was red, white and either black or blue, they were not sure. Goldie decided to do nothing, feeling that his 'hands were absolutely tied by the pledge I had given through the Foreign Office' and by his promise to conclude the Ilorin war before the river became too low. Yet, he reported to his fellow-directors, he felt very tempted to ignore both pledges and occupy the country from Bussa to Ilo in strength, driving out the intruders.[2] Nevertheless, when the troops, about half the total force, who were to invade Ilorin arrived at Jebba, Goldie marched them off to the south.

The march on Ilorin was a repetition of the tactics which had defeated the Nupe armies. Moving forward in square formation the troops beat off the repeated charges of the Ilorin cavalry, and by the morning of 16 February they were outside the walls of Ilorin city. After an abortive attempt to negotiate a surrender the city was shelled, and in the strong wind it was soon blazing from end to end. At half-past three in the afternoon the troops marched into the smoking ruins of the town.

[1] FO 2/167, no. 238, Treaty with Nupe 1 Ramadhan 1314 A.H. (A.D. 5.2.1897).
[2] FO 27/3368 Goldie to R.N.C. 26.2.97 enclosed in R.N.C. to F.O. 8.4.97.

The political settlement with Ilorin was even more lenient than that with Nupe. Goldie had been reluctant to fight the Emir from the first, convinced that the fault lay as much with Lagos as with Ilorin. He had continued to correspond courteously with the Emir throughout the fighting. There were no rival claimants among the Muslims for the Ilorin throne, and to resurrect someone from the old Yoruba dynasty would be to play into the hands of Lagos. Emir Suliman was therefore persuaded to surrender himself, and presented with a treaty which he promptly signed. It was an elaborated version of the Nupe treaty containing the same stipulation that he would obey such directions respecting the administration of Ilorin as might be given him 'from time to time' by the company's officials. In addition the Emir promised to make no war without the consent of the company, to accept such a frontier with Lagos 'as the company may decide', and to prevent the liquor trade, destroying all stocks of gin and rum to be found in the country.[1]

Soon after the signature of this treaty the troops marched out of Ilorin. Goldie left no European resident, though it appears that an African official was left in charge. The troops went to Jebba, from where they were shipped down the Niger to engage in punitive expeditions against Lafiaga, the Idda people, and the Patani of the delta, before the officers were disbanded and returned to England.

Meanwhile Goldie had received more news of the foreign expedition at Ilo. On the day after the signature of the Ilorin treaty news was brought that the expedition had now occupied Bussa, had hoisted its flag, and had threatened to burn down the King's house and drive him from the town if he refused to cooperate. From the Emir's palace at Ilorin Goldie sent off a carefully worded letter to the leader of the expedition, whoever he might be, pointing out that Bussa was under the company's protection, and that this had been recognized by France when

[1] FO 2/167, no. 329, Treaty with Ilorin 15 Ramadhan 1314 A.H. (A.D. 18.2.1897).

she evacuated Fort D'Arenberg. Goldie asked for details of the
expedition, and reminded its leader that he must ask permission
if he wished to enter the Niger Territories, and that if he wished to
trade he must submit to the company's commercial regulations.[1]

When the troops had left Jebba Goldie set out overland for
Fort Goldie, taking no soldiers with him so that he could not
later be accused of breaking his pledge. When he arrived at the
fort there was a reply to his letter. It was headed 'Résidence de
Boussa' and disclosed that this was Lieutenant Bretonnet's
expedition. Mizon's erstwhile companion now signed himself
'French Resident of the Middle Niger', and announced that his
orders were to 'effectively occupy and organise' the new
administrative circle of the Middle Niger. Bretonnet denied
that Bussa was in any way subordinate to the company and concluded by practically challenging Goldie to remove him by
force—'I have taken possession in the name of the French
Republic and I occupy effectively the territory of Bussa.'[2]
Goldie was in no position to take up the challenge. He could
only reply courteously to Bretonnet, upholding his previous
claims, and passing responsibility for a final settlement to their
respective governments.[3]

Before leaving the Niger Goldie had one more task. At Asaba
he issued a proclamation abolishing the legal status of slavery in
the company's territories. Practically the proclamation had no
effect, for it simply meant that slavery was no longer recognized
in the company's courts, which in any case did not exercise
jurisdiction in the emirates. The proclamation was intended to
be the beginning of the attempt which Goldie now made to
rally public opinion to the Niger Company to force the Government to reform the company on the lines of the Kirk scheme.

This campaign of publicity merits a little closer study. Goldie
had coincidentally timed things well, his military victories on

---

[1] FO 27/3368 Goldie to Officer commanding the European expedition reported
to be at Bussa 17.2.97, enc. 2 in R.N.C. to F.O. 8.4.97.

[2] *Ibid., loc. cit.* enc. 3. Bretonnet to Goldie 23.2.97.

[3] *Ibid.* enc. 4. Goldie to Bretonnet 8.4.97.

the Niger came at a time when British public opinion had swung away from its earlier distrust of empire, and was preparing to celebrate the Queen's Diamond Jubilee with a veritable orgy of imperial self-congratulation. The British press had fallen in with this mood, had indeed helped to create it, and no newspaper more than *The Times*. Here Miss Flora Shaw, confidante of Cecil Rhodes and later to become Lugard's wife, now dealt with colonial news and articles. In the spring of 1897 *The Times* ran a series of articles on the Niger Company. They were designed to present the company in the most favourable possible light. In April there were two full length feature articles giving a history of the company to date, written in a style which suggests that they were based on drafts submitted by Goldie. There was no criticism of the company's monopoly, even though this subject was being aired at this time in the paper's own correspondence columns. Other reports on the military campaign itself stressed that the campaign was directed against the Fulani slave-raiders, and lauded Goldie's 'abolition' of slavery. An editorial on 19 April compared Goldie to Clive, Bida to Plassey, and the establishment of the Niger Company to the spread of British rule in India.[1]

This was crude propaganda; Goldie himself was capable of better things, directed to a more sophisticated public opinion. He presented his views in the introduction to Lieutenant Vandeleur's account of his experiences of fighting in the Sudanic region both on the Nile and in the campaigns against Nupe and Ilorin.[2] In it he elaborated his theories about the nature of the peoples of the Sudan, their political beliefs and attitudes, and the proper methods by which European powers ought to administer such regions. The result was Goldie's most brilliant piece of writing, revealing an incisive and critical understanding of the pattern of Nigerian history and politics. Almost every book which has had cause to touch on Goldie's career makes use of it, and the essay is the most often quoted of all Goldie's

[1] Miss Perham, *Lugard*, p. 648, suggests that these articles were written by Flora Shaw. See *The Times* 1.3.97; 16.3.97; 30.3.97; 17.4.97; and 19.4.97.

[2] Vandeleur, S., *Campaigning on the Upper Nile and Niger*, London, 1898, with an introduction by Sir George Goldie.

few published writings. But like all his activities, whether practical or theoretical, it cannot be taken simply at face value,[1] but
needs to be put into the context of Goldie's plans, ambitions and
difficulties at the time when it was written. Nevertheless, just as
the Niger Company's administration was laying the foundations
for Lugard's system of indirect rule in the emirates; so did this
essay of Goldie's lay the basis for the theoretical and moral
arguments which Lugard was to elaborate and refine in the
Political Memoranda and the *Dual Mandate*.[2] We have seen that
the new treaties in Ilorin and Nupe were a reflection of the
company's lack of administrative power and resources. Goldie's
essay bears all the marks of these same pressures and limitations.
Indirect rule was not a theory dreamed up by bold administrators as a humanitarian experiment. It was a system which grew
out of the normal processes of historical evolution, out of the
pressure of events which the administrators could control only
imperfectly.

Goldie began his analysis by stressing the unity of the Sudanic
region from Senegambia to the frontiers of Ethiopia, a unity
which he felt had been obscured by the use by the general public
of the word 'Sudan' to denote only a small segment of the
region, the Anglo-Egyptian Sudan. Goldie characterized the
whole region as 'the lost thirteenth of the human race'. Its
people were organized in powerful states, they were intelligent
and industrious, and controlled a fertile soil. What had not
until now been realized, said Goldie, was that the Sudan could
never have a proper and adequate commerce with the rest of
the world 'until a sound basis was substituted for that on which
the social system in those regions has hitherto rested'. By this he
did not mean the institution of slavery, for Greece, Rome and
the Southern States of the U.S.A. had demonstrated that progress and slavery were compatible. Nor did he mean the slave

---

[1] As it is in almost every work which makes use of it, e.g. Wellesley and Gwynn,
Sir George Goldie: Founder of Nigeria, London, 1934, which prints the essay as an
appendix; Burns, *History of Nigeria*, 4th ed., London, 1948, pp. 154–5.

[2] Lugard, F. D., *The Dual Mandate in British Tropical Africa*, London, 1923. Once
again I would stress that I do not wish to suggest that Lugard in any way copied
Goldie's theories, but that he was greatly influenced by them, and driven by
experience to the same, or similar, conclusions.

trade, for that was an inevitable adjunct of any region where there was slavery. The barrier was slave *raiding*, a system which destroyed all the normal incentives to economic progress. Various schemes had been put forward to eradicate the evil, but Goldie rejected them all. Railways would not touch the root of the problem, for slaves in West Africa and the Sudan were not used exclusively as transport animals. Legitimate commerce had lost its lustre:

> It is, I fear, useless to hope that commerce with Europe will, by itself, suffice to alter a social system so deeply ingrained in the Sudanese mind; for the creation of commerce on a large scale is impossible until slave raiding is abated.

The only answer lay in 'the same vigorous means which we employ in Europe for the prevention of crime and violence'. He did not thereby advocate the complete military conquest and close administration of all the Sudanese states:

> The policemen of our towns do not have their batons habitually drawn, though they do not hesitate to use them on occasions. There is probably no part of the world where diplomacy is more effective than Negroland, provided it is known that behind diplomacy is military power.

At this point we can see the motives behind Goldie's argument peeping through. The assumption is that the Nupe and Ilorin campaigns were fought to suppress slave raiding; the qualification that direct military action ought to be a last resort —like the undrawn truncheon of the policeman. Basically Goldie was trying to spike the guns of the French; anticipating the coming threat as one of French military occupation. He is arguing that military rule is not the best form of rule, and therefore not a superior claim to title. This is revealed even more clearly by a long, and apparently irrelevant, aside which follows, in which he argues that the Berlin Conference stipulations about effective occupation applied only to the coasts of Africa,[1] and not to the interior.

---

[1] Incidentally on this point Goldie was absolutely correct. The idea that the Berlin Conference set up 'rules' for 'effective occupation' is widespread among students and writers on African history even today. As the 'rules' applied only to

Goldie went on to deal with objectors from the other extreme, those who 'questioned the morality of "mowing down natives with artillery and maxim guns" '. His argument was that the end justifies the means:

Now, these 'natives' were the fighting organisation of great regions which they—though in a comparatively small minority—held down with a hand of iron, treating the less warlike inhabitants as cattle to be raided when wanted. The death of each Fulah killed at Bida secured the lives and liberty of scores of peaceful and defenceless natives. If Europe had no material interests to protect and develop in Africa, it would still have the same right, the same duty to extirpate slave raiding that a man has to knock down a ruffian whom he sees maltreating a woman or child in the street.

These sentiments may now seem a little bombastic and self-righteous. In the context of 1898, however, there was much obvious truth in the argument. It seems clear that the common people of Ilorin and Nupe, to say nothing of the pagan peoples who had risked their lives in using the opportunity of the campaign to rebel against their overlords, would have heartily agreed with Goldie.[1]

But he did not claim that humanitarianism was the only motive of the campaign. He went on to examine the economic possibilities of the region between the Niger and Lake Chad which he called the 'Niger-Soudan'. Cut off by the monopolist tribes of the Sahara and the 'savages' of the Niger delta, the region had hitherto been isolated and prevented from fulfilling its proper role in the human family. Now that these barriers were broken and the social canker of slave raiding soon to be

new acquisitions on the coasts of Africa, and as the coasts were already almost completely occupied, these stipulations, like all the others of that memorably absurd gathering, were known to be of no practical effect. Miss S. E. Crowe made this very plain in her *Berlin West Africa Conference*, published in 1942, but the myths persist.

[1] In Lugard's campaigns in the north in the first decade of this century the neutralism of the subject Hausa populations was very marked. Mary Smith, *Baba of Karo*, London, 1954, shows that Baba, herself a young girl at the time, was decidedly pro-British, and shared this attitude with most of the Hausa in her district. Her story is full of the terror of constant slave-raiding by the Fulani, and the struggles of a 'good family' to scrape together ransom money to buy back various captured relatives. The fact that the Hausa were Muslim, and only infidels may be enslaved, made no apparent difference.

overcome, Goldie estimated that the population would soon treble itself, and live at an increased standard by concentrating its efforts on production, some of whose fruits would be exported to Europe to buy manufactures. This argument is in effect that of Lugard's 'dual mandate', reduced to purely economic terms. The indigenous people has a duty to the world to exploit its resources effectively through trade; Europe, or the power controlling the region, has a duty to administer wisely and reform the social system so that the society may properly perform its duties.

All this could be achieved, Goldie argued, only by avoiding 'vital errors of policy'. Rough and ignorant handling of Sudanese political susceptibilities could breed religious fanaticism and revolts like that of the Mahdi in the Egyptian Sudan. These people possessed a kind of patriotism difficult for the European mind to grasp. They did not object to the assertion of a 'protectorate' but when asked to concede complete sovereignty 'they invariably stipulated that their local customs and systems of government shall be respected'. This led him to his advocacy of indirect rule, in a passage which has often been partially quoted. It is so striking in the way in which it anticipates the future system of Lugard that it bears quotation in full.

It is therefore certain that even an imperfect and tyrannical native African administration, if its extreme excesses were controlled by European supervision, would be in the early stages, productive of far less discomfort to its subjects than the well-intentioned but ill-directed efforts of European magistrates, often young and headstrong, and not invariably gifted with sympathy and introspective powers. If the welfare of the native races is to be considered, if dangerous revolts are to be obviated, the general policy of ruling on African principles through native rulers must be followed for the present. Yet it is desirable that considerable districts should be administered on European principles by European officials, partly to serve as types to which the native governments may gradually approximate, but principally as cities of refuge in which individuals of more advanced views may find a living, if native government presses unduly upon them; just as, in Europe of the Middle Ages, men whose love of freedom found the iron-bound system of feudalism intolerable, sought eagerly the comparative liberty of cities.

Goldie closed his essay on an imperialist note more akin to French than current British ideas of the purpose of African colonies. This was the military possibilities of the region, in which Goldie claimed a greater interest than in its commercial development. The campaign had fully demonstrated the fighting qualities of the Hausa, and his ability to absorb training and discipline. Britain had for too long relied on India as a reservoir of military manpower; this was not healthy in view of the awakening nationalism of that sub-continent. A new source of strength could be found here on the edges of the Sahara. The expansion of empire always brought with it 'more than equivalent accession of wealth, vigour, and strength to maintain it'. By the military expansion of her empire Britain could avoid declining to the position of a second-rate power in the world.

12

Crisis

THE French occupation of Bussa was the spark which fired the
Anglo-French crisis of the succeeding months. The occupation
of Bussa was different in character from the French moves which
had preceded it at Nikki and elsewhere in Borgu. Bussa was not
a territory which Goldie claimed by recent and highly debatable
treaties, but had since 1885 been assumed to be a country over
which the Niger Company had clear and secure rights. The
French occupation was an open attack on the principle of controlling protectorates by treaty and a test case to determine
whether effective occupation gave a better title than treaty
alone. The real danger to Goldie's company was even more
basic. Bussa controlled territory which was open to navigation
up the Niger from the sea, and the British monopoly of the Niger
trade was in jeopardy. Goldie had been criticized in the past for
concentrating on controlling the navigable waterway to the
neglect of areas away from the river banks. In this crisis the
British Government, and particularly Joseph Chamberlain,
were to display an attitude almost as protectionist as Goldie's
was monopolist, thus, in a way, justifying Goldie's previous
strategy. The realities of geography could not be ignored.

In earlier days the British reaction might not have been so
firm. The personal influence of Joseph Chamberlain will be
seen as a factor which asserted itself with increasing frequency
and weight as the crisis developed, until in the end Chamberlain was virtually controlling all the elements involved. For the
first time Britain had a Colonial Secretary willing to use imperial funds, and even to organize new units of imperial troops,

to defend and expand British influence on the Niger. This was a new experience for the French, and they resented it. Intelligent French politicians read deep and aggressive designs into the British moves. Gabriel Hanotaux, Foreign Minister in the unusually long-lived Méline ministry, which lasted from April 1896 to June 1898, interpreted British policy as a grand plan for the overthrow of the Boer Republics, the acquisition of the bankrupt Portuguese African possessions, and the linking of these, through Central Africa to the Nile valley and Egypt.[1] Chamberlain's counter-moves in West Africa seemed to indicate that Britain was not even prepared to give ground in areas which were to her of secondary importance, but was bent on wrecking the French design for a compact block of North and West African territory. The only way, it seemed to him, to resist these claims was to occupy regions in force before the British could move. The Marchand expedition was already on its way to Fashoda to forestall Kitchener's advance on the upper Nile as the Niger Crisis progressed. Seen against this wider background, the Bussa affair was a kind of rehearsal for Fashoda, all the more important because its settlement would establish precedents for dealing with the crisis over Fashoda which the French knew was inevitable. The Niger Crisis was thus brought to the forefront of international politics, pushed by the colonial parties and their journals in each country to extremes, and for a time became the chief question occupying the minds of the British and French Foreign Ministries. At the height of the crisis new alignments of the powers of Europe, and even war between France and Britain, were not far from the minds of the Cabinets.

All this had a weakening effect on the position which Goldie could hope to maintain. Despite his earlier triumphs in diplomacy, he could not expect to shape policies which had to take account of world-wide interests. When imperial troops made their appearance in the company's territories, even Goldie's influence on purely local issues was seriously undermined, for it now appeared that the chartered company had lost its usefulness

---

[1] Perham, op. cit., pp. 626–7, discusses Hanotaux's position from his own writings, especially his Fachoda, Paris, 1909.

in sheltering the Government from expense and responsibility. Moreover, the presence of these troops, needing all kinds of help from the company's administration and organization, itself produced a delicate situation. The Niger Company was, after all, a commercial enterprise seeking to acquire profit, and not a Society for the Rendering of Gratuitous Assistance to the Imperial Government. Goldie's reluctance to risk his shareholders' capital in support of imperial troops, without some assurance for the future of the company, produced bitter quarrels and a catastrophic collapse of relations between the company and the British Government. Before the crisis was over the Government had definitely determined to get rid of the chartered administration. This was a decision which materially assisted the conclusion of an agreement with France.

The French made no attempt to meet British protests against the occupation with evasion. Hanotaux, supported by the Colonial Ministry, insisted that Bussa was now in the French sphere, and refused to take up the carefully laid hint that perhaps Bretonnet had exceeded his instructions. The French press supported these claims, and carried reports that Bretonnet was under the direct orders of Governor Ballot of Dahomey. Throughout April, May and June 1897 the British protests continued, but no satisfaction was obtained.[1] In these circumstances the Niger negotiations stagnated, though Salisbury continued to carry on an inconclusive discussion with the French ambassador, and in March had made a private visit to Paris to try to persuade Hanotaux to submit the whole question to arbitration.[2] Joseph Chamberlain therefore determined that the time had come to take counter-measures to force the French to negotiate. If France claimed title by 'effective occupation', Britain could play the same game; with British and French posts established side by side across Borgu she could bring about a situation

---

[1] FO 27/3338 Monson to Salisbury, 98 Af. 5.4.97; *ibid.* Monson to Salisbury, 187 Af. 19.6.97; *Débats* 22.3.97 and *Politique Coloniale* 23.3.97.
[2] Kennedy, A. L., *Salisbury*, London, 1953, pp. 280–2.

which would expose the absurdity of such claims. To achieve this Chamberlain needed Goldie's co-operation, not only for the company's forces to take part in the counter-offensive, but also so that imperial forces could use bases on the Niger. He therefore approached Goldie with his plans in May.

To understand Goldie's reaction it is necessary to examine the position of the Niger Company somewhat more closely. It has been seen that Goldie was full of high hopes for the future. At this very moment *The Times* and other newspapers and journals were publicizing the Nupe and Ilorin victories, Goldie felt that public opinion was now on his side, and that he was in a position to force the Government to implement a reform of the company on the lines of Kirk's proposals.

His hopes were a mirage, arising from wishful thinking and a complete misunderstanding of the Government's attitude. The victories in Nupe and Ilorin, far from making the Foreign Office more sympathetic, cleared the air for schemes to get rid of the company. Whilst the Ilorin problem remained unsolved these had been postponed for fear Goldie would sit back and allow his successors to deal with Ilorin. Moreover, the very success of the campaign increased the jealousy and hostility of Lagos. Even as Goldie and his troops were marching on Nupe, Foreign Office officials, in consultation with the Treasury, were working together on 'the immediate financial effect of withdrawing the rights and functions' of the chartered company. The Kirk scheme was not discussed at all, the assumption was that the charter would be revoked outright. The officials envisaged the payment of £500,000 in compensation, not for the loss of the monopoly, which was technically illegal by the charter, but disguised as 'repayment' for 'administrative deficits' since the grant of the charter (£200,000) and repayment of the 'Niger Government Loan' of £250,000. The other £50,000 could cover any assets which the new administration would wish to take over.[1]

---

[1] See FO 83/1520 R.N.C. to F.O. 19.1.97 sending administrative budget for 1895, sent to Treasury for 'inquiry into the Company's position'. FO 83/1521 Brett to Hill 10.2.97. FO 83/1523 mem. by G. L. Ryder and Hill 12.3.97.

The Foreign Office officials sensed that Goldie would use the publicity from the Nupe campaign to make it difficult for the Government to get rid of the Niger Company. Clement Hill advocated counter-measures designed to put Goldie in a difficult position from which the Government would appear justified in buying the company out. He wanted to use the Brass question for this purpose, telling Goldie that he must open up the Niger to the Brassmen's trade:

Goldie will resist this and argue that it will open up the Niger to the spirit trade, that he would rather resign, etc., but it is possible that it may bring him to make some practical proposal and may lead up to the idea of buying out the administration. . . .[1]

In May 1897 it was decided to exclude Goldie from meetings to be held at the Colonial Office to decide on policy in the rear of the Gold Coast, a region which touched western Borgu.[2] At the same time there were public indications that the Government intended to get rid of the company. Salisbury began to drop hints to this effect in answer to questions in Parliament, hints which the Liverpool press regarded as 'gratifying'.[3]

When Goldie had his first meeting with Chamberlain on 27 May 1897 he already had more than an inkling that the policy was to jettison the Niger Company, not to reform it. This was a bitter disappointment, and Goldie took it as a personal blow. He therefore approached the meeting in a truculent and defiant mood, determined to exploit any advantages he possessed to the full. If the Government intended to get rid of the company then Goldie must be wary of committing the company to help imperial forces, unless Chamberlain were prepared to promise that the financial losses to the company would be fully recoverable. Again, this was perhaps the last chance Goldie would have to bring the Kirk scheme within realizable distance. Chamberlain would need all the help which the company's staff, steamers and resources could provide in getting the imperial troops into action. He might be willing to pay a high price.

[1] FO 83/1525 minute by Hill 15.4.97 attached to Hill to Bertie 26.4.97
[2] FO 83/1526 mem. by T.H.S. received 13.5.97.
[3] *Liverpool Journal of Commerce* 26.5.97.

At the interview Chamberlain asked Goldie to concert with the Colonial Office on measures for the joint defence of the company's territories by the company's constabulary, forces from Lagos, and those of the Gold Coast. He also asked what measures Goldie intended to take to preserve Sokoto from French aggression. Goldie in reply denied that there was any danger to Sokoto, and refused to commit the company to give any assistance to imperial forces.[1] Chamberlain had taken a tough line at the interview, and annoyed Goldie so much that he wrote to both Salisbury and Chamberlain a day or so later protesting at the way he had been cross-questioned.[2] But he had also read the writing on the wall, and he went to the Foreign Office asking that if the end was nigh, then it should be speedy. If the Government really intended to get rid of the Niger Company he would have to consider how far he would be justified in continuing to run the administration at its present scale. Sir Clement Hill noted that similar doubts made the East Africa Company let their administration 'run down'.[3]

Unfortunately for Goldie, a speedy revocation of the charter was not so simple to accomplish. The Treasury, notorious for its time-wasting procedures, would have to be consulted, and it was a dangerous manœuvre to replace the company just at the time when the French were challenging its borders. The Colonial Secretary had in the meantime to try to get Goldie's co-operation. Early in June the British counter-measures had been set in motion. The Governor of the Gold Coast was instructed to occupy places in the north, and Chamberlain wrote to inform Goldie of the new policy. Of one thing Chamberlain was sure; that was that the old policy of relying on treaty rights must be dropped or the French would soon have not only Borgu and Bussa, but Sokoto and Gandu as well. As to the alternative Chamberlain was confused and hesitant, and placed before Goldie the choice of seizing posts in the French sphere as retaliation, occupying what was left of the British

<hr>

[1] CO 147/127 interview with Goldie 27.5.97, used by Perham, *op. cit.*, p. 632.
[2] Perham, *op. cit.*, p. 632.
[3] FO 83/1527 mem. by C.H.H. on interview with Goldie 29.5.97.

sphere in force so as to prevent any further losses, or trying to get an agreement with France by conceding access to the Niger. At this stage he preferred concession and a diplomatic settlement. Unless Goldie could think of a better policy, said Chamberlain, concession of access to the Niger would have to be tried. Above all 'the present policy of drift' would have to be abandoned.[1]

Before Goldie had a chance to reply to this, the position of the Niger Company deteriorated further. Lord Salisbury consented to receive a deputation from Liverpool and adopted a most conciliatory attitude to them. They had 'much obliged' him by coming to 'explain matters', for they were 'in a position which is not shared by any other body of men . . . able to give us information and facts upon which we can confidently work'. Though he insisted that there would be no 'harsh treatment' of the Niger Company, and refused to give details of proposed changes on the Niger, he gave a definite undertaking that responsibility for the region would soon be transferred to the Colonial Office. Goldie was seriously worried, and the Liverpool press openly jubilant.[2] Meanwhile, without consulting Goldie, and with a cavalier disregard for the company's juridical rights, Chamberlain had asked the Governor of Lagos to suggest strategic points which the Lagos forces could occupy in order to secure the return of Bussa.[3] It appeared that Lagos forces were to be used to defend the company's treaty sphere; now it seemed that it was the Imperial Government which was prepared to spend money and assume responsibility, and the chartered company which counted pennies and shirked responsibility.

When he received Chamberlain's letter Goldie was in a state of physical exhaustion from overwork, and was unable to reply until mid-July. This must be taken into account in assessing his

[1] CO 96/308 C.O. to Goldie 1.7.98, compare Miss Perham's analysis of this letter, *op. cit.*, p. 633.

[2] *The Times* 7.7.97; *Liverpool Journal of Commerce* 2.7.97 (leader); *Liverpool Post* 2.7.97 (leader); *Liverpool Courier* 7.7.97. Goldie was worried enough to set his allies in motion to protest at the affair, see FO 83/1529 Millers to F.O., tel., 8.7.97 and African Assn. to F.O., tel. and letter, 5.7.97.

[3] FO 83/1530 see enclosures in C.O. to F.O. 16.7.97.

extraordinary reply, a mixture of impossible and contradictory proposals apparently deliberately framed to delay and obstruct. Arguing that the French might well evacuate Bussa under diplomatic pressure, just as they had previously abandoned Fort D'Arenberg, he went on to suggest a plan which must have made even the bellicose Chamberlain blench. He proposed to lead a thousand African troops against Bussa as soon as the dry season permitted:

All that the Company would ask of Her Majesty's Government would be to prevent any attack on its frontier from the Niger Coast Protectorate, and to prevent French Dahomey being reinforced by sea. . . .

With this help he promised to annihilate the French garrison in Bussa.

Goldie went on to challenge the rest of Chamberlain's arguments. He was only 'too well aware' of the 'policy of drift', to which the Niger Company had been a notable exception. If the Crown colonies had displayed 'a tithe of the energy put forward by the Company with its slender resources' they would not today be hemmed in and encircled by French possessions. Chamberlain had said that there could be no war with France over Bussa; Goldie could not agree. If France had earlier been convinced that in the last resort Britain would fight for her claims, enormous diplomatic labours, and considerable losses of territory, would have been saved. In any case France would not make war for Bussa. Her Government was unstable and would soon give place to one less militant. Above all he deplored the suggestion that Britain should concede access to the navigable Niger. This would only allow the French to flood the Fulani empire with gin and fire-arms, allowing the Muslims to crush the British and creating a vacuum which the French would then fill. To cede Bussa would be the most fatal blunder since Majuba (a nasty hit at Chamberlain's Liberal past). If anything had to be conceded then Britain should cede the northern parts of Bornu and Sokoto. Control of the river was essential.[1]

[1] CO 96/308 Goldie to C.O. 19.7.97, used by Perham, *op. cit.*, pp. 633-4.

Such ideas were anathema to Chamberlain, bent on 'developing the Imperial estate'. Were vast and populous areas to be bartered away merely to allow the Niger Company's steamers to ply unmolested and unrivalled through a narrow section of the Niger, admitted to be poor and thinly peopled? Probably at Chamberlain's request, the Foreign Office administered a stinging rebuke. France had now demonstrated beyond all doubt that she intended to base her claims on effective occupation. The Niger Company would have to change its methods and do likewise. Neglect of imperial interests in favour of commercial monopoly must stop:

> Apparently the efforts of the Niger Company in this respect are confined to one matter only, namely, keeping in their hands the water-way of the Niger below the rapids. It may be open to question whether it will be possible for the Niger Company to maintain this principle, for, though it is undoubtedly of great importance from a commercial point of view, foreign countries refuse to admit that it is reconcilable with the Act of Berlin of 1885, and it is not in accordance with the policy usually pursued by this country in dealing with river communication. On the other hand the Niger Company do not profess to protect possessions which are not necessary for this one primary object. . . .

The great danger was that France would cross the Niger and occupy places in Sokoto and Gandu which now had nothing but a treaty to protect them. Was Goldie prepared to occupy with the company's forces all the most important places on the left bank of the Niger to prevent any French crossing?[1]

Goldie was at this time on his way abroad for a recuperative holiday, and the Foreign Office letter overtook him at Dover as he awaited ship. He immediately cancelled his holiday and returned to London. In his reply he again urged the need for negotiations, but he repeated his earlier offer to lead an attack on Bussa if the Royal Navy would blockade the coast of Dahomey.

In defence of the company he went much further than he had gone hitherto in resisting Chamberlain:

[1] FO 27/3370 F.O. to R.N.C. most confidential 23.7.97.

I submit that the issue of a Charter by Her Majesty's Government forms a contract with the Chartered Company by which the latter agrees, among other things, to undertake all internal native wars and maintain domestic order without charge on the Imperial Treasury, while the Imperial Government contracts to defend the Chartered Company against the aggressions of foreign Powers. The Niger Company has admittedly performed its obligations to the full, and it feels itself entitled to call on the Imperial Government for protection against foreign invasion, which it cannot adequately combat.

Juridically Goldie may well have been right, but in the realm of actual politics this was a grave admission that the chartered company was now useless to the Imperial Government. If the Government must fight the company's battles, and pay the cost, it might as well administer the territories directly and at least try to recoup some revenue from them.

Goldie went on to refuse to occupy the left bank of the Niger. He had always followed a policy of keeping the constabulary concentrated, to split them into small garrisons would weaken the force, and in any case a sphere in which the company occupied posts side by side with other posts in French hands would have 'no fiscal value'. If France was to be given access to the Niger in any way at all, then the whole territory was useless to Britain. Why not cede the whole of the Niger Territories above Lokoja in return for the French cession of Madagascar and her recognition of British control of the upper Nile? This would be preferable to voluntarily abandoning the Niger after it had been ruined by conceding access to the French. As for the charge that the company had neglected its imperial mission for the sake of the monopoly, Goldie pointed out that all the regulations which permitted that monopoly to be created had been put into force without any objections from the Foreign Office. As for Bussa itself, the company's policy since 1889 had been supported, and at times prompted, by the Foreign Office. If it had not been for the pledge not to move into Bussa extracted from the company at the time of the Nupe Campaign, there would be no crisis now. The Foreign Office was as much responsible for any difficulties as the company.[1]

[1] FO 27/3370 R.N.C. to F.O. 27.7.97.

T

Chamberlain, undaunted by Goldie's refusal to co-operate, went ahead with his plans. If the company refused to defend its own territories then imperial forces would have to do so. Five days after receiving Goldie's refusal Chamberlain sent instructions to the Governor of Lagos which amounted to a detailed plan whereby Lagos would defend the company's sphere. The Imperial Exchequer would pay the cost of two thousand additional men for the Lagos constabulary. The Governor was given copies of all the company's treaties and told to begin the occupation of places in Borgu, and if possible in French Dahomey. His base would have to be on the Niger, probably at Leaba, so as to secure a short supply line. The Admiralty was to provide two gunboats on the river, and the Niger Company, it was hoped, would assist in providing Hausa recruits and river transport.[1]

The problem of obtaining the necessary minimum of co-operation from Goldie was one which from this time forward dominated the relationship between the Niger Company and the Government. Goldie was by now convinced that his administration was heading for destruction. Only by using the need for co-operation could he force the Government at best to prolong the company's administrative powers, at worst to secure a generous financial settlement. There was an element of blackmail in this attitude, but in fairness to Goldie it must be stressed that there were greater dangers in Chamberlain's plan to use imperial troops than the mere loss of administrative authority. If the company were forced to turn over its entire fleet and personnel to assist the imperial force then trade would cease. Even if the Government played fair and paid the cost, goodwill and trading habits might disappear in the meantime. Goldie therefore pressed for a quick settlement of the basic problem—the future of the administration. He still demanded the implementation of the Kirk scheme, but he was prepared to go further, and agree to the complete disappearance of the

[1] CO 147/115 Chamberlain to McCallum 23.7.97.

company's administration, but on condition that Colonial Office rule did not take its place. Instead he wanted self-government by the merchant community on the lines laid down by Mary Kingsley,[1] and 'at the risk of appearing presumptuous' he echoed her strictures on Colonial Office administration:

> It seems to me that, whatever may be the present activity of the Colonial Office, it cannot be permanently a creative machine. Its main business in all parts of the British Empire, except to a limited extent in West Africa, is that of control—the 'governor' of the steam-engine, and not the boiler. Its officials are brought up from the first in this all-important work of control, which develops an entirely different habit from that of initiating and administering.

He therefore suggested a plan for a 'Permanent Administrative Council for West Africa', appointed by the Colonial Secretary from 'men of African experience' who should hold their seats permanently. The Council would administer a united Nigeria after the company had been bought out, and would rule directly through officials appointed by it, and would itself be responsible to the Colonial Secretary.[2]

All this was very well, but the Government could not be expected to undertake far-reaching reforms in the middle of the crisis, which was now mounting in intensity. In early August news reached London that the French had occupied Kishi, in the rear of Lagos, and Say, north of Bussa, Chamberlain therefore intensified the preparations for sending an imperial force. In these final proposals the West African Frontier Force was born, though it was still referred to vaguely as 'a West African Force'. Now it was to be independent of Lagos, under the command of a 'Commissioner and Commandant' with the political function of representing imperial interests in the region in which the force operated. This region was defined to include all the company's territory west of the Niger except Ilorin. The Commissioner would be 'independent of the Company' and receive his orders direct from the Colonial Office. His task would be to

---

[1] For a discussion of Mary Kingsley's influence at this time see Chap. 13, pp. 303–6.
[2] CO 147/127 R.N.C. to C.O. 21.7.97, note the minute by Chamberlain insisting on direct C.O. rule.

advance and establish posts in Borgu, and if necessary in the
Dahomey hinterland, in order to compel the French to retreat.
If the French retaliated by crossing the Niger and invading
Gandu or Sokoto, them it might be necessary to give the Com-
missioner command east of the Niger, and relieve the company
of its administrative functions, but this was not 'necessary or
advisable' at present. The Foreign Office was asked to secure
Goldie's co-operation in implementing the plan.[1]

So easy to ask, so difficult to achieve. Salisbury advised
Chamberlain to tread delicately, and suggested that Goldie be
invited to a conference with representatives of the Foreign and
Colonial Offices, and the War Office Intelligence Division. To
this Chamberlain agreed, and the conference began its work in
early September. The War Office put forward a scheme, not
unlike Goldie's plan for attacking Boussa in force, except that
the company's forces, pending the arrival of the Frontier Force,
were to invest Bussa and starve the French out. Chamberlain
supported this, and made provision to pay the cost to the company, since it might be a long process. But now Goldie rejected
this, and put forward a plan to occupy places in Borgu with
small detachments, exactly the policy which he had condemned
when it was suggested by Chamberlain. The main point, however, was that any action by the company was 'subject to some
prospect of stability in the present administration'.[2]

Goldie continued to develop this theme in face of protests
from the Foreign Office. He insisted that he would do nothing
without 'full prior knowledge' of the future position of the company. He continued to argue that it was the Imperial Government's duty to defend the company from aggression by foreign
powers, and complained bitterly of the way he had been treated.
After concentrating all the company's resources on the desperate
gamble of a war with Nupe and Ilorin he had expected some
gratitude. Instead he had been '*immediately* met by a reopening
of that Brass question' and rumours that the Government
intended to get rid of the company. He now learned that the

[1] CO 147/124 C.O. to F.O. 14.8.97.
[2] FO 83/1533 mem. of meeting at F.O. 7.9.97.

Admiralty intended to put two gunboats on the Niger, yet nothing had been said to the company about such a plan. It would be 'a real breach of trust' if he and his fellow-directors embarked on any operations without safeguarding the interests of the shareholders. He would move, and move quickly, if he could be given an assurance either that the company could continue to administer, preferably on a reformed basis, or be bought out at once. In the latter event—'an operation which could be arranged in a few hours discussion'—Goldie offered personally to direct the proposed operations after the revocation of the charter, 'of course without pay'.[1]

Chamberlain was angered by this attitude; Goldie must be taught a lesson:

... it looks as if he was trying to force our hands in favour of the Company. I think this is a shortsighted policy and will not really advance his interests. His best course is to work cordially with us, and to make friends of us, but he will not do so without all sorts of terms and conditions—which will require great discussion and involve long delay. I should like to tell him that the British Government does not understand the contract with the Company as he does, nor do they agree that he is to take all the profits and that we are to spend hundreds of thousands or possibly millions in securing his claim against the French, and that he is then to step in and enjoy without cost all the security that we have gained for him.

If this is his view our best course will be to expropriate him at once, stock, lock and barrel—paying the capital value of his property but allowing nothing for goodwill or future profits, since these are altogether dependent on the expenditure we are to make.

In fact I should take a very high line with him and tell him that in this crisis he must be with us or against us and that we cannot allow him to dictate terms. Bear in mind that his Company is very unpopular and that he could find few friends to defend him either in Parliament or in the country.

I think he might be brought into line and then the plan of concentration can at once be carried out ... we must stick to the concentration and do it ourselves, if necessary, as soon as we have got a sufficient force together.[2]

[1] *Ibid.* Goldie to F.O. 14.9.97.
[2] A copied extract of this letter from Chamberlain to Salisbury appears in FO 83/1533 where it is dated 22.9.97. It is quoted partially in Garvin, J. L., *Life of Joseph Chamberlain*, Vol. III, pp. 209–10, and by Perham, *op. cit.*, p. 637, quoting

Salisbury did as Chamberlain asked, though he toned his despatch down somewhat. Goldie was told that the Government refused to accept his assertion that it was responsible for the defence of the company's territories, but noted his argument 'reserving to another opportunity the consideration of its general effect upon the relations between the Company and the Government'.[1] Goldie replied by reiterating his demand to know what was to be the company's future. The officials would have liked to continue the argument, but Salisbury overruled them—'Better leave the matter where it is.'[2]

Angry as he was Chamberlain had not lost his head. He had begun to play a delicate and dangerous game, in which success depended on his being able to see more into the minds of other intriguers than they into his. Already in July he had asked Lugard to take command of the Frontier Force. Lugard had two essential qualifications; he was the only figure of any stature whom Goldie might permit to march over the company's territories without obstruction, and to the French his appointment would indicate that they could expect firm opposition. Yet both these assets were dangerous. Lugard might intrigue with Goldie to preserve the Niger Company, indeed he might succeed as he had in his political campaign for the retention of Uganda earlier in the decade. Or his appointment might arouse such a clamour among the French colonial group that France might be stampeded into war.[3]

Probably Chamberlain was well aware that Lugard was at this time fully under Goldie's quasi-hypnotic influence. But in appointing Lugard Chamberlain obtained a hold over Goldie, who was now loath to make things difficult for the only man he could trust not to use the Frontier Force to destroy the company's administrative position. Thus in October 1897 Goldie

Garvin. She thus, with Garvin, dates the letter 19.9.97. The discrepancy may be due to the fact that Garvin worked from a draft written on the 19th, but not sent until the 22nd.

[1] FO 83/1533 draft by Salisbury 23.9.97.
[2] FO 83/1534 R.N.C. to F.O. 24.9.97 with minutes by T.H.S. and Salisbury.
[3] Cf. Perham, op. cit., p. 637, where a slightly different view of the significance of the appointment is taken.

made a specific offer to lend 300 men to the Frontier Force, and to supply it with stores. Chamberlain eagerly followed this up, though he was careful to insist that Goldie should not be allowed to dictate terms.[1]

Meanwhile, however, Goldie and Sir John Kirk (now in effect a director of the Niger Company, though his name did not yet appear on the company's reports) had been meeting Lugard, and letting him know of their plans. Lugard was completely won over, and wrote to his brother that he was now 'absolutely at one with Goldie' and would 'fight on his side all I can (though necessarily secretly)' against any attempt at 'arbitrary confiscation'.[2] When Lugard met Chamberlain on 12 November to discuss the tactics and strategy to be followed he must have appeared to be little more than Goldie's spokesman. He argued against Chamberlain's military plans, and insisted that Lokoja, the company's main station in the north, and not Leaba, which Chamberlain wanted, should be the base of operations. When Chamberlain announced that Goldie had promised 300 men and stores, an official intervened to say that Goldie had now withdrawn his offer, and Lugard chipped in to say that Goldie intended to resign from the company. Chamberlain grew very angry and told Lugard that if the company refused help 'it will be the worse for them'. When Chamberlain asked Lugard what he would do if the negotiations in Paris broke down, he was given a rehash of Goldie's plan for the cession of the northern part of Sokoto, which Chamberlain 'vehemently and angrily' rejected. After a stormy end to the meeting Lugard decided to resign the post. But Chamberlain's judgement was sound. It was Goldie who persuaded Lugard to go on; the prospect of any other commander horrified him.[3]

Matters had now come to a head. The officers who were to command the Frontier Force had been recruited, and Chamberlain wanted them to leave for the Niger on 27 November. They could reach the mouth of the Niger easily by the regular

[1] FO 83/1534 Goldie to Sanderson 7.10.97; FO 83/1536 C.O. to F.O. 30.10.97.
[2] Lugard to E. J. Lugard 16.11.97 quoted by Perham, *op. cit.*, p. 652.
[3] This interview is dealt with in more detail by Perham, *op. cit.*, pp. 641-2, on which the above account is based.

steamers, but the company, with its monopoly of transport on
the Niger, would have to take them up to Lokoja. This Goldie
refused to do unless a full settlement of the company's future
position were first agreed upon. Either the Government should
take over the company as soon as possible, or implement the
much superior scheme advocated by Sir John Kirk.[1] Chamberlain tried to side-track this awkward demand, and again asked
merely for help in getting the officers up the Niger, promising
full payment for transport. But Goldie replied in even more
extreme terms threatening to call a general meeting of shareholders to receive his resignation and decide how to protect the
shareholders' interests. Chamberlain pointed out that if the
company refused to transport the officers it could hardly expect
good treatment when the time came for it to be compensated for
the loss of its charter. Nevertheless, Chamberlain's chief concern
was to get the Frontier Force into action, and he tried to do
what he could for Goldie, asking the Foreign Office to arrange a
'speedy settlement' so that the Frontier Force might get some
co-operation.[2]

The Foreign Office did its best to do so, and Goldie actually
discussed the rate of financial compensation with Sir Thomas
Sanderson, the Permanent Under-Secretary. Goldie's claims
were huge, and probably intentionally inflated to alarm Hicks
Beach, the Chancellor of the Exchequer, who was already
worried at the high cost of Chamberlain's West African plans
and might be anxious to seize upon the Kirk scheme as an alternative to outright revocation and compensation.[3] Once in the
hands of the Treasury, however, all hope of a rapid settlement
vanished; though the papers were received in November, and
marked 'immediate', nothing was done except to summarize
their contents. Meanwhile Chamberlain continued to press
Goldie to transport the officers up the river, and again Goldie

[1] FO 83/1537 R. L. Antrobus to Sanderson 17.11.97, Goldie to Sanderson
18.11.97 enc. Goldie to Chamberlain 17.11.97.

[2] FO 83/1537 C.O. to F.O. 25.11.97 enc. C.O. to Goldie 18.11.97, Goldie to
C.O. 19.11.97 and C.O. to Goldie 22.11.97.

[3] *Ibid.* mema. by J.H.S., G.L.R. and C.H.H. 20.11.97 and Sanderson to Goldie,
private, 23.11.97. For Hicks Beach's attitude see Hicks Beach, Lady V., *Sir Michael
Hicks Beach, Earl St. Aldwyn,* London, 1932, Vol. II, p. 47.

refused unless he were told 'the terms of the revocation of the charter'.[1] It was not until December that Goldie grudgingly withdrew his demand to know the final details of the compensation to be paid, and allowed the officers to proceed. In return he demanded and was given assurances that the troops would not be used to injure the interests of the shareholders.[2]

Having agreed merely to transport the officers, this did not mean that Goldie was prepared to co-operate generally. The Treasury was reluctant to give any guarantees until a settlement had been reached with France, so that Goldie was still completely in the dark as to the Government's plans for compensation. He continued to obstruct, and, with Lugard, staged an elaborate correspondence designed to show how completely dependent the Frontier Force was on the Niger Company.[3] When the two gunboats to be provided by the Admiralty were ready Goldie refused to assist them in any way—the company's fleet was 'quite adequate' to protect the Niger.[4]

The whole situation was really very silly, and Chamberlain had the good sense to realize it. He recognized that Goldie was a very able man, wasting his talents in this futile bickering at a time when the French threatened the very existence of the British in northern Nigeria. Why could not Goldie receive the assurances he wanted, or better still, the charter be revoked at once. The Law Officers had reported that upon revocation the company's treaties would automatically pass to the Crown, though they advised that revocation should await a settlement with France as the French would undoubtedly argue that the treaties had lapsed if revocation were attempted. Chamberlain tried to evade this difficulty by suggesting an agreement with

[1] Treasury papers TI 9213c/17217 Ryder to Mowatt 24.11.97 with enclosures. FO 83/1539 C.O. to F.O. 14.12.97 enc. C.O. to R.N.C. 30.11.97 and R.N.C. to C.O. 30.11.97.

[2] This assurance was given by both the Colonial Office and the Treasury, see Treasury Papers TI 9213c/18457 comments and minutes with C.O. to Treasury 15.12.97.

[3] See the correspondence enclosed in papers referred to in the above footnote, and correspondence quoted by Perham, *op. cit.*, p. 663.

[4] FO 83/1606 Goldie to F.O. 10.1.98 enc. correspondence with Admiralty and C.O.

Goldie which should be kept secret until after a settlement had been reached with France. Once Goldie had been conciliated his talents could be put to real use; 'it might even be possible' to employ him 'as Her Majesty's High Commissioner in the Niger Territories'. Though the Treasury refused to conclude a secret agreement at once with Goldie, they did agree that Goldie's fears were in the circumstances reasonable, and gave Goldie an assurance that fair payment would be made for any losses, direct or indirect, which the company sustained by assisting the Frontier Force.[1]

Goldie, now guaranteed against losses, agreed to co-operate with the Frontier Force, and in the weeks which followed began personal talks with Hicks Beach, the Chancellor of the Exchequer, which eventually resulted in the secret agreement that Chamberlain had asked for. At first Hicks Beach was hostile. In a letter to Salisbury in February he agreed that the Niger Company was entitled to fair compensation for rights to which it was justly entitled. 'But,' he asked, 'how can we ask Parliament to compensate it for the loss of an indefensible monopoly on the Niger, or to pay for treaty rights, many of which are, in the opinion of the Foreign Office, of very doubtful value.' He was not disposed to be generous, in view of Goldie's refusal to co-operate hitherto.[2] Nevertheless the Chancellor overcame his scruples, and by mid-March 1898 Goldie received the assurances he wanted. In a 'strictly confidential' letter to Goldie, Hicks Beach laid down the terms for revocation of the charter which would eventually be laid before Parliament. The company would receive £150,000 for the rights relinquished and the dislocation of its trade due to the revocation, £300,000 as compensation for the losses on administration since 1886, one half of all mineral royalties collected in the company's Sokoto, Gandu, and Benue treaty spheres, a fair price for any administrative assets taken over by the new administration, and the Government would assume responsibility for the 'Niger Government

---

[1] FO 83/1538 F.O. to Law Officers 13.12.97; FO 83/1539 same to same 28.12.97; FO 83/1606 C.O. to F.O. 24.1.98 with minute by Salisbury; Treasury Papers T1 9336/1442 C.O. to Treasury 24.1.98 and Treasury to C.O. 29.1.98.

[2] Quoted by Lady Hicks Beach, op. cit., p. 87.

Loan' of £250,000. In return Goldie must promise to place all the company's resources at the disposal of the Government until the charter was revoked, for which the Government would guarantee the company a dividend of six per cent per annum from 1 January 1898.[1]

Thus Chamberlain succeeded in getting Goldie's co-operation. Lugard could now no longer delay, and left England to join the already partly-organized and half-trained forces at Lokoja.[2] Goldie was as good as his word, and telegraphed orders to the company's forces to obey Lugard as their commander.[3] In April Lugard heard with consternation that Goldie now endorsed the 'chessboard' policy of piecemeal occupation, and he was compelled to set the force in motion. Forces from Lagos had already occupied a line of posts in the south, and fomented rebellions in some towns, which drove out the French and allowed British forces to occupy them. Lugard's forces, led by Colonel Willcocks, marched through Borgu establishing posts and finally linking them to Kishi. On the march back he found that the French had hoisted the tricolour 400 yards from one of these posts. After consulting Lugard, Willcocks retaliated by hoisting the Union Jack 400 yards from the French-occupied Kiama, under the guns of the French garrison. At another place British troops were opposed by fixed bayonets, and at another shoved their way bodily through a cordon of French soldiers, who howled provocative insults at their fellow-Africans as they did so. But nowhere did the bullets fly. Chamberlain had guessed correctly that the French would not start a war for Borgu.[4]

•   •   •   •

[1] FO 83/1611 Treasury to F.O. 20.7.98 enc. Hicks Beach to Goldie 17.3.98.

[2] Perham, *op. cit.*, pp. 678 and 684.

[3] This order was much disliked by the Agent-General and the Commandant of Constabulary, who grumbled and made conditions, and actually succeeded in involving Lugard's forces in operations in the Niger Delta. See Perham, *op. cit.*, p. 686 and CO 446/1 Lugard to C.O. 9.5.98.

[4] Perham, *op. cit.*, pp. 676–97 gives such a full and well-written account of these operations that it would be futile to do more than summarize them briefly. Willcocks described his own part in the campaign in *From Kabul to Kumasi*, London, 1904. Lugard chronicled the campaign in full detail in his despatches to the Colonial Office which may be found in CO 446/1.

The real battle for Nigeria's western frontier was fought not in Borgu, but in the conference room in Paris, between the departments of state in London, and between the Foreign Ministers and ambassadors. Here, as in Borgu, it is possible to trace increasing influence from Chamberlain which eventually dominated the negotiations. Goldie, in contrast to the position he had obtained in the early 'nineties, played almost no direct part. Yet in this sphere, in contrast to his attitude on the question of counter-measures, Chamberlain acted as a kind of indirect advocate for Goldie, sharing his views on the need to control the navigable Niger and forcing them through against stiff opposition.

The manner in which Chamberlain secured control of these negotiations was part of his wider political plans and ambitions. In 1895, on joining Salisbury's Unionist Government, Chamberlain had deliberately chosen the Colonial Office, then as now considered as one of the more junior Cabinet ranks, in order to impart a more colonial emphasis to British policy.[1] The chief obstacle to these ambitions was the Prime Minister, Lord Salisbury, who had since the 1880's displayed a cynical light-heartedness towards colonial expansion, and as one of Europe's leading exponents of diplomacy was accustomed to using colonial issues in the interests of larger power politics, and not vice versa. He was not, therefore, predisposed to allow Chamberlain to divert British policy towards an attitude of 'colonies first'. But Chamberlain had advantages. The chief of these was his position in British party politics. As the chief personage of the Liberal Unionists he had to be placated to secure solid support in the Commons; and as the foremost exponent of the Caucus system in party organization his influence on the electorate was much to be feared. If the Liberal party were to drop its plans for Irish home rule it was quite possible that Chamberlain and his flock might rejoin the fold. Thus Salisbury was willing to allow Chamberlain to acquire a few 'barren tracts' if this did not unduly complicate the international

[1] Garvin, *Chamberlain*, Vol. III, pp. 3–8.

situation.[1] Yet Salisbury, in the event, was forced to concede more than this. In the years after 1895 Britain almost went to war with the United States over the question of British Guiana's frontier, faced war with France first on the Niger and then on the Nile, and finally became committed to a warlike solution of the South African problem. In the new age of aggressive colonial expansion heralded by the Jameson Raid, the seizure of Bussa, and the Fashoda crisis, Salisbury was out of his depth and unsure of himself. He had always been able to see the importance of Egypt and the Nile basin, and of strategic routes like Suez and the Cape. But passions were now aroused which he failed to understand. Public opinion became incensed about issues which he once thought slightly comic. Gone were the days when a few jokes with the French ambassador at the expense of the colonial madmen were enough to produce an amicable and appropriately vague settlement. Where Salisbury resisted Chamberlain now, it was usually at the behest of officials and ambassadors, and these seemed so often to be proved wrong-headed by Chamberlain.

The chief official resistance to Chamberlain came from the ambassador in Paris, Sir Edmund Monson, supported by the British Niger Commissioners, Gosselin, Monson's deputy, and Colonel Everett of the War Office Intelligence Division. Monson, after an early failure to enter party politics as a Liberal, had served nearly thirty years in the diplomatic corps, and after a period as ambassador in Vienna now held the premier ambassadorial post. His advice therefore carried much weight, especially with Salisbury. His first concern was Britain's position in the international power structure. He was an admirer of French culture and sensed the menace from Germany and Austria. It seemed to him that by her traditions Britain must move closer to France and Russia in resisting the ambitions of the Central European powers. His ambition was, therefore, to secure a settlement of Anglo-French colonial disputes, which he

---

[1] Cf. Salisbury to Monson 19.10.97 quoted by Perham, *op. cit.*, p. 668, where he writes of the impossibility of going to war 'for the sake of a malarious African desert'.

regarded as red herrings in the diplomatic situation, so as to clear the air for a reorientation of alliances. His natural instincts seemed to tell him that Borgu or control of Niger navigation were not worth the sacrifice of this settlement with France. The thought of war with France over such issues appalled him. In August 1897 Monson seized upon an offer of resumed negotiations made by Hanotaux to voice his doubts as to the wisdom of Chamberlain's counter-measures in West Africa, and argued that the offer to negotiate ought to be accepted. It was a mistake to look at West Africa in isolation, 'however indisputably important that sphere may be'.[1] Chamberlain, though he refused to modify his plans in Africa, was forced to accept Salisbury's suggestion that the negotiations be resumed, adding the comment that it was British military preparations which had forced the French to resume talks.[2]

The renewed negotiations did not go at all to Chamberlain's liking. It seemed to him that the British delegates allowed the French to make the most exaggerated claims and say the most outrageous things, without protest. There were long tirades against the Niger Company, its objects were 'simply commercial and self seeking', its agents merely 'private individuals, the hired servants of a Trading Company'. Not so the gallant Frenchmen, who were commissioned by the state, and made their treaties in full dress uniform, 'with the honourable object, not of gain, but of promoting the civilisation of the native races'. What comparison could there be between the activities of such men and those of the Niger Company, engaged in supplying the Africans with arms and ammunition 'to resist the advance of French civilisation'?[3] The French insisted on access to the navigable Niger, and on one occasion declared that 'where the French flag was once planted, there it must remain'.[4] By early November 1897 the negotiations were stagnant, and

[1] FO 27/3343 Monson to Salisbury, 15 Af. tel. most conf. 16.9.97 and FO 27/3339 Monson to Salisbury, 273 Af. very conf. 17.9.97.
[2] FO 27/3372 F.O. to C.O. conf. 21.9.97 and C.O. to F.O. 27.9.97.
[3] This was the line taken by Hanotaux, see FO 27/3340 Monson to Salisbury, 330 Af. 22.10.97 and same to same, 334 Af. 22.10.97.
[4] FO 27/3340 Gosselin to Salisbury, 345 Af. conf. 30.10.97 with enclosures.

the commissioners were back on the well-worn track of discussing yet again their respective treaty rights.

This was Chamberlain's cue to protest at the way the British delegates were conducting themselves. Why did they not protest vigorously at all these extravagant claims, particularly the claim to establish title by flag-hoisting. They should call on the French to abandon Bussa, if they refused then they should be asked to 'elect a principle on which they will stand'. If they chose effective occupation then the British delegates should inform them that the talks would be broken off for six months, by which time the British expected to be in effective occupation of as many places in the French sphere as they were in the British sphere. The whole West African hinterland would then be chequered with the Union Jack and the Tricolour. If the French saw the absurdity of this then they could opt either for treaty rights or the 'hinterland' theory; in either case Bussa would be British. If the French refused to meet these arguments, then the negotiations should be broken off.[1]

Monson resisted these arguments strenuously. The hinterland theory was useless, for the coast was curved and every inland point must lie in several hinterlands. As for treaty rights the British commissioners had exhaustively examined all the Niger Company's treaties on the middle Niger and had come to the conclusion that 'none of these claims can be established'. Monson went on to demand for himself and the commissioners a freer hand to offer concessions, otherwise he foresaw the breakdown of negotiations.[2] Chamberlain replied point by point, attacking particularly Monson's lack of faith in the treaties; Lugard's own evidence about the Borgu treaties outweighed 'any amount of *ex post facto* assertions by negroes'.[3]

Salisbury now made the first of a series of decisions which mark the steady progress of Chamberlain towards control of the negotiations. New instructions were sent out to Monson on 23 November ordering him to ask the French to choose a

[1] FO 27/3373 C.O. to F.O. 12.11.97.
[2] FO 27/3340 Monson to Salisbury, 368 Af. conf. 14.11.97.
[3] FO 27/3373 C.O. to F.O. 22.11.97.

principle, either 'hinterland' or treaty rights, on which to base
their claims. Where facts were in dispute they might be submitted to the judgement of 'some impartial arbitrator'. A few
days later Monson received a paraphrase of the Colonial Office
criticisms of the conduct of the negotiations, and a refusal to
give him the 'freer hand' he had requested.[1] This was but the
first of many dispatches Monson was to receive which had in
effect been drafted in the Colonial Office.

No one was more surprised than the British delegates themselves at the reception given by the French to the new approach
prompted by Chamberlain. The British now put forward the
most extravagant and fanciful claims, most of which they themselves thought unjustifiable, and hinted that a failure to accept
them would lead to 'serious complications'. Instead of replying,
as was expected, with redoubled invective, the French delegates
adopted a 'distinctly apologetic' tone. In addition they agreed
to recommend a major concession, which Hanotaux later
accepted officially; namely that if the frontier line west of the
Niger were settled by agreement, France would recognize the
Anglo-German frontier from the sea to Lake Chad, claim no
territory east of the Niger, and recognize the Say–Barruwa line
subject to delimitation and a British recognition that the
northern shores of Lake Chad were French.[2] Monson was
forced to admit that the military preparations were having their
effect on the French attitude.

This French concession effectively narrowed the dispute to
its most difficult aspect, that of Niger navigation. The French
now asked that the regulations for Zambezi navigation, forced
on Portugal by Britain in the interests of the Nyasaland and
British South Africa Company protectorates, should form the
basis for the Niger navigation regulations, and that in addition
France should be given a concession near Leaba, similar to the
British Chinde concession on the Zambezi, which would be
linked to Dahomey by a corridor.[3] This proposal gave rise to

---

[1] FO 27/3336 Salisbury to Monson, 367 Af. 23.11.97 and same to same, 374 Af.
26.11.97.

[2] FO 27/3341 Monson to Salisbury, 393 Af. 27.11.97 with enclosure.

[3] FO 27/3341 Monson to Salisbury, 393 Af. 27.11.97 and same to same, 400 Af.
28.11.97.

PLATE 3

Sir John Kirk
From *The Exploitation of East Africa*, R. Coupland,
Faber and Faber

another disagreement between the diplomats and the Colonial Office, but this time it took the form of a direct argument between Chamberlain and Salisbury. Salisbury thought that the French claim for access to the Niger and a 'Chinde' near Leaba was a cheap price to pay for the recognition of all the frontiers of the Niger Company, and cynically dismissed as rubbish Goldie's arguments that the French would flood the Niger Territories with arms and spirits.[1] On the following day Chamberlain replied with a vigorous attack on Salisbury's arguments which was practically a rehash of all that Goldie had said against conceding access to foreigners. The most that Chamberlain was prepared for was to draw up new navigation regulations, without the guarantee of a 'Chinde'. Again he complained of the weak attitude of the British negotiators, and demanded that they press British claims to the full.[2] Once more Chamberlain's view triumphed, and dispatches went off to Paris repeating word for word the policy he advocated.[3]

The negotiations entered a new phase with the British proposals made in January 1898. Britain offered to recognize Mossi and Gurunsi, in the rear of the Gold Coast, as French, to concede Nikki to France, but to retain Bussa. The idea of a corridor to the Niger was excluded, but the French were offered a lease of land on the Niger to erect wharves and warehouses. New navigation regulations would give free transit for all goods except arms and spirits. In return the French were asked to agree to identity of treatment for British and French merchants from the Ivory Coast to the Niger Coast Protectorate. The proposals are an interesting indication of the way in which commercial considerations still lay behind British policy, even in the hands of Chamberlain. Just as in Gladstone's day, Britain was prepared to make large territorial concessions provided British merchants could maintain free action. It was just for this reason that these proposals could not be expected to commend

[1] FO 83/1538 mem. by Salisbury 30.11.97.
[2] FO 83/1538 mem. by Chamberlain 1.12.97.
[3] FO 27/3336 Salisbury to Gosselin, 438 Af. 30.12.97 (printed in Gooch and Temperley, *British Documents on the Origin of the War*, London, 1927, Vol. I, p. 132, no. 157, cited hereafter as *British Documents*).

U

themselves to the French, whose merchants looked to territorial frontiers for protection against British competition. Moreover the British proposals were not generous in what they conceded; they offered only territories like Nikki and Mossi already in French occupation, yet asked the French to withdraw from Bussa and Ilo on the Niger. Only in the Gold Coast did Britain offer to withdraw from occupied territory, but this had been publicly acknowledged by Britain as legitimately French.

Yet once again the French reaction was mild and conciliatory. Hanotaux confessed to Monson that he was very worried that the officers in West Africa might lose their heads and precipitate a war 'for objects which in themselves cannot be worth so grave a calamity'. He promised to do all he could to get approval for the tariff proposals, though he warned of the strong protectionist feelings in the Cabinet, Premier Méline in particular being 'an enraged protectionist'.[1]

These British proposals were in fact the basis for the final agreement. The French replied by asking for a lease for ninety-nine years, with the right to transport goods (excluding arms and spirits) free of duty.[2] Chamberlain now began to see his way to accepting a settlement. He agreed to the idea of a lease of land, and was prepared to liberalize the navigation regulations, though he would not go so far as to base them on those for the Zambezi.[3] By the end of March 1898 the French had elaborated their proposals into the sketch of a Convention which accepted most of the British territorial proposals, the plan for a lease, and gave a ten-year fiscal concession to British merchants in the French West African colonies.[4] The rest of the negotiations, though occupying three more months of fiercely contested argument, was spent in modifying these general bases. Chamberlain continued to dominate the policy of the British. In May he was prepared to break off negotiations if the French did not

[1] *British Documents*, I, no. 164, p. 139; FO 84/3411 Monson to Salisbury, 75 Af. conf. 20.2.98.
[2] FO 27/3412 Monson to Salisbury, 106 Af. 11.3.98 with enclosure.
[3] FO 27/3438 C.O. to F.O. Secret 17.3.98.
[4] FO 27/3408 Salisbury to Monson, 150 Af. 22.3.98 reporting interview between Balfour and Courcel; FO 27/3412 Monson to Salisbury, 116 Af. 22.3.98.

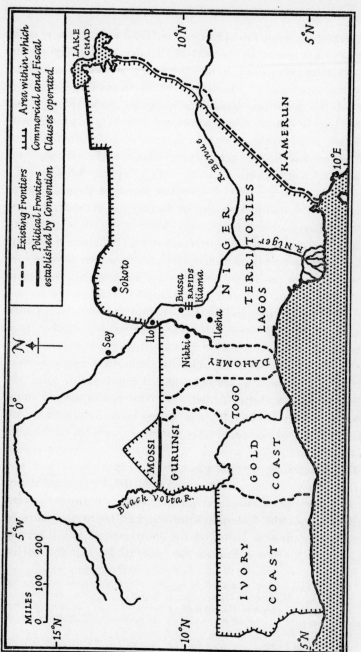

6. The Anglo-French Convention of June 1898

Existing Frontiers

Political Frontiers established by Convention

Area within which Commercial and Fiscal Clauses operated.

MILES
0   100   200

N

LAKE CHAD

Sokoto

Say

Ilo

Bussa
RAPIDS
Iliama

Nikki

Ilesha

MOSSI

GURUNSI

Black Volta R.

TOGO

DAHOMEY

IVORY COAST

GOLD COAST

NIGER TERRITORIES

LAGOS

R. Niger

R. Benue

KAMERUN

5°W

0°

10°E

15°N

10°N

5°N

10°N

5°N

10°N

drop their demand for 'Zambezi' navigation rules. It is worth noting that despite all the official criticism of the Niger Company's monopoly, the Colonial Secretary should be so insistent that the Government should inherit all the political power to exclude foreign trade which the company had built up since 1886. Indeed Chamberlain was now so much in sympathy with Goldie's views on this topic that he actually sent him to Paris to bolster up the British negotiators, who, he alleged, had 'not enough stiffening in the lot to hold up a paper collar'.[1]

Another question was that of Ilo, north of Bussa, where a French officer had lost his life 'in the cause of civilisation'. The French negotiators argued that sentimental public opinion would be enraged if Ilo were returned to Britain. (In fact the French officer had been murdered by an irate African husband, who had been put in jail so that the officer might more easily make love to his wife, but had escaped!)[2] The real reason behind the French demand for Ilo was that some experts, Toutée among them, had argued that the Niger was navigable up to this point. The Ilo question produced another argument between Salisbury, who felt that the military tension in West Africa had gone far enough, and Chamberlain, who was prepared to go even further and order Lugard to move into Dahomey.[3] Chamberlain once again triumphed, and Monson was told he could offer not Ilo, but places in the Gold Coast.[4]

Once more the French gave way. Their position was now rapidly deteriorating, and it seemed likely that France might have to face the critical situation on the Niger without a Government. Lebon, the Colonial Minister, had failed to secure re-election on the first ballot on his constituency, and it seemed likely that he would lose on the second. In fact the Méline

---

[1] CO 537/15 minute by Chamberlain 25.5.98, quoted by Perham, *op. cit.*, p. 698.

[2] FO 27/3413 Monson to Salisbury, 193 Af. 3.6.98.

[3] Garvin, *Chamberlain*, Vol. III, pp. 218–19, prints Salisbury's exchange of letters with Chamberlain on this subject, and they are reproduced in Perham, *op. cit.*, pp. 700–1.

[4] FO 27/3416 Salisbury to Monson, 16 Af. tel. 4.6.98, this telegram is in fact merely a precis of C.O. to F.O. Secret 4.6.98 in FO 27/3440.

Cabinet fell from power on the day after the Convention was actually signed on 14 June.[1]

The Convention settled the frontier disputes in both the Gold Coast and Nigeria, and established the broad outlines of their modern frontiers. In Nigeria the 1889 boundary between Lagos and Porto Novo (now Dahomey) up to the ninth parallel was retained, from whence it curled through Borgu, leaving Nikki to France, and Kiama and Bussa to Britain, striking the Niger at Gere, the port of Ilo. It then curved northwards in an arc one hundred miles from the city of Sokoto, then along the fourteenth parallel for seventy miles, where it dropped down to 13 degrees 20 for a further two hundred and fifty miles, then once more along the fourteenth parallel to meet Lake Chad just north of Barruwa. All this was to be delimited by a Boundary Commission in detail as soon as possible. Each party agreed not to victimize chiefs who had signed treaties with the other, and to abstain from any political action in the other's sphere. The last two articles contained the commercial agreements. Britain was to grant two leases to the French, one near Leaba, and one at the Niger mouth. Britain promised to discuss new navigation regulations with the French. British and French subjects and protected persons, their products and merchandise, would be given equal treatment in an area extending from the Ivory Coast to the German frontier with the Niger Coast Protectorate. An exchange of notes attached to the Convention provided for the withdrawal of all troops from each other's spheres.[2]

The Anglo-French Convention, like the Declaration of 1890, was a British triumph. The only sacrifice of any importance was Nikki, but here the British title was weak, and the country economically worthless. In keeping the rest of eastern Borgu Britain retained political control of the Niger. Sokoto and Bornu, vast and important areas, were now guaranteed against foreign occupation. The idea of international participation in

[1] FO 27/3413 Monson to Salisbury, 185 Af. 23.5.98, reports on the French political situation. In fact there was an attempt by the French to get the Convention signed before 22 May, the date of Lebon's second ballot. This failed too due to an illness of Hanotaux.

[2] For text see Hertslet, *Map of Africa*, Vol. II, pp. 785 ff.

SIR GEORGE GOLDIE

framing rules for Niger navigation was scotched for all time. Even the leases and the new navigation rules were worthless concessions, for which the French had bartered a valuable one in the shape of the thirty-year fiscal identity, for within a few years railways were to displace the river as the best form of bulk transport. It is hardly surprising that there were complaining voices raised in France and demands for its modification. In fact the Convention was never out of danger until it was finally ratified, in March 1899, against the fierce opposition of the French colonial group.

The British triumph was peculiarly and personally that of Joseph Chamberlain. His policy of negotiation from strength seemed to have been brilliantly justified. He had carried it through with consummate skill, manipulating individual actors in the drama to suit his own purposes almost without their knowing what he was doing. If the political system in Britain was still partly oligarchical, it was also increasingly democratic, and here too Chamberlain's flamboyant oratory had been tuned to the emerging imperialism of the masses, popularizing the idea that there were urgent issues at stake in Nigeria, warning France that 'the people' were with him. His political judgement that the French would not fight for Borgu had been brilliantly justified.[1]

Success is the yardstick in politics. But it is well to pause and consider what Chamberlain staked in the crisis. The 'weakness' of Salisbury, Monson or the Niger Commissioners would have cost Britain Ilo, perhaps Kiama, and given the French a corridor and free access to the Niger. On the other hand if France had imitated Chamberlain, and met strength with strength, intransigence with intransigence, war would almost certainly have followed. The result would have been catastrophic not only for Britain, but for a Europe divided in the face of German militarism and expansionism. No British interest in Nigeria was really worth this.

---

[1] Perham, *op. cit.*, p. 705.

13

Decline and Fall

IT is usually stated that the decision to revoke the Niger Company's charter was agreed secretly as a concession to France during the negotiations for the Convention of 1898. Mary Kingsley went so far as to complain that the French had 'secured Goldie's head on a charger'.[1] We have seen that this was not so; the decision to revoke the charter had to be made on grounds of policy long before the negotiations with France had begun in earnest, and even the basis of the final compensation to be paid to the company had been thrashed out with Goldie long before the signature of the Convention. It might be imagined that once the Convention had been signed, the transfer of administration to the Crown would have been rapidly accomplished. In fact the charter was not revoked for another eighteen months. Despite Chamberlain, the mills of the Colonial Office still ground slowly.

In these last months of the charter the Niger Company's administration lapsed into near-chaos. Knowing that the administration would soon come to an end, there was no incentive for Goldie to spend more than an absolute minimum on government. The company's staff and steamers were diverted almost completely to trade, there was a huge increase in turnover, and profits rose by fifty per cent.[2] But even if Goldie had continued as before, it seems likely that his efforts would have had very little effect on the political situation in the northern Emirates. The process begun by the victories in Ilorin and Nupe

[1] Gwynn, S., *Life of Mary Kingsley*, London, 1933, p. 182.
[2] See Appendix I for details of profits.

had to be continued to be effective, and the fact that Goldie had stopped short destroyed the company's influence. Until 1897 the Emirs had regarded the company as little more than a group of traders who had their uses, particularly as suppliers of arms and ammunition. After the campaigns against Nupe and Ilorin they were alarmed at the company's new-found military prowess, and suspected that its objects were now political and religious, its concealed aim being the establishment of Christian domination. Even more disturbing for the Sultan of Sokoto were the company's intrigues with Rabeh Zobeir, the upstart conqueror of Bornu and ever-present threat to the Fulani empire. British Intelligence in Cairo conceived a plan to solve all problems from the Nile to the Niger by allying with Rabeh and placing him under British protection. Zobeir Pasha, Rabeh's foster-father and once the arch slave-dealer of the Egyptian Sudan, was employed as a go-between and wrote letters to try to revive Rabeh's old loyalties. These were carried by Egyptian messengers whom the Niger Company tried to smuggle into Bornu via the Niger.[1] These intrigues, and the war against Nupe and Ilorin, turned Sokoto hostile at the very time when the French threat to the Niger bend was becoming intense. In October 1897 the Sultan sent out letters to all the Emirs on the Benue, ordering them to drive out the company:

> You have seen what the Company has done to Bida and Ilorin—my territory. You are not to allow the Company to remain in any part of the country over which you have jurisdiction.

Later, with a piece of bluff designed to bolster up his shaky authority, the Sultan announced: 'Behold! I have another vassal. Rabeh has joined me.'[2]

The Emirs, much to the relief of the company's officials, seem to have taken very little notice. Yola did nothing, though the company's local official reported home that would have to 'go

---

[1] For the whole story of this scheme, 1893–6, see the fascinating series of documents in FO 2/118 *Messages to Rabeh Zobeir*. The messengers seem to have been more interested in living well at the company's expense than in delivering the letters. This volume is a mine of information on Rabeh, and even contains the accounts of visitors to his court, some written in Arabic.

[2] Kirk-Greene, A. H. M., *Adamawa Past and Present*, Oxford, 1958, p. 49.

or stay as he says'. At Muri, where the company had managed to patch up the disruption caused by Mizon's intervention with a tacit agreement not to interfere with the Emir's internal affairs or slave raiding, the Emir was in two minds. He wanted the company's trade, but feared that if he disobeyed the Sultan his neighbour, the Emir of Bakundi, would use this as a pretext to devour him with the aid of other Fulani princes near by. His mind was finally made up for him when the Emir of Bakundi wrote to say that he was going to ignore Sokoto. Thus the company escaped disaster on the Benue. The Fulani political structure was too weak and disunited to act.[1]

A greater danger was that Sokoto, aided perhaps by Gandu, would act in territories directly under their authority. Here the situation was complicated by the presence of the French in Borgu, by the fact that British authority was divided between the military officers of the Frontier Force and the civilian officials of the company, and by the dissolution of the Sokoto-Gandu power system itself. The Hausa were still unconquered in Gobir, where the *jihad* had originally begun, and now they began to expand their territory for the first time. The Emir of Kontagora defied Gandu and defended his territory by force, whilst Rabeh continually menaced from the east. Internal weakness alone explained why Sokoto and Gandu failed to intervene in the explosive situation on the middle Niger, despite continual threats that they would do so. Goldie was studiously inactive, and strongly resisted all Chamberlain's suggestions that he should establish a resident in Sokoto. Chamberlain was wise enough to understand that he could not expect Goldie to embark on new policies now, and the matter was allowed to drop.[2]

In Nupe the breakdown of the Niger Company's authority was total. After the battle of Bida the company had 'deposed' the Emir Abu Bokari, and replaced him with the *Markum* Mohamedu, but without a garrison or other tangible evidence

---

[1] *Ibid., loc. cit.*

[2] CO 446/1 Lugard to Chamberlain, tel. 9.5.98, same to same, tel. 21.5.98 with minute by Chamberlain, Lugard to Chamberlain 29.5.98; FO 83/1610 R.N.C. to F.O. 22.6.98; FO 83/1611 F.O. to C.O. 25.6.98.

of support from the company Mohamedu was powerless to
resist the legitimate Emir. By August 1897 Abu Bokari was once
more in control of Bida. Goldie had no illusions about this, and
followed a policy of supporting Mohamedu in the south where
he had the support of the 'pagans', the riverain tribes, and the
restored shadow-king Idirisu. The basis of Goldie's policy was
commercial; 'what happens in northern Nupe is not vital to us
so long as we hold the waterway,' he explained to his deputy,
Lord Scarbrough.[1]

The lack of effective authority in Ilorin led to serious quarrels
between the company's officials and the officers of the Frontier
Force. We have seen that the conquest of Ilorin resulted in
practically no political changes, even the refractory Emir himself was allowed to continue his reign. The Emir was thus able
to continue as before, and in August 1898 the Lagos authorities
began to complain of renewed attacks on the Yoruba, and interference with caravans. But now Lagos could complain not
simply to the Niger Company, but also to the military officers of
the Frontier Force. At this time Lugard was in England for
consultations on the future administration of Nigeria, and
Colonel Willcocks was left in charge. His first act was to send a
corporal with a letter demanding the Emir's co-operation. This
was not very diplomatic and the Emir was offended that one so
lowly should attempt to deliver messages to him. The corporal
was therefore badly treated and beaten and kicked by the
Emir's men.[2] Willcocks could not let this pass; he was naturally
concerned that the prestige of the Frontier Force should be made
apparent to the local African people, and he was concerned for
the safety of the telegraph line from Lagos to Jebba which had
just been completed and ran through Ilorin. He therefore
despatched Captain the Honourable Richard Somerset with
fifty men to deliver protests. The Emir was not to be bullied; he

[1] Goldie to Scarbrough 30.8.97 inc. telegrams to and from Wallace (in the
possession of the Earl of Scarbrough). Nupe was not conquered until Lugard's
forces occupied it in 1901. Bokari continued to be a threat until 1906, when he was
defeated in battle and exiled to Lokoja, where he died soon afterwards. Burns,
History of Nigeria, pp. 169–70; Nadel, *A Black Byzantium*, p. 84.

[2] CO 446/1 Willcocks to C.O. 8.11.98 enc. Somerset to Willcocks 7.11.98 which
summarizes the early stages of the affair.

returned the letters of protest unopened, had Somerset's interpreter beaten up, ordered a boycott of food supplies to the party,
and saw that their water was poisoned. Hearing all this Willcocks telegraphed home for permission to march on Ilorin.
Lugard, having seen the Niger Company in action in Nigeria,
supported Willcocks. But Willcocks was told that he could
attack Ilorin only if the Niger Company's Agent-General
concurred.[1]

To hope for agreement between Willcocks and Agent-General
Watts was over-optimistic, to say the least. Watts had done his
best to impede the activities of the Frontier Force from the first,
on one occasion he had even gone to the length of organizing
'picquets' among the Africans to prevent the sale of food to the
soldiers. The two men had quarrelled over this and general
relations with the company's employees were very bad. For the
most part the military officers affected aristocratic habits,
whereas the company's men were of 'low class' origins. This
led to bitter misunderstandings and jealousies. In these circumstances Watts resisted Willcocks' request that he be allowed to
march on Ilorin. Instead, whilst admitting that Somerset had
been badly treated, he urged Willcocks to withdraw the soldiers
and trust to the Emir's goodwill to protect the telegraph. Willcocks angrily rejected this idea, and telegraphed home asking
to be allowed to deliver a week's ultimatum to the Emir.[2]

These rivalries were duplicated in London. Goldie vehemently
defended Watts, and asked that he be allowed to telegraph the
Agent-General that he need fear no 'aggression' against Ilorin.
He protested at the discovery that officers of the Frontier Force
were not subject to the company's courts of justice, because they
were technically 'on active service' in a 'foreign country'—the
protectorate being out of the Queen's dominions. There had
been no insult to Somerset's men; to the Emir they were foreign
troops who had no right to be there, in behaving as he did the
Emir was merely showing his fidelity to the company—'the only

[1] *Ibid.* Willcocks to C.O. 30.9.98 with minutes; FO 83/1614 C.O. to F.O. 5.10.98
and same to same 15.10.98 enc. tel. to Willcocks.
[2] CO 446/1 Willcocks to C.O. tel. 16.10.98.

Imperial representative he knows'. The Emir was 'a fine fellow', and unless the Frontier Force was prepared for a general campaign against the Fulani it would be folly to attack him. 'Statesmanship' was the only alternative. Goldie telegraphed orders to Watts to go to Ilorin city and negotiate a settlement with the Emir, and in the meantime he asked the Colonial Office to inform Willcocks that Watts had full authority in matters of native policy. He did not get quite as much as this, but Willcocks was told to sit tight and see what Watts could achieve.[1]

Agent-General Watts' visit did indeed settle the matter for a time. He persuaded the Emir to write an apology and pay a small fine, and though Willcocks thought the whole thing inadequate he was anxious to withdraw Somerset and his men, who were in poor shape after nearly a month in the inhospitable city. Goldie agreed to garrison the town with an officer and fifty men of the constabulary, and the imperial force withdrew.[2]

This was not quite the end of the affair. Somerset was young and forthright, and he was an aristocrat with friends in high places. He was so embittered by the whole business that he sent a long private letter to a friend in the Colonial Office attacking the Niger Company in the most extreme terms. Despite its obvious bias, Somerset's account of Ilorin is interesting as a reflection of the attitudes of a young Englishman of the type who was about to take over the administration of Nigeria. His main charge was that the company was not an administration at all, but a mere trading company masquerading as such, using deceit and sharp practice to maintain this fiction. Ilorin had '*never been subjugated*', slavery was rampant 'and you can see the lines of poor manacled devils working in the fields'. The Emir had done everything in his power to impede the Frontier Force; a chief who had helped in the construction of the telegraph line was arrested by the Emir and set to work in the field with his ankles

[1] CO 446/3 Goldie to C.O. 13.10.98, R.N.C. to Selborne 14.10.98 and R.N.C. to C.O. 14.10.98. CO 446/1 Willcocks to C.O. tel. 16.10.98, Goldie to Antrobus annexed, minutes on tel. to Willcocks 16.10.98. It is interesting to note that in one of the Emir's messages to Willcocks he refused further communication because Willcocks represented 'the Government at Jebba'.

[2] CO 446/1 Willcocks to C.O. tel. 29.10.98 and minutes, same to same 1.11.98 tel. (misdated 1.10.98).

chained together so that he could not move his feet more than five inches apart. Slaves could be openly purchased in a public market. One of the officers saw a man lying in front of the Emir's palace with his head cut off and his private parts laid on his stomach. When questioned, the Emir had roared with laughter and said that the man had committed suicide. Watts knew all about this kind of thing; in fact he had arranged with the Emir to make sure that a visiting bishop of the Church Missionary Society saw not a single slave when he visited Ilorin; the Emir thought this a fine joke. Somerset concluded by asking his friend to use his influence against the company:

I do hope Mr. Chamberlain is not lead by Sir G. Goldie. I've no doubt the latter is a very honest and delightful gentleman but he *can't* know what is going on here—the absolute robbery of the native and the brutes most of the Niger Company's employees are. . . . I came out here with the greatest possible admiration for the Niger Company but that changed very quickly indeed.

One cannot help suspecting that pride and arrogance played a big part in forming Somerset's judgement. He gave himself away in the most impassioned paragraph of this wholly passionate letter:

Can you imagine what it is to be an officer of the Imperial Forces to sit down and see the British flag insulted, and the British prestige suffering (as it is for they all say in the town that we are afraid of them!) to please a rotten, cheating trading company, with a man of Watt's stamp *over* me?[1]

Somerset sent in the same account in an official report to Willcocks, though the language was toned down. In commenting on it Lugard, who was still in England, showed that his views on the company had altered. He demanded that the company should give an explanation of Watt's conduct, praised Somerset's self-control and courage, and condemned Watts for discriminating between the company and the Frontier Force, and allowing the Emir to think Somerset of no importance.[2]

. . . . .

[1] F.O. Conf. Print 7653 Somerset to Oliver 22.10.98.
[2] CO 446/1 Willcocks to C.O. 8.11.98 inc. Somerset's report on visit to Ilorin 7.11.98; Lugard to Antrobus 29.12.98.

If the division of authority in Nigeria were not enough to convince the Colonial Office of the need for a speedy transfer of the
administration, the traditional opponents of the Niger Company
added their arguments. They could now assume that transfer
would soon take place, so that in the main their complaints were
not so bitter as in the past, and concentrated on the delay in
opening up the river to free trade. There were fears that the
terms of the transfer might leave the company with a monopoly
of the land, or at least in control of the landing places on the
banks of the rivers.[1] There was also a final acrimonious flare-up
of the liquor question. Behind this agitation was the more
general struggle between the Liverpool traders, for whom the
forthright pen of Mary Kingsley was busily defending the liquor
trade, and the missionary and radical interests who attacked the
trade as immoral and debauching to the African. Goldie had
allied himself to the missionary party by his fierce taxation of
spirits, and their prohibition in the north, and in his speeches
and writings. This attitude had considerable propaganda value,
but it laid Goldie open to isolation if his Liverpool opponents
could show that the company itself did a large trade in spirits.
In January 1898 John Holt alleged that the company had been
shipping out 'enormous quantities' of spirits during the high-
water of 1897 to avoid any duties which the new administration
might impose.[2] James Pinnock, the renegade ex-director of the
Niger Company, made similar charges in the 1898 season,
alleging that in the first three months of the year the company
had shipped 900,000 bottles of gin by the regular steamers alone,
and that in one sailing the company had shipped seventy-five
tons of gunpowder for sale to Africans.[3] The accusations were
reported in the press,[4] and Sir Charles Dilke began asking questions in Parliament. He forced the Government to give statistics,
and Goldie, in providing them, blundered by sending in two

[1] This pressure was steady and continuous until the announcement of the date
for revocation. A full list of all the complaints would be too long to set out in detail.
For an example, see FO 83/1608 Liverpool Chamber of Commerce to F.O. 3.3.98.

[2] FO 83/1606 C.O. to F.O. 21.1.98 enc. Holt to C.O. 10.1.98.

[3] FO 83/1614 Pinnock to F.O. 19.10.98; FO 83/1615 Pinnock to F.O. 9.11.98,
each with enclosures.

[4] E.g. Daily Chronicle 4.2.98.

different sets of figures. Hence Dilke was told in February 1899 that the Niger Company had shipped 900,000 bottles in 1898 as Pinnock had alleged, whilst in March Dilke was told that 1,500,000 was the correct figure. In memoranda sent in to assist in answering these questions Goldie gave two completely different sets of figures of the company's liquor shipments since 1892:[1]

	Version of October 1898	Version of February 1899
1892	218,646	169,116
1893	318,834	266,303
1894	nil	21,250
1895	142,250	162,275
1896	159,830	126,275
1897	138,037	162,892
1898	not given	178,180
	(in gallons)	

In much of this opposition there was an air of unreality. With the exception of small firms such as Pinnock's, the Liverpool interests were now concerned more with the shape of the future administration than with abusing the dying Niger Company. They were not enthusiastic at the prospect of direct Colonial Office rule, even though they preferred it to that of the Niger Company. Crown colony rule, particularly when implemented by Chamberlain, who never seemed hesitant in spending large sums, spelt high taxation. Increased taxation would fall directly on the trade, or take the form of a hut or poll tax on the African. Many of the traders feared taxation of the African more than they feared taxation of themselves, for it was felt that taxation would cut the African's purchasing power, and it was widely believed that the hut tax had caused the recent revolt in Sierra Leone. As the day for the Colonial Office assumption of the Niger Company's administration drew nearer, feelings towards Goldie began to mellow. Whatever might be said of him, he had at least looked after the interests of the Niger merchants who had banded together under his leadership in 1879. Why could

[1] Compiled from FO 83/1614 R.N.C. to F.O. 18.10.98 (first version) and FO 2/242 R.N.C. to F.O. 10.2.99 (second version).

he not be given wider interests to manage? Why not the whole of the trade? Could not the old amalgamation discussions be revived to create a new kind of administration to replace the chartered company, run by, with, and through the traders, and presided over by the greatest statesman the African trade had yet produced—Goldie himself?

Such were the vague ambitions running through the minds of John Holt, Alfred Jones, and the Members of Parliament for Liverpool and Manchester. It was left to Mary Kingsley to give coherence and a chance of success to the movement. A brilliant theorist, she was able to hammer the unformed aspirations into workable schemes of administration. She had every opportunity to publicize the scheme, both through her widely read books published by Macmillans, and through the weekly and quarterly journals to which she was a regular contributor. Even more important was her position within the narrow circle which determined colonial policy. She was a close friend of Goldie, despite her Liverpool connexions, and the only person who might have brought him round to work with his old enemies. Politically she was equally well-connected, invited to meet the 'Balfour set', well known amongst parliamentarians, and popular with the imperialist group which ran the Royal Geographical Society. She was friendly with many of the Colonial Office officials and their wives, and above all she had the ear of Chamberlain, who even asked her for details of her administrative scheme for Nigeria before she herself had prepared it for submission.[1] This scheme eventually came to nothing,[2] but its conception represents the last brilliant glow of the chartered company idea in West Africa.

Mary Kingsley's schemes grew out of her support for the declining Niger Company, and their growth can be traced in her letters to John Holt. In December 1897, attacked in a Liverpool paper for her support of the company, she replied by

---

[1] J.H.P. 16/2 Mary Kingsley to John Holt 23.5.98.

[2] In practice, that is. It has not hitherto been realized how much the imminent downfall of the Niger Company lay behind her criticisms of Crown colony rule in *West African Studies*, published early in 1899, usually regarded as a work of study and reflection.

PLATE 4

(b) Mary Kingsley

From *Life of Mary Kingsley*, S. Gwynn, Macmillan

(a) F. D. Lugard, 1893

Reproduced by permission of Eliot and Fry Ltd.

arguing that the Niger Company was a living demonstration that 'mere traders' were capable of ruling and expanding territory without violence to the African, and that it would be better if the rest of West Africa were under similar rule.[1] Early in 1898 she began writing to Holt to try to persuade him to heal the breach with Goldie, arguing that the Government was deliberately fostering the quarrel 'lying to both and grinning to itself at having so good an excuse for neglecting W[est] A[frica], which it detests. . . .'[2] In March she suggested the formation of a Liverpool school of political economy to replace the declining influence of Manchester, and a week later urged that Goldie should go into Parliament, supported by the traders as 'member for Africa'.[3] By April she had begun to elaborate the scheme of merchant rule in detail, asking Holt how he liked the idea of a sort of House of Commons for West Africa, composed of the traders, who would handle the finances. Prices would be fixed, and each trader be paid a uniform profit (she suggested thirty-three and one-third per cent) the surplus to be used for administration. The Imperial Government would be responsible only for defence from external aggression. Once more she put Goldie forward as the leader—'a splendid weapon both to fight red tape and foreigners'.[4]

In the autumn of 1898 the scheme was receiving active support from the merchants. Both the Liverpool and Manchester Chambers of Commerce began to press for the creation of representative machinery, and Holt wrote to Goldie asking him not to retire from West African affairs and to assume leadership of the merchant interests.[5] At the end of the year there was a flutter of activity when a by-election occurred in the Kirkdale division, and Holt asked Mary Kingsley to find an eminent figure to stand as leader of the West African interests in Parliament. Goldie was the ideal man, but he refused to stand until

---

[1] J.H.P. 16/1 contains a draft of Mary Kingsley to *Liverpool Journal of Commerce*, 3.12.97.
[2] *Ibid*. Mary Kingsley to Holt 2.2.98.
[3] *Ibid*. same to same 23.1.98, 13.3.98, 21.3.98.
[4] *Ibid*. Mary Kingsley to John Holt 26.4.98, 29.4.98 and 5.5.98.
[5] J.H.P. 3/7 Goldie to Holt 26.7.98 (his reply).

X

the charter revocation was completed. Other distinguished men either could not or would not stand. Too late, Mary Kingsley spotted a young man 'full of go, no doubt full of foolishness, but he will like his father make the fur fly'. He was a Mr. Winston Churchill.[1]

By 1899 the movement had spent itself, and the old antagonisms emerged once more as the Colonial Office intention to establish official rule became obvious to all. Mary Kingsley did manage to persuade Alfred Jones to join Holt in asking Goldie to lead them, but Goldie was tired of the business:

'I believe he means it really,' he wrote to Scarbrough, 'for I have been told lately that both he and John Holt—my persistent assailants since July 1886—are now converts, and say that they are ready to follow me anywhere in West African politics.

'I am very grateful to Jones (who I believe has bought a great many R.N.C. shares) for his appreciation. But how this letter confirms what I have lately suspected but what my vanity prevented me thinking in former days—viz. that Liverpool thought I had made a slave of myself for twenty years for increase of pelf and not very successful at that.'[2]

Mary Kingsley still seems to have believed that Goldie might achieve her ambitions, but her tragic death in South Africa was also the death of the scheme for merchants' rule.[3]

Chamberlain did not take these schemes very seriously, and the delay in revoking the charter was not due to any hesitancy as the form of the future administration. The tardiness of the French Chambers in ratifying the Anglo-French Convention partly explains the delay, the rest was sheer inertia and red tape. Here one of the chief impediments was lack of space in the Colonial Office and the refusal of the Foreign Office to lease a

[1] J.H.P. 16/4 Mary Kingsley to John Holt 10.5.99.
[2] Goldie to Scarbrough 23.10.99 in the possession of Lord Scarbrough.
[3] Among the numerous biographies of Mary Kingsley, Gwynn, S., *Life of Mary Kingsley*, London, 1933, is perhaps still the fullest. Howard, C., *Mary Kingsley*, London, 1957, contains a great deal of new material, and the author has used the letters to John Holt.

room and allow a hole to be knocked in the wall which separated the two offices.[1]

Both Chamberlain and the Treasury assumed that Goldie would accept the Governorship of the new colony.[2] He refused, precisely why we do not know, although three years later he characterized the work of a colonial governor as 'very mechanical' and killing to initiative and energy.[3] Lugard was thus left as the obvious choice, despite his unpopularity among the merchants.

In May and June 1899 Goldie concluded the final negotiations with Hicks Beach about the financial compensation to be paid to the Niger Company. The Chancellor carried out all the promises which he had made in order to secure Goldie's co-operation with the Frontier Force. The company was relieved of all its administrative powers and duties, and assigned to the Government the benefits of all its treaties, land and mineral rights. It retained all its plant, assets, stations and wharves, but undertook to transfer certain war materials, steamers and stores to the new administration for £115,000. The Government assumed liability for the interest on the 'Niger Government Loan' of £250,000, with the alternative of redeeming the stock at £120 giving three months' notice. The company was to receive £150,000 for transferring its rights and for dislocation of business as a consequence of revocation, and £300,000 as compensation for 'administration losses' since 1886. Finally the company was to receive one-half of the royalties which the Government undertook to impose on all minerals mined in an area between the main Niger and a line through Yola and Zinder, providing they were exported through a British customs house. This concession was to last for ninety-nine years. The total compensation paid to the company was thus £865,000 plus

[1] FO 83/1616 C.O. to F.O. 14.12.98, note the unanimous F.O. minutes resisting the proposal.

[2] T1 9336/1442 Treasury to C.O. 27.1.98.

[3] J.H.P. 3/7 Goldie to Holt 27.10.1903. Mary Kingsley reported that she was told by the wife of a colonial official that Goldie also refused the Governor-Generalship of all the West African colonies (J.H.P. 16/4 letter to Holt, July 1899, n.d.).

the mineral royalties. These extraordinarily generous terms were accepted by Goldie almost immediately.[1]

As the agreement involved the spending of Government moneys it had to be embodied in a Parliamentary Bill. Thus, for the first time in its history the Niger Company had to run the gauntlet of a Parliamentary debate. There was little to fear from the Liverpool critics of the company, who welcomed the policy of revocation, and were prepared to pay the price, but there were doubts about Radical and Irish reaction. The task of defending the Bill fell to Sir Michael Hicks Beach, and he was not pleased with the prospect. The policy of revocation was Chamberlain's, not his, and he had only accepted it 'by *force majeur* of the Foreign and Colonial Offices', yet Chamberlain insisted that as a shareholder in the company he could not defend the Bill. Hicks Beach therefore asked that the papers presented to Parliament should include a reasoned statement from the Foreign Office on the policy followed, and perhaps of Goldie's complaints and demands, although 'we must not say anything more than can be helped about their misdeeds'.[2]

An official despatch from the Foreign Office to the Treasury, advocating a policy of revocation, was therefore concocted and inserted in the Parliamentary paper.[3] It was clearly designed to placate the company's enemies, and to give the impression that their opposition had triumphed. It gave most space to the significance of the Anglo-French Convention and the need for imperial control now that the French had special rights on the Niger. It also stressed the way in which the company had impeded its rivals, 'which, though strictly within the rights conferred upon it by the charter' had created 'a practical monopoly

[1] T1 9480A/10710 Treasury minute on revocation 28.6.99; T1 9480A/10833 R.N.C. to Treasury 28.6.99.

[2] FO 2/244 Hicks Beach to Salisbury 15.6.99.

[3] Written, of course, long after the financial agreement had been concluded, though members were not to know this. I have found scores of examples of this kind of 'doctoring' in the Parliamentary papers of this period, sometimes involving the suppression of parts of documents, rewriting of parts or of whole documents, altering of dates on them, or, as in this case, concoction of new documents. For colonial and diplomatic affairs in this period Parliamentary papers are most unreliable.

of trade'. It was also stated that the 'manner in which this commercial monopoly presses upon the native traders', as exemplified by the rising in Brass had influenced the decision. The Parliamentary paper also contained a Treasury minute setting out the sums to be paid to the company, notes on the company's history, a copy of the charter, lists of treaties and specimen forms of treaties, and the revenue and expenditure accounts and balance sheets since the charter. All this information was more than the opponents of the company had been able to obtain in fourteen years of opposition. Its presentation was not well thought-out, and much of the information contradicted other parts of the paper.[1]

Nevertheless the debate in Parliament from 26 July to 4 August was politically a tame affair. The Liverpool men and the main body of the Liberal opposition kept silent. The only fireworks came from the Irishmen and the Radicals. Their main attack came in committee, where Dillon, the member for Mayo East, moved an amendment to reduce the amount of compensation from £865,000 to £400,000. Dillon had analysed the balance sheets of the company and concluded that most of its capital was 'water'. He also noted the curious fact that the Government was to pay £115,000 for a *part* of the company's assets in Nigeria, whilst the company's own balance sheet valued its *total* assets in Nigeria at only £113,282! He went on to attack the proposal to pay the company £300,000 as compensation for 'administrative losses'. This was a bad precedent which might result in the House facing the prospect of finding millions for the administrative losses of Cecil Rhodes' company, and in any case these were 'a bogus deficit which the Company have manufactured while they were paying enormous dividends, and carrying enormous sums to reserve'. If the Niger Company had lost so much on administration, why was it necessary to compensate them for the loss of the losing part of the business? Dillon attacked the view that the company ought to be treated generously because it was handing over a ready-made and cheaply-won empire—'I refuse to recognise as a great gift to

---

[1] P.P. 1899, LXIII (c. 9372).

this country the addition of thirty-five millions of unknown people . . . nobody can forecast the extent of the evil that may result.' Dillon was supported by Henry Labouchere, who rested his arguments mainly on the monopolistic nature of the company. It was 'monstrous' that having acquired an illegal monopoly and violated the charter, 'the Government should come forward and pay them for it'. The Government was acting generously in 'not turning the Company out neck and crop without compensation'.

Hicks Beach's reply was hesitant and confused. He accused the opposition of arguing that any cession of territory to the Crown was to be deplored, and of believing that 'all chartered companies behaved badly'—here Labouchere interjected his hearty agreement! The Chancellor thought the allegation that men like Sir George Goldie risked their capital merely for gain was 'a scandalous statement to make about such gentlemen'. Their intention had been 'to extend the British Empire, British trade and British commerce in territories which appeared to them of great value to the civilised world.' He agreed that the monopoly was the 'one exception' to the 'admirable manner' in which the Niger Company had behaved, but stressed that the charter itself 'enabled the Company to obtain that monopoly', a curious argument when article fourteen expressly forbade monopoly.[1]

The Chancellor's defence of the settlement seems to have aroused more suspicion than the allegations of the Radicals. Mr. Sydney Buxton, who had earlier praised the company for its humanitarianism, was so puzzled by Hicks Beach's reply that he asked for a Committee of the House to examine each item in the financial agreement in detail, and then walked out of the chamber and refused to vote. Others, though critical, were not disposed to make issues at this late stage. This was no haggling matter, said Mr. Gibson Bowles—'Off with his head; so much

---

[1] But note that Lord Wrenbury, one of the greatest modern exponents of company law, writes that a chartered company 'even if the charter by express words forbids any particular act . . . can nevertheless at common law do the act', the only penalty for a breach of a charter is revocation of the charter. *The Law and Practice of the Companies Acts*, 11th ed., 1930, p. 9.

for Buckingham.' W. F. Lawrence, speaking for Liverpool, expressed his willingness to 'forgive and forget', and voted against Dillon's amendment, which was defeated by 143 votes to 57. The minority consisted entirely of Radicals and Irish members, and included Labouchere, Dilke, and the young David Lloyd George. In further divisions in committee the dissidents gained some ground, mustering 78 against 171 votes, and 89 against 160. On the third reading they continued their opposition, Dillon denouncing this 'monstrous waste of public money' and asking that the Bill be rejected in the hope of a better bargain in another year. In his closing speech Hicks Beach refused to answer objections to the financial provisions and contented himself with the general statement that

it was never my belief that it was my duty, on behalf of the country, to endeavour to get the better of the Company in this matter. I always thought my duty was to act fairly as between the taxpayers and the Company, with the full understanding that the Company has deserved well of the country, having regard to the fact that but for the action of the Company the country would not be in possession of these territories.

The House then divided, and the Bill passed the Commons by 181 votes to 81.[1]

In the Lords the Bill had a much smoother passage. On the second reading Salisbury summarized a note he had received from Goldie complaining at the tone of the Parliamentary paper:

He thinks that the effect was to give an impression that the Niger Company was much more a commercial company and much less a political company than it really was, and he claims that the main object of the founding of the National African Company, which was the original form of it, was political, but for which, Sir George Goldie says, he would have had no connexion with it.

Salisbury accepted this view, and delivered a short eulogy of the company, concluding by 'expressing our deep gratitude and high esteem for the adventurers and patriots to whose efforts the preparation of this territory [for Imperial rule] is due'. The

---

[1] *Hansard*, 1899, Vol. X, cols. 370–542.

Liberals in the Lords made no challenge, the Earl of Kimberley expressed his entire agreement with Salisbury, and with Goldie's claims. The Bill then passed its final stages without a division.[1]

The date is 1 January 1900, the place Lokoja on the Niger. It is morning, and men have gathered around the flagstaff at the barracks. Most of them are uniformed Africans of the Niger Company's constabulary or of the Frontier Force, with a sprinkling of British officers in full dress uniform, among them Frederick Lugard. The Niger Company's flag, with its device of the three-legged Manx emblem, each foot bearing a word of the motto *Ars, Jus, Pax*, is hauled down; the Union Jack slowly rises in its stead. The African military band strikes up 'God save the Queen' and the men cheer. So passed away the Royal Niger Company, Chartered and Limited.

[1] *Ibid.* cols. 1002–4, col. 1241, and col. 1449.

14

Years of Retirement

SIR GEORGE GOLDIE was not yet fifty-four when the Royal Niger Company lost its charter. Since the military campaigns in Nupe and Ilorin and the Anglo-French Crisis which grew out of them, he had been a famous public figure. None of those who had dealings with him, whether private or official, could fail to see that he was a brilliant, if difficult, person. Had he determined to build for himself a second West African career he would certainly have succeeded. Probably he could have had an official career—and what an interesting prospect—Goldie as one of Chamberlain's pro-consuls! If the Government had spurned his services there were many avenues open for the unofficial career in which he had already demonstrated his abilities. He might have stayed with the Niger Company as its leader in the difficult decades ahead, and would then have directed the battle with the Lever combine in the 'twenties. Or he might have done much earlier what Lord Leverhulme subsequently achieved, and created a West African trade combine, with profound effects on the shape of the international soap and margarine industries. Or perhaps, as Mary Kingsley and Holt had urged him to do, he might have entered Parliament to lead the African traders—a formidable prospect for any Colonial Minister to face.

But he was tired of West Africa. In March 1898 his wife Mathilda died of sudden heart failure. Though he had long suspected that she was not strong, her death shocked him profoundly, and coming at the time of the crisis in Borgu when he had to keep working, it seems to have imparted an unhappy

aura to his West African work. In August, after the signature of
the Anglo-French Convention, Goldie went to South America
'to try and forget Africa, and still more England—for a time'.[1]
After his return this revulsion persisted, and perhaps increased,
despite the pressures put on him to continue working in West
Africa after the charter should be revoked. The strongest claim
was that of the Niger Company itself, whose directors wanted
him to continue in charge, but during 1899 he determined to
leave the company, and sell out his interests. During the next
three or four years his connexion with the Niger gradually
evaporated as questions arising from the transfer of administration were cleared away. His family still retained a large shareholding in the company, but by 1904 he could declare that he
'no longer' took 'a special interest in West Africa'.[2]

This did not mean that he had lost all ambition; in fact he
may have been over-ambitious. What really fascinated him was
the prospect of repeating his triumph on the Niger elsewhere,
and perhaps on a vaster scale. The contemplation of huge rivers
especially enthralled him; they were highways of empire. He
was always looking for the familiar combination of private
commerce, easy river transport, and British imperial expansion.
Since about 1897 he had seriously considered the prospect of
moving on to the upper Nile, but Kitchener's victories and the
establishment of the Anglo-Egyptian Sudan destroyed the
possibility. Some time after 1900 the Government of Brazil
asked him to take charge of the administration of the upper
Amazon, but he wanted to work inside the British Empire, and
turned it down. As early as 1899 he had begun to turn his mind
to China.

The Manchu dynasty of Emperors in China was clearly unstable, European powers and the Japanese had already extorted
numerous concessions, both territorial and commercial, and it
seemed as if events in Africa would repeat themselves and China
be partitioned among the great powers. China too was a country
of great rivers. Goldie began to read as much as he could about
the country, and especially about the great Yangtze Kiang and

[1] J.H.P. 3/7 Goldie to Holt 1.8.98.   [2] *Ibid.* Goldie to Holt 8.12.1904.

the interior regions which could be reached from it. In January 1900 he set out to study the river at first hand, arriving at Canton in February. There he hired an interpreter and two 'boys' and planned his journey. He intended to go up to Wuchow by water, thence overland for nearly a thousand miles through Kwangsi, Kweichow and Szechwan to Chungking, where he would strike the Yangtze River. From here he proposed to work back to the coast by junk to Ichang, thence by steamer and railway to the sea. But his plans misfired, for he arrived in Canton just at the time of the so-called 'Boxer' rising, a violent outbreak of resentment against foreigners and their encroachments, and the interior over which he proposed to travel was in turmoil. The journey had to be abandoned.[1]

His mind filled with such adventurous prospects, it is not surprising that offers of official appointments seemed dull by comparison. In April 1901 Goldie was offered the choice of the Governorships of New South Wales or Victoria. The Australian colonies had just banded together in the Federation, so that the Governor of a State responsible to the State legislature had little real power and was in effect merely a local figurehead. Goldie was well aware of this, nevertheless he was tempted to accept. His children had now married and set up their own homes, and he felt that there was little to bind him to England. The job 'may be (in a modest way) useful to the Empire' and he neither knew nor cared what the salary might be, for he was now quite rich. He did not know what to do—'if I refuse, the Government will be vexed and never offer me anything else. On the other hand, if I go to Australia, will they ever remember me again?' He therefore left it to Scarbrough to decide, though his friend was much younger than he. In the end the offer was declined.[2]

Later in the year Goldie was offered and accepted membership of the Royal Commission which inquired into the military preparations for the South African War. Whilst he was *en route*

[1] My sources for the China travels are letters Goldie wrote to Scarbrough on 10.1.1900, 26.1.1900, and 8.2.1900, the second of which is quoted in Wellesley, *Goldie*, p. 77.
[2] Goldie to Scarbrough 25.4.1901, in the possession of the Earl of Scarbrough.

for South Africa, visiting East Africa on the way, and reading voraciously about both areas, Scarbrough took the opportunity afforded by Goldie's absence to press for some recognition of his past achievements. Goldie had been knighted in 1887 for his work at the Berlin Conference, and in 1898 he was given a K.C.M.G. for his victories in Nupe and Ilorin. But Scarbrough refused to acknowledge that either his present temporary appointment, or the honours already conferred were sufficient recognition. He therefore wrote to Lord Salisbury's private secretary suggesting that Goldie had been passed over owing to the pre-occupations of the Boer War. He could not imagine that the Government intended to let Goldie's talents and administrative experience lie fallow for ever, but in the meantime at least he might be allowed to take a seat in the House of Lords. But the Coronation of Edward VII came and went, and Goldie's name was not in the honours list. Scarbrough continued to press the matter, complaining that Goldie 'did not even receive a word of thanks either verbally or by letter from the Prime Minister' for his work in Nigeria, but nothing was done.[1]

In 1903 Goldie's opportunity at last seemed to present itself. Cecil Rhodes had died before the Boer War had ended, and since his death the affairs of the British South Africa Company, chartered rulers of Rhodesia, had not gone well. Earlier hopes of untold wealth from diamonds and gold had failed to materialize, the administration was run at a constant loss, and settlers and shareholders were discontented and restless. Earl Grey, the British South Africa Company's administrator, approached Goldie and asked him to visit Rhodesia and advise the company on its policies. Grey was so impressed with Goldie that he and his fellow-directors invited him to join the Board of the South Africa Company. Here was the kind of chance Goldie had been waiting for, and after two nights of long talks with Grey he had almost agreed to join the company. 'I want work—that's the fact,' he confessed to Scarbrough. 'After all it is Imperial work, and I fancy the distant picture is good, although they may have

---

[1] Papers in the possession of the Earl of Scarbrough, Scarbrough to Barrington 7.11.1901, same to Balfour 14.2.1903.

dark days before them for a time. But I do not mind dark days. A storm makes me buck up.' He was tired of dilly-dallying with the Colonial Office, and felt that the time had come to beard Chamberlain. He therefore wrote to Chamberlain to tell him about the offer, and asked him to give him a definite idea whether he would be given official work; if there was no prospect he would accept the directorship, 'for I feel that I need something into which to throw my surplus energies'. But he was not committed yet, and wrote to Scarbrough to ask his advice.[1]

Scarbrough was far from enthusiastic, and warned Goldie against hasty action. The South Africa Company, since Rhodes' death, was 'like a ship without a rudder', and Goldie ought not to join them without an 'absolutely free hand'. If the directors came to him and frankly asked him to assume Rhodes' mantle then he should accept and state his conditions. But if this were not clear then he would face the unpleasant task of pushing his way to the top, which was what the South Africa Company really needed from him. He must also try to find out the real position of the company; was the transfer of its administration to the Crown imminent? If so, then Goldie might have to conduct yet another battle with the Government on financial compensation. Finally Goldie must assure himself about the company's methods of finance. The South Africa Company's record was a shady one. 'Their hands have not always been clean.' Were they still tied up with mining companies of doubtful repute? Could the administration go on indefinitely losing money, now that Rhodes's private purse was not readily open? Scarbrough felt that Goldie's letter to Chamberlain was unwise—'You have risked a good deal on that letter. A fox does run straight sometimes. I trust that he will on this occasion.'[2] This advice seems to have decided Goldie against the idea. He went to Rhodesia in 1904 to conduct the inquiry as he had promised, but he did not join the South Africa Company's directorate. Nor did he obtain definite acceptance or refusal from Chamberlain. After 1904 his imperial work and hopes were at an end, though he did serve on

[1] Goldie to Scarbrough 6.8.1903, in the possession of the Earl of Scarbrough.
[2] Scarbrough to Goldie, n.d., draft, in the possession of the Earl of Scarbrough.

the Royal Commission on the disposal of South African War stores from 1905 to 1906.

He now came to terms with his fate and accepted it. For the rest of his life he was retired from national or commercial affairs, except for the years of the First World War, when he returned as Honorary Advisor to the Niger Company whilst Scarbrough was away at the war. In the years before the war he became an alderman of the London County Council, and Chairman of its Finance Committee. Here he found an exciting and pugnacious political life, in company with such political giants of their day as Will Crooks, George Lansbury, and Sydney Webb. Goldie was perhaps happiest of all at this time. He was healthy in body and vigorous of mind, and used his fortune [1] to travel widely in Europe and America. He had a London house in Queen's Gate Gardens, and spent some of his leisure in the Nunnery, the family house in the Isle of Man. His friends were few, but he was a self-sufficient person who did not crave the esteem of others, and the few friends he possessed were very close and completely trustworthy. Sometimes he would spend an evening with a colleague from the County Council talking of the old days on the Niger, and of the fighting in Bida and Ilorin. At one time he began to prepare notes for an autobiographical account of his work with the chartered company, but the war came, and afterwards he felt that opinion was no longer in sympathy with the imperial idea. The papers he had collected were burned, and he spurned the approaches of would-be biographers.

Soon after the war his health began to fail. He was now well over seventy, and began to be attacked by emphysema, a chronic condition in which air enters the tissues around the lungs, causing great pain and difficult breathing. Despite this, his mind was still keen and active. He followed the struggle between the Niger Company and the Lever group with keen interest, and in 1921 offered Scarbrough £20,000 in cash to fight the 'soap boiler'. By this time he was unable to lie prone, and had to sleep in a sitting position, yet he was 'perfectly

---

[1] On his death Goldie left £70,000.

happy' and an incessant reader.[1] But his condition worsened. He was forced to spend his winters in Italy to avoid the cold, and travelling was very difficult for him. Returning in the summer of 1925 he became so ill that he had to be carried from the boat at Dover. He got as far as London, but had to abandon his plan to go on to his son's house in the country. One of his friends described a last meeting some few days before he died. He lay alone in a small room in the hotel just off Picadilly where he had been forced to halt his journey. He breathed with difficulty and was in terrible pain. He was unable to get up and had no apparent consolations, not even books. His friend asked what he did with himself all day. He replied that he spent his time thinking, mainly about his career and the meaning of his life. It gave him the greatest pleasure to do just this—to contemplate the past. He was perfectly happy, just as he had been for many years.

A few days later, on 20 August 1925, in this same room, unshaken in the belief that there was no God and no life to come, Sir George Goldie came to the end of his seventy-nine years of life.

[1] Goldie to Scarbrough 4.11.1921, 13.1.1922, in the possession of the Earl of Scarbrough.

SELECT BIBLIOGRAPHY

MANUSCRIPT SOURCES

I. IN THE PUBLIC RECORD OFFICE, LONDON

Foreign Office Records

Slave Trade Papers (F.O. 84) under 'Domestic Various', 'Africa West Coast', 'France' and 'Germany', 1870–92.

General (F.O. 83) under 'Africa Various', 1893–9.

France (F.O. 27) under 'Africa' and 'Africa Various', 1893–8.

Germany (Prussia F.O. 64) under 'Africa' and 'Africa Various', 1893–8.

Africa (F.O. 2) under 'Niger Coast Protectorate', 1893–8, and under 'France' and 'Germany', 1899–1900.

Colonial Office Records

Niger Coast Protectorate (C.O. 444), 1899.

Africa West: West African Frontier Force (C.O. 445), 1898–1900.

Nigeria Northern (C.O. 446), 1898–1900.

Supplementary Correspondence: Africa West (C.O. 537), 1897–1899.

Treasury Records

Under classification T1, 1887–9.

Granville Papers

Papers of Lord Granville containing many confidential Foreign Office prints of the period 1880–5 (P.R.O. 30/29).

2. OTHER COLLECTIONS

Registrar of Joint Stock Companies

Papers originally seen at Bush House, Strand, London, many of which are now partially destroyed, some transferred to Public Record Office. 1875–99.

Church Missionary Society, 6 Salisbury Square, London, E.C.4

Niger Mission Papers.

Y

At Rhodes House, Oxford

Niger Company Papers presented by the Earl of Scarbrough. These are mainly concerned with the period since 1900, but Volumes I, IV and X contain material on the chartered company.

In the possession of John Holt and Company (Liverpool) Ltd.

The John Holt Papers.

In the possession of the Earl of Scarbrough

Miscellaneous correspondence from Goldie to Scarbrough, 1890 to 1925.

II PRINTED SOURCES

1. PARLIAMENTARY PAPERS

1884–5 LV 133 *Protocols and General Act of the Berlin West African Conference.*

1886 XLVII *General Act of the Berlin Conference.*

1888 LXXIV 141 and 1892 LVI. 763 *Return of Customs Duties Levied by the Royal Niger Company.*

1896 LIX 361 *Report by Sir John Kirk upon the disturbances at Brass* (omits his recommendations for reform).

1899 VI 697 *Royal Niger Company Bill.*

1899 LXIII 417 *Papers of Revocation of the Royal Niger Company's Charter and the Government of the Niger Districts*, etc.

2. COLLECTIONS OF DOCUMENTS

Documents diplomatiques français. Première Série. 1871–1900, Paris, 1929–.

Gooch, G. P. and Temperley, H., eds., *British Documents on the Origins of the War*, Vol. I, London, 1927.

Hertslet, E., *The Map of Africa by Treaty*, 3 vols., London, 3rd ed., 1909.

Palmer, H. R., ed. and trans., *Sudanese Memoirs*, Lagos, 1928.

Reports of the Council and Ordinary General Meetings of the National African and Royal Niger Companies. 1884–1900.

3. BOOKS (PUBLISHED IN LONDON UNLESS OTHERWISE STATED)

Beach, Lady V. Hicks, *Life of Sir Michael Hicks Beach, Earl St. Aldwyn*, vol. II, 1932.

Bovill, E. W., *The Golden Trade of the Moors*, 1958.

Burns, Sir A., *History of Nigeria*, 4th ed., 1948.

Cecil, Lady G., *Life of Robert, Marquis of Salisbury*, vol. IV, 1933.

Cook, A. N., *British Enterprise in Nigeria*, New York, 1943.

Lord Crewe, *Lord Rosebery*, 2 vols., 1931.

Crowe, S.E., *The Berlin West Africa Conference, 1884–1885*, 1942.

Dike, K. O., *Trade and Politics in the Niger Delta*, Oxford, 1956.

Elias, T. O., *Nigerian Land Law and Custom*, 1951.

Garvin, J. L., *The Life of Joseph Chamberlain*, Vol. III, 1934.

Greene, T. Kirk, *Adamawa, Past and Present*, 1958.

Gwynn, S., *Life of Mary Kingsley*, 1933.

Hanotaux, G. and Martineau, A., *Histoire des colonies françaises et de l'expansion de la France dans le monde*, Tome IV, Paris, 1931.

Hobson, J., *Imperialism, a study*, 3rd ed., 1938.

Howard, C., *Mary Kingsley*, 1957.

Kingsley, Mary, *West African Studies*, 1899.

Kingsley, Mary, *The Story of West Africa*, 1899.

Langer, W. L., *European Alliances and Alignments, 1871–1890*, New York, 1931.

Langer, W. L., *The Diplomacy of Imperialism, 1890–1902*, 2nd ed., New York, 1951.

Masson, P., *Marseilles et la colonisation française*, Paris, 1912.

Meek, C. K., *The Northern Tribes of Nigeria*, 2 vols., 1925.

Moon, P. T., *Imperialism and World Politics*, New York, 1937.

Nadel, S. F., *A Black Byzantium, The Kingdom of Nupe in Nigeria*, 1942.

Orr, C. W. J., *The Making of Northern Nigeria*, 1911.

Perham, M., *Lugard, The Years of Adventure 1858–1898*, 1956.

Wellesley, Dorothy, *Sir George Goldie, Founder of Nigeria*, 1934.

Woolf, L., *Empire and Commerce in Africa*, 1920.

de Wiart, C., *Les Grandes Compagnies coloniales anglaises du XIXme siècle*, Paris, 1899.

4. ARTICLES

Baillaud, E., 'La Compagnie Royale du Niger et son evolution', *Annales de l'Ecole libre et de science politique*, July 1898, p. 493.

Chauveau, J., 'Mizon à Yola', *Revue d'histoire des colonies*, XLI, 1954, pp. 227–44.

Y*

Darwin, L., 'Sir George Goldie on Africa', *Journal of the African Society*, XXXIV, 1935.

Goldie, Sir G., 'Britain's Priority on the Middle Niger', *New Review*, June 1897.

Goldie, Sir G., 'The Future of the Niger Territories', London Chamber of Commerce Pamphlet, 1897.

Lugard, F. D., 'An Expedition to Borgu on the Niger', *Geographical Journal*, Vol. VI, 1895.

Lugard, F. D., 'England and France on the Niger, the Race for Borgu', *Nineteenth Century*, XXXVII, 1895.

Maxse, F. A., 'The acquisition of Nigeria', *National Review*, December 1903 and January 1904.

Tepowa, A., 'A Short History of Brass and its People', *Journal of the African Society*, VII, 1907–8.

Thomson, J., 'Up the Niger to the Central Sudan', *Good Words*, XXVII, 1886.

APPENDIX I

The Financial History of the Niger Company

THIS book has been concerned with the political and administrative aspects of the Niger Company's history, but the course of the narrative should have made it plain that the company's financial activities were basic to its history. Without trading profits there could be no chartered administration. Not the least of Goldie's achievements was the success with which he husbanded his shareholders' capital through the years of fierce competition, from the French companies in the early 1880's, and from the African Association in the early 1890's; and finally secured favourable terms of compensation from the Government upon revocation of the charter. The Niger Company's financial success outshone the record of any African chartered company; the Imperial British East Africa Company went practically bankrupt, and the British South Africa Company paid no dividends for many years. The British North Borneo Company was finally successful, but its early years were not fruitful. No investor who held shares throughout the chartered history of the Niger Company had reason to complain of Goldie's stewardship.

The years of the National African Company, the formative years, were also the most critical in all the Niger Company's history. Before it received its charter the company could on no account be regarded as a solid prospect by the cautious investor. Factors absorbing profits were the competition of the French companies, the increased emphasis on non-remunerative political and administrative activity, particularly treaty-making, and the general depression of produce prices in England. Due to slowness of transport, and time lag in the company's book-keeping system, the full impact on the accounts was not felt until after 1885. For 1882 (July–December) the company paid a dividend equivalent to 10 per cent per annum and this was increased for the first half of 1883, actually a dividend of 12 per cent for the eight months November 1882 to June 1883, less the proportion of the 10 per cent dividend from July to December 1882 already paid. There was some restiveness among shareholders at this payment, but they were quieted by a 15 per cent dividend for the second half of 1883. By 1884 dividends were feeling the pinch, the first half-year's interim dividend was reduced to 10 per cent and the last half-year paid slightly under 10 per cent. By this time profits were scarcely sufficient to cover dividends. No dividend was paid in 1885, and the company sustained a loss of nearly £40,000 on the year. Reserves and the Insurance Fund which had been built up to £29,730 had by this time disappeared. In 1886 the company earned only £8,255 in profits, still leaving a deficit of £30,634 to be earned before a dividend could be paid. It was not until 1888 that dividend payments were resumed, a 5 per cent interim for the first half of the year.

Merely to examine dividends in these years, however, would give a completely false idea of the company's progress. Though heavily in debt (principally to Goldie himself, who lent his own fortune) and though a call of £1 per share was made in 1884, the money was used to build up a formidable commercial organization. By June 1883 the company had spent £22,700 on new steamers (far more than the value of the existing fleet in 1882) and £34,000 on building and plant. The number of steamers was doubled, and the number of stations rose from nineteen in 1882 to thirty-nine in 1883. This was apart from the steamers and fleet of the French companies, acquired at a cost of £160,000 in 1884.

The acquisition of the charter was a financial, as well as a political, turning point. Lord Aberdare announcing the charter at the Ordinary General Meeting in July 1886, gave some hints to restive shareholders that the charter would have financial value:

As to the prohibition of monopoly and the equal treatment of traders of all nationalities, that might appear to some of the shareholders rather formidable, as letting in the competition from which they had suffered, but the Government had given them power 'to levy customs duties and charges'. . . .

for administrative purposes, and he gave a hint that the expenses incurred in treaty-making since 1881 could be charged to this account. Some shareholders had asked why it was necessary to have political rights at all, and urged that the company should continue as a mere commercial concern, but Aberdare's answer was

that such rights were absolutely necessary for arrangements must be made with native princes. They had found already, with the comparatively small competition offered to them, that constant expenditure had been necessary in having agents everywhere to counteract the proceedings of competing agencies.

It would have been difficult to state more plainly, without openly admitting the intention, that administrative powers would be used to exclude competitors. Any doubts were dispelled by Aberdare's remarks on produce prices. The company, he avowed

had every desire to treat the natives with perfect fairness and to give them what they were entitled to for their produce, but they now had a power of reducing the prices of produce which they did not before possess, and that power they would exercise.

The charter resulted in an immediate improvement of the balance sheets, though not in dividends. At the end of 1885 the company had a debit balance on the profit and loss account of £38,890 and was in debt for £111,423, a total debt of £150,313. By the end of 1886 this figure had been reduced to £78,916, a debit balance of £30,634 and debts of £48,282. Aberdare, in his speech at the Ordinary General Meeting in July 1887, explained the improvement as due to lower prices paid for African produce, and denied allegations that this had provoked rebellions on the Niger:

What had happened, unfortunately, had been that there had been a very considerable reduction in the price of the produce. A charge had been made against the company that they had availed themselves of their position, by their charter, to 'grind down' the natives, and to make them part with their property at the lowest possible value. He, however, denied that they had carried the reductions further than was indicated by the fall in prices at home.

This improvement steadily continued throughout the years from 1887 to 1890. Gross trading profits rose from £46,765 in 1887, to £58,680 in 1888, to £60,095 in 1889, to £66,363 in 1890, from a steady figure of about £340,000 turnover. This made it possible not only to eradicate the debt, but to build up a reserve and insurance fund to £20,000 by 1890. Dividend payments were resumed, 2½ per cent only in 1888, but 6 per cent for 1889 and 1890. It must be remembered that these payments were made on a paid-up capital increased from £383,650 to £443,350, by the creation of £60,000 in shares to purchase the *Compagnie française de l'Afrique equatoriale*; and that each shareholder after 1889 received 1½ per cent in addition as interest on 'Niger Government 5 per cent Stock', to be secured from revenues as a recompense for administrative and treaty-making costs before the charter, which was distributed in the proportion of £3 for each £10 of capital held.

This growing prosperity was challenged, with almost disastrous results, by the entry of the African Association into competition on the Niger in 1891 and 1892. Though the Niger Company stepped up its turnover of goods and produce, its gross trading profits fell from the £66,363 of 1890, to £51,891 in 1891 and to £43,167 in 1892. Though the dividend was maintained at 6 per cent in 1891 and 1892, it was found impossible to put money into reserves, and these, standing at £20,000, were entirely absorbed in payment of the reduced 5 per cent dividend of 1893.

The successful purchase of the African Association's Niger assets, put an end to competition. After 1894 the monopoly was complete, no other firm exported from the Niger, and the few hundred pounds' worth of goods imported by rival firms were insignificant.

Complete commercial monopoly did not mean that the company was able to leap ahead and double or treble its profits. The inhibiting factor appears to have been the political difficulties of the years from 1894 to 1897, and the need to divert men and plant into non-remunerative work of this kind. In 1893, when the company had a monopoly for part of the trading season, profits soared by over 50 per cent of the previous year's figure to £69,293. In 1894 this figure was almost maintained at £64,909, but gross profits dropped to £56,974 in 1895, probably as a result of the Brass attack on Akassa. In 1896 and 1897 profits rose to £65,398 and £68,555 respectively, they might have been higher had the company not been obliged to collect men and stores, arms and ammunition for the Nupe and Ilorin campaigns of 1897. Nevertheless, the years from 1893 to 1897 showed steady and solid financial achievement. Despite the increase of paid-up capital to £493,680 by the creation of £50,330 in £10 shares paid to the African Association, dividends were increased to 8 per cent for 1894, 3½ per cent in 1895, 6 per cent in 1896 and 9 per cent in 1897. Dividend figures do not give an adequate picture of growth. In each of these years there was a steady growth of reserves from the £5,000 set aside in 1894 to a total of £74,000 in 1897, in which year alone over £25,000 was set aside.

Financially the year 1898, a difficult and depressing one from the political and administrative aspect, was the most profitable in all the company's history. This paradox is explained simply by the fact that the company had practically resigned all administration into the hands of the West African Frontier Force, which undertook not only the control of the north, but was even used on punitive expeditions on the lower Niger. In 1898 the company was able to have its cake and eat it, the cost of administration had been the price paid for monopoly, but in this year the company was able to transfer administrative costs to the Frontier Force, whilst continuing to en-force the customs regulations. Profits rose to the record figure of £94,531. The company paid only 6 per cent in dividend, putting £39,000 into reserves to raise that fund to £113,000, and carrying £36,396 over to the balance sheet.

Thus, by the time of revocation the Niger Company was in a strong position financially. If the company had wound itself up, dividing its assets and the £865,000 received from the Government as compensation, there would have been about £3 to distribute for each £1 of paid-up capital. As it was, the company continued as a purely com-mercial concern after 1900, as the Niger Company Limited.

It is ironical to note that in doing so, it retained its practical monopoly of the Niger trade for several more years. John Holt, writing to E. D. Morel in 1902,[1] analysed the reasons for the persistence of the monopoly. The huge sum given as compensation allowed the Niger Company to expand and renew its plant. The large stocks of goods in Africa built up before revocation were free of duty to the new government, and its stations and wharves were free of government charges. In addition the Niger Company controlled all the chief trading centres. New competitors had from the first to pay customs duties, and found great difficulty in obtaining land for stations. The new government made it illegal to buy land from natives, and leases, short in duration, carried a fine on entry and heavy annual rents. If a competitor established himself at a trading centre, he had to face the Niger Company locally, if he tried to move away and make new centres of trade this was a speculation which might prove catastrophic, for the lessor government had power in the leases to prevent him removing his buildings. Thus, argued Holt, the Government had strengthened the Niger Company's monopoly, which, ostensibly, it had 'spent so much money to make free'.

[1] Holt to Morel 2.2.1902, E. D. Morel Papers in The London School of Economics.

APPENDIX II

Royal Charter granted to the National African Company, later called the Royal Niger Company

VICTORIA, by the Grace of God, of the United Kingdom of Great Britain and Ireland, Queen, Defender of the Faith. To all to whom these Presents shall come Greeting:

Whereas an humble Petition has been presented to Us, in Our Council, by the National African Company, Limited, of 34 to 40, Ludgate Hill, in the City of London (hereinafter referred to as 'the Company').

And whereas the said Petition states (among other things) that the Petitioner Company was incorporated in the year 1882, under the Companies Acts, 1862 to 1880, as a Company limited by Shares. And that the Capital of the Company is 1,000,000*l.*, divided into 100,000 Shares of 10*l.* each, with power to increase. And 91,675 of such Shares have been subscribed for and issued; and a further 6,000 of such Shares have been subscribed for and are about to be issued, making in all, 97,675 of such Shares. And that the objects of the Company as declared by the Memorandum of Association of the Company, are (amongst others) the following, that is to say:

To carry on business and to act as merchants, bankers, traders, commission agents, shipowners, carriers, or in any other capacity, in the United Kingdom, Africa, or elsewhere, and to import, export, buy, sell, barter, exchange, pledge, make advances upon, or otherwise deal in goods, produce, articles, and merchandise according to the custom of merchants, or otherwise.

To form or acquire and carry on trading stations, factories, stores and depôts in Africa or elsewhere, and to purchase, lease, or otherwise acquire, carry on, develop, or improve any business or any real or personal property in the United Kingdom, Africa, or elsewhere, or any undivided or other interest whatsoever therein respectively.

To apply for, acquire, and hold any Charters, Acts of Parliament, privileges, monopolies, licences, concessions, patents, or other rights or powers from the British Government, or any other Government or State, or any potentate or local or other authority in

RESTRICTION OF TRANSFER BY COMPANY

4. The Company shall not have power to transfer, wholly or in part, the benefit of the Cession aforesaid, or any of them, except with the consent of Our Secretary of State.

FOREIGN POWERS

5. If at any time Our Secretary of State thinks fit to dissent from or object to any of the dealings of the Company with any foreign Power, and to make the Company any suggestion founded on that dissent or objection, the Company shall act in accordance therewith.

SLAVERY

6. The Company shall, to the best use of its power, discourage and, as far as may be practicable, abolish by degrees any system of domestic servitude existing among the native inhabitants; and no foreigner, whether European or not, shall be allowed to own Slaves of any kind in the Company's territories.

RELIGIONS OF INHABITANTS

7. The Company as such, or its Officers as such, shall not in any way interfere with the religion of any class or tribe of the people of its territories, or of any of the inhabitants thereof, except so far as may be necessary in the interests of humanity; and all forms of religious worship and religious ordinances may be exercised within the said territories, and no hindrance shall be offered thereto except as aforesaid.

ADMINISTRATION OF JUSTICE TO INHABITANTS

8. In the administration of Justice by the Company to the peoples of its territories, or to any of the inhabitants thereof, careful regard shall always be had to the customs and laws of the class, or tribe, or nation to which the parties respectively belong, especially with respect to the holding, possession, transfer, and disposition of lands and goods, and testate or intestate succession thereto, and marriage, divorce, and legitimacy, and other rights of property and personal rights.

TREATMENT OF INHABITANTS GENERALLY

9. If at any time Our Secretary of State thinks fit to dissent from or object to any part of the proceedings or system of the Company relative to the people of its territories, or to any of the inhabitants thereof, in respect of slavery or religion, or the administration of Justice, or other matter, and to make the Company any suggestion

founded on that dissent or objection, the Company shall act in accordance therewith.

FACILITIES FOR BRITISH NATIONAL SHIPS

10. The Company shall freely afford all facilities requisite for Our Ships in the harbours of the Company.

FLAG

11. The Company may hoist and use on its buildings, and elsewhere in its territories, and on its vessels, such distinctive flag indicating the British character of the Company as Our Secretary of State and the Lords Commissioners of the Admiralty shall from time to time approve.

GENERAL POWERS OF THE COMPANY

12. The Company is hereby further authorised and empowered, subject to the approval of Our Secretary of State, to acquire and take by purchase, cession, or other lawful means, other rights, interests, authorities, or powers of any kind or nature whatever, in, over, or affecting other territories, lands, or property in the region aforesaid, and to hold, use, enjoy, and exercise the same for the purposes of the Company, and on the terms of this Our Charter.

QUESTIONS OF TITLE

13. If at any time Our Secretary of State thinks fit to object to the exercise by the Company of any authority or power within any part of the territories comprised in the several Cessions aforesaid, or otherwise acquired by the Company, on the ground of there being an adverse claim to that part, the Company shall defer to that objection.

PROHIBITION OF MONOPOLY

14. Nothing in this Our Charter shall be deemed to authorise the Company to set up or grant any monopoly of trade; and subject only to customs duties and charges as hereby authorised, and to restrictions on importation similar in character to those applicable in Our United Kingdom, trade with the Company's territories under our protection shall be free and there shall be no differential treatment of the subjects of any Power as to settlement or access to markets, but foreigners alike with British subjects will be subject to administrative dispositions in the interests of commerce and of order.

The customs duties and charges hereby authorised shall be levied and applied solely for the purpose of defraying the necessary expenses of government, including the administration of justice, the maintenance of order, and the performance of Treaty obligations, as herein mentioned, and including provision to such extent and in such a manner as Our Secretary of State may from time to time allow for repayment of expenses already incurred for the like purposes or otherwise, in relation to the acquisition, maintenance, and execution of Treaty rights.

The Company from time to time, either periodically or otherwise, as may be directed by Our Secretary of State, shall furnish accounts and particulars in such form, and verified, in such manner as he requires, of the rates, incidence, collection, proceeds, and applications of such duties, and shall give effect to any direction by him as to any modification of the description, rate, incidence, collection, or application of such duties.

CONFORMITY TO TREATIES

15. The Company shall be subject to and shall perform, observe and undertake all the obligations and stipulations relating to the River Niger, its affluents, branches, and outlets, or the territories neighbouring thereto, or situate in Africa, contained in and undertaken by Ourselves under the General Act of the Conference of the Great Powers at Berlin, dated the twenty-sixth February, One thousand eight hundred and eighty-five, or in any other Treaty, Agreement, or Arrangement between Ourselves and any other State or Power, whether already made or hereafter to be made.

FOREIGN JURISDICTION

16. In all matters relating to the observance of the last preceding Article or to the exercise within the Company's territories for the time being of any jurisdiction exercisable by Us under the Foreign Jurisdiction Acts, or the said General Act of the twenty-sixth February, One thousand eight hundred and eighty-five, the Company shall conform to and observe and carry out all such directions as may from time to time be given in that behalf by Our Secretary of State, and the Company shall, at their own expense, appoint all such Officers to perform such duties and provide such Courts and other requisites for the administration of Justice as he directs.

GENERAL PROVISIONS

And We do further will, ordain, and declare that this Our Charter shall be acknowledged by Our Governors, and Our Naval and Military Officers, and Our Consuls, and Our other Officers in Our Colonies and possessions, and on the high seas and elsewhere, and they shall severally give full force and effect to this Our Charter, and shall recognize and be in all things aiding to the Company and its Officers.

And We do further will and ordain, and declare that this our Charter shall be taken, construed, and adjudged in the most favourable and beneficial sense for and to the best advantage of the Company, as well in Our Courts in Our United Kingdom, and in Our Courts in Our Colonies or possessions, and in Our Courts in Foreign Countries, or elsewhere, notwithstanding that there may appear to be in this Our Charter any non-recital, mis-recital, uncertainty or imperfection.

And We do further will, ordain, and declare that this Our Charter shall subsist and continue valid, notwithstanding any lawful change in the name of the Company, or in the Articles of Association thereof, such change being made with the previous approval of Our Secretary of State signified under his hand.

And We do, lastly, will, ordain, and declare that in case at any time it is made to appear to Us in Our Council expedient that this Our Charter should be revoked, it shall be lawful for Us, Our heirs and successors, and We do hereby expressly reserve and take to Ourselves, Our heirs and successors, the right and power, by writing, under the Great Seal of Our United Kingdom, to revoke this Our Charter, without prejudice to any power to repeal the same by law belonging to Us or them, or to any of Our Courts, Ministers, or Officers, independently of this present declaration and reservation.

SCHEDULE OF TREATIES

[Here follow the numbers of treaties made by the Company on certain dates in 1884.]

In witness whereof We have caused these Our Letters to be made Patent.

Witness Ourself at Westminster, the tenth day of July, in the fiftieth year of Our Reign.

By Warrant under the Queen's Sign Manual,
MUIR MACKENZIE.

The
Great
Seal

INDEX

Nupe, 15; *jihad* in, 16–17; British policy towards (1871), 23 ff.; French traders in, 36 ff.; rebellion in, 38 ff.; agreement with National African Company, 88–9, Germany and, 114 ff.; agreement with company investigated, 140–1; slave raiding, 240; Niger Company plans war against, 240 ff.; defeated by company's troops, 247 ff.; political reorganization and indirect rule in, 254–5; breakdown of company's authority in, 297–8

Oil Rivers, 11–12, 27, 47–8, 54, 57, 58, 59, 95, 97, 98, 99; plan for charter to rule area, 102 ff.; Macdonald in, 130 ff.; recommendations for future administration, 153–4
Onitsha, 20, 25, 28, 38, 88, 90, 101, 137, 194
Opobo, 27, 133–4

Palm kernels, 97, 122–3, 194
Palm oil, 10–11, 20, 27, 28, 31, 97, 98, 194
Parliament, Government's dislike of legislation on colonial matters, 81; opposition to Niger Company in, 189–90; debates on revocation of charter, 308–12
Pauncefote, Sir Julian, 72 ff., 77, 78, 79, 83, 110–11, 113, 125
Pepple, King George, 126, 132–3
Pinnock, James, 30–3, 127, 302
Protectorate, concept of, 53; authority in, 55–6

Quinine, 11, 17, 19

Rabeh, 296
Radicals, 102, 309
Revenue, 119 ff.; investigation of, 142 ff., 191–2
Rhodes, Cecil, 5, 124, 197, 316
Rogerson, Stanley, 106 ff., 124
Rosebery, Lord, 83, 91, 174, 190–1, 204

Salisbury, Marquis of, 76 ff., 83, 109–10, 118, 119, 120, 123, 125, 135, 148, 165–7, 214, 241, 242, 266, 270, 282, 284–5, 287–8, 289, 292, 311–12
Scarbrough, Earl of, 235, 245–6, 298, 315, 316, 318
Selborne, Lord, 73–4

Semellé, Compte de, 36–8
Shaw, Flora, 258
Shea-butter, 17, 20, 24, 26, 80, 97, 145
Sierra Leone, 40, 51, 95, 97, 105
Slave trade, 9, 12, 20, 259–60
Slavery, 86, 135; declared abolished, 250, 257–8; Goldie's views on, 259–60; in Ilorin, 300–1
Soap, 10, 33
Sokoto, 16, 89–90, 136, 146, 269, 271, 272, 276, 279, 293, 296; treaty of 1890, 162–3; treaty of 1892, 220
Somerset, Richard, 298–301

Tariff regulations, 96 ff., 99, 100, 101, 120, 152
Taubman family, 2–3, 29, 33
Taubman, George Dashwood Goldie, see Goldie
Thomson, Joseph, 189–90
Times, The, 207, 246, 258, 267
Toutée, Captain, expedition on Niger, 226–30
Trading licences, 97 ff., 100, 120, 150–1
Treasury, 48, 49, 56–9, 63, 80–1, 267, 269, 280, 281, 282, 307
Treaties, with African rulers, 59 ff., 88–9; expenses of, 113; validity of, 136–40; see also Akassa, Bonny, Borgu, Bornu, Brass, Bussa, Calabar, Forcados, Gandu, Ilorin, Nupe, Sokoto, Yola

Umoru, Emir of Nupe, 36, 38
United African Company, formation, 31–3; struggles with French, 34 ff.; reformed as National African Company, 44–6
Uthman dan Fodio, 16

Victoria, Queen, 199, 209, 235

Wallace, William, 115, 148, 177–9, 220, 229, 249
Warri, 189
West Africa Company, 26, 30 ff.
West African Frontier Force, 275–6, 278 ff., 283, 298–301

Yola, 136, 139, 146; French in, 172, 175, 177–9; Germans and, 181–5; and Sokoto, 296–7
Yoruba, 22, 232 ff.

Zweifel case, 147–9

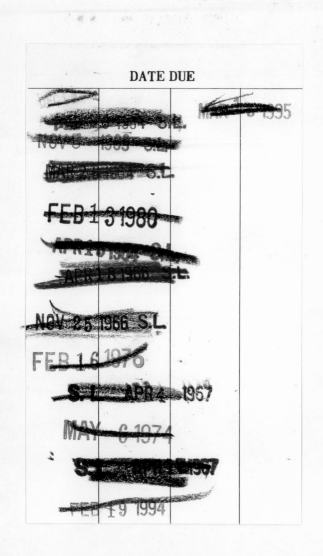